CHANGING THE SUBJECT

ROSALIND ROSENBERG

CHANGING THE SUBJECT

HOW THE

WOMEN OF COLUMBIA

SHAPED THE WAY WE THINK

ABOUT SEX AND POLITICS

COLUMBIA UNIVERSITY PRESS / NEW YORK

COLUMBIA UNIVERSITY PRESS
Publishers Since 1893
New York   Chichester, West Sussex

Library of Congress Cataloging-in-Publication Data

Rosenberg, Rosalind, 1946–
  Changing the subject : how the women of Columbia shaped the
way we think about sex and politics / Rosalind Rosenberg.
    p.   cm.
  Includes bibliographical references and index.
  ISBN 0-231-12644-1 (cloth : alk. paper)
    1. Columbia University—History—20th century.   2. Columbia
University—Admission—History—20th century.   3. Feminism and
higher education—New York (State)—New York—History—20th
century.   4. Women in higher education—New York (State)—New
York—History—20th century.   5. Coeducation—New York (State)—
New York—History—20th century.   I. Title.
  LD1250.R28 2004
  378.747'1—dc22

                                                          2004055135

Designed by Lisa Hamm

c 10 9 8 7 6 5 4 3 2 1

To the Memory of Mirra Komarovsky

CONTENTS

ACKNOWLEDGMENTS

I BEGAN this book in 1998, when my colleague Robert A. McCaughey invited me to present a paper on the "woman question" at the Columbia University Seminar on the history of the university. The evening of my presentation came and went, but the challenge of trying to explain the importance of women to the history of the university and the world beyond continued to preoccupy me. I am indebted to the Publication Committee of the Columbia 250th Anniversary Celebration for the support and encouragement it gave me to turn that preoccupation into the book that follows. Committee Chairman Ashbel Green, as well as the committee members, Wm. Theodore de Bary, Eric Foner, Kenneth T. Jackson, Robert A. McCaughey, Jerry Kisslinger, Marilyn Pettit, Michael Rosenthal, and Fritz Stern, and the executive directors of the 250th Committee, Roger Lehecka and Claudia Bushman, gave me complete freedom to say what I wanted, knowing that what I wanted to say might not always reflect well on Columbia.

I wish also to acknowledge the help of the librarians and archivists at Columbia and its affiliated colleges. I relied most heavily on Marilyn Pettit, Jocelyn Wilk, and Jennifer Ulrich of the Columbia University Archives–Columbiana Library; Jean Ashton and Bernard Crystal of the Rare Book and Manuscript Library; Ron Griele and Mary Marshall Clark of the Oral History Research Office; Jane Lowenthal and Donald Glassman of the Barnard College Archives; Whitney Bagnall of Special Collections in the Law School Library; David Mink and Bette Weneck of the Teachers College Special Collections; and Stephen E. Novak of Health Sciences Archives and Special Collections. Columbia Senior Research Analyst Rebecca Hirade provided me with data on students and faculty, while Betsy Esch and Tom Mathewson found key documents for me in the files of the Columbia University Senate.

Many of the Barnard and Columbia College students who took my course American Women in the Twentieth Century in recent years found themselves roped into research for this project. Thanks in particular to

Aimee Arciuolo, Elvita Dominique, Sarah Harper Nobles, and Ambika Panday, whose diligent, enthusiastic, and often inspired sleuthing made this a much better book than it otherwise would have been.

Several Columbians with particularly long memories helped me frame my project. Eli Ginzberg (Columbia, B.A. 1930, Ph.D. 1933) of the Business School gave me an insider's view of Columbia that stretched back to the 1920s. Marion Jemmott, who began work at Columbia in 1952 as a secretary in the Department of Philosophy and rose through the ranks to become secretary of the university with responsibility for the Board of Trustees minutes, provided a running tutorial on everything from the history of tenure to life as a female staff member. Eleanor Elliott (Barnard 1948) and Helene Kaplan (Barnard 1953), longtime members of the Barnard College Board of Trustees, gave me particularly candid reports from the west side of Broadway. Patricia Albjerg Graham, a Teachers College–trained historian (Ph.D. 1965), did the same for the north side of 120th Street. Joan Ferrante (Barnard 1958, Columbia Ph.D. 1963) and Gillian Lindt (Columbia Ph.D. 1965) helped me understand the importance of the School of General Studies to female faculty and nontraditional students. George Fraenkel, former dean of the graduate faculty; Jonathan Cole (Columbia, B.A. 1964, Ph.D. 1969), the second longest serving provost in Columbia's history; and Michael Sovern (Columbia College 1953, Law School 1955), president of the university during the pivotal 1980s, offered a wealth of knowledge about the inner workings of the university over many decades.

Others willing to share their memories of their time at Columbia greatly enriched my understanding of the university. For consenting to interviews and for responding to my queries with often lengthy letters and e-mails, I wish to thank Barnard College President Judith Shapiro, as well as Provost Elizabeth Boylan, Associate Provost Flora Davidson, Dean of the College Dorothy Denburg, Dean of Students Karen Blank, Counsel Michael Feierman, Vice President for Planning Lew Wyman, Registrar Constance Brown, and the secretary to the Barnard Board of Trustees, DiAnn Pierce. Also helpful were former Barnard Presidents Martha Peterson and Ellen Futter, former Dean of Students Barbara Schmitter, and former Dean of Admissions Christine Royer. In recounting the history of women in the School of General Studies, I benefited from the memories of former administrator Joseph Kissane; and I learned a great deal about the history of the professional schools from former Columbia Law School Dean Barbara Black and from the founder and director of the Partnership for Women's Health at Columbia, Marianne Legato.

Thanks, also, to the former students and faculty members who shared their recollections with me: Ivar Berg, Carol Berkin, Ronald Breslow, Caroline

Bynum, Carl Degler, Carolyn (Rusti) Eisenberg, Estelle Freedman, Herb Gans, Nina Garsoian, Renee Gene, Henry Graff, Maxine Greene, Ruth Taubenhaus Gross, Helen Meyer Hacker, Jacquelyn Dowd Hall, Carolyn Heilbrun, Sylvia Ann Hewlett, Frances Hoffman, Gerda Lerner, Barbara Low, Gita May, Christia Mercer, Betty Millard, Lucille Nieporent, Anne Prescott, Eugene Rice, Joseph Ridgely, Louise Rosenblatt, Doris Rosenberg, Dorothy Ross, Alice Rossi, Elspeth Rostow, Paula Rubel, George Stade, Betsy Wade Boylan, and Virginia Heyer Young. For insights into the life of Mirra Komarovsky, I am grateful to her sister Dolly Cheser, her niece Ana Silbert, and her neighbor Anne Lowenthal.

I could not have told the story of the creation of Columbia Women's Liberation and of Columbia's embattled relations with the United States Department of Health, Education and Welfare in the late 1960s and early 1970s without the help of former students, staff, and junior faculty members Barbara Buonchristiano, Rachel Blau DuPlessis, Amy Hackett, Ann Sutherland Harris, Kate Millett, Catharine Stimpson, and Harriet Zellner. Rachel Blau DuPlessis also inspired the title for this book by directing me to her essay "Reader, I Married Me: A Polygynous Memoir," in *Changing Subjects: The Making of Feminist Literary Criticism*, edited by Gayle Green and Coppelia Kahn. DuPlessis's essay and the book in which it appeared helped me make the connection between the intellectual and the political in the lives of many Columbia women in the 1970s. Generous, too, in sharing their memories, were several who served in the Columbia administration in the early 1970s: Provost Wm. Theodore de Bary, Vice President for Administration Paul Carter, and Deputy Vice President for Academic Affairs James S. Young. Essential to understanding the view from Washington, D.C., were my interviews with J. Stanley Pottinger, former chief counsel of the Civil Rights Division of the Department of Health, Education, and Welfare, and Beatrice "Bunny" Sandler, who more than any other person became the voice of academic women in Congress in the early 1970s.

In piecing together the story of how Columbia College came to admit women, I benefited from interviews with former Columbia Provost Fritz Stern, former Columbia College Dean of Students Roger Lehecka, former Assistant Dean of Columbia College Michael Rosenthal, former Columbia College Dean of Admissions James McMenamin, and former President Michael Sovern.

In writing this book, I accumulated debts to a number of fellow historians whose knowledge of Columbia proved particularly helpful. I wish, in particular, to thank Linda Kerber (Barnard 1960, Columbia Ph.D. 1968) and Estelle Freedman (Barnard 1969, Columbia Ph.D. 1976), whose memories of Barnard and Columbia from the 1950s through the 1970s deepened my understanding of those years. Thanks also to Janet Alperstein, Lois Banner, James Boylan, Desley Deacon, James Farr, Grace Farrell, Helen Horowitz, Marion Hunt, Herbert Wechsler, Lynn Gordon, Caroline Niemczyk, and Andrea Walton.

I owe a special debt to Robert A. McCaughey, who not only inspired this book, but also provided help at every step along the way, often taking time from work on his own book, *Stand Columbia: A History of Columbia University in the City of New York, 1754–2004,* to help with research and read drafts. I am indebted, as well, to Judith Shapiro, Gillian Lindt, Margaret Vandenberg, Susan Ware, Herb Sloan, Mia Bay, Thomas Bender, Claire Potter, and Nancy Woloch, who read all or parts of the manuscript and suggested changes. Thanks to my colleagues in the Barnard history department—Mark Carnes, Lisa Tiersten, Kathryn Jay, Deborah Valenze, and Joel Kaye—as well as those at Columbia—Roger Bagnall, Elizabeth Blackmar, Eric Foner, William Harris, Kenneth T. Jackson, Alice Kessler-Harris, and Marcia Wright—for help along the way. Other colleagues who gave much of their time include Demetrios "Jim" Caraley, Helene Foley, Serge Gavronsky, Robert Hanning, Peter Juviler, Barbara Schatz, Vivian Taylor, and Kathryn Yatrakis.

Friends who have no relationship to Columbia but who nonetheless listened patiently as I tried out ideas on them deserve particular credit. Special thanks, therefore, to Patrizia Chen, Catherine Clinton, Dan Michael McDermott, Regina Park, Rick Schaffer, Susan Schlechter, and Clarence Walker.

Thanks to the editors at Columbia University Press, especially to Jamie Warren for his encouragement and guidance. Thanks, also, to my copy editor, Naomi Loeb Lipman (Barnard 1951, Columbia M.A. 1952), who brought to the manuscript not only her eagle eye but also her detailed knowledge of the subject of this book, and to Irene Pavitt for shepherding the book through production.

Finally, I want to thank my family, and I do so despite their comments about my hearing. My hearing is fine. If I do not always respond when addressed, it is because I have strengthened my powers of concentration over the years. Thanks to my grandson, Henry, for insisting that I accompany him down the slide; to my daughter-in-law, Kim, for her help in matters large and small; to my son Cliff for his historical perspective; to my son Nick for his psychological insights; and, above all, to my husband, Gerry, for his wry wit, unfailing support, and daily reminders that there is more to life than work.

CHANGING THE SUBJECT

INTRODUCTION

THIS IS a book about the women of Columbia and the changes they made as they took their place within the university. The story begins in the years following the Civil War, when women first established a series of beachheads on Columbia's periphery, and it unfolds over the course of the century that followed, as new generations fought for inclusion. In the course of their struggle, women turned Columbia into a uniquely structured research university, one in which they were able to challenge prevailing ideas about sex, as well as accepted views of ethnicity, race, and rights. In doing so, they laid the foundation for what we now know as "gender," the idea that biological sex is distinguishable from its cultural expression; played a central role in the rise of modern feminism; and contributed importantly to political reform. Innovative thinking about sex and its relationship to politics developed in many places in those years—in Vienna, Paris, London, Boston, and Chicago, to name just a few—but nowhere was that thinking more productive over a longer period of time than in New York, and no New York institution provided a more important forum for debate than Columbia.

An economic boom transformed New York into a great metropolis in the years after the Civil War. By the turn of the twentieth century, it was the country's most ethnically diverse city, its cultural center, its economic leader, and its principal haven for ambitious, rebellious, heterodox women. Men came, too, but never in the same numbers. Because of its emphasis on commerce and culture, New York became a women's city. Men gravitated in relatively greater numbers to cities like Pittsburgh, Detroit, and Chicago, places that boasted heavy industry and demanded of their workers brute strength.

Recognizing the opportunities concentrated in New York, a women's movement, begun in upstate New York in the 1840s and emboldened by the egalitarian rhetoric of the era of the Civil War, gravitated to Gotham in the 1860s and made the opening of higher education to women one of its chief demands. As New York's leading institution of higher learning, Columbia came under early, heavy, and persistent fire. Lillie Devereux Blake, a prominent suffragist (and descendent of two Columbia presidents), initiated the battle in 1873. She won a sympathetic response from Columbia's progressive president, Frederick A. P. Barnard, but ran into stiff opposition from trustees and faculty.

One Columbia professor, John W. Burgess, proved an especially vigorous foe. A specialist in the politics of Reconstruction in the post–Civil War South, Burgess blamed the economic turmoil and physical violence then plaguing the South not on the desperate attempts of traditional white leaders to hold on to their positions, but rather on the black men and their radical white allies who were struggling to assume power. The middle-class white women knocking at Columbia's door, Burgess believed, threatened a similar disruption at the college. In the context of New York City, with its burgeoning immigrant population, opening Columbia's door to women risked opening it to other dangerous groups: Jews, Catholics, perhaps even African Americans. Burgess would devote much of the final three decades of his career at Columbia to building a school of political interpretation that linked race, sex, and radicalism as the three forces most responsible for undermining an otherwise orderly American polity. He did everything he could to block those forces at Columbia.

Burgess's opposition did nothing, however, to quell the demands of women's rights advocates. By the early 1880s they had generated enough support among prominent New Yorkers to force the Columbia Board of Trustees into a compromise. In 1883 the board grudgingly created a Collegiate Course for Women, under which they granted women the right to take exams, though not to attend classes. One of the first women to enroll, Annie Nathan Meyer, found this halfway measure wholly unsatisfactory and launched a campaign to open an affiliated college for women. Barnard College, founded in 1889, was the result. Two years later, the reformer Grace H. Dodge succeeded in creating an affiliated training school for teachers, named Teachers College, out of which grew a school for adults called the School of General Studies. Using Barnard, Teachers College, and General Studies as staging areas, female students gradually infiltrated the rest of the university. So successful was this effort that over the course of the next century, Columbia awarded more doctoral degrees to women than did any other university in the country.

This study has its roots in my book *Beyond Separate Spheres* (1982), which examined the work of the first generation of social scientists in America. At the turn of the twentieth century those scholars began to question the prevailing Darwinian idea that sexual orientation, masculinity and femininity, social roles, and even social structure were the products of biology. A disproportionate number of those early social thinkers worked at Columbia, a fact that I initially attributed to Columbia's rapidly increasing size, as it grew from a small college into a major research university in the early years of the twentieth century. Since then, I have concluded that more was at work than sheer numbers. Columbia was different, not just because it was big; the University of Wisconsin and the University of California at Berkeley were far larger, and yet they generated little research on gender and trained far fewer female academics. Nor was Columbia's location in a large city enough by itself to explain its difference. The University of Chicago was an urban school that paralleled Columbia in many ways, attracting large numbers of talented women and generating important work on gender and social reform.

And yet Columbia outdistanced Chicago, first, because the city of New York offered a broader array of opportunities to women with advanced training, and, second, because of the university's unusual structure. Unlike Chicago, where women were included with relatively little controversy from the university's founding in 1892, Columbia—an all-male institution from its creation in 1754—fought women's admission for decades. Moreover, when Columbia's trustees finally gave in to women's demands for admission, they sought to contain them in separate schools, with their own faculties, for as long as possible. Ironically, the flip side of containment was consolidation. Those separate schools provided continuing bases of protest and critical thinking from the 1890s forward. They encouraged students to claim the right to further training and provided jobs for talented graduates, at a time when academic employment was largely closed to women. In challenging traditional assumptions about *who* could be a subject in the educational system, Columbia women began to question *what* could be a legitimate subject of intellectual inquiry to a much greater extent than did women at any other university.

Columbia gained a further edge over Chicago because New York City possessed a public system of higher education segregated by gender up until World War II. The only school to send more women on to graduate training at Columbia than Barnard College was Hunter College, New York City's elite public college for women. Filled with the ambitious daughters of immigrants and taught by a faculty that included many women who had earned their degrees at Columbia, Hunter nurtured the academic talent of its female students to an unusual degree.

Because Columbia became an important training ground for women, it also became a significant source of women-centered political reform at a time when politics was coming to rely increasingly on expert knowledge. Through links to the city's public-school system and its scores of settlement houses, women with ties to Columbia (as students and faculty) played a key role in bringing women of different classes together to rethink the institutions of marriage, motherhood, work, and politics. At a time when marriage usually meant the end of an ambitious woman's career, Elsie Clews Parsons, who graduated from Barnard in 1896 and won her Ph.D. in sociology in 1899, campaigned on behalf of married women, including mothers, who wanted to continue working. At a time when politics was an overwhelmingly male preserve, Frances Perkins, who earned her M.A. in economics at Columbia in 1910, became the first woman to serve as secretary of labor of the United States and in that position played a critical role in expanding the American government's approach to social welfare. And at a time when journalism was a male club, Iphigene Ochs Sulzberger, who graduated from Barnard in 1914 and went on to do graduate work in journalism and history, lobbied tirelessly to broaden the scope of her father's newspaper, the *New York Times*, to hire women and to include attention to issues of interest to them.

The women who first demanded the right to study at Columbia were predominantly Protestant whites, like the men who had built the university. But in the years preceding World War I, an accelerating influx of ambitious and talented immigrants challenged that racial and religious exclusiveness. By the 1920s Columbia's graduate faculties and professional schools—most particularly Teachers College—were enrolling more Jews, Catholics, and African Americans than any other major research university. This increase did not take place without resistance. Indeed, fear over the loss of ethnic homogeneity in the student body was widely expressed by admissions officers and played an important role in keeping the number of minority students much lower than Columbia's location—a subway ride away from the Lower East Side and next door to Harlem—should have allowed. Resistance proved especially great at the two undergraduate colleges. Columbia College did not enroll its first black student until 1906. Barnard College waited until 1925.

The resistance of Columbia admissions officers to greater diversity provoked a spirited response among scholars who saw the university's growing diversity as something to celebrate rather than regret. Teachers College, under the leadership of James Earl Russell and Mabel Carney, prepared more black students for careers in higher education than any other school in the country, while Columbia's department of anthropology, under the direction of Franz Boas and Ruth Benedict, introduced the idea of culture to the American public as a way of understanding and accepting differences in behavior and attitudes. Among Boas's and Benedict's students, Margaret Mead and Zora Neale Hurston had an influence that resonates to this day.

The sexual freedom of Manhattan in the 1920s and 1930s inspired these scholars further to question conventional assumptions about sexuality. Margaret Mead's *Coming of Age in Samoa* (1928) issued a call for greater sexual freedom in the guise of an ethnography of adolescents in the South Pacific. Ruth Benedict's *Patterns of Culture* (1934) opened the way to a more tolerant view of sexual difference in America through its sympathetic treatment of the *berdache* (men who dressed as women) among the Plains Indians. And Zora Neale Hurston's *Their Eyes Were Watching God* (1937), with its freewheeling literary style, provided a pioneering depiction of female autonomy and sexual expressiveness in African American literature.

Columbia women's questioning intensified during World War II and its aftermath, as a labor shortage created both opportunities for women and new thinking about them. The Manhattan Project opened jobs to women scientists, including two future prizewinners, Maria Goeppert-Mayer and Chien-Shiung Wu, and the need for "trained brains" in Washington led to concern over "womanpower" on the Columbia campus. In the 1950s, Columbia became the leading employer of female scientists in the country; in the process, the idea of science as a male preserve began to weaken.

In those same years, a period famous for its celebration of domesticity, scholars began to lay the theoretical foundations for a new women's movement. The Barnard sociologist Mirra Komarovsky challenged conventional thinking about the assumed naturalness of women's domesticity in her pathbreaking research on "role strain." Finding deep discontent among college-trained women who had gone on to lives as full-time wives and mothers, Komarovsky called for the transformation of social mores and institutions to enable women to combine family and work in her pioneering book *Women in the Modern World* (1953). A decade later, Betty Friedan's *Feminine Mystique* drew heavily on her work.

Attention to women's concerns at Columbia accelerated in the early 1960s. Beginning with the "Bermuda Shorts Affair" at Barnard College in the spring of 1960, the balkanized structure of Columbia University, together with the cosmopolitan atmosphere of New York City, enabled women on campus to challenge the way the university controlled their lives—from the clothes they wore, to where they lived (and with whom), well in advance of the resurgence of modern feminism. This challenge was an overwhelmingly white affair, until Barnard, inspired by the civil rights movement, embarked on a campaign to recruit black students. Between 1963 and 1969 the number of African American students entering Barnard each year rose from eight to forty-two. As a critical mass of black students gathered at the college, they founded the Barnard Organization of Soul Sisters (BOSS), which, in the wake of student uprisings at Columbia in the spring of 1968, proceeded to challenge both black men at Columbia and white women at Barnard with marginalizing black women's concerns.

These racial protests helped ignite further critical reflection about gender. Gerda Lerner, who had won a doctorate in history in 1966 with her biography of the abolitionists Sarah and Angelina Grimké, embarked on a documentary collection of black women's writings, while in English, Kate Millett, a graduate student (and Barnard College instructor), built on the idea of racism to show how sexism provided a way of structuring power relations in society in her best-selling dissertation *Sexual Politics* (1970), and Carolyn Heilbrun explored the social construction of gender in her pathbreaking work *Toward a Recognition of Androgyny* (1973). In the reciprocal pattern that had long characterized the relationship of Columbia's women to the city of New York, these works influenced feminist debates in the city, which, in turn, inspired feminist organizing at Columbia and new thinking about the relationship of women not just to the university but also to the state.

One of the transforming events of the second half of the twentieth century, and the event that, next to the admission of women, John W. Burgess had most feared in the years after the Civil War, was the intercession of the federal government into everyday life. Columbia played a pivotal role in producing a new intercession in the 1960s and early 1970s, as women at the university appealed to the federal government to help them win more jobs. In 1969, while completing her dissertation, Kate Millett helped found Columbia Women's Liberation (CWL). One of the organization's first projects was to investigate the status of women at Columbia. When the investigators discovered that only 5 percent of the university's full professors were women, they turned to the federal government for help in improving women's job prospects. By 1971, CWL had persuaded the United States Department of Health, Education, and Welfare to withhold $33 million in federal contracts from Columbia until the university devised an acceptable affirmative-action plan for women and minorities. Through women at Columbia Law School, most importantly Ruth Bader Ginsburg, the feminist challenge to the traditional conception of gender, together with the legal successes of the civil rights movement, inspired new thinking about constitutional rights and the obligations of citizenship.

The importance of the civil rights movement to the emergence of modern feminism was further underscored in the debates that began to take place over the future of Columbia's college for women. Although some of the most innovative thinking on gender at Columbia had been produced either at

Barnard College or by those who had studied there, the idea of a separate college for women began to seem increasingly anachronistic by the late 1960s, as many involved in the civil rights movement and the sexual revolution questioned whether separate could ever be equal. Elsewhere, schools that had long been single-sex began to adopt coeducation. Vassar and Connecticut College admitted men; Yale, Princeton, Wesleyan, Amherst, and Williams admitted women; Harvard and Radcliffe, Tufts and Jackson, Brown and Pembroke merged. A century after Lillie Devereux Blake demanded that Columbia College admit women, a new campaign for coeducation took shape on Morningside Heights.

This time, however, men led the way, while women, for the most part, resisted. The resulting debate contributed further to the resurgence of feminism at Barnard (which was unique among affiliated colleges in having its own faculty) and to an explosion of new work on women throughout the university. By the time Columbia College decided to admit women, in 1982, Barnard's annual conference, "The Scholar and the Feminist," and Columbia's University Seminar, "Women and Society," had become important venues for some of the country's most important new feminist scholarship. In that context, the leaders of Barnard College came to believe that maintaining a separate voice within the university would be a positive step and they resolved to remain—as they had been since 1889—an independent college for women, affiliated with the larger university.

John W. Burgess would have been dismayed by this result. The steps he had taken to arrest the coeducational tide in the 1880s and 1890s produced what to him would have been the worst possible consequences. Ironically, if he had been willing to see women admitted to Columbia College, there would have been no separate undergraduate female student body, conscious of its own identity. If he had been willing to provide Barnard students with Columbia faculty as their teachers, or if he had supported the incorporation of Teachers College into the university in the 1890s, there would have been no separate faculties outside the graduate school and therefore no critical mass of academic women and sympathetic men, free to ponder the narrowness and masculine bias of conventional academic disciplines. But Burgess insisted on his own vision of what a research university should be, and in so doing he unintentionally helped lay the foundation for modern thinking about gender, the modern women's movement, the imposition of federal regulations on university life, and, in the wake of Columbia's decision to admit women in 1982, the instant creation of a student body with a greater proportion of women than existed at any other university in the country—a far cry from the racially homogeneous, all-male bastion he had fought so hard to secure.

ONE

THE BATTLE OVER COEDUCATION

ON OCTOBER 4, 1873, the writer and suffragist Lillie Devereux Blake escorted her two teenage daughters and a friend to Columbia College, then located at Forty-ninth Street and Madison Avenue. Intent on a meeting with President Frederick A. P. Barnard, she believed she had "an especial claim" to be heard. Samuel Johnson, her maternal great-great-grandfather, had served as Columbia's first president (1754–1763), when it was still Kings College, and William Samuel Johnson, her great-grandfather, had led the college after the American Revolution, from 1787 to 1880. Their portraits hung in the college library. In common with each of those presidential ancestors, as well as every president down to and including President Barnard, Blake was a member of the Episcopal Church and learned in Greek and Latin. Her education, acquired through a Yale College tutor in the 1840s, had been advanced for its time. But individual instruction, she believed, could not serve as a model for the expanding needs of the post–Civil War world. She therefore wished to make a formal application on behalf of five young women for admission to Columbia College.

According to her petition, one had just graduated first in her class from the Female Normal School (later Hunter College) and now aspired to the classical education available in New York City only at Columbia. Another had graduated from the University of Michigan and wanted to enter Columbia's "medical department." The others, who probably included her older daughter (seventeen-year-old Bessie) and the other young woman who came with her that day, were "qualified and earnest students." According to Blake's reading of Columbia's original charter, her candidates had every right to attend. The charter dedicated the college to the education of "youth," a group that surely included young women as well as young men. Moreover, although Columbia was a private institution, much of its endowment, including a valuable plot of land just to the north and west of the college (where Rockefeller Center now stands), had been received from the citizens of New York. These women and men "might naturally wish to have their daughters benefited by the wealth they bestowed."[1]

THE CITY OF NEW YORK

The time seemed right. New York City's unique position as the connecting link between the American hinterland and European commercial centers had transformed it, in the decades leading up to the Civil War, from a relatively modest urban cluster at the southern end of Manhattan into the financial, mercantile, and cultural capital of the country. From a total population of only 150,000 in 1820, before the opening of the Erie Canal, the city had grown to 1.5 million by 1865.[2] The laying of the transatlantic cable in 1866 and the completion of the transcontinental railroad in 1869 promised an even brighter future. Women were playing an increasingly important role in Gotham's economic boom. Ellen Louise Demorest's style-setting magazine, *Mirror of Fashions,* reached sixty thousand readers every month. The stories of Sara Willis Parton (Fanny Fern) became the chief circulation draw for the *New York Ledger,* a family weekly. Margaret Getchell, superintendent of Macy's department store, oversaw two hundred mostly female employees and did an annual business of $1 million.[3]

None of those women had needed a college degree to achieve success. Indeed, few men, other than those destined for the clergy, viewed higher education as worth pursuing. That view began slowly to change, however, with the scientific and technological advances and the soaring cultural aspirations of the second half of the nineteenth century. Gradually, growing numbers of men turned to college and professional training to improve their prospects. Women tried to follow, but in New York, at least, few were able to crack the male educational establishment. Mary Putnam Jacobi, daughter of the publisher George Palmer Putnam, had to travel to Paris to gain medical training equal to that available to men at home. Women who wanted to be lawyers faced even greater hurdles. To practice New York law, one had to train in New York, but the law schools fiercely resisted female encroachment. When three young women applied for admission to Columbia Law School in 1869, Trustee George Templeton Strong responded, "No woman shall degrade herself by practicing law, in New York especially, if I can save her."[4]

Another rejection, the indirect result of a reading tour by Charles Dickens, led to an organized response. In 1868, the Press Club of New York sponsored a dinner at Delmonico's to honor Dickens at the end of his American visit. Eager to see the famous writer, Jane Cunningham (Jennie June) Croly, the editor of *Mirror of Fashions*, wrote to reserve a place. The Press Club rejected her request on account of her sex. Outraged, Croly demanded the "extension of the same privilege upon the same terms as men." Horace Greeley, the editor of the *New York Tribune*, took her part, refusing a request that he preside at the dinner unless the "women had a chance" as well as the men. At the last minute, the organizers of the dinner agreed to allow women to attend but suggested that, to avoid embarrassment, they sit behind a curtain, out of sight. Outraged anew, Croly set out to organize a club of women of "literary and artistic tastes" who would "promise to exert an important influence on the future of women and the welfare of society." She called the club Sorosis, a botanical term for any plant that produces clusters of flowers out of which grows a single, compound fruit, like a pineapple. "Sorosis" seemed the perfect metaphor for a group of women intent on turning a collection of supposedly fragile creatures into a united, vital presence in the public sphere. Within a year, the club's membership included six artists, twenty-two authors, six editors, one historian, eleven poets, nine teachers and lecturers, eight philanthropists, two physicians, four scientific writers, and a number of journalists. Rejecting convention, they used no Miss or Mrs. when they listed their names in their official documents. It was to be Mary C. Greeley, not Mrs. Horace Greeley. Although most of the women were writers, they did not want a purely literary club; they wanted something broader, more involved in the world, more dedicated to changing the gender relations of the day. Sorosis quickly spawned sister clubs all over the country, beginning with the Boston-based New England Woman's Club, founded by the noted suffragist Julia Ward Howe. In 1873, Sorosis sponsored the Woman's Congress, which attracted more than four hundred women from across the country who had "conquered an honorable place in any of the professions or leading reforms of the day" and who wanted to discuss problems they were encountering, like winning access to higher education.[5]

Sorosis was part of a larger women's rights movement, begun in upstate New York in the 1840s. That movement gravitated to New York City in the 1860s, when Henry Stanton, the husband of the suffragist Elizabeth Cady Stanton, received an appointment at the New York Customs House in 1862. Moving into a brownstone on West Forty-fifth Street with her husband and seven children, Elizabeth Cady Stanton joined with her friend Susan B. Anthony (who boarded with the family) to turn New York City into a base of operations for an expanded women's movement. They launched campaigns for women's suffrage on both the state and the federal level, created the Working Woman's Association for female wage earners, and established the Woman's Bureau for middle-class professionals in a large townhouse near Gramercy

Park. At the Woman's Bureau, they founded *Revolution*, a journal dedicated to the slogan "Men Their Rights and Nothing More; Women Their Rights and Nothing Less," and published articles "not only on the ballot," but also on "bread and babies." They educated their readers to their feminist heritage by reprinting the work of Mary Wollstonecraft and argued on behalf of women's economic independence from men. Only when fully self-sufficient, they maintained, could women marry and remain married out of choice rather than economic necessity. To gain self-sufficiency, they added, would require a revolution in the way men and women thought about themselves and their relationship with one another. Marriage would have to become less a sacrament and more a civil contract, easily dissolved in the case of desertion, cruelty, drunkenness, adultery, or simple incompatibility. Men would have to learn to adhere to the same high moral standard expected of women and refrain from sexual relations when their wives did not choose to have them. Women would also have to be guaranteed equal rights under the law and greater economic opportunity. In service to all these goals, society would have to provide coeducation in schools and colleges.[6]

THE SPREAD OF HIGHER EDUCATION

Oberlin College had been educating women together with men ever since 1837. Founded by militant abolitionists, the college had envisioned a Christian community of men and women, black and white, working together for a better world. Although there were limits to the gender equality the college promoted—women were expected to retain their traditional role as help-meet to their husbands—Oberlin's model of women and men educated together influenced other religious groups, which founded coeducational liberal arts colleges throughout the Midwest in the years that followed. Their example influenced, in turn, the decision of state universities to admit women, beginning with the University of Iowa in 1855. In 1862, President Abraham Lincoln accelerated the movement toward coeducation when he signed the Morrill Land Grant Act, which made public lands available to endow state colleges and universities. After the Civil War, as an expanding public-school system outstripped the supply of male teachers, the demand for female teachers mounted. For training, women turned first to newly opened normal schools, but many soon found their appetites whetted for the greater challenge of, and the enhanced remuneration made possible by, a classics-based liberal-arts education. Although the Morrill Act did not refer to women specifically, many claimed a right as citizens to enroll in universities enlarged or newly created by federal largesse.

Where principle did not work, practical considerations often carried the day. In a state struggling to establish its first university, the prospect of building a second institution just for women made little financial sense. Principle and practicality combined to win women admission to state universities in Wisconsin in 1867; in Kansas, Indiana, and Minnesota in 1869; and in Missouri, Michigan, and California in 1870. Neither principle nor practicality proved compelling in the South, however, where racial and gender prejudice reinforced each other so powerfully that integration of one kind seemed to threaten integration of the other. Moreover, public education, as yet, barely existed there. Nor did either argument work especially well in the East, where all-male private colleges—like Harvard, Yale, Princeton, and Columbia—were long established and well endowed. Education for women had received an early boost with the creation of female seminaries, such as Mount Holyoke in Massachusetts in 1837 and Judson in Alabama in 1838. More advanced instruction took hold after the Civil War, when Vassar opened its doors in 1865. In the following decades, many female seminaries evolved into rigorous colleges, and new colleges for women, like Smith and Wellesley, joined them. But most women's rights leaders looked on separate education for women as a second-best solution to women's educational aspirations and argued that coeducation was the wave of the future. Julia Ward Howe and Elizabeth Cary Agassiz spearheaded the campaign for coeducation in New England; Elizabeth Cady Stanton and Susan B. Anthony led the way in New York. In 1870, after twenty years of struggle (and with the help of Horace Greeley), Cornell University agreed to admit women. By 1873, women had won admission to Boston University, Wesleyan, and Syracuse, and they were knocking at the door of Harvard College.[7]

New York City, with its intellectual energy and political ferment, presented an inviting but difficult target to those hoping to extend coeducation further. Unlike most of the Midwest and Northeast, New York City had not a single public high school as of 1873. The reason for this delay was the extreme economic, ethnic, and religious heterogeneity of the city. Public high schools opened first in the reasonably homogeneous communities of the Northeast and Midwest, where the schools were essentially the secular arm of a dominant white Anglo-Saxon Protestant sect. New York was the last major city in the Northeast to extend public education beyond grammar school. In 1878, two high schools, one for boys and the other for girls, finally opened. Significantly, they were in thoroughly Protestant Brooklyn (a separate city until 1898). As of 1873, the only college preparation available for girls in New York City was through a handful of private (mostly religious) academies or tutors.[8]

Opportunities for women at the college level barely existed. New York University, founded in 1831, did not admit women. City College, founded in 1847 as the Free Academy and renamed in 1866, barred women also. The only options were the private Rutgers Female College, founded in 1838 as an institute and renamed a college in 1867, and the public Female Normal School, created in 1870, which became Hunter College in 1914. Neither offered the traditional classical curriculum of Greek and Latin, and the Normal School did not even grant a degree. At midcentury, most academics still believed that the principal goal of a college education should be the development of "mental discipline." Such development depended on the vigorous exercise of the brain through the study of mathematics and classical texts. Since many doubted that the female brain was capable of the intense mental training expected of college students, the only way to prove them wrong was to undertake the same work on the basis of which men had staked their claim to superiority. For a New York woman to do so in 1873, she had to leave town.[9]

LILLIE DEVEREUX BLAKE

Lillie Devereux Blake did not believe that New York parents should have to send their daughters away to college. Born in Raleigh, North Carolina, in 1833, the daughter of a wealthy planter, George Pollock Devereux, and his Connecticut cousin, Sarah Elizabeth Johnson, Blake spent her early childhood on her family's plantation. In 1837, however, her father died, and her mother returned with her children to New Haven, Connecticut. There, Blake entered a world of Whig politics, Episcopal ritual, and social influence. She attended Miss Apthorp's school for girls until she was fifteen and then studied the Yale College curriculum with a tutor. Determined to find an "occupation in life," she yearned to be a writer but recognized that winning the attention of men offered a more certain avenue to power. An uncommonly pretty and spirited young woman, she set out to conquer the drawing room. "I live to redress the wrongs of my sex," she wrote at sixteen in a moment of protofeminist pique; to do so, "men's hearts must be attached and then trifled with."[10]

In 1855, she married Frank Umsted, a lawyer from Philadelphia, and settled briefly in St. Louis, where, after the birth of her first daughter, Elizabeth, in 1857, she began writing short stories and essays for *Harper's Weekly* and the *Knickerbocker Monthly*. In her fiction, Blake subverted conventional courtship narratives by portraying heroines as courageous figures and heroes as vulnerable creatures, easily dominated but quick to disparage women

Lillie Devereux Blake (1833–1913)
Writer, suffragist, and leader of the first
campaign to open Columbia College to
women. Portrait by William Oliver Stone,
1859. Gift of the estate of Florence L.
Robinson. (Columbia Art Properties)

as "mere playthings." After moving to New York and giving birth to a second daughter, Katherine, in 1858, Blake published her first novel in 1859. A book that linked male selfishness to domestic failure, *Southwold* showed off the erudition of its author by cramming quotations from fifty-four authors in six different classical and modern languages into the text. Three months after its publication, her twenty-six-year-old husband, having squandered her inheritance, killed himself with his revolver.[11]

Traumatized, penniless, and with two daughters to support, Blake resisted remarriage as a solution to her troubles and turned, instead, to writing. When the Civil War began, she moved to Washington, D.C., to work as a war correspondent, after marching into the editorial offices of Parke Godwin of the *New York Evening Post* and talking him into paying her $10 an article.[12] In between writing her "Letters from Washington," she produced a blizzard of essays and short stories, published mostly under pseudonyms. Her writing seethed with rage against a society that could take so many talented human beings at birth and turn them into mere women. In "The Social Condition of Woman," published anonymously in the *Knickerbocker Monthly* in 1862, she argued that women needed self-fulfilling action in the world as much as men, but that society robbed them of that chance by pressuring them into marriage as the only means of earning their livelihood. The only remedy, she insisted, was that women be granted "entire equality on every point—politically, legally and socially." In 1866, she married Grinfill Blake, a businessman several years her junior, who encouraged her writing and, when she protested against women's legal disabilities, urged her to join the suffrage movement.[13]

In 1869, she did. Although she feared the ridicule of friends, she visited Stanton and Anthony's Woman's Bureau one day and returned home to report with surprise, "Grinfill, *they're ladies!*"[14] She quickly became a close friend of the two pioneering women's rights leaders and a vital presence at the National Woman Suffrage Association. She published articles in *Revolution*, drafted countless speeches, and coined the slogan "The ballot is denied to idiots, lunatics, and women!" She was considered an electrifying speaker. The *New York Times* found her "forceful and eloquent"; the *New York Herald* judged her "the most brilliant lady speaker in the city"; and the *Albany Sunday Times* wrote that "there are very few speakers on the platform who have the brightness, vivacity and fluency of Lillie Devereux Blake."[15] Some of her rivals resented that success. In 1873, fellow suffragist Charlotte Wilbour grumbled, "I do not like to be the tail to your kite," and refused to continue sharing the platform with her.[16] Despite such tensions, Blake found that her skills as an organizer and orator catapulted her to positions of leadership. She served as president of both the New York State Woman Suffrage Association, from 1879 to 1890, and the New York City Woman Suffrage Association, from 1886 to 1890.

Blake focused much of her energy on suffrage, winning important battles that paved the way toward full suffrage, such as an 1880 law that allowed women to vote for school trustees; however, she never saw the ballot as the only goal worth fighting for. She wrote and spoke extensively against women's unequal treatment in the workplace and in marriage, and she advocated liberalized divorce laws. Through her lobbying of the state legislature, Civil War nurses came to receive for pension benefits, women became eligible for civil-service positions, and mothers gained the right to be joint guardians of their children. Moreover, under her leadership women began to sit on school boards and work in women's prisons. Blake parted company with Stanton and Anthony in the 1870s only once, when they sided with the radical Victoria Woodhull and her sister Tennie C. "Tennessee" Claflin in their celebration of "free love." Blake detested the sisters' brash personal style: their short hair, abbreviated skirts, mannish jackets, and loud neckties. She also deplored their argument that people might have more than one "natural mate," a view that they seemed eager to support in their own, not so private, lives. In Blake's judgment, an alliance with these women only played into the hands of conservatives like Anthony Comstock and threatened the goal of advancing women's rights to social, economic, political, and educational equality.[17]

FREDERICK AUGUSTUS PORTER BARNARD

When Columbia president Frederick A. P. Barnard met Blake, he was, at sixty-four years, old enough to be her father. Standing six feet tall, with a white beard, he hardly looked like a man interested in what he would later call "an innovation on immemorial usage," which the introduction of coeducation to Columbia would certainly be considered to be.[18] But Barnard was more flexible than he looked. When the Columbia College trustees had gone looking for a new president in 1864, the country's foremost scientists had championed him for the job as a man who could bring the institution into the modern age. At the time, Columbia College amounted to little more than a day school for the sons of the local Episcopal elite. Located at Forty-ninth Street and Madison Avenue, on the northern edge of the city's development, it looked out over railroad tracks to the east and cattle fields to the north and west. A board of trustees, dominated by Episcopalians, presided over Columbia's affairs. In addition to the undergraduate college, those affairs related to the newly established School of Mines (1864); the Columbia Law School (1858), located downtown near the courts; and, since 1860, a medical department, only loosely affiliated at the time, known as the College of Physicians and Surgeons, on Twenty-third Street, in Chelsea. Undergraduates, having begun their education at local academies, transferred to Columbia for college, while continuing to live at home. In 1865, the college enrolled 150 young men and employed a faculty of 10 professors, 1 adjunct professor, and 1 tutor. The day began at 9:45 A.M. with chapel exercises and continued with three hours of recitations in a prescribed curriculum, dominated by mathematics, Greek, and Latin. The college library, presided over by a librarian who disliked helping those who asked for assistance, was open for fewer than three hours each day. What little time the students spent at the college, they often devoted to imaginative pranks. But misbehavior was the least of the problems that Barnard encountered when he arrived at Columbia. More worrisome was the fact of falling enrollments.[19]

Columbia faced three problems. First, as of midcentury, there were simply too many schools competing for too few students. Second, many wealthy families, even Episcopal families, had begun to regard Columbia as too parochial and were sending their sons to Yale and Harvard. Third, families were growing increasingly concerned about the temptations to which their

Frederick A. P. Barnard (1809–1889)
Graduate of Yale College (1828), scientist,
president of Columbia College (1864–1889),
and namesake of Barnard College. Portrait
by Eastman Johnson, 1886. Commissioned
by the Columbia College Board of Trustees.
(Columbia Art Properties)

sons were subjected in the city. Parents who believed that they could adequately chaperone their daughters in New York City felt that they had to ship
their sons to more-pastoral settings to ensure that they would reach maturity
away from the dangers of the city. As Barnard saw it, "there exists a class of designing and plausible knaves [in New York City] who are ever on the watch
to inveigle and mislead the unsophisticated, and whose malignant natures
are never fully satisfied unless to the plunder of their victims they can add
their moral ruin."[20] Columbia's dwindling enrollment threatened Barnard's
ambition, as he told the trustees in his annual report of 1866, to make Columbia College "the nucleus of what will one day be the great university of
the city—possibly the continent."[21] If he could make Columbia the center of
technological, scientific, and intellectual innovation, he could reverse the
college's downward slide. To accomplish that feat, however, would require
strong, innovative leadership on his part. Although his own college education
and teaching had been at all-male institutions, aspects of his past made him
receptive to Blake's plea that innovation might include coeducation.

Born in 1809 in Sheffield, Massachusetts, Barnard had been particularly
close to his mother, who taught him to read before he was three and inspired in him a lifelong love of mathematics. In her honor, he later added
her maiden name, Porter, to his own. At fourteen, Barnard headed for Yale
College, where, though the youngest member of his class, he led the entire
school in mathematics and science. A fun-loving student, he gradually

turned away from the austere Congregationalism of his upbringing in favor of the Episcopal Church. Given the prominence of the Johnson family, he would have known of them, but he left New Haven more than a decade before Elizabeth Johnson Devereux brought her daughters back to live there. As a student, Barnard also played sports, wrote poetry, and found himself much attracted to "the charms of the opposite sex." Barnard had the opportunity to enjoy those charms, first at Yale, where his favorite professor, the chemist Benjamin Silliman, regularly invited female auditors to attend lectures, and later in Hartford, where, in the course of teaching mathematics at the Hartford Grammar School for boys, he met Catherine Beecher, headmistress of the neighboring female seminary. Barnard soon became a regular at Beecher's weekly soirées, where he came to know some of the foremost female writers of the day, including Lydia Segourney, Harriet Beecher, and Sara Willis (Fanny Fern), women who would, in a few years, inspire young Lillie Devereux Blake to become an author.[22]

Barnard's positive assessment of intelligent women developed further after he accepted a professorship in mathematics and natural philosophy at the all-male University of Alabama in 1838. The pistol-toting, knife-wielding students at Alabama were so wild that the university had been forced to close down the year before, when the entire faculty resigned. Barnard was part of the new president's plan to bring order to the institution. Taking advantage of the white southern male's code of chivalry, and recalling the example of Silliman at Yale, Barnard opened his classes to young women from the community in the hope that, as at Yale, they would have a civilizing influence.[23]

One female visitor made an especially strong impression on Barnard. She was Margaret McCurry, a twenty-three-year-old British-born woman from Ohio, who came to Alabama to visit a cousin and promptly fell in love with the thirty-eight-year-old professor. Although respected for his scientific accomplishments in mathematics and astronomy, Barnard was widely known in Tuscaloosa as a man with a drinking problem. Indeed, the university president had found it necessary to reprimand him on more than one occasion. According to family lore, Barnard was drunk the day he proposed to McCurrry, and she accepted him only on condition that he henceforth abstain from alcohol. He agreed and, at his wife's urging, took the further step of joining the temperance movement. Although the couple never had any children, they seem to have enjoyed a close relationship, and Barnard clearly valued the steadying influence that his new wife provided. Never good with money, he had regularly overspent his salary on his numerous scientific projects, books, the "pleasures of the day," and loans to friends. Once his funds were spent, he relied on credit. His new wife took firm control of his financial affairs, instituted stringent economies to pay off his debts, taught him to live within his means, and inspired him to focus on his career. In 1854, he took a position as professor of physics, astronomy, and civil engineering at the University of Mississippi, where he was ordained an Episcopal priest in 1856 and became chancellor of the university in 1859.[24]

In Oxford, Mississippi, rising southern nationalism and a crisis in his household forced him to confront the tangle of race and gender in a way he had avoided up to that time. In two decades of living in the South, Barnard had tried to fit into the ruling white community. Although he regularly criticized the South for its failure to capitalize on the technological revolution of the day—to build up its public schools, expand its universities, and provide scientists with research funds—he remained silent on the slavery issue. In fact, he owned at least one female house slave. In the spring of 1860, Barnard came home one day to discover from Margaret that this slave had been beaten and raped by a student from the university. Barnard immediately demanded that the faculty dismiss the student. The faculty, unwilling to take the word of a slave against the denial of a white student, refused. Barnard, acting on his own authority, insisted that the student's parents remove him from school. A member of the faculty declared that Barnard himself should be dismissed for being "unsound on the slavery question." While Barnard demanded and got a trial before the board of trustees, which cleared him of the charge, the whole experience embittered him toward his adopted home and the institution of slavery.[25] When the university closed the following year at the outbreak of war, Barnard made his Unionist sympathies known to scientific colleagues in the North. Visiting friends in Virginia, the Barnards slipped through Union lines and made their way to Washington, D.C., where Frederick's younger brother led Union troops who were protecting the capital. Frederick found a temporary position chairing the map and chart department of the United States Coastal Survey in Washington, D.C., and Margaret helped him make new acquaintances who could help him find a suitably prominent academic position in the North. Barnard, in sum, had ample cause to admire strong, intelligent women.[26]

He had one other reason to be sympathetic to the appeal of those who felt unjustly disadvantaged. Almost completely deaf since early adulthood, Barnard understood what it meant to be an outsider. Before going to Alabama, he had taught for five years at the New York School for the Deaf and Dumb, into whose building on East Forty-ninth Street Columbia College moved in 1857, after its previous occupants moved farther uptown. When Barnard accepted the presidency of Columbia, he was, in effect, returning to a place in which he had dedicated himself to helping others. But more than sympathy drew Barnard to the idea of admitting women to Columbia.

Doing so, he believed, would have three clear benefits: it would improve discipline in the college, add welcome revenue, and place Columbia at the forefront of educational reform in the United States. Barnard told Blake that he would support her petition to the board. The decision about whether to adopt coeducation, however, was not his to make. The board of trustees would have to consider Blake's request.[27]

THE BOARD OF TRUSTEES

The Columbia College Board of Trustees had a troubled relationship with Barnard. They hired him in 1864, despite concerns about his deafness, because he was the one candidate around whom they could build a consensus. The conservative trustees, who wanted to maintain Columbia's traditions, found reassurance in his ordination as an Episcopal priest; the progressives, who wanted to modernize the college's curriculum and turn Columbia into a university, saw promise in his scientific work. He seemed a good compromise: a minister who championed science. George Templeton Strong, a lawyer who sided with the progressives, quickly came to admire the new president. "I predict he will prove the most efficient president we have had in thirty-five years," he declared partway through Barnard's first year at Columbia. In 1867, he praised Barnard's efforts "to raise the moral tone of the undergraduates" and bring "vigor" to the college.[28]

But Barnard's drive also created problems. The trustees, accustomed to managing the smallest details of Columbia's administration, suddenly had a president who threatened to take control of Columbia's future. To their consternation, Barnard was able to use the deafness they had feared would hamper his leadership to increase his power. At board meetings, trustees sat at a long table, speaking into tubes connected by long cords to Barnard's ear trumpet at the head of the table. The cumbersomeness of this system of communication made objecting to Barnard's resolutions so difficult that the trustees usually let minor disagreements pass and gave the new president much greater authority than he could otherwise have commanded.[29] The result was a piling up of projects that some feared the college could ill afford. "Were he as wise as he is fertile in suggestions for expenditures," the board chairman, Hamilton Fish, declared, "the college would have a valuable financial leader at its head."[30]

Some trustees also had reservations about Margaret McCurry Barnard. In the beginning, Strong, for one, rather liked the weekly soirées that she hosted for leading statesmen and distinguished authors, as well as her "simple agreeable heartiness of manner." But in 1870, he objected to her "heavy fire of talk." She had turned into the kind of figure he most disliked—a "strong-minded" woman.[31] Times were changing, however, and so was Strong. More than seventy colleges and universities had decided to admit women by 1873, and active campaigns for coeducation were under way at both Harvard and Yale. Moreover, as anyone who read the student press knew, three of Columbia's science professors—the physicist Ogden Rood, the chemist Charles Arad Joy, and the geologist John S. Newberry—admitted women to their lectures. Strong was an enthusiastic supporter of these scientists because of their work in the School of Mines, which he saw as the vehicle by which Columbia could break out of its traditional insularity, connect with the larger business community, and become a leading university. Mining created opportunities for engineers in the West, while construction in New York City produced an even more dramatic explosion of jobs at home. To Strong, the School of Mines stood for progress and so did its science faculty.[32]

With so much change afoot, President Barnard had reason to hope for a respectful hearing from the trustees when he presented Blake's petition for coeducation on October 6, 1873.[33] Strong listened. While the "mere suggestion of young ladies among our Freshmen and of 'sweet girl-graduates' on the stage at commencement shocks all my conservative instincts," he confessed to his diary that evening, "I cannot shut my eyes to considerations in its favor, strange as the innovation would be." The father of three college-age sons, Strong had contact with young women only through his niece, Lucy Derby. Only a few months before the trustees considered Blake's petition, he had proudly observed her host a party for a "semi-literary, semi-Bohemian set" of young journalists and editors from the *Times*, *Tribune*, and *Post*. This was the crowd from which Sorosis was then drawing many members. They were not Strong's kind of people, but love for Lucy had begun to soften him somewhat to their advanced views.[34]

The Reverend Benjamin Haight, who chaired the board's meeting the day that Barnard presented Blake's petition, also indicated a willingness to listen. Saying that the question of coeducation should be "respectfully considered," he referred the matter to the Reverend Dr. Morgan Dix, the forty-six-year-old rector of Trinity Church and chairman of the Committee on the Course and Statutes. From the time of Columbia's founding as King's College in 1754, the rector of Trinity Church had claimed a position on the college's board and a disproportionate influence over its affairs. Dix, an 1848 graduate of Columbia College, had served as rector and trustee since 1862, and was widely known for his orthodoxy in a climate of growing unbelief. Dix worried about the negative consequences of the city's commercial growth: the growing ranks of the poor, the extravagance and dissipation of New York's new commercial class, and the erosion of religious feeling. He was especially troubled by the secularizing trend in universities, the placing of "rationalistic professors in the chairs once occupied by the great theologians of the Church." The most dangerous were scientists like Ogden Rood, whose atheistic tendencies and practice of admitting women to lectures, Dix believed, was part of a dangerous march of democratic ideas that threatened nothing less than revolution.[35]

Dix agreed to consider Blake's petition, but warned his colleagues at the outset of his deep disapproval. All he shared with strong-minded women like Blake was a mutual respect for the Sisters of St. Mary, whose school for Episcopal girls operated under his jurisdiction. Dix had served as the sisters' chaplain since 1866 and supported their work among the sick and poor, as well as their school, which trained the daughters of the Episcopal establishment for their future roles as Christian wives and mothers.[36] Blake, as a matter of fact, had enrolled both of her daughters in their school. Horace Greeley (the recently deceased editor of the *New York Tribune*, defender of Sorosis, and unsuccessful presidential candidate) had a daughter there as well. "These young ladies submit kindly to the influences of the Church," Dix reported.[37] Coeducation, Dix implied to his fellow trustees, was a passing fashion, part of the radicalism spawned by the tumult of Civil War and Reconstruction. He was not at all surprised to find it championed by women like Blake and men like Greeley. But as long as the Church could shape the next generation, this radicalism would pass. The sisters were doing all that was necessary or wise to protect women's legitimate interests.

Morgan Dix (1827–1908)
Graduate of Columbia College (1848), rector of Trinity Church (1862–1908), and member of the Columbia College and University Board of Trustees (1862–1908). (Columbia University Archives–Columbiana Library)

The following month, Dix returned to the board with the recommendation that Blake's petition be rejected. Whatever consideration Strong may
have given the matter of coeducation did not, in the end, overcome his
reservations, for, as he reported in his diary, the board "unanimously agreed
to decline the honor" of admitting women to Columbia. This would be his
last chance to vote on the matter; he died in 1875.[38]

If the vote was unanimous, Barnard must have voted with the others. It
seems unlikely that he had changed his mind since meeting with Blake, but
he may have concluded that the moment was not right to press the issue. Becoming the first college in New York City and—apart from Cornell, Syracuse,
and Boston Universities—the first in the Northeast to admit women would
have been a major departure from tradition. As long as Harvard and Yale held
out, it would be hard to prod the conservative trustees to action. Seeing that
his trustees were adamant, Barnard probably decided not to waste valuable
capital on trying to boost admissions with women students at that time. He
stood a better chance at winning their support for another pet project: enlarging the new School of Mines, which at 136 students had outpaced the college
at 123 and seemed poised for dramatic growth.[39] The women could wait.

For the most part, Columbia students approved the board's negative judgment. Apart from one editorial in February 1874, which urged that Columbia's doors be "thrown open" to women auditors for the benefit of all, the student press denounced coeducation. The general sentiment seemed to be that
New York women who wanted a collegiate education should "go to Vassar."[40]

Never easily deterred, Blake patiently set about organizing support for her
cause. She turned first to Elizabeth Cady Stanton, who praised her efforts a
couple of weeks later at the 1873 Woman's Congress, organized by Sorosis,
in New York. Three years later, in recognition of the centenary of the signing of the Declaration of Independence, Sorosis agreed to support the re-
newal of Blake's petition to open Columbia College to women. Sorosis pe-
titioned the University of the City of New York (later New York University)
at the same time, without success. Jennie June Croly wrote that President
Barnard "warmly endorsed" the Sorosis petition, but on December 4, 1876,
the trustees tabled it without further debate.[41]

THE ANNUAL REPORT

From the beginning of his presidency, Barnard closed each academic year
with an annual report to the board of trustees. At first, the board was delighted by his detailed assessment of the college's progress, as well as his analysis
of the challenges that lay ahead. The trustees readily footed the expense of
printing a thousand copies for distribution to the public. One suspects that

the board's largesse may have been prompted by more than institutional pride. According to George Templeton Strong, who frequently complained about Barnard's prose and speaking ability, any expense was better than having to listen to the president drone on for the several hours that an oral presentation required.[42]

The publication of Barnard's reports gave him an important weapon when the board resisted his reforms. If he could not persuade the trustees, he could go over their heads to the general public. In 1879, he chose to do so when he inserted into his yearly report an extended essay, "On the Expediency of Receiving Young Women as Students in Columbia College." In a sly dig at what Strong used to call the "fogies" on the board, Barnard recognized that he was not likely to succeed in changing the minds of those afflicted with the "spirit of conservatism." Such men could not accept "innovation upon immemorial usage," no matter "how cogent the arguments" in its favor, "because feeling is not controlled by judgment." Barnard addressed himself instead to objections susceptible to reasoned argument. He took as his guiding principle that "the mental culture of women should not be inferior in character to that of men," because as American society became increasingly dependent on technology, it could ill afford wasting any mind capable of the finest training.[43]

Barnard conceded that space constraints had posed problems for Columbia in the past but that a newly completed building on the corner of Madison Avenue and Forty-ninth Street—Hamilton Hall—offered ample room for growth. To those who said there were other, more suitable institutions for women, he responded that the "finishing schools," then available, were "ornamental" and "superficial," while the new women's colleges could not possibly give as good an education as "that given by the long-established and well-endowed colleges of highest repute" then monopolized by men. Moreover, Barnard deplored the proliferation of colleges, which pitted schools against one another in competition for a limited number of students. He looked with greater favor on Harvard's recent decision to set up an "Annex," under which female students would have access to Harvard's faculty. But he criticized the duplication of effort (and unnecessary expense) involved in Harvard's decision to teach women and men in separate classes. To Barnard, the increasingly popular solution of coeducation was much the best practice, especially at Columbia, which had the advantage of not having to house its students. To add women would mean simply adding "more names to the class-roll."[44]

To those who believed the "female intellect is inferior in native capacity" and that "association of the sexes will depress the standard of scholarship," he responded that in his experience women actually made better students than men because of their "quickness of perception" and "diligence." Moreover, evidence from Cornell University demonstrated that the addition of women had raised the standard of scholarship, while decreasing attrition. Since the arrival of the first woman student at Cornell in 1872, the dropout rate had fallen from 26 percent to 16 percent, even as admissions requirements had been tightened and examinations made more rigorous.[45]

Some critics of coeducation warned that the level of work required at the traditionally male colleges demanded too much of the "delicate constitutions of young women." This warning drew principal support from a little book by a Harvard Medical School professor, Dr. Edward Clarke, written in response to a campaign in the late 1860s to open Harvard to women.[46] Clarke's *Sex in Education* (1873), which went through eleven editions in six years, built on Herbert Spencer's theory that the body is a closed energy system to make the case that mental training in women used energy needed for the proper functioning of reproductive organs.[47] Women would never be scholars without putting their health and future as mothers at risk. The implication was clear: if women's future as mothers was jeopardized, there would soon not be enough sons to go to Harvard. Supported by a flurry of counter-studies published in the six years since Clarke's tract, Barnard replied that too much work can harm anyone, but the exercise of the mind required for the interpretation of a passage from Homer is no greater than that required for "drumming on an ill-tuned piano" or conjugating an irregular French verb.[48]

Women, Barnard firmly believed, would thrive at Columbia. Moreover, he claimed, "the presence of young women in colleges is distinctly conducive to good order. Nothing is more certain than that the complete isolation of young men in masses from all society except their own tends to the formation of habits of rudeness, and to disregard the ordinary proprieties of life." His experience as a student at Yale and a professor at Alabama confirmed that.[49]

Some worried that college would destroy a woman's "delicacy and reserve" and produce instead a "romping hoyden or self-asserting dogmatist," Barnard acknowledged. Observation of the coeducational high schools of the country, however, did not confirm this. As for the fear that the association of the young of both sexes would lead them to be more occupied with each other than with their books, he appealed again to experience. Young people who were segregated from one another were far more likely to have their imaginations excited than were young men and women who became acquainted in an academic setting, especially in a nonresidential college like Columbia, where students would have contact only in lectures.[50]

"Whatever may be the fate of the present suggestion," Barnard concluded, " I cannot doubt that the time will yet come when the propriety and the wisdom of this measure will be fully recognized." If only the trustees would follow his lead and build Columbia into a great, cosmopolitan university that offered "instruction in every branch of human knowledge," he could imagine a future in which Columbia would "open widely her doors to all inquirers without distinction either of class or sex."[51]

The prospect of a university that drew no distinction of either class or sex proved too much for the conservative sensibilities of his board. According to Nicholas Murray Butler, then a sophomore at the college, the reaction to Barnard's report was "panic."[52] But Barnard was convinced that his arguments on behalf of coeducation would eventually persuade any reasonable person. In October 1879, he approached the trustees once more, this time with a proposal that they give formal recognition to the, by then, longstanding practice in the sciences of allowing female auditors to attend lectures. The auditors included, among others, Margaret McMurray Barnard, the daughters of former Professor of Botany John Torrey, the daughters of Congressman Abram Hewitt, and the daughter of a Columbia trustee, Dr. Cornelius A. Agnew, who was also a trustee of the College of Physicians and Surgeons. One day, Agnew, having occasion to read Columbia's by-laws, discovered language that barred from attendance at lectures anyone who was not matriculated in the college. The punctilious Agnew instructed his daughter to cease going. Barnard tried to persuade Agnew that the language of the by-laws could not apply to women, since women were not allowed to register. The point of the rule was to protect the college from freeloaders, not keep women out, but Agnew was not to be persuaded. Not even his wife, a passionate supporter of women's education, could change his mind.[53]

At about this time, Caroline Reed, headmistress of the exclusive school for Episcopal girls located around the corner and sometime employer of Columbia instructors in search of a little extra income, asked Barnard's permission to send one of her classes to Columbia to sit in on the lectures in chemistry. Barnard agreed, but then, worried about the trustees' reaction to his annual report, decided that he had to clear the way by introducing a resolution to the board that would regularize the practice of female attendance. To his dismay, Dix refused to consider any modification of the rules, and even sympathetic trustees like Agnew decided that a formal change could have dangerous consequences, chief among them the admission of women to the Law School, which continued to receive applications from women.[54]

Butler later recalled seeing Barnard come from trustee meetings in that period of his administration, with his "face flushed and muttering to himself, as a result of some recommendation which he thought important having been either pigeonholed or negated." Barnard must have been beet-red the after-noon of November 3, 1879, when the board announced its refusal to take what, to Barnard, seemed the modest step of recognizing the status quo.[55]

The students sided with the trustees. The editors of *Acta Columbiana*, the forerunner of the *Columbia Spectator*, equated all-male colleges with pres-tige and coeducation with downward mobility. On the one hand, "Oxford, Cambridge, Harvard, Yale, Princeton, exclude women," they observed. On the other hand, "some fifty colleges in the United States whose halls are half empty admit young women." With a rhetorical flourish they inquired, "To which of these two classes shall Columbia belong?"[56]

Convinced that he was right, and believing that the public would support him if he could just reach them, Barnard persisted. In June 1880, he began a second essay, "The Higher Education of Women," with the deadpan com-ment that while his effort the previous year had "failed to attract the serious attention of the Trustees," he believed that "it did not altogether fail to ex-cite interest." In the meantime, history was passing the college by. In Eng-land, University College, London, had opened its lectures to women, and, with the opening of colleges for women at both Cambridge and Oxford, Barnard felt certain (with undue optimism, as it turned out) that coeduca-tion would soon extend to those institutions as well. Coeducation was not a midwestern practice only; the most elite schools in the English-speaking world were moving in that direction. The English movement had begun rel-atively late, compared with the United States, but it had moved quickly, Barnard argued, because of public pressure. Addressing the larger audience he hoped would read his report, he mentioned a group of British women and men who had formed the Association for Promoting the Higher Edu-cation for Women to gain women access to Cambridge. That kind of out-side pressure, he implied, would likely be required to speed change at Co-lumbia. Barnard closed by saying that he did not press the case for coeducation simply for the sake of throwing young women and men to-gether. His intent was simply to "secure for women opportunities for an ed-ucational culture as large and liberal as is provided for the opposite sex." In New York City, Columbia provided the best education available; women should have access to it, without restriction.[57]

It would not be the best education for long, the students responded, if women were allowed to share it. The editors of *Acta Columbiana* called co-education a "monstrous evil" that had already destroyed the prestige and in-fluence of many a promising institution.[58]

Again, the trustees failed to be moved by Barnard's appeal. Undaunted, Barnard issued a third report, also titled "The Higher Education of Women," in June 1881. For him, the case for coeducation had grown still stronger.

Women students were performing brilliantly wherever they were given the opportunity to study; their health had not suffered; the men's academic performance had not suffered; admitting women to previously all-male colleges was obviously better for the country than building new ones that would further crowd an already overpopulated field; the "public mind is prepared" for coeducation; a "majority" of "our most enlightened citizens demand it"; "our circumstances are such as to make it easily practicable"; "the members of our faculty without exception demand it."[59]

JOHN W. BURGESS: AN "AMERICAN SCHOLAR"

Not quite. Far from supporting coeducation "without exception," the faculty was badly divided on the issue. The scientists, led by the physicist Ogden Rood, favored it and had been slipping women into their lectures for years. Trained at Yale and in Germany, Rood was generally regarded as the genius of the faculty. Witty and worldly, he was also a notorious freethinker and a longtime friend of Lillie Devereux Blake. But the scientists stood alone in the early 1880s against their more conservative colleagues, most of whom had spent their entire adult lives at Columbia, drumming Greek, Latin, and mathematics into a mostly reluctant student body. One mathematics professor, John Howard Van Amringe, opposed coeducation unequivocally. "You can't teach a man mathematics if there's a girl in the room," he declared. "And if you can, he isn't worth teaching," he added in a homophobic flourish.[60] Also opposed to the admission of women was the relative newcomer John W. Burgess.

Although few scholars today have heard of John W. Burgess, and fewer still have read his work, Burgess exercised enormous power in his time, a power that affects us even now. One of the country's early political scientists, he specialized in constitutional law and its relation to state formation following the Civil War. Through his teaching and writing, he exercised a significant influence on how two generations of historians and political scientists wrote about politics and race relations in the United States. Burgess's influence stemmed in part from the power of his prose and the vigor of his teaching but even more from his entrepreneurial zeal. Recruited to Columbia in 1876 by Trustee Samuel Ruggles and President Barnard to breathe new life into the little college, Burgess founded one of the country's first graduate programs at Columbia in 1880. Over the course of the next half century, Burgess's Columbia turned out more Ph.D.'s than any other school in the country.[61]

To an important degree, Burgess and the faculty he hired seeded the American professoriate with men who bore his professional and intellectual

John W. Burgess (1844–1931)
Professor of history, political science, and
international law (1876–1912) and dean
of Columbia College and University
(1880–1912), as photographed in 1878.
(Columbia University Archives–Columbiana
Library)

stamp. His most influential student was William A. Dunning, who earned a
Ph.D. in history in 1885 and went on to make Columbia the center of the
study of southern history in the United States. Although Dunning claimed
to be dedicated to historical objectivity, he believed that white Southerners
had a special empathy for the history of their region and he attracted large
numbers of them, including, most famously, Ulrich B. Phillips (Ph.D. 1902),
to study with him. These students, known collectively as the "Dunning
School," argued that, in the years after the Civil War, a helpless white population had been tyrannized by ignorant blacks and manipulated by venal
northern carpetbaggers and southern scalawags.[62]

   As part of his effort to secure Columbia's standing as the nation's leading
site for the professional training of political leaders and scholars, Burgess vigorously opposed the campaign to admit women. He conceived of his position
as part of a larger strategy to hold onto Columbia's core constituency of male,
white, Anglo-Saxon Protestants. To Burgess, the dangers posed by women
and non-WASPs to the future of Columbia and to the professionalization of
the social sciences were linked. In resisting the adverse effects of women, he
believed that he was protecting the future of his university and the social sciences more broadly from the malign influences of minority men.

   Born in 1844 into a Tennessee slave-owning family, Burgess later recalled
a youth populated by a hierarchy of "intelligent, proud, and courteous slave
barons"; "ignorant, slovenly, poor white trash"; and, "at the bottom of all, the

vast mass of African slaves which served as the base of the political, economic, and social structure." Women, to the extent that they figured at all in
Burgess's race- and class-bound recollections, appeared chiefly as trophies
and victims. In youth, they were "beautiful maidens" who, through an implied process of Darwinian sexual selection, served as "the prizes of zealous
and sometimes fierce competition between the coxcombs of the country
and the beaux of the towns." As married women, these aristocratic "maidens" turned into the sole victims of an otherwise benign slave system. "The
person of my father's household who endured the greatest hardships of life,"
Burgess recalled, was "my dear good mother, who was called upon to minister to every black who might have a pain in the tip of his toe at any time of
day or night."[63]

Despite growing up in the slave-owning South, Burgess was a Northerner
"by instinct and heritage." His father was a nationalist, "old-line Whig" who
taught him that the Constitution of 1787 had created not a "confederation of
sovereign states," but a "nation holding exclusive sovereignty." When the
South seceded, Burgess fought on the Union side in the Civil War. In 1865,
at the age of twenty-one, he ventured north to Massachusetts, attended
Amherst, studied law in nearby Springfield, married, and taught briefly—and
unhappily—at coeducational Knox College in Illinois. In his experience,
having women around did not raise the moral and intellectual level of the experience, as Barnard insisted it would—just the reverse. Leaving Knox,
Burgess pursued graduate work in Germany before returning to Amherst,
where he tried and failed to persuade the trustees to turn the college into a
university. In 1876, a frustrated Burgess moved to Columbia, where he believed he stood a better chance of building a European-style university.

Burgess fought two battles in the 1870s. The first was against the old-guard
"College crowd" among the trustees. Impressed by the European system of
education, which prepared students for graduate study in gymnasiums and
lycées, Burgess believed that American high schools should be encouraged
to take over the work then being done in college, leaving university faculties
free for advanced research. Although Burgess never succeeded in his goal of
abolishing Columbia College, he did eventually make the graduate school
the center of Columbia University. Far more than any other school in what
would later be known as the Ivy League, Columbia College came to occupy an uneasy, marginal place within the shadow of the much larger and
more powerful graduate faculty.

Burgess's second battle was against the forces that he thought threatened
his nascent project: immigrants and women. He believed that the biggest
challenge facing the country was the political corruption he attributed to the

inclusion of African Americans in southern state governments and the growing number of immigrants in northern cities like New York. Only by creating new administrative structures within the United States, patterned on the bureaucratic models then being developed in Germany and France, Burgess argued, could America's traditional leaders, WASP males, secure their standing and protect the republic, two goals he took to be coterminous. Among his early students Burgess counted a future Columbia president, Nicholas Murray Butler, and a future United States president, Theodore Roosevelt. Both epitomized the virtues he worked to inculcate: administrative expertise, incorruptibility, and the kind of military masculinity that Burgess had come to value as a result of service in the Civil War.[64]

Women had no place in this plan. As important as Burgess had found study in Germany for his professional development, he had been deeply disturbed by the political radicalism that he had encountered there, especially among the few women students, most of whom he later recalled as Russian Jews with socialist convictions. He proudly described himself as an "American Scholar," a person untainted by the radical beliefs then infecting Europe. Creating a research university in America would allow future generations to pursue advanced study at home, rather than having to go abroad and risk exposure to dangerous ideas.[65]

Near the end of his life, Burgess wrote in detail about his reasons for fearing the presence of women. In addition to the standard worries that they would "distract the attention of the male students from their proper work" and debase the school's reputation by their intellectual weakness and "physical infirmities," Burgess laid out a demographic—and, to his mind, clinching—concern. Since New York fathers usually sent their sons to colleges outside the city, while preferring to keep their daughters at home, a decision to admit women to Columbia, he feared, would "make the college a female seminary"—not a female college, but a lesser school, a seminary. No institution on the way to becoming the world's greatest research university could risk such a threat.[66]

But that was not all. As early as the 1870s, an accelerating immigration into New York City was beginning to drive out the white Anglo-Saxon Protestant population that had long governed the metropolis. This change meant that the daughters who attended a coeducational Columbia could not be guaranteed to be Episcopalian, or even Unitarian. If immigration continued its present course, Columbia could be flooded by Catholics or, worse, by Jews. His ultimate fear was that the college would be reduced to a "Hebrew female seminary."[67] Burgess was not alone in his fear of a Jewish influx. In 1874, Columbia trustee George Templeton Strong had argued in favor of increasing admissions requirements to the Law School, by requiring a college degree and proficiency in Latin, to "keep out the little scrubs (German Jew boys mostly) whom the School now promotes from grocery counters in Avenue B to be 'gentlemen of the bar.'"[68] A greater threat, in Burgess's view, were the well-to-do Jewish families that, by the early 1880s, were knocking at the door of Caroline Reed's school for girls, just around the corner from Columbia. Reed's son and biographer later recalled that his mother "had great difficulty in resisting the insistence of the Jews to get their daughters into her school."[69] Should Caroline Reed's resolve fail, Jewish daughters would soon be knocking at Columbia's doors, a prospect that would create, Burgess feared, a breeding ground for women's rights and socialism.[70]

The admission of Jewish daughters could also serve as a breeding ground for civil rights. Burgess had left the South, but the South had never left Burgess. The only political concern that troubled him more than women's suffrage and socialism was the effort of radical Republicans after the Civil War to place political power into the hands of southern blacks and their white supporters. It was a "soul-sickening spectacle," he later wrote, one that he did not want to see encouraged in his adopted home.[71] It must have pained him to listen to Barnard say, in his most expansive moments, that Columbia should be open to all "seekers after knowledge, of whatever age, sex, race, or previous condition."[72] Opening Columbia's door to women would mean opening it to Jews; opening the door to Jews would, by Barnard's logic, entail opening it to blacks. That he could not risk.

THE "MONSTER PETITION"

Having failed to move the Columbia community with the appeal of the suffragist Lillie Devereux Blake or even that of the less radical Sorosis leader Jennie June Croly, Barnard seems to have concluded that he might stand a better chance if he had the support of the reform-minded wives of New York's business elite, women like Mrs. J. P. Morgan, for instance, who would never dream of using her own name, Fanny, in public. If the trustees could see that even so respectable a woman as Mrs. Morgan supported the admission of women to Columbia, then they might see how far behind the times they really were. In November 1881, he wrote to Mrs. Henry E. Pellew, a friend of Margaret Barnard's, urging her to work with Mrs. Morgan and others to persuade the trustees that the public favored opening Columbia to women. "The trustees do not open the college to women because they do not believe that the intelligence of New York is interested, he explained. "If that impression can be removed from their minds, they will hesitate no longer."[73]

On January 20, 1882, Barnard received a letter from eight women, including Mrs. Pellew, Mrs. Morgan, and Mrs. Cornelius Vanderbilt, asking him to "collect and reprint in pamphlet form" the essays that he had included in the annual reports of the past three years on "the admission of women to the educational advantages of Columbia College." Barnard replied the next day that he would gladly comply with their request and was encouraged to learn that "influences more powerful than any I am able to exert" were being marshaled on behalf of coeducation. On Saturday, April 22, 1882, an organization called the Association for Promoting the Higher Education of Women in New York held its first meeting. Revealing its debt to Barnard, the group adopted the same name as the British group then seeking the admission of women to Cambridge. Barnard had praised the British association in his 1880 report as an organization that worked to win women "not merely university education, but education in the university."[74]

To host the first meeting, the committee turned to Parke Godwin, who recently had succeeded his father-in-law, the poet William Cullen Bryant, as publisher of the New York Evening Post and who had been Lillie Devereux Blake's first employer. Godwin arranged for the organization to meet in the theater of his club, the palatial Union League Club on Fifth Avenue and Thirty-ninth Street, and he chaired the first meeting. Established in 1863 to support the Union cause, the Union League Club (not to be confused with the older, more restrictive Union Club) had sponsored a black regiment, supported the founding of the Metropolitan Museum of Art, and battled on behalf of good government. The club's membership, 1,400 strong by 1880, included the leading merchants, railroad magnates, and bankers of New York, as well as its newspaper publishers and leading literary lights. Many of the association's members were either members of the Union League Club or wives of members.[75] The fact that Hamilton Fish, the club's immediate past president, was currently the chairman of the Columbia College Board of Trustees enabled members of the association to exercise maximum influence.

The program included speeches by the Reverend Dr. Richard Storrs, of the Congregationalist Brooklyn Church of the Pilgrims; Joseph H. Choate, one of New York's leading corporate lawyers and a future ambassador to the Court of St. James, whose extensive contacts in England made him familiar with educational reform for women there; and the Reverend Henry C. Potter, not yet bishop of New York, or yet trustee of Columbia College, but rector of the Episcopalian Grace Church. The organization's founding objectives were "to secure the admission of women in Columbia College" and "to raise the standard of instruction in existing schools for girls." Clarifying the association's coeducational intent, Choate delivered a speech that lifted liberally from remarks delivered three weeks earlier by a Harvard Annex junior, angry at the way women were being treated by Harvard. In Choate's version, "If you ask why we insist on Columbia's actually opening her doors to women, we answer because there is no reason why they should submit to gather in an annex the crumbs which fall from their master's table, when they have a right to an equal seat at the board."[76] The members, who included Caroline Choate and Margaret Barnard, resolved to circulate a petition calling on the trustees to admit women as their first step toward achieving those goals.[77]

President Barnard did his part, behind the scenes. In June 1882, he wrote to Caroline Choate to be patient with the slow progress of the movement for coeducation: "In revolutions of traditional opinions, time is an element of incalculable power." He sent a letter to educators throughout the United States endorsing the work of the association and requesting the educators to reply to a survey on the subject of women and education. And he took advantage of his many contacts among journalists in the city to "keep the press stirring." As he told Caroline Choate, "Luther would never have carried through the reformation but for the incessant shower of pamphlets the reformers poured out from the press. We want as many different hands in the work as possible also."[78]

The Reverend Dr. Morgan Dix heard about the first meeting of the Association for Promoting the Higher Education for Women in New York in a conversation with Caroline Reed. In his judgment, the participants were "all fanatics on the subject of female education." Helpless in the face of this public organizing, Dix sought petty ways to punish Barnard: refusing him the secretary he needed to handle his mounting paperwork, wondering if it might not be a good idea to stop publishing Barnard's annual reports because they departed so significantly from the policy that the board wished to set, and deploring Barnard's efforts to make a public campaign out of a private, institutional matter.[79]

Columbia students were just as dismayed by the threat of coeducation as the trustees. The *Spectator* published an editorial, as well as a series of articles, that, in contrast to published reaction from students in 1873, offered no dissent from the prevailing belief that coeducation would destroy the institution. The students feared having to compete with women. They worried about the loss of prestige that attending a coeducational school would entail. They warned of the threat that coeducation would pose to the "morals of the fair sex." And, despite Barnard's confident pronouncements about space not being a problem, they believed it would be. One student, out of sorts after the inconveniences of several years of steady construction on campus, suggested hopefully, "When coeducation has been disposed of, perhaps the room in the basement of the Anonymous Building will no longer be reserved for a 'ladies cloak room,' but provided with a lunch-counter and tables." Other students reported that the "belligerent and demonstrative outcry" against coeducation in 1879 had been replaced by "a settled and reasonable belief that coeducation would not only be financially unprofitable and unsuccessful, but positively detrimental to the welfare of the University." They stressed that they did not oppose higher education for women per se. They were simply opposed to "the mingling of the sexes in the same recitation and lecture rooms," which "would be disastrous to all college feeling and order." If the "college has money to waste in the experimental running of an 'Annex' in some other part of the city, well and good, but that is for the Trustees to decide, and not for an association of charitable but misguided ladies."[80]

By early 1883, the "monster petition," as Dix called it, was complete. Among the 1,352 people who signed it were President Chester A. Arthur and former president Ulysses S. Grant, as well as fifty physicians, many clergy ("mostly Presbyterians," grumbled the Columbia trustees), principals, and teachers in several girls' schools.[81] One of the ministers who signed the petition was the Reverend Arthur Brooks, rector of the Episcopal Church of the Incarnation at Thirty-fifth Street and Madison Avenue. Underscoring the fact that the city's Episcopal clergy were by no means all as conservative as the Reverend Dr. Dix, the Reverend Dr. Brooks endorsed the petition not only on behalf of the women who sought professional careers but also on behalf of the growing number of aimless young women who filled his pews each week—a leisured class generated by the great wealth drawn to New York City as the economic center of the country. He wanted to see these women engaged in some productive activity and publicly deplored the fact that a woman in New York City could "obtain the gratification of every want, wish, or whim, save one—she could not get an education."[82] On February 5, 1883, Hamilton Fish, having received the association's petition, duly presented it to the board of trustees and appointed the Select Committee of Five, which included Dix, to consider it.

THE LENTEN LECTURES

The Reverend Dr. Morgan Dix was furious. He blamed the petition on a "persistent set of agitators" made up of a "little knot of persevering women, most of whom are Unitarians of the Boston type or freethinkers." Dix was referring to the congregation of the Unitarian All Souls Church on Chambers

Street, whose largely New England membership included William Cullen Bryant and his son-in-law, Parke Godwin, as well as many of the women active in organizing the Association for Promoting the Higher Education of Women in New York. Unitarian women of the Boston type not only were "freethinkers," but condoned what in the late nineteenth century was widely known as a "Boston marriage," one in which two women lived as lifelong partners. Dix may have given Boston Unitarians more credit than they deserved for the relentlessness of the campaign to open Columbia to women, but he was onto something. The membership of the Association for Promoting the Higher Education of Women in New York overlapped substantially with the membership of the New York Committee on the Harvard Examinations for Women and the Boston Women's Education Association. One of the women Dix thought to be most fanatical on the subject of coeducation was Eliza Theodora Minturn, a member of all three groups and the chief link among them. The daughter of the Union League Club's first president, Robert Minturn, and the friend of the Harvard Annex student Elizabeth Briggs, Minturn made sure that nothing happened in either Boston or New York with respect to women's education that was not the subject of intense scrutiny in the other city within a few days.[83]

Just as troubling to Dix as Boston Unitarians were New York Episcopalians like Lillie Devereux Blake, whose public careers, in his view, inevitably threatened traditional family life. Although in the early 1880s Blake focused most of her energies on the suffrage movement, she continued to see President Barnard and press the cause of coeducation. John W. Burgess later complained that in this period he "could scarcely enter the private room of our own President Barnard without finding Mrs. Lillie Devereux Blake seated in front of his famous trumpet exerting all the power of her beauty, her art, and her eloquence to persuade him that this great movement [for women's education] had at last struck New York and that Columbia must open its doors to women or be left behind."[84]

As word of the petition circulated around New York, Dix resolved to fight back. In February 1883, he chose as the topic of his annual Lenten lectures "The Calling of a Christian Woman." He began on February 9 at Trinity Chapel on West Twenty-fifth Street, the uptown appendage of Trinity Church, where New York's most fashionable faithful then worshipped and where Edith Wharton would marry in 1885. Dix's first lecture, in which he idealized maternity and the importance of women's confinement to the domestic sphere, was not well covered in the press. His second lecture, however, in which he spoke of women's degradation under paganism and their "restoration under Christianity," was widely reported.

Blake read a report of it at breakfast with her younger daughter, Katie, the next morning. "Why, this is outrageous," she exclaimed. Dix had placed the blame for all the evil in the world on Eve and her female descendants. Blake had to respond. She immediately rented Frobisher Hall, on Fourteenth Street, publicized a lecture of her own, and stood ready to answer him on the Sunday evening following his third Friday sermon. On each of the successive Fridays, Dix gave a new lecture on his theme of women's place. And on the following Sunday, Blake rebutted his arguments.[85]

Dix's lectures were clearly a response to the "monster petition," which had just been dumped in his lap. The subject of education," he noted, "has of late been much discussed." The newspapers "teemed" with articles about it. At least "one public meeting has been held to make or direct opinion on the subject." Everywhere people spoke of "The Higher Education of Women" and "Coeducation," as though they were linked. But, he warned, they were not. Coeducation, in trying to make woman "what she was not meant to be and can not be, will be not a higher education, but a lower." The whole campaign was part of an "organized attempt" to "remove woman from her proper place of work [the home]." Were this effort "to succeed, the way would be open to success on every other line of the programme of revolution." Admit a woman to Columbia today, he implied, and the socialists would be in power tomorrow.[86]

Dix insisted that God was on his side. Sin had entered the world through Eve and had been kept at bay since the beginning of Christianity only by the sacrifice of the Virgin Mary. Coeducation threatened to return woman to her original condition. Dix recognized that he lived in an age of science and that God could not serve as his only authority. Fortunately, he found science on his side as well. As Edward Clarke had warned in his response to the agitators at Harvard, coeducation would destroy women by forcing them to an intellectual effort, easy enough for men, but that their bodies could not withstand. Taking no account of a decade's worth of scientific rebuttal to Clarke's anecdotal account, Dix declared, "Nature herself forbids coeducation and protests against it." At the same time, coeducation would destroy morality, for it would "throw the young of both sexes together at an age when the passions are strong and the interest in each other is inevitable." Where coeducation had been introduced, moral decline had quickly followed. In the Midwest, he had heard, men and women spent their time kissing, and in Zürich, it was said, "women walked about in trousers, smoking cigarettes, and chatting with the professors." This should occasion no surprise: "the entrance of Athene into our collegiate halls will be inevitably followed by the advent of Aphrodite."[87]

Coeducation engendered lust but never true love, Dix insisted. By encouraging women "to know all that men know," "to go wherever men go," "to go down and strive in the streets, to vote, to fight, to act the man," to press for married women's property acts that "make married persons practically independent of each other," and to compete "with men on a field which God reserved for men only, in work not suited to the woman, and in the professions already overstocked," coeducation made woman "offensive and detestable in men's eyes."[88]

Dix conceded that there were "instances in which women have done notable things" that have "profited mankind." But, he insisted, "they are exceptions."[89] The advocate of coeducation was guilty of trying to turn an exception into a rule and thereby threatened society at its very foundation. There was no greater threat to the home, he averred, "than the woman who, under the selfish idea of lifting herself up into a higher intellectual position, deliberately unfits herself for social and domestic duties, and persuades others to follow that example." This was the sort of woman who was most likely "to defeat the objects for which marriage was instituted," by avoiding (through birth control or abortion, one assumes) "first the pains, and next the cares and duties of maternity." These attitudes fed the "growing indifference to the chief of all social abominations, divorce." The only threat to human welfare that could compete with coeducation, in Dix's view, was "fashion," which lured the young away from their religious duty to waste themselves on frivolous parties and dissipation. In the midst of his Lenten lectures, this frivolity had reached new heights in a party given by Alva Vanderbilt in her bid to wrest social recognition from Caroline Astor.[90]

In place of coeducation, Dix supported schooling that "develops the true ideal of womanhood, as distinct from that of manhood." He praised "the convents and religious houses of our American and English sisterhoods," where "many women have found a true and worthy mission." He honored the "good wives and devoted mothers" who read and visited museums in their spare time, "only we say that these things should follow after higher and more sacred duties." But they must not "be sought for themselves." The principal work of the Christian woman was "to resist the forces of secularism and naturalism, and maintain the old Christian ideas." Dix therefore deplored the new colleges for women—like Vassar, Wellesley, Smith, Mount Holyoke, and Bryn Mawr—nearly as much as the coeducational institutions. Their only redeeming virtue was their isolation from male centers of learning. In all other respects, they stood guilty of the same misguided ambition of turning women into men that was being threatened at Columbia. In conclusion, Dix urged his female listeners to abandon their call for coeducation, devote themselves to their families, pray in silence, and, finally, "let the world alone; let things alone which do not concern you."[91]

WOMAN'S PLACE TODAY

Lillie Devereux Blake delivered her response, week by week, in a white heat of righteous anger. Witty, eloquent, and forceful, she raked Dix over her feminist coals. This was personal. There he stood, at the head of the wealthiest church in New York, declaiming against higher education for women. And here she stood, a descendent of Columbia presidents, in hastily rented Frobisher Hall. Despite having published some five hundred articles, short stories, and lectures, as well as five novels, she was so hard-pressed financially that in some years she had to sell pieces of her family's remaining silver to pay the rent. Laying responsibility for Columbia's decade-long refusal to admit women entirely at Dix's feet, Blake told her listeners of her unsuccessful efforts ten years before to win women the right to attend Columbia. What she did not tell her audience was that, as a result of Dix's obstruction and because her husband was gravely ill and able to work only intermittently, she could not afford to send her daughters to a residential college out of town. They ultimately had enrolled in the Female Normal School, and in 1876 they had become teachers in the primary grades of the city's public-school system for $41.75 a month, the most that a woman without a college degree could then earn. Dix's suggestion that all women had a home to which they could retire in silence galled her. So, too, did his suggestion that women like her were an exception. In the state of New York in 1883, there were 73,000 more women than men; moreover, there were 400,000 women over twenty-one who were single, widowed, or divorced—about one-third of the adult female population. And that did not count the women who were forced to support their husbands.[92]

In a drumbeat of steady sarcasm, Blake lambasted "this Reverend stumbling block," "this simple-minded rector," "this respectable fossil," this "theological Rip Van Winkle," "this pulpit dictator." Drawing on her youthful training in Greek and Latin, her wide reading, and her lifetime in the Episcopal Church, she gave tit for tat in classical allusion and scriptural exegesis. Women had been better off under the pagan Egyptians, Romans, and Teutons than they had ever been under Christianity, she asserted. And they would not be so abused under Christianity but for the biblical interpretations offered by the Reverend Dr. Dix and every other male religious leader since the Middle Ages. Genesis did not prove that women were inferior and leaders in sin. Rather, the biblical text said that "'male and female' both were created 'in the image of God,' and . . . given 'dominion' over the earth, showing that they were absolute equals." The angel had persuaded Eve to eat forbidden fruit "by the promise of knowledge." Adam, who was present, "expected her to take the leading part . . . and meekly followed her lead." If Eve was inferior to Adam because he was created first, then Adam was inferior to the fishes, because they preceded him. Contrary interpretations were "at the root and foundation of every idea of woman's inferiority which afflicts us today," as well as at the root of every argument used against coeducation. Given that girls had for so long been forbidden to romp, compressed by corsets, hampered by skirts, kept indoors, and forced to spend many hours each day at the piano, Blake thought that "we may really found a claim for woman's superiority on the fact that, in spite of this monstrous act of destruction, our girls are as bright as they are. I fancy boys would hardly come out as well."[93]

Blake castigated the obstructionist rector for persisting in this opposition despite mounting and overwhelming evidence that coeducation was a success everywhere it had been tried. Blake cited testimony from the presidents of Cornell, Michigan, Wesleyan, and Boston, and that of professors throughout England in support of her claim. She added that coeducation, far from destroying the home, had improved it, as educated women had "carried into their domestic life sounder knowledge, higher tastes and aspirations, stronger interest in the truth, and greater power of influencing for good the lives and character of those they love." How could a reasonable man object? The modern man did not want "a silly goose" for a wife, but "a woman on whom he can rely . . . who shall be his wife, his friend, and his companion."[94]

In response to Dix's fears of moral decline, she conceded that there was much vice in the world but declared that the way to end it was not by hiding women away in the home, but by giving them the intellectual resources to combat it and encouraging them to go out into the world to reform it. Women turned away from marriage and motherhood not because they wanted to, but because men "usurp all authority," "beat their wives," and fail to support their families. As for Dix's criticism of those women who wasted their time at parties, she spoke for her girlhood self when she declared that Dix "denies to our young women all higher education, closes to them all active careers, and then blames a gifted girl for wishing to achieve success in the only arena open to her"—that is, in society.[95]

Blake derided Dix for his arrogance in presuming to judge that there were professions "unsuited" to women and that there were professions, like medicine, that were "overstocked." Why should it be women who must give way? Why must the advantage go unquestioningly to men? She acknowledged that it had been a "favorite sneer to declare that 'strong-minded' women neglected their duties," but she denied that this was true. "If you find a woman full of energy as a writer, as a speaker, in her reform work," she said, speaking obviously of herself, "you may be sure she will carry that same energy into the administration of her house."[96]

As far as the press was concerned, Blake won the battle of the lectures handily. Her witty caricature of Dix delighted editorialists around the country. Publishers clamored to print Blake's lectures as a book. Since she had delivered them from notes, she relied on newspaper accounts to help her prepare a manuscript for publication. She did so in three weeks. The volume appeared by the end of April as a 20-cent paperback entitled *Woman's Place To-day*, and it quickly became a handbook for suffragists both in the United States and in England. But the reaction of the press came too late to change the outcome of the debate over coeducation at Columbia.[97]

THE COLLEGIATE COURSE FOR WOMEN .

On March 5, 1883, the day after Blake delivered her first stinging attack, and before the press had been able to do anything more than praise her "Effective Sarcasm" against the Reverend Dr. Dix, the rector reported to the board his committee's recommendation that the petition of the Association for Promoting the Higher Education of Women in New York be rejected. With the sole exception of President Barnard, the board voted to approve the reverend's report. As Dix noted in his diary, he had engineered a "complete and thorough triumph over the coeducation scheme."[98]

The students and alumni did not think so. They were furious about what they saw as an "entering wedge" to coeducation in the committee's report to the full board. They had some reason for concern. If Dix had been able to respond to the petition on his own, he would have done what he had always done in the past: reject it out of hand. But board chairman Hamilton Fish, who had served as secretary of state under Ulysses S. Grant (a signer of the petition), recognized the need for diplomacy.[99] When in early February he received the "monster petition" from the Association for Promoting the Higher Education of Women, he decided to appoint a committee to review it. Fish did not want Columbia to admit women, and he did not want Barnard on the committee, but he did try to appoint members who represented the basic divisions of the board. Three of the committee members—Dix and the Reverend Talbot W. Chambers, together with William C. Schermerhorn—favored outright rejection. But John Townsend, who had at first favored rejection, had come to approve establishing an annex, and Cornelius Agnew supported coeducation. Although Agnew had proved to be a disappointing ally to Barnard in the 1879 struggle over recognizing women's right to attend lectures, he assured the president that this time he was "ready for the fray" and looking forward to "fighting."[100] Given Dix's statements in his Lenten lectures against women's being educated like men, the report that the committee produced was a triumph for the dissenters.[101] First, the report included a request that the board authorize a course of study—to be pursued outside the college—that could lead to a "suitable testimonial or diploma." Second, it invited those with the means to do so to raise funds for a college for women, and, it promised, the board would "carefully consider how best to develop the growth of so interesting a foundation." Hardly a wringing endorsement of educational opportunity for women, but a more conciliatory statement than the board had been willing to consider in the past. When the board rejected coeducation on March 5, 1883, it approved these provisions and authorized the Select Committee of Five to draft plans for what came to be known as a Collegiate Course.[102]

These concessions, painful though they must have been for Dix, did little to shield him from public criticism. Although editorialists recognized that the trustees had offered a "first step" toward coeducation for those who wanted to pursue the matter, the city's newspapers excoriated the board for its failure to respond more fully to public opinion. As Dix reported in his diary, "The press is teeming with comments most of them one-sided, and many extremely bitter, on the refusal of the Board of Columbia College to allow coeducation. The extent to which the public mind had been debauched by the women and President Barnard on this subject is evident from the tenor of the articles pouring from the press; never was there a grosser delusion." The coverage from the *New York Tribune* was especially critical, perhaps in part because Blake's nephew, Jimmie Umsted, worked there and took a special interest in the topic. As reports of Dix's lectures on a Christian woman's calling began to circulate, the negative judgments mounted. A few days later, Dix reported: "Received newspapers today, one from Auburn, N.Y., another from St. Augustine, Florida, and another from Rochester, N.Y., filled with most abusive expression about my lecture."[103] Even within the Episcopal community, his views were beginning to seem extreme, a fact that may have contributed to his defeat for the position of coadjutor of the Diocese of New York that year.

By May, under further encouragement from Agnew, whose resolve was, in turn, stiffened by Barnard, Dix relented a bit more. In a report to the board on May 7, 1883, he went so far as to say that when those interested in higher education for women had raised enough money to establish a separate college "conducted with due regard for the laws of physiology and hygiene and reverence for the principles of the Christian religion," he thought that "a way will be found to connect it with our University System and . . . secure to it the advantage of the personal attendance of our College Faculty in its several branches of instructions." Meanwhile, his committee was willing to authorize a collegiate course of study, patterned on the Columbia curriculum, for any young woman who had reached the age of eighteen (later lowered to seventeen). If, studying outside the college, she could pass the same exams that the faculty gave to male students, then she would "receive a certificate stating the subjects which she has pursued and with what success."[104] This was the recognition that Harvard was then giving to women enrolled at the Harvard Annex, which was a far cry from what Frederick Barnard, Lillie Devereux Blake, and Caroline Choate had hoped for—indeed, a massive disappointment, but a step in the right direction.

Blake, for her part, continued to fight for women's rights with mounting success. She became the leading suffragist in New York, and very nearly in the country. Elizabeth Cady Stanton pushed her for the presidency of the National Woman Suffrage Association in 1890, but Susan Anthony preferred Carrie Chapman Catt, who shared Anthony's single-minded dedication to the suffrage struggle. Blake and Stanton's insistence that the vote was simply part of a much larger set of necessary projects, one of which was a woman's version of the Bible they published in answer to Dix, did not sit well with Anthony. For many decades, Stanton and Blake were given short shrift in histories of women's suffrage. But in the long run, their comprehensive approach to women's rights would prove more valuable than Anthony appreciated. By regarding politics as just one aspect of a total system of exclusion and refusing to work on that aspect alone, they helped create a broad framework for understanding women's collective disadvantages.[105]

In the meantime, women kept knocking at Columbia's gates, and Frederick Barnard did what he could to let them in. He won female students the right to use the library and arranged for those admitted to the Collegiate Course to consult with faculty members at the beginning of each semester to clarify expectations regarding what was to be learned that term. He fully expected that, as women demonstrated their ability to do advanced work, opposition from students and faculty would turn to support, and the trustees would have to admit them to the full privileges of the university.[106] There were signs he might be right. Six women passed the entrance exam in 1884, and, by 1888, twenty-eight were enrolled.[107] Despite the trustees' prohibition of class attendance, professors at the School of Mines continued to welcome women to their lectures.[108] Most promising of all, in 1883 Melvil Dewey, inventor of the

Dewey Decimal System, arrived from Wellesley College with six Wellesley graduates to modernize Columbia's library and began talking about establishing a library school open to women and men alike.[109]

Barnard had long believed that Columbia's future depended on the quality of its library. On this matter, at least, he could count on the support of John W. Burgess. In 1883, Burgess had recommended, and Barnard had concurred, that they recruit Melvil Dewey to take charge of Columbia's newly completed library.[110] Dewey believed that the development of modern libraries depended, in turn, on the training of professional research librarians, and in 1886, with the enthusiastic support of President Barnard, he persuaded the Columbia College Board of Trustees to establish a professional school of "library economics," open to students who had completed two years of college. After two years of further study, they would be awarded the bachelor of library science degree.[111]

Before coming to Columbia, Dewey had spent a year at Wellesley College, where he had married the head librarian and been converted to the idea that professional training should be open to women as well as men. As he set about establishing his new school, he therefore actively recruited women for the first class. Word of his efforts eventually reached the trustees, who, reminding him of their steadfast opposition to coeducation, ordered him not to use any Columbia classrooms. Dewey used the college chapel instead, but the trustees were not satisfied. In late 1888, with President Barnard in failing

Columbia College Library
The reading room at Columbia, when the college was at Forty-ninth Street and Madison Avenue. (Columbia University Archives–Columbiana Library)

health and no longer able to protect Dewey, the board pressed him to resign. On April 1, 1889, they reached an agreement with the regents of the State University of New York that Dewey and his school be officially transferred to the State Library in Albany.[112] Although twenty-three students, twenty women and three men, had completed the library course at the time the school was closed, the trustees refused to recognize their accomplishment. Columbia would not offer library training again until 1926.[113]

THE "ABSOLUTELY EXCEPTIONAL" WINIFRED EDGERTON

Dewey succeeded better on another front. Soon after arriving in New York City, he had occasion to introduce to President Barnard a nineteen-year-old math prodigy in search of a telescope. Winifred Edgerton, one of the many young women forced elsewhere for college by the absence of opportunity in New York City, had attended Wellesley College, where she had excelled in mathematics and astronomy. Following graduation in 1883, she had returned home to complete a project for the Harvard Observatory that involved making an independent calculation of the orbit of a comet from data that Harvard furnished. Through Melvil Dewey, whom she had known at Wellesley, she met Barnard and asked about the possibility of continuing her studies. Edgerton was twice lucky. Not only was Barnard an ardent advocate for women, but he also had a special fondness for astronomy. In 1846, he had persuaded the trustees at the University of Alabama to build him an observatory, and he had been championing the cause of practical astronomy ever since. He quickly agreed to take up Edgerton's cause with Professor of Astronomy John Krom Rees at the School of Mines.[114] Eager to have an assistant, Rees became Edgerton's supporter. Recognizing his own failure to win the board's support on behalf of women students by frontal assault, Barnard next advised Edgerton to visit Columbia's trustees individually to plead her case. The trustees had only just approved the Collegiate Course and had never discussed graduate study for women, but Edgerton won the favor of all, including even Dix. It helped, no doubt, that Edgerton worshipped at Trinity Church. Influenced by her piety as much as her brilliance, Dix persuaded himself that her studies would interfere with neither her domestic obligations nor her religious devotions. This was no Lillie Devereux Blake.[115] Convinced that she presented a case that was "absolutely exceptional in nature," Dix supported her request to pursue graduate research.[116]

For the most part, Edgerton worked alone in the observatory, as the trustees intended, accompanied by only a chest full of dolls. But the trustees' rule against class attendance by women seems to have been so widely flouted that

Winifred Edgerton (1863–1931)
Graduate of Wellesley College (1883),
astronomer and mathematician, and first
woman to receive a Ph.D. from Columbia
(1886), as photographed in 1883. (Wellesley
College Archives)

even the pious and deferential Edgerton took classes with male students without word getting back to the board. Two years later, the science and mathematics faculty, including even John Van Amringe, recommended that she be permitted to present a dissertation and take doctoral exams. There was some precedent for doing so. Boston University had bestowed the first Ph.D. on a woman in 1877. Three years later, Cornell, Syracuse, and the University of Pennsylvania each had awarded a degree.[117] At Columbia, however, Edgerton was the first woman to qualify for a doctorate. She succeeded so well that on June 7, 1886, the Columbia trustees voted without dissent to award her the Ph.D. cum laude—the first Columbia degree ever given to a woman. At the same meeting, the trustees bowed to President Barnard on a second key point. In contrast to Harvard, which still refused to honor course work completed in the Harvard Annex with a Harvard degree, the Columbia trustees agreed that those women who completed the Collegiate Course would be awarded the same degree given to Columbia men.[118] At commencement, according to local papers, the Columbia students gave Edgerton an ovation that lasted for fully two minutes.[119]

In 1887, Mary Parson Hankey earned a bachelor of literature degree for her completion of the nonscience portion of the undergraduate curriculum. Unfortunately, she died of pneumonia within a year, giving ammunition to those who believed that women could not withstand the rigors of serious academic study. But the women kept coming. In 1888, Alice Louise Pond completed the Collegiate Course, science and all, and became the first woman to receive a B.A. Her appearance on the commencement platform brought forth such a storm of applause that the exercises had to be interrupted, at which point the class of 1888 gave her the Columbia cheer. In the next six years, another six women earned the Columbia bachelor's degree.[120]

With the public seemingly so supportive of the women students, with a growing number of faculty welcoming them to their classes, with the undergraduates now cheering women at commencement, and with the trustees willing to award women the same degrees they awarded men, President Barnard believed that coeducation was within reach. At least one young woman who had enrolled in the Collegiate Course, however, thought Barnard a poor political analyst; in her judgment, coeducation at Columbia seemed about as close as "doomsday."[121]

TWO

ESTABLISHING BEACHHEADS

ANNIE NATHAN enrolled in the Collegiate Course in 1885. The daughter of Robert and Annie Florence Nathan, she represented the advance guard of what John W. Burgess most feared, an incursion of Jewish women. A member of New York's Sephardic community, which had played an important role in New York's commercial and cultural life since before the American Revolution, she was descended from Rabbi Gershom Seixas, the only Jew ever to have served on the Columbia College Board of Trustees. This world of privilege and influence was marred for her in childhood, however, by her father's business reverses and philandering, and by her mother's suicidal despair, drug addiction, and early death. She cared for her brothers and father from the age of thirteen, retreating into her books whenever time allowed.[1]

Like many young women of her class and time, Annie Nathan acquired her education not from schools but from tutors and her family's library. With this preparation, she passed Columbia's entrance examinations at the age of eighteen and enrolled in the Collegiate Course. Twice a year, once in the fall and again in midwinter, she was "granted interviews with various august professors," who told her what to read. Dutifully, she did so, but when it came time to take the examination in one of the courses, she realized that she had never encountered the material on which part of the exam was based. Coolly, she answered what she could and then added, "certain of the questions evidently referred to the Professor's lectures, which I had not had the privilege of hearing." The professor, having a sense of justice, or perhaps a sense of humor, passed her. But she found the whole experience exasperating, even "futile." It wasn't just the exams. Braving the stares of young men as she entered the library, steering clear of the professors known to be hostile to the presence of women, and knowing all the while that the male students benefited from the daily guidance of faculty in classrooms and laboratories while she did not—it all wore on her. Columbia was simply not a welcoming institution; it did not even have a restroom for women. President Frederick Barnard had carefully planned one when Hamilton Hall was de-

Annie Nathan Meyer (1867–1951)
Student in the Collegiate Course
(1885–1886), founder of Barnard College
(1889), and member of the Barnard College
Board of Trustees (1889–1951). Portrait, 1885.
(Annie Nathan Meyer, *Barnard Beginnings*
[Boston: Houghton Mifflin, 1935], frontispiece)

signed back in the early 1880s, but the students had successfully lobbied to convert it to a men's dining room as soon as the trustees rejected the petition from the Association for Promoting the Higher Education of Women. Gradually, Annie Nathan grew disenchanted with education for women at Columbia. On February 15, 1887, she married Dr. Alfred Meyer, a prominent doctor thirteen years her senior, and withdrew.[2]

Meyer did not intend to make a choice, when she married, to give up hope of a career, any more than Lillie Devereux Blake or Jennie June Croly had before her. Like them, she wanted to be a writer. She had been drawn to the idea of attending school, in the first place, because she thought it would provide a good excuse for avoiding all the domestic and social obligations that interfered with her writing. Marriage to a sympathetic and supportive husband, she believed, would provide an even better cover for her literary ambitions. But writing was not enough; she needed a project. Knowing that in marrying she had given comfort to those who opposed women's education, she resolved to do something about Columbia's unfairness toward women students. Being married and a college dropout, she thought, would make her crusade easier, since no one would suspect her of seeking change for her own benefit. She could assume the high moral ground and hope for the glory that would come with success.[3]

Meyer went first to Melvil Dewey, who, as the college librarian, was the one person with whom she had enjoyed regular contact while pursuing the Collegiate Course. Having spent time at Wellesley, and having married the

Wellesley librarian, Dewey was more enthusiastic about women's colleges than was his friend and mentor, President Barnard. Dewey encouraged Meyer to try to found a separate women's college at Columbia. She quickly learned whom to contact and whom to avoid. She avoided President Barnard. Quietly, she began organizing "Certain Friends of the Higher Education of Women" to press for "a college for women to be affiliated with Columbia College." Meyer made much of the fact that, unlike women at the Harvard Annex, Columbia women had the right to a university degree. All they needed was a college to go with it.[4]

In January 1888, Meyer published an article in the *Nation* in which she called attention to the fact that there were currently sixty-seven young women from New York and its suburbs who had been forced to go elsewhere to attend college. There were two at Cornell, four at Bryn Mawr, thirteen at Smith, seventeen at Vassar, and thirty-one at Wellesley. She mentioned a local girls' preparatory school that had at least five students who were ready to attend college the following year but who would not be able to because their parents would not allow them to leave home. Another thirty-three were pursuing a college course with the Cambridge-based Society to Encourage Studies at Home, and there were 1,600 women enrolled in the Female Normal School, many of whom would love to attend college. The time had come, she declared, "to begin to organize an association for the collegiate instruction of women by the professors and other instructors of Columbia College."[5]

With the help of Melvil Dewey and Mary Mapes Dodge, the editor of the popular children's magazine *St. Nicholas,* Meyer next wrote a memorial to the Columbia College Board of Trustees that "respectfully" noted "the great desirability of establishing in connection with Columbia College some provision for the instruction of women whereby the examinations and degrees [B.A., M.A., and Ph.D.] recently opened to them may be made truly available and many-fold more valuable." Such a "connection" she wrote, could be established through an "annex" similar to the women's colleges of Cambridge and Oxford, England, and the Harvard Annex in the United States. If the Columbia board would but give its consent, the Society for the Instruction of Women by the Professors and Other Instructors of Columbia College could be incorporated and would raise the funds necessary to make the undertaking a success. She then set out to collect fifty signatures from the city's business, professional, and cultural elite.[6]

She won over many of the women and men who had organized the Association for Promoting the Higher Education for Women, including Caroline Sterling Choate. From the beginning, members of the association appear to have been less dedicated to the idea of coeducation than President Barnard. At the time, both private and public schools in New York City were still segregated by sex, which made coeducation a more radical innovation there than in places where boys and girls shared the same classrooms in the primary and secondary grades. Caroline Choate shared Barnard's desire to see women admitted to Columbia, but she seems to have been concerned that the president's insistence on coeducation might be too radical for New York City. Following the rejection of the association's petition, she redirected her energies to other projects. Most important, she helped found the Brearley School for girls in the hope of giving talented girls the preparation they needed to succeed in Columbia's Collegiate Course as well as in other colleges that had begun to admit women.[7] Meyer also secured the signature of another association member, the Reverend Dr. Arthur Brooks, whose position as rector of the Church of the Incarnation gave him standing with Columbia's Episcopal trustees. She tried to win the endorsement of a mix of wealthy women and men who could finance a new school, and professional women who could give the new institution the intellectual seriousness she wanted it to have.[8]

Armed with her memorial, Meyer followed Winifred Edgerton's example and set out to visit the Columbia trustees one by one. She left Morgan Dix for last. Given the views he had expressed in his Lenten lectures opposing education for women modeled on the college studies of men, Dix could not have been pleased to see Meyer. But he was facing new problems that, in addition to the persistent pressure for coeducation of the past two decades, seem to have made him more open to the idea of endorsing a separate college for women. Melvil Dewey, with President Barnard's blessing, was pressing for a professional school of "library economics" open to women and men alike. At the same time, Nicholas Murray Butler, who, having graduated from Columbia College, had earned a Ph.D. and joined the teaching staff, was suggesting, with the enthusiastic support of Barnard, that Columbia begin offering professional training for teachers, an enterprise that Dix feared would also attract an undue number of women. Finally, Dix was beginning to encounter dissatisfaction even from some trustees over Columbia's policy of barring women from its classes. Sentiment seemed to be growing at least to admit women to graduate classes.[9] Fearful of further coeducational threats, Dix began to see the creation of a separate women's college, one that would take responsibility for preparing women for all Columbia degrees, B.A. through Ph.D., as the only way to stop the agitation. At a time when white Southerners were turning increasingly to legal segregation as a way of containing the social, economic, and political ambitions of blacks, what had seemed only a half-dozen years earlier to be a dangerously progressive idea began to seem appealingly conservative.[10]

Dix assured Meyer that he was not against women's education. "I am against wild women," he explained, in a not very subtle allusion to Lillie Devereux Blake. "I disapprove," he continued, "of unwomanly tactics, of creatures who are not men and certainly not women." In other words, he hated women who gave public speeches (especially ones that attacked him), campaigned for women's suffrage, or agitated for coeducation. In those respects, he had nothing to fear from Meyer. While she wanted women to have access to the same educational privileges available to men, she abhorred politics and, to the dismay of many later Barnard women, was a staunch antisuffragist.[11]

Meyer's antisuffragist stance remains something of a mystery. She believed deeply in individual freedom and condemned both religious and racial discrimination throughout her life. She fought as hard for women's right to men's educational privilege as any suffragist fought for women's right to men's political privilege. She had both suffragist and antisuffragist friends. And she was asked by leaders of each faction to contribute her considerable journalistic talent to their respective sides. Meyer later attributed her position to what she considered the suffrage movement's anti-male attitude and claim of moral superiority. In advancing this characterization, Meyer had to create something of a straw woman, especially in New York, where—under the leadership of Lillie Devereux Blake, Susan B. Anthony, and Elizabeth Cady Stanton—the suffrage movement remained resolutely rights-based from the 1870s onward. Stanton might occasionally speak in exasperation of "the male beast," in fighting for fairer divorce laws, but she did so not out of a belief in men's innate depravity but out of the conviction that the powerful tend to exploit the powerless.[12] A more likely justification for Meyer's antisuffragist stance was personal. She blamed Blake for the Columbia trustees' refusal to extend educational privileges to women. Meyer was convinced that a more diplomatic person, one willing to settle for a separate college for women affiliated with Columbia, could have succeeded a decade earlier and would have spared her the frustrating experience she had been forced to endure in the Collegiate Course. Seth Low once called Meyer a "regular Brooklyn politician"; she was a resolutely practical person.[13] It would be a mistake, however, to regard Blake as the only source of Meyer's antisuffragist stance. Even more important was the intense jealousy she felt toward her older sister, Maud, especially following the death of their mother. That jealousy led the sisters in different directions as adults. While Annie was battling for women's education, Maud was fighting for women's suffrage and helping to found the Consumers League, an organization that marshaled the nation's female consumers to fight for the rights of working women. For Annie Nathan Meyer, the political was personal.[14]

THE FOUNDING OF BARNARD COLLEGE

On March 5, 1888, board chairman Hamilton Fish transmitted Meyer's memorial to the board and referred it to a committee headed by Dix. On May 7, 1888, Dix reported his committee's approval in principle of Meyer's proposal, as long as it was understood that her group would have full financial responsibility for the proposed "annex" and would have to present the board with an acceptable plan for organizing the new institution before the board would grant its "official sanction." At the same meeting, the board received a letter of resignation from President Barnard, whose failing health had left him increasingly incapacitated. Because of the departure of the board's secretary, Meyer did not learn of the board's action until the following fall and assumed that the proposal had been tabled. But, as soon as Meyer learned that the board would consider establishing a college for women affiliated with Columbia, she organized a committee. She chose its members with care. As an implicit challenge to the all-male, overwhelmingly Episcopalian Columbia board, she decided to lead the committee herself. Next, she persuaded Frederic Coudert, a widely respected corporate lawyer and a Catholic, to join her committee. For added weight, she persuaded a second lawyer, Francis Lynde Stetson, known as J. P. Morgan's attorney general for his work counseling the banker on his corporate reorganizations, to serve as well. For gender balance, she invited two women: Ella Weed, the principal of the academically rigorous Miss Brown's School, and Columbia's star female graduate, Winifred Edgerton.[15]

Edgerton had come close to accepting a professorship at Smith College in 1887, but at the last minute, she had decided to marry John Hamilton Merrill, an 1885 graduate of Columbia's School of Mines with an 1890 Ph.D. Edgerton accepted the prevailing social norm that marriage precluded a teaching career, but, like Meyer, she wished to remain engaged in the world and eagerly joined Meyer's committee. When John Merrill discovered that committee meetings were being held downtown in men's offices, however, he demanded that his wife resign. A few years later, when he secured a position as New York State geologist and the couple moved to Albany, he barred her once more from public activity. Knowing of Edgerton's accomplishments, the lieutenant governor asked her to serve on the local school board. John Merrill said no, and again Winifred acquiesced, turning her energies to rearing four children. She later founded a girls' school but never again pursued either scientific research or social reform. The contrasting experiences of Winifred Edgerton Merrill and Annie Nathan Meyer revealed how important the choice of a husband could be to the future of a talented woman who decided to marry. Merrill's choice sharply circumscribed her ambitions. Meyer's led to a vigorous and successful public career.[16]

Working quickly, Meyer's committee wrote by-laws for its proposed school, organized a board of trustees, secured a building, and presented its plan to the Columbia trustees on February 4, 1889. At Meyer's suggestion, the committee's proposal included a recommendation that the new women's college be named for President Barnard, then near death, in recognition of his long campaign on women's behalf.[17]

On April 1, 1889, the same day that the trustees shipped Melvil Dewey and his library school up to Albany, Dix's committee recommended that the board accept the plan proposed by Meyer's committee. The trustees insisted, however, on one change. The founders of the new "annex" had proposed that their school's faculty be composed of "professors and instructors designated or approved by the trustees of Columbia College," but the Columbia trustees feared that such a provision could lead to different instruction in the two schools. Although Meyer's memorial called for a women's college modeled on the Harvard Annex, which depended on Harvard faculty exclusively for its teachers, the suggestion that the new college might be free to hire other faculty, who had merely been "approved" by Columbia, seemed to suggest that the committee planned to follow the practice of Bryn Mawr, which had just opened its own graduate program with its own faculty.[18] Not wanting to follow the Bryn Mawr model, the trustees therefore insisted, and the college proponents readily agreed, that all instruction be provided "exclusively" by the "professors and instructors of [Columbia] college." The training of a female student would mirror in every particular the education of her male counterpart, but it would be pursued in a separate building, and all expenses would be the responsibility of the board of trustees of the new institution.[19] With that change made, the Columbia board approved the creation of Barnard College.

Frederick Barnard died on April 27, 1889, never having commented publicly on the proposed school. Meyer never asked his permission, or even that of his wife. Margaret McCurry Barnard later told Meyer that she believed he "never would have approved of it." Her husband, she emphasized, "was for opening to the full limit every asset of Columbia College, freely and unequivocally to women and upon the same terms as for the men."[20] Barnard consistently had argued that the separate instruction of women and men was not merely less efficient, but also less effective pedagogically than coeducation. He fervently believed that men and women learned better together. As Nicholas Murray Butler later remembered his saying, "inter-training and equal training take the simper out of the young woman and the roughness out of the young man."[21] But it was too late for him to protest, and, as Margaret Barnard conceded to Meyer, "now that you have done my husband the honor of naming the College for him, you have taken the wind from my sails. I cannot very well fight a College which bears his name."[22] For her part, Meyer insisted that she did not oppose coeducation in principle; she simply believed that real coeducation could be more fully achieved in a separate college dedicated to women's interests than in Hamilton Hall, where women were likely to be lost in an atmosphere of male privilege.[23]

Annie Nathan Meyer believed that the success of the new enterprise depended on her being able to assemble a board of trustees that would chart a middle course between the ultraradicalism, or "queerness," as she put it, of Lillie Devereux Blake and the ultraconservatism—at least on gender matters—of the Columbia board, especially the Reverend Dr. Morgan Dix. One of Meyer's advisers, Frances Fisher Ward, who was the president of the Vassar alumnae association, wanted a board made up entirely of women (to mirror Columbia's board of all men). "There was no doubt," Meyer later affirmed, "that to have followed this policy would have won for the young institution the support and friendship of a certain type of feminist." Meyer maintained, however, that the financial future of the college depended on its including men, who were more likely than women to hold "the purse strings" and possess essential legal skills. She therefore insisted on a board that was evenly divided between eleven women and eleven men. All the members of her founding committee, save Edgerton, joined the board. Mindful of the insularity created by Columbia's Episcopal-heavy board, Meyer continued her insistence on religious balance. A liberal Episcopal priest, the Reverend Dr. Arthur Brooks, served as chairman of the board. The genteel Unitarian agitator Caroline S. (Mrs. Joseph H.) Choate served as vice chairwoman. The Jewish banker Jacob Schiff took on the responsibility of treasurer. Meyer and Schiff were the only Jews on the twenty-two-member board, but that was two more than the Columbia board could claim. Frederic Coudert provided a Catholic presence. Laura Spelman (Mrs. John D.) Rockefeller, in addition to her wealth, had the distinction of being a Baptist. The complete board of eleven women and eleven men included religious leaders, bankers, political leaders, lawyers, authors, educators, and philanthropists. The heterogeneity of the board was particularly notable at a time when gender, racial, and religious exclusiveness was on the rise. In 1892, the Union League Club, which had long welcomed members without regard to religious affiliation, black-balled Theodore Seligman from membership, even though his father had been a founder. The club's remaining Jewish members then resigned en masse. Four years later, in 1996, the Supreme Court affirmed the constitutionality of racial segregation in *Plessy v. Ferguson*. It was in this context that Meyer created Columbia University's first genuinely coeducational institution: the Barnard College Board of Trustees.[24] To commence operations, Treasurer Schiff announced that the board would need at least $5,000 in yearly income, plus a projected $2,000 in tuition. That meant acquiring assets of at least $100,000 before opening the college's doors. Even that sum, however, would not cover the projected expenses of $7,500 a year, plus the costs of heat, electricity, and janitorial services. Barnard opened, instead, with a little less than $10,000, half provided by J. P. Morgan, with most of the rest generated by the promise of thirty-six people to donate $100 each for five years. That paltry sum so discouraged Schiff that he proposed delaying a year before accepting any students. His fiscally reckless but passionately committed colleagues voted him down.[25]

The trustees rented a brownstone at 343 Madison Avenue, between Forty-fourth and Forty-fifth Streets, five blocks south of Columbia College, and they set out to hire Columbia instructors who would shuttle back and forth between the two schools, teaching their courses once for the men, and then again for the women. The brownstone on Madison Avenue mirrored thousands of other houses, in which New York's upper middle class lived in the 1880s. A narrow hallway and stairs led to three floors above. There was a small room to the right, and a larger room in back, furnished with chairs with writing arms purchased from Columbia. The trustees gladly permitted the building's owner to live on the top floor in exchange for a reduction of the rent. They also rented the parlor on the second floor to the Women's University Club to save a little more money. The accommodations were spartan compared with the lavish surroundings at Vassar or Wellesley, but it was a start.[26]

Ella Weed, chairwoman of the academic committee of the board of trustees, oversaw the day-to-day academic affairs of the new college, until a permanent dean could be hired. A Mrs. Kelly ran the house, standing watch if a student seemed to be spending too much time in conference with an attractive young male instructor. Mrs. N. W. Liggett, another Vassar graduate, by way of the Packard School in Brooklyn, served as registrar and bursar.[27]

In the fall of 1889, fourteen young women passed the Columbia entrance exams and arrived at Barnard to begin college.[28] Barnard offered the same curriculum and the same teachers available at Columbia: mathematics with Thomas Scott Fiske, Latin with Nelson G. McCrea, Greek with Mortimer

Barnard College
The first home of Barnard College, at 343 Madison
Avenue, as photographed in 1889. (Barnard College
Archives)

Lamson Earle, English with Edward B. Wasson, and a choice of either
French with Bernard O'Connor or German with William H. Carpenter.
The college also admitted a number of so-called specials, students who
wished to take a class or two in a particular subject. Fearing that the new college would soon be swamped if it opened its doors generally to special students, Ella Weed decided to admit only the limited number who wished to
study botany, and she hired an instructor specifically for them.[29]

Weed faced a number of challenges in helping young women navigate
through the foreign cultural territory of a Columbia education. First, there
was the embarrassing problem, faced whenever a female student entered the
Columbia library, of how to comport herself should a young man chival-
rously open a door. Propriety barred her from speaking directly to a man to
whom she had not been properly introduced. But to ignore a display of courtesy seemed rude. After much consultation, the consensus settled on a simple acknowledgment as the appropriate response.[30] Beyond the chance encounter, women students faced the culture shock of moving from one of the
girls' schools of New York to the Columbia College classes taught at Barnard
by male instructors used to teaching men. Schoolgirls were accustomed to
reading *Silas Marner* and being asked a few questions about it relating to content and grammar. At Barnard, they were subjected to the Columbia style of
English instruction: daily themes, promptly returned and red inked with
"Trite," "Lacking in Unity," "What of it . . . ?"—not the gently encouraging

comments of their former schoolteachers.[31] Columbia instructors were by no means unique in their brusque treatment of female students. In Cambridge, one student at the Harvard Annex submitted a theme to her Harvard instructor that took the form of two letters written to a boy named Robert. In them, she challenged the prevailing double standard in social relations between men and women and argued that young men should adhere to the same code of conduct expected of young women. Her instructor dismissed her argument as one that rested "upon the notion of the world which exists in a well-brought up feminine mind, and not upon the world as it is." Being told that her experience counted for naught, she must have found it difficult to conclude that she had anything to offer. Gradually, the students adapted to their professors' insistence on critical analysis, if not always to their opinions about gender norms. As Alice Duer Miller (Barnard 1896) later recalled, "A Barnard girl, even when she returns from a consultation with an essay patterned in red ink, manages to derive pleasure from that excitement."[32]

From the start, Barnard attracted a cosmopolitan group of students. In contrast to other women's colleges, which drew their students overwhelmingly from Protestant families, Barnard also attracted the daughters of Jews and Catholics. It included women from a remarkably broad range of economic backgrounds as well. In addition to the well-off daughters of the business and professional classes, Barnard enrolled students from two groups that did not then typically consider college: the wealthy daughters of the city's elite who wished to remain in New York City so as not to forgo the social life of the New York debutante, and young women who had to stay in New York because they could not afford the cost of a residential campus. To attend Mount Holyoke meant paying $425 for tuition, room, and board, while registering at Barnard College brought a charge of only $150 for tuition. To broaden its base still further, the Barnard trustees began immediately to raise scholarship funds. Barnard offered its students exposure to a diversity of backgrounds uncommon for women's colleges at that time. In 1890, the Reverend Arthur Brooks, president of the board of trustees, proudly announced that "Barnard College is for women of every class . . . those who are to earn their living and those who are not can meet here, each class, nay, better, each woman, helping the other, without patronage, without condescension, without bitterness."[33]

FOUNDING A COLLEGE FOR TEACHERS

Brooks exaggerated Barnard's inclusiveness. Few families were able to afford all that sending a daughter to Barnard required: paying for the extra classes in Greek, Latin, and mathematics that she needed to win admission, and forgoing her earnings while she remained in school. There was a much greater demand for training that did not require such extensive preparation. As of the 1880s, New York City offered the Female Normal School to prepare young women for jobs in the city's public schools. But as the growth of New York City in the late nineteenth century put growing pressure on the city's public-school system, and as educational reformers began to criticize traditional methods of pedagogy, support began to grow for a school dedicated specifically to the training of teachers in modern pedagogical methods.

New York had always had its poor and never had seemed able to muster the resources to resolve their problems. In the final decades of the nineteenth century, as political persecution and economic dislocation drove immigrants from eastern and southern Europe to America's principal port, the city's population soared and the misery of its slums deepened. By the turn of the twentieth century, four out of every five residents either were foreign born or had a parent who was foreign born. The tenements into which the poor crowded were built without thought to sanitation, light, or air. In good times, children worked long days alongside mothers and fathers for a bare subsistence. During economic downturns, they roamed the streets or sought entry to schools where classes of sixty to a hundred children were common.

On the theory that teaching the youngest children required the least skill, principals assigned the first graders to the least experienced teachers, usually female, just out of grammar school themselves, with certificates bestowed by a local Tammany official. Untutored in pedagogy, they lined up their charges in rigid rows and drilled them in arithmetic and simple word recognition. Those conditions so shocked the conscience of well-off New Yorkers, whose own children were taught in private academies, that they finally responded by founding a reform movement, led largely by women, aimed at relieving the poverty, illiteracy, disease, and vice that threatened to swamp the city. Although they worked on a broad range of interrelated problems, from public health to civil-service reform, almost all reformers shared a belief in the importance of education. For Grace Hoadley Dodge, education reform became a personal crusade.[34]

Dodge, born in 1856, was the eldest of six children of Sarah (Hoadley) and William Earl Dodge Jr. For generations, the Dodge family had combined evangelical zeal and civic mindedness with exceptional business success. William E. Dodge was a partner in the metals firm of Phelps Dodge and an active supporter of the Young Men's Christian Association, the Young Women's Christian Association, the Metropolitan Museum of Art, the New York Children's Aid Society, the American Museum of Natural History, the Union Theological Seminary, and the American Sunday School Union.[35]

Grace Hoadley Dodge (1856–1914)
Founder of Teachers College (1892) and member
of the Teachers College Board of Trustees and
treasurer of Teachers College (1892–1914), as
photographed around 1900. (Columbia University
Archives–Columbiana Library)

Large and awkward as a child, Grace Dodge was known as the "giant" to
her younger siblings. Had she been a man, her size would likely have helped
her make a mark in business. There was certainly plenty of opportunity in
the family's various enterprises. As the demand for copper in indoor plumb-
ing and electrical wiring soared in the final decades of the nineteenth century, Phelps Dodge extended its investments into copper extraction in Arizona and became the largest mining company in the United States.[36] Grace
also seems to have had the necessary talent. J. P. Morgan once claimed that
she had the best business mind of his acquaintance.[37] Barred from business
by her gender, however, Grace developed an acute self-consciousness about
her imposing size. Tutored at home as a child, she went dutifully to Miss
Porter's fashionable boarding school in Connecticut at the age of fourteen.
After two lonely years, however, she persuaded her parents to let her return
home to help her mother, a semi-invalid, run the household and to assist her
father in his religious projects. She became a teacher in the Sunday school
and sewing classes of the Madison Square (Presbyterian) Chapel and in the
industrial schools of the Children's Aid Society. She volunteered as a reader at the Yonkers hospital and served as a manager of the New York Infir-
mary. Finding satisfaction in those activities, while recoiling from the
prospect of making the debut expected of young women of her class, she
told her father, "You have taught me to be a follower of Jesus, to love God
and man . . . I must love through work."[38]

Respectful of his daughter's wishes, William E. Dodge introduced her to
Louisa Lee Schuyler, who, with Josephine Shaw Lowell, was turning chari-

table work into a career for women in the 1870s. From Schuyler, Dodge gained confidence in her managerial skills, as she directed the Bellevue Training School for Nurses, served as chair of the State Charities Aid Association's Committee for the Elevation of the Poor in Their Homes, and organized a large network of Working Girls Clubs. But she also came to realize that she was a very different person from her mentor. Schuyler saw herself as the general of an elite corps of volunteers, dedicated to making charity more efficient; Dodge saw herself as an educator seeking to reform society.

Her own travails made her especially sensitive to the burdens of gender. In her view, men's exploitation of women—economically and sexually—united women more than class differences divided them. She referred to the working "girls" who came to her sewing classes as her "sisters" and stressed the interdependence of rich and poor women, whatever their religious, class, or ethnic background. "They need us and we need them," she declared. In embracing sisterhood across class lines, Dodge tended to ignore the extent to which her solutions to female vulnerability were rooted in her class background. She saw herself as a working girl, too, one whose wages had simply been "paid in advance," without appreciating the psychological freedom and social power that being paid (so securely and so handsomely) "in advance" entailed.

Repelled by the cheap dance halls that abounded in New York, she found it difficult to understand their attraction to the young women with whom she worked. Confident in the moral superiority of middle-class households, she was baffled by young working-class women's tendency to avoid domestic service in "good" homes in favor of what were, to her, the morally treacherous though admittedly better-paid realms of the factory. Dodge never lost her piety or her belief that young women had to be protected. Her network of Working Girls Clubs gave young working women safe places to socialize. She supported the Woman's Municipal League in a study of employment agencies that sometimes consigned immigrant girls to houses of prostitution. She supported the American Committee for the Abolition of State Regulation of Vice in an effort to stamp out prostitution. And she consolidated several church-supported organizations into the New York Traveler's Aid Society to ensure the more effective protection of young women, new to the city, from the predations of men.[39]

Dedicated as she was to working "with" her "sisters" and learning from them, however, Dodge could not help observing that her lectures on moral purity and her efforts to protect women from vice were not having much impact on the misery that surrounded her. Like the college graduates who were establishing the country's first settlement houses on the Lower East Side,

Dodge came to see poverty as a social rather than an individual problem. The great need of the day, she believed, was to bridge the social and economic gap between native-born and immigrant, rich and poor, for the benefit of both.[40]

Of all the work Dodge tried, the most influential proved to be her teaching in the industrial schools of the Children's Aid Society, which offered a basic primary education to children not able to gain entry to the city's overcrowded public schools. Through this work, Dodge met Emily Hutchinson, who introduced her to the ideas of the German educational reformer Friedrich Froebel. Emphasizing the importance of learning through doing, Froebel sought to harmonize emotional and mental development. Hutchinson adapted Froebel's ideas to the education of little girls through her system of the "kitchen garden," in which she taught domestic skills by substituting miniature household utensils for toys. To spread Hutchinson's teaching, Dodge formed the Kitchen Garden Association in 1880, when she was twenty-four years old. Four years later, having come to see this work with girls as a model for education in general, she formed the Industrial Education Association (IEA), through which she campaigned to make manual training part of the public-school curriculum.[41]

Dodge wanted to avoid the one-sided, spiritually deadening pedagogy of the traditional schoolteacher, who treated intellectual development as separable from emotional and physical development, who taught children to sit still and recite rather than allowing them to discover the world through play, who force-fed them the names of trees rather than taking them into the forest or parks to discover nature for themselves, and who, in the process, robbed society of its children's creative spark. Dodge thought that the learning-by-doing approach to education should be an integral part of education for everyone. Manual training, she believed, was an "essential aspect of general education." Without it, children receive an education that "trains the memory too largely, the reasoning powers less, the eye and hand too little."[42]

Dodge recognized the political value of securing male support for her project. She created a board of managers for the IEA, to which she recruited prominent men, including her father; Columbia's president, Frederick Barnard; and a Columbia trustee, Seth Low. She persuaded Alexander Webb, president of City College, to assume the presidency of the organization, while she undertook principal administrative responsibilities herself and looked for a suitable site for it, which she found it at 9 University Place, in Greenwich Village. She also publicized industrial education with a large exhibition of the work children were doing in IEA-sponsored classes. The exhibit, attended by 70,000 people, appealed to a broad constituency. To progressives, manual training offered a way to make education more mean-ingful to children, while to conservatives it provided the basis for a system of vocational training that could lead quickly to employment. In short, it soon became a popular panacea for curing the ills of the city's schools.[43]

In 1880, Lillie Devereux Blake had won women in New York State the right to vote for and serve on local school boards. That victory had special meaning for Blake, whose daughter, Katherine Devereux Blake, having been denied admission to Columbia, had turned to the Female Normal School to prepare for work as a teacher. The Normal School offered only a two-year training course to girls who had completed grammar school, a far cry from the collegiate education that Lillie originally had sought for her. By the 1880s, she was struggling, with thousands of other underprepared women, to teach in the overcrowded, poorly funded, badly lit, and meager-ly supplied schools of New York. Lillie Devereux Blake's school suffrage vic-tory had no immediate effect in New York, because the Board of Education was appointive. But public pressure following Dodge's IEA exhibition forced Mayor William R. Grace to appoint the board's first two female members. He chose Grace Dodge and Mary Nash Agnew, wife of the Columbia trustee Cornelius Agnew, the ardent advocate of coeducation at Columbia whose daughters' attendance at science lectures in 1879 had precipitated the first major debate on the Columbia board over whether Columbia should be opened to women.

Dodge served as a member of the New York Board of Education for three years, during which time she investigated the maintenance of school build-ings, promoted industrial education, and demanded that teachers' salaries be raised. She also made herself the female teachers' special representative. Visiting them and encouraging them to visit her in return, she came to the conclusion that they needed training as much as their students did.[44] She envisioned schools staffed with expert teachers who, through manual train-ing, would transform society. To accomplish this goal, Dodge well under-stood the political importance of establishing an academic alliance. Through her contacts at Columbia, Dodge met Nicholas Murray Butler, who had just earned his Ph.D. in philosophy and was interested in educa-tional reform. In 1887, she recruited him to serve as president of the Indus-trial Education Association.

Born in 1862, Nicholas Murray Butler grew up in Paterson, New Jersey, the son of a small textile manufacturer. He entered Columbia at the age of sixteen, having graduated from Paterson's coeducational public high school and studied Greek and Latin with tutors. His parents had hoped to send him to Williams College or Princeton University, but financial reverses brought on by the depression of the 1870s forced them to settled on less-expensive Columbia. Butler's father paid the $100 tuition fee for the first year; Butler earned the rest by teaching at local private schools and writing for the *New York Tribune*, while living with relatives in Brooklyn.[45] A star student and campus leader, Butler attracted the attention of both President Barnard and Professor John W. Burgess. Barnard detected a promising educator; Burgess, a gifted politician.[46] Butler fulfilled the ambitions of both. As president of Columbia from 1902 to 1945, he led the university to greatness in the early twentieth century, and, although he never held political office, he exercised far-reaching influence in both domestic politics and international relations, as a prominent figure in the Republican Party, an adviser to presidents, and president of the Carnegie Endowment for International Peace.[47]

Burgess's most immediate impact on this product of New Jersey's public schools was to help turn him against the coeducation of his childhood. In the spring of 1882, Butler drafted a senior-class resolution against admitting women to Columbia. "It is the fixed opinion and firm conviction of the senior class," the petition read, "that the coeducation of the sexes is undesirable from an educational as well as from a social and moral point of view, and that its introduction here would be a fatal blow to the future welfare and prosperity of the institution."[48]

Barnard must have been irritated by his protégé's defection on the woman question, but he gained the upper hand when it came to shaping Butler's career. Butler entered Columbia with the intention of attending law school and pursuing a career in politics, a goal that Burgess worked to encourage. Barnard altered his plans. "Why not do something distinctive, something that is really worthwhile, something new and constructive?" the president asked, as he set forth a course of reading in German on the history, philosophy, and moral purpose of education.[49]

Pedagogy was much on Barnard's mind. As he counseled Butler, he was lobbying the Columbia trustees to found a professional school for teachers. Nowhere, he lamented in his 1881 annual report, was education treated as a science; nowhere was there "an attempt made to expound its true philosophy." In an obvious reference to the medical and law schools, Barnard deplored the fact that "our leading sciences concern themselves very little about human beings unless they are ill and we want to cure them . . . or unless they commit crimes and we want to punish them." He called for a school of pedagogics, the first of its kind in this country, "designed to prepare teachers for their work." A school that taught the history, theory, and practice of teaching, he insisted, "would bring the College more directly and to more effective purpose into contact with the outside world than almost any other."[50]

A year later, Barnard lamented the failure of the trustees to respond favorably to his plea. Even a proposed course of lectures had met with no success. Undaunted, he pointed to the desperate plight of New York City's teachers: "At the present time they have, as a rule, no adequate knowledge of the nature of their task, and certainly they have no proper preparation for it." He conceded the existence of the city's Female Normal School, which took students who had completed grammar school, but he questioned its sufficiency. The trustees, ever cautious of any innovation that might be costly or might bring women into Columbia's halls, declined to follow Barnard's lead.[51]

Already in his seventies, Barnard understood that the success of his campaign depended on finding a lieutenant to carry on the fight. He therefore awarded Butler a three-year graduate fellowship so that he might prepare to carry on the work he had begun. Between 1882 and 1884, Butler read philosophy under the direction of Columbia's Professor Archibald Alexander; read classic works on education in English, German, and French with Barnard; and met with Barnard's cousin Henry Barnard, who, with Horace Mann, had been an important builder of America's common schools. With a dissertation entitled "An Outline of the History of Logical Doctrine," mysteriously lost when Columbia moved to Morningside Heights, Butler earned his Ph.D. in 1884, a mere two years after his B.A. With a degree in hand, but with one year yet to run on his graduate fellowship, Butler set sail for Europe to round off his education in Berlin and Paris. In 1885, he returned to Columbia, only to find that the college had no place for him except as a lowly assistant in philosophy. Determined to create a permanent place for himself, he began lobbying the trustees to create a department of pedagogy.[52]

By the 1880s, more than 60 percent of all teachers in the Northeast were women; in New York City, the figure was over 90 percent.[53] Those interested in taking courses in pedagogy were therefore likely to be female. Given his spirited opposition to coeducation as an undergraduate, Butler must have experienced at least some difficulty in supporting a curricular innovation that would inevitably bring women into Columbia's classrooms. Nonetheless, he well understood that if he was to stay at Columbia, a job had to be created. Winning the trustees over to the idea of a department of pedagogy seemed his only chance.[54]

In April 1886, Butler offered to give a course of four lectures on Saturday mornings on the history of education in the hope of demonstrating a demand for pedagogic instruction. The trustees agreed to his use of the Law School's large lecture hall as part of Columbia's program of free lectures. To everyone's surprise, the hall was filled to capacity and 1,500 requests for tickets had to be refused. The following year, Butler took a tentative second step.

He proposed to teach a course at Columbia, open to seniors as well as interested members of the public, on pedagogics. Always suspicious of any schemes costing money or threatening to bring women into the college, the trustees studied Butler's proposal with care. The number of Columbia seniors interested in a course in pedagogics was likely to be small, they concluded. The proposed course could not therefore be defended on economic grounds—except, of course by admitting outsiders. But the outsiders were likely to be "nine-tenths" women who were "either already engaged in teaching or training for that profession."[55] The answer was no. Blocked by the trustees, Butler followed Barnard's established practice of looking outside Columbia to the women of New York to find support for his plans. He found that support from Grace Dodge.

In 1887, Butler agreed to accept Dodge's offer to be the director of the Industrial Education Association if she would agree to shift its aim toward the training of skilled teachers and the study of education. Dodge agreed and further approved changing the organization's name to the New York School for the Training of Teachers. There was a lingering tension between them, however, that reflected their divided purpose. Butler was principally interested in training a professional cadre of educators; Dodge was more directly interested in social reform. He was first and foremost an academic administrator; she remained, at heart, a social worker. But they would continue to collaborate and, in the process, turned the New York School for the Training of Teachers, renamed Teachers College in 1892, into the largest professional school at Columbia, and later, in the world.

ANNIE CURTIS AND SETH LOW

Women and their supporters had achieved no more than a tentative foothold on the periphery of Columbia College, when Frederick A. P. Barnard died in 1889. It fell to Seth Low to achieve Barnard's dream of turning Columbia into a research university and securing a permanent place for women in it. Low's appointment was by no means a foregone conclusion when Barnard died. Barnard had hoped that the trustees would choose a university man to succeed him, someone like General Francis A. Walker of the Massachusetts Institute of Technology, but Walker was not an Episcopalian. Supporters of the college favored Henry Drisler, senior professor of Greek and acting president following Barnard's retirement. The board settled on their fellow trustee Seth Low, because he pleased both sides. A loyal alumnus of the college, he could be trusted to protect its interests; but he also had a vision of Columbia as a great university.[56]

Seth Low (1850–1916)
Graduate of Columbia College (1870) and
president of Columbia College and University
(1890–1901), as photographed in 1901. (Columbia
University Archives–Columbiana Library)

Annie Curtis Low (1847–1929)
Member of the Barnard College Board of
Trustees (1891–1912), as photographed around
1880. (© Bettmann / Corbis)

Low, though nominally an Episcopalian, was descended from New England Unitarians. In the early nineteenth century, his family had migrated to Brooklyn, where Low's father, Abiel Abbot Low, built a shipping business and made a fortune in the China trade. Born in 1850, Seth Low grew up in a mansion on Pierrepont Street in Brooklyn, from which he could see his father's clipper ships at anchor. He attended Columbia, where he led his class and graduated in 1870. President Barnard called him "the first scholar in college and the most manly young man we have had here for many years."[57] After college, Low toured Europe, joined the Episcopal Church, went into the family business, and became active in alumni fund-raising. Preferring public service to business, he joined the Columbia College Board of Trustees in 1881 and served as mayor of Brooklyn from 1883 to 1888, president of Columbia University from 1890 to 1901, mayor of New York City from 1901 to 1903, and a leader in the progressive National Civic Federation thereafter. Many of Low's background feared the massive immigration that was beginning to change the face of New York in the 1880s; they saw it as a threat to democracy. But Low disagreed. What threatened democracy, he believed, was not the immigrant but the faulty machinery of government. It had to be modernized so that it could better serve the people. He recognized that Tammany Hall could be replaced only by the expansion of municipal services. As mayor of Brooklyn, he raised the property taxes of the wealthy; integrated the public schools and made textbooks free to all; applied civil-service principles in the hiring of teachers; established a normal school; invested heavily in new schools; expanded and modernized the police, fire, and sanitation departments; and established the "rule of common sense" regarding the Sunday closing of saloons in immigrant neighborhoods. As Lincoln Steffens wrote of him, Low "always gave more than he took."[58]

In December 1880, just before joining the Columbia board, Low married Annie Wroe Scollay Curtis. Born in 1847 in Boston, Annie Curtis was the eldest child of Benjamin Robbins Curtis and Anna Wroe Scollay Curtis, distant cousins who traced their roots back to the founding of Massachusetts and who had been sending men to Harvard for generations. Benjamin Curtis (Harvard College 1829, Harvard Law 1832) was a prominent lawyer, respected member of the Whig Party, and justice of the Supreme Court, from which he resigned in 1857 following his dissent in the *Dred Scott* case. Sometime in the early 1860s, Curtis and his family converted from Unitarianism to Episcopalianism and became prominent members of Trinity Church in Boston, where Annie became a close friend of the Reverend Dr. Phillips Brooks, brother of New York's Reverend Dr. Arthur Brooks, the first chairman of the Barnard College Board of Trustees. Family members later remembered that Annie Curtis was "one of the few women of her time able to take verbatim reports of the torrential words of [Trinity's] great preacher [Phillips Brooks]."[59]

Annie Curtis belonged to the generation of Boston women from professional families whose formal education stopped short of college. Learning continued, however, in frequent attendance at the lyceum lectures and public lectures given by Harvard professors. Annie Curtis was related to Charles Eliot, president of Harvard; George Ticknor, the first professor of modern languages at Harvard; and Anna Eliot Ticknor, founder of the Society to Encourage Studies at Home, the forerunner of the Harvard Annex and Radcliffe College. She shared her husband's commitment to political reform and education and seems to have given him the courage to leave business for public service soon after their marriage. Her nephew, Benjamin Low, later recalled her as "a woman of rare mind, poise, and sagacity," who was Seth Low's "chief happiness in a singularly happy life" and the principal source of his success. "There were few if any of his problems," Benjamin Low believed, "which he did not submit to her wise and judicious appraisal, and in no smallest detail did he range beyond her tender and helpful concern." Childless, like her predecessor Margaret McMurry Barnard, she worked tirelessly, and for the most part anonymously, to win women a place at Columbia's table.[60] An associate member of the Barnard College Board of Trustees from the beginning, she joined the board as a full member in 1891 and served until 1912. She sat on both the finance and academic committees of the board. She was also a member of the New York chapter of the Daughters of the American Revolution (then an organization committed to social reform), which raised the funds to hire Professor J. F. Jameson as a lecturer in American history at Barnard before the Faculty of Political Science at Columbia consented to supply an instructor. Barnard students so appreciated her efforts on their behalf that in 1894 they dedicated their first publication, the *Barnard Annual* (forerunner of the *Mortarboard*) to her. No one did more to secure the future of Barnard College as both a refuge and a beachhead for young women.[61]

OPENING THE GRADUATE FACULTIES TO WOMEN

As soon as he assumed office in February 1890, Seth Low called the faculty together to discuss the future of Columbia College. For twenty-five years, President Barnard had sought to build Columbia into a great research university. But, as he often complained to university leaders who were enjoying greater success in this effort elsewhere, he faced the resistance of both faculty and trustees.[62] Low found that two-thirds of the faculty still favored keeping Columbia a small college, while only one-third advocated building it into a university of graduate and professional schools. Low sided with the university faction, and, despite having to deal with a board unwilling to spend money and a campus that was already overcrowded, he built a great university in less than a decade. He increased the faculty fivefold, moved the campus to Morningside Heights, launched an ambitious fund-raising and building campaign, and took decisive steps to make the university the center of public life in New York City. He forged formal links to Union Theological Seminary, Jewish Theological Seminary, Cooper Union, the Metropolitan Museum of Art, the American Museum of Natural History, and the New York Botanical Garden.[63]

Not a scholar, Low recognized that his principal gifts were political. As he wrote to his father, his contribution would be "to bring the College into closer touch with the community; and this happens to be the one thing which especially needs to be done at this time."[64] He continued Barnard's practice of sponsoring public lectures as a way of establishing a dialogue with the many constituencies of the city. He reached out to all, whatever their race, class, ethnicity, or gender. As he wrote in his article "The University and the

Workingman," he "should be glad to have it known by the workingmen of America that at Columbia College . . . the disposition exists to teach the truth . . . without fear or favor, and we ask their aid to enable us to see the truth as it appears to them."[65] His administration was to be one that encouraged dialogue as a way of achieving betterment for all. Barnard had worked mightily to force Columbia out of its Episcopalian day-school cocoon, but his stubbornness, and perhaps his deafness, had set limits to his political success. Low, by contrast, was able to make people work together toward a goal that the majority had long resisted. He was the consummate reform politician.[66]

Fitting women into this transformation proved to be one of the biggest problems he was to face as president. The difficulty of the task struck him forcefully in the spring of 1890, when Ella Weed presented him with Barnard College's request for faculty for its second year. Virtually from the start, the effort to match Columbia College's curriculum posed a "formidable" challenge, not only to the Barnard trustees, who had to raise the necessary funds to pay instructors, but also to the Columbia trustees, who had promised to release instructors from their Columbia duties to teach their courses a second time at Barnard College.[67]

Harvard was having trouble meeting the Harvard Annex's curricular needs, despite having twice the number of faculty that Columbia had in 1890: 109, compared with Columbia's 45.[68] In fact, students at the Harvard Annex had only one-quarter as many courses to choose from as did students at Harvard. In its first year, Barnard College made do with six Columbia instructors, as well as a botanist to teach special students, who enrolled only to take selected science courses. The following year, however, Barnard administrators asked for four more teachers to teach the freshman- and sophomore-year classes and an additional ten faculty to teach graduate classes to New York City women who held degrees from other schools. It is not clear how Barnard came to assign itself responsibility for women's graduate instruction, since its charter spoke only of collegiate study and a bachelor's degree. The only other women's college to offer graduate training, as of 1890, was Bryn Mawr. The Harvard Board of Overseers did not open graduate instruction to women until 1894 and then only under "certain conditions" and without prospect of an advanced degree.[69] The Barnard College Board of Trustees seems simply to have concluded that the Columbia trustees' agreement in 1886 to award the B.A. and Ph.D. to any woman who qualified, their acceptance in 1888 of the memorial calling for "instruction of women whereby the examinations and degrees recently opened to them may be made truly available," and their agreement in 1889 to provide faculty for any necessary course work added up to the right to offer a graduate program.[70]

Perhaps for this reason, the Barnard request for faculty to teach graduate courses did not, in itself, provoke any protest from the Columbia trustees. Everyone seemed to agree that the problem Barnard was creating was a function of the number of faculty it was suddenly requesting, not the level at which the faculty were being requested to teach.

Hoping to soften the blow, Barnard officials alerted the trustees to an opportunity. Emily Gregory, an unusually well-qualified botanist, had just completed a fellowship at the University of Pennsylvania and had applied to teach at Barnard. Born in Portage, New York, in 1841, Gregory had grown up just a few miles from Seneca Falls, amid the intense ferment of abolitionism and women's rights. She came to botany late, taking it as only a minor subject at Cornell, from which she graduated in 1879, at the age of thirty-nine, with a major in literature. Like so many women who sought higher education in the late nineteenth century, she probably had spent the previous two decades working as a schoolteacher to support herself. She pursued her new interest in botany, first at Harvard, then at various German universities, and finally at the University of Zürich, one of the few institutions in the world willing to award the Ph.D. to women at that time. Earning her doctorate in 1886, she was the first American woman to receive a Ph.D. in botany and one of the first to receive it in the sciences. For several years after earning her doctorate, Gregory held temporary positions at Smith, Bryn Mawr, and Radcliffe. She then accepted the first postdoctoral fellowship ever awarded to a woman at the University of Pennsylvania. In 1888, she joined the Torrey Botanical Club, named for the early-nineteenth-century Columbia botanist John Torrey, and opened up to women in 1879 by Elizabeth Knight, a graduate of the Female Normal School and an expert on mosses, who later married the Columbia botanist Nathaniel Britton. By the time Gregory joined the club, 40 percent of the members were female. When Barnard College opened, the club offered to equip a botany laboratory, and Gregory offered her own services for free to set it up and give instruction.[71]

If Barnard College could hire Dr. Gregory to teach botany, the college could make do with nineteen Columbia faculty. After two months' deliberation, a special committee of the Columbia board, chaired by Low, delivered its report. Given the trustees' insistence in 1889 that Barnard hire only Columbia professors or instructors, the committee saw no alternative but to allow the requested instructors to teach at the women's college the following year. Low and his fellow committee members hastened to stress, however, their concern about "how burdensome, nay, how injurious, to the best interests of Columbia, the increased demand for instructors, augmenting naturally in the future, will prove." They therefore urged the board to suggest

Emily Gregory (1841–1897)
Graduate of Cornell University (1879)
and University of Zürich (Ph.D. 1886),
botanist, and lecturer (1890–1895) and first
professor (1895–1897) at Barnard College,
as photographed around 1890. (Barnard
College Archives)

that the by-laws of Barnard College be amended to revert to the original language proposed by Barnard's founders in 1889: that Barnard's faculty "consist of Professors and Instructors to be approved of by the President of Columbia College." To ensure the quality of Barnard instruction, Columbia faculty would continue to give all exams, but Barnard could hire its own faculty (with the president's permission) when no Columbia teacher was available. The trustees readily complied with the committee's recommendation and, at the same time, approved Barnard's hiring of Gregory. The first woman ever to teach at any school affiliated with the university, Emily Gregory assumed the position of lecturer on the anatomy and physiology of plants and director of the botany laboratory at Barnard College.[72]

This plan evoked an immediate protest from Alice Freeman Palmer, former president of Wellesley; wife of a Harvard professor, George Palmer; friend of the Harvard Annex; and soon-to-be dean of women at the new, coeducational University of Chicago. Palmer worried that Barnard College was making a concession that would destine it to second-class status and, as a by-product, might encourage Harvard to abandon its obligation to staff courses for women at the Harvard Annex.[73]

Seth Low had the same concern and tried throughout the 1890s to press the Columbia faculty to provide Barnard with adequate faculty. To do so, however, meant placing a strain on Columbia's faculty resources just when he was trying to build the graduate program. The only solution, in his mind, was to follow the lead of Frederick Barnard and John W. Burgess and cut back undergraduate course work at both Barnard and Columbia by allowing all seniors to take courses in the expanding graduate faculties and professional schools. But he faced two obstacles: the still-powerful supporters of the college, who feared that it would be destroyed, and the continuing prejudice among the trustees and some faculty against admitting women to any Columbia course, be it undergraduate or graduate.

Low's first step, in the spring of 1890, was to establish the University Council, on which he placed the deans of the various faculties: law, political science, philosophy, mines, and the college. The cleverness of this institutional reform, from the point of view of the university builder, was that it reduced the political power of the college, whose dean had only one vote. In June 1890, Low pushed a resolution through the council asking the schools to open their graduate courses to seniors. This maneuver cut back on the demand of the college for faculty resources, but it did not solve the problem of increasing demand from Barnard.[74]

Low accepted the prejudice in New York against coeducation for younger students, but he argued that, as the specialization of course work and the maturity of the students increased, duplication of course offerings became increasingly hard to justify. Proceeding cautiously, Low introduced the topic of coeducation indirectly the following year by alerting the trustees to a problem that had arisen with the Saturday morning University Lectures.

As part of an effort to increase Columbia's presence in New York City and to build public support, President Barnard had begun a course of free lectures on assorted topics in the 1880s. The lecture series had been a big success, especially among women, for whom they provided one of the few opportunities available for continuing their education. During the winter of 1890/1891, however, Low had been "mortified to learn" that the lectures, given in the Law School, had become a kind of pickup spot—"a pleasant rendezvous for a morning's entertainment"—such that in several cases the lecturers had found it almost impossible to continue amid the hubbub. Low had made it his business to attend all subsequent lectures, "and that put an end to the disorder." But something more had to be done. The problem, he believed, stemmed from mixing public entertainment with serious scholarship. He proposed that Columbia fulfill its duty to the public by sponsoring a series of free lectures, geared to a popular audience, at Cooper Union, in Greenwich Village. These lectures would satisfy the interest of the casual listener, and their location far from Columbia's campus would shield the university from whatever adverse publicity might follow on any disruptions.[75]

But the "earnest listeners who have been in attendance on the lectures delivered at the college," Low pointedly added, "might not be so reached." To meet the needs of these "earnest listeners," he proposed that "all university lectures be thrown open to the public on the payment of a small fee at the discretion of the professor . . . and the president." The earnest listeners Low had most in mind were prospective Barnard seniors and graduate students. If the trustees did not accept his proposal, he warned, they would be compelled, by their agreement with Barnard, to make Columbia faculty available to mount, in effect, a second graduate program for the exclusive use of Barnard students. This would mean taking time away from their own research or having to teach, in addition to their other classes, a class of what was likely to be a very small number of women. At its next meeting, in December 1891, the trustees voted to approve Low's proposal and thereby authorized the Faculties of Philosophy and Political Science to open their classes to women.[76]

It was a masterful political maneuver. From the start, opposition to coeducation at Columbia had been reinforced in the minds of many trustees by fears associated with Columbia's urban setting. One reason that so many families preferred to send their sons away to college was to limit their exposure to young women from the wrong background. To throw open Columbia's doors to women, many believed, would greatly complicate the policing of male students.[77] In informing the trustees about problems that had developed with the Saturday morning lectures and in laying out his proposed solution, Low was able to acknowledge long-standing trustee concerns about the need to maintain sexual order, while legitimizing coeducation for "serious" women, who had completed at least three years of college, as the fiscally prudent solution. It is difficult to believe that Low would have succeeded without the resolute campaigning of Lillie Devereux Blake, Frederick and Margaret Barnard, and the women and men who made up the Association for Promoting the Higher Education of Women. He built on their foundation. But he built with skill that few could equal.

Nicholas Murray Butler, newly promoted to dean of the Faculty of Philosophy, immediately implemented this policy with the explanation that it "saves my time and Barnard's money."[78] Gradually, he persuaded his colleagues in the Faculty of Philosophy to admit female students.[79] A few years later, Butler revealed how much his thinking had changed since he was a Columbia senior. The "woman who grows up surrounded by women and taught only by women, and the man who grows up surrounded by men and taught only by men, are a long time maturing. Both are abnormal." He continued to believe, however, that in the New York context, where even the public schools were segregated by sex, Columbia's solution of perpetuating that segregation at the college level, "with equal opportunities," and providing "common opportunities" in graduate school was the best way to way to deal with fixed prejudices.[80]

In maneuvering to win admission to graduate courses for women, Low benefited from the example being set elsewhere. Most major universities that had not already done so began admitting women as doctoral candidates in the early 1890s. Yale and Pennsylvania admitted women to graduate study in 1891, while continuing to bar them as undergraduates. Both Chicago and Stanford announced the same year that they would institute full coeducation for both graduates and undergraduates. Brown admitted women to graduate work and established a coordinate college, Pembroke, for undergraduate instruction by Brown faculty. The German universities, which were then producing the best scientists in the world and had been admitting women to lectures without awarding them degrees for some years, succumbed to the pressure of American women in 1895 and began to award them the Ph.D. Margaret Maltby (Oberlin, B.A. 1882, M.A. 1891; MIT, B.S. 1891), who taught at Wellesley from 1887 to 1893 and would go on to head the Barnard physics department, won the first Ph.D. in physics from the University of Göttingen in July 1895. Harvard proved more resistant to pressure. By 1894, it was allowing a handful of Radcliffe College graduates to take a few select classes, and in 1902 it allowed the creation of the Radcliffe Graduate School and accorded it the right to give its own degrees, but it did not grant women the Harvard degree until 1963. Johns Hopkins succumbed to the pressure to admit women in 1907, but Princeton and the University of Virginia held out until 1970.[81]

Not everyone in the graduate departments welcomed women into their courses. Dean Burgess, for one, objected strenuously to the new rule and bullied those of his junior colleagues in the Faculty of Political Science who already had admitted women to reverse course and allow only male auditors to attend classes in government, history, and economics.[82] Professor John Howard Van Amringe, in math, also refused to teach women.

A frustrated Seth Low reacted by dipping into his own pocket to create the nation's first chair in sociology at Columbia, "to take advantage, so far as possible, of the special opportunities for sociological study incident to our location in the City of New York."[83] In 1886, Low had been among the founders of University Settlement, the settlement house modeled on Toynbee Hall in London and the first to be established in the United States. Since that time, scores of idealistic young people, mostly college-educated women, had flocked to University Settlement and other settlement houses like it in search of meaningful work and more democratic solutions to the deepening problem of poverty in the city. Convinced that women were playing an important role in extending social services to the poor of New York, · Low believed that courses in sociology would be particularly valuable to Barnard students. The first person to occupy the new chair was Franklin Giddings, a former journalist and a pioneer sociologist, who was then teaching political science at Bryn Mawr. Happy to offer courses at Barnard as a condition of his employment, Giddings joined the Columbia faculty. Inspired by the liberal evolutionism of such figures as Lester Frank Ward, Giddings believed that social progress occurred through an ever-greater "consciousness of kind." He encouraged his students to venture into the city to carry out studies of the poor that could be used as the basis for devising better ways of addressing the problems they faced. Low saw Giddings as helping advance his vision of a practical, democratic, and socially responsible social science, while meeting the teaching needs at Barnard College.[84]

EMILY JAMES SMITH

Ella Weed, chairwoman of the academic committee of the Barnard College Board of Trustees, made do with the resources available, but, distracted by illness and her duties as principal of her own school, she was not able to give Barnard her full attention. When she died in January 1894, the board decided that it was past time to hire a dean for the college. A committee made up of Barnard trustees Annie Curtis Low, Annie Nathan Meyer, and George Plimpton (who replaced Jacob Schiff as board treasurer in 1893) searched for someone with the academic credentials needed to handle the awkward relationship with the Columbia faculty. They settled on twenty-nine-year-old Emily James Smith, a member of the first class to graduate from Bryn Mawr, in 1889; a former student of Franklin Giddings; one of the first American women to study at Girton College, Cambridge; and a graduate student of Paul Shorey in Greek at Chicago. Although she was young, her excellent academic training and wide experience, together with her wit and sparkle, made her a fortunate choice to lead the still-struggling school. The fact that she was a specialist in Greek added to her luster. One of her first students, Virginia Crocheron Gildersleeve, later remembered her "rapier-like mind and satiric wit" and credited her with setting the intellectual tone of the college.[85] As dean, she accomplished three things. First, she dramatically increased Barnard students' access to Columbia's graduate classes in their senior year. Second, she added courses to the Barnard curriculum that she thought necessary to meet the needs of her students. And third, she won Barnard the right to hire its own faculty.

Emily Smith Putnam (1865–1944)
First dean of Barnard College (1894–1900).
(Barnard College Archives)

Pressured by Dean Smith (and, no doubt, by his wife), President Low returned to the subject of opening graduate courses to women at the October meeting of the University Council in 1894.[86] Citing the examples of Yale, Harvard, a number of state universities, and a growing number of European universities that recently had opened graduate classes to women, he urged the council to admit Barnard seniors, as well as any interested women college graduates, to all Columbia graduate courses. As Low explained to his deans, "Unless Columbia throws open to [women] her doors in the graduate courses, the City of New York must depend altogether for the influence of highly educated women, upon women who receive their training outside of the city."[87] For a generation, the principal argument used to justify the advanced training of women was that a certain number of middle-class women would never marry and would have to support themselves as teachers. Low, the urban reformer, intent on securing for the city the specialists necessary to run an efficient, modern government, looked on women as an untapped resource for city betterment. Low's recommendation brought forth an indignant response from Burgess, who was absent from the meeting at which Low made his proposal, but who came to the next meeting in December armed with a twenty-six-page screed against Low's plan.[88]

Burgess disputed Low's contention that there was a "world movement for coeducation." He dismissed its existence in the state universities as no more than an unfortunate concession to economic and political pressures, and he derided the coeducational graduate instruction at Harvard, Yale, Oxford, and Cambridge as too limited in scale to take seriously. As correspondence between President Charles Eliot of Harvard and both Low and Burgess makes clear, Low's effort to open Columbia classes to Barnard seniors was causing alarm among the Harvard Board of Overseers. Indeed, Harvard's decision not to grant Radcliffe graduates the Harvard degree seems to have been inspired, at least in part, by the fear that doing so would force the university down the path that Low had charted at Columbia, where some forty courses had opened to women in only two years. As Eliot reassured Burgess, when the latter wrote him an urgent note following Low's proposal to the University Council, "I have not changed my opinion about co-education at all." He conceded that a few graduates of newly founded Radcliffe College, "six this year," had been admitted to "certain specified graduate courses in Harvard University." But he emphasized that "the authorities of both Harvard and Radcliffe disbelieve in co-education, and have no purpose in using that method." To make clear his preference for the approach he was taking at Harvard, compared with Low's campaign at Columbia, Eliot concluded his letter by saying, "Thus far there has been nothing in either the scholarly life or the social life of Radcliffe College which could even suggest co-education. I believe that the Radcliffe method is the safest one which has yet been devised—decidedly safer than that of Columbia for example."[89]

As for the example of the German universities, where Burgess had pursued his own graduate instruction, he recalled only "some half-dozen women [who attended] lectures, chiefly under the medicine professors." They were, he recalled, "Russian women of advanced political opinions, who had worked [their way] into the lecture rooms by persistently soliciting the individual professors." One of the principal reasons that Burgess had urged the creation of graduate training at Columbia in political science in the first place was to discourage young American men from pursuing graduate work in Germany, where they would likely pick up socialist ideas. He had no intention of undermining his own efforts by admitting women, who, if they had the temerity to muscle their way into a graduate classroom, might well harbor the very radical ideas that Columbia was designed, in his view, to protect against. In closing, Burgess cited the unfortunate experience of the Columbia Law School dean, Timothy Dwight. Fifteen years earlier, Dean Dwight had been approached by "a nicely appearing woman" who, inspired no doubt by Lillie Devereux Blake, had observed that the school statutes did not include the word "male" in them and that, therefore, she had the "*right*" to attend Law School lectures. "Professor Dwight was greatly disturbed and excited about the matter," Burgess recalled. "He put a detective upon her track and traced her finally to a house of prostitution." Having raised the twin bogeymen of radicalism and sexual license in defense of his views, Burgess persuaded the University Council to table Low's proposal.[90]

If Burgess was right on his dates, the female applicant to the Law School would have appeared in about 1879, the year in which Barnard began calling for coeducation at Columbia in his annual reports and the trustees refused to sanction women's attendance at lectures, even as auditors. One wishes, of course, that Burgess had elaborated. Was this "house of prostitution" a figment of Dwight's or possibly Burgess's overwrought imagination, stimulated by the popular late-nineteenth-century association of radicalism, feminism, and sexual license? Or did a hard-working woman of the sex industry really seek to better her lot by becoming a lawyer?

Frustrated about the difficulties they were experiencing in meeting Barnard's instructional needs, Seth and Annie Low concocted an elaborate scheme. Insisting on anonymity, they gave Barnard $12,000 in three successive years, beginning in 1895, with which the college offered to pay the salaries of three new full professors—two in political science and one in pure science—at Columbia. There seems to have been at least some support at Barnard for using the money to follow the practice already established at Bryn Mawr of hiring a separate graduate faculty, but the trustees evidently concluded that no college could compete with a research university in the hiring of graduate faculty and that Barnard students' interests would be better served if they were incorporated into the Columbia graduate program. So, it was agreed, the Low money would be used to hire Columbia faculty. In exchange, Columbia agreed to make those hired, or other professors, available to teach Barnard students. Barnard's Dean Emily Smith worked with the Lows and faculty at Columbia to recruit three of the most distinguished scholars in the country: James Harvey Robinson in history, John B. Clark in economics, and Frank Cole in mathematics. As Low had hoped, Burgess could not resist the opportunity of gaining two luminaries for the Faculty of Political Science, even on a shared basis, and he agreed to the plan.[91]

At the same time that Dean Smith was working to recruit new faculty to fulfill the terms of the Low gift, she asked the president to promote Emily Gregory to professor of botany at Barnard College. By training, experience, and accomplishment, Gregory obviously deserved promotion. Not only did she teach all the undergraduate courses at Barnard in botany, but she also directed women doing graduate work and pursued her own research. Low recognized Gregory's achievements, but he hesitated. He continued to hope that through steady pressure and persuasion. he would be able to convince the Columbia faculty to meet its obligations to Barnard, through teaching separate classes to the younger students and welcoming the more mature students into the graduate classes. As Low wrote to Smith on January 17, 1895, "I cannot consent to anything which will relieve our own professors of responsibility for the educational work of Barnard College." True, Barnard's by-laws, at his own insistence, clearly provided that the women's college could appoint non-Columbia faculty with Low's approval. But Low firmly believed that whenever he allowed the college to do so, he lessened the pressure he could exert on the Columbia faculty to teach at Barnard. Moreover, he implied, Barnard would never be able to attract men to professorial appointments at Barnard who were as good as those Columbia could attract, and before long Columbia would no longer be willing to give its degree to Barnard graduates.[92] Despite those reservations, and perhaps because Gregory was not a man (and could not therefore be expected to be hired by Columbia), Low was willing to make an exception in this one case. He approved her promotion to professor of botany at Barnard. Throughout the 1890s, Gregory remained the only faculty member whom Barnard could properly call its own, except for Dean Smith, whom Low permitted to teach Greek to the first- and second-year students. Tragically, Gregory served Barnard as a professor merely from the time of her promotion in 1895 to her sudden death at the age of fifty-six in 1897.[93]

As Low had hoped, the opposition of members of the Columbia faculty to greater coeducation did decline as they were drawn increasingly into the teaching of Barnard students. In 1896, the Faculty of Pure Science (organized separately from the School of Mines in 1892 to house mathematics, physics, and biology) opened its classes to Barnard seniors and graduate students, with the understanding that propriety would be observed by confining their laboratory work to a time when no man was present.[94] The problem of laboratory work may have been the reason that the scientists, who had been the first to admit women to their lectures, were almost the last to admit them to graduate research. In a lecture hall, the women could sit decorously to one side. In the tight quarters of a laboratory, however, they risked physical contact with male students. At first, Barnard solved the problem by having its own botany and chemistry laboratories, but those labs could not compare with the much better equipped Columbia facilities. Finally, the problem was solved by granting Barnard students access to Columbia laboratories on Saturday mornings, when no Columbia student was around.[95]

In 1898, the Faculty of Political Science finally agreed to admit women to its classes, with the permission of the instructor. Not every faculty member chose to give that permission. John W. Burgess, for one, kept his classes in

American constitutional history closed to women until the day he retired in 1911. For Burgess, the point of graduate training in political science continued to be the grooming of the country's governmental elite. But as the graduate faculties grew, the emphasis shifted to the training of research scholars, a role for which women did not seem so obviously disqualified by virtue of their disfranchisement. Younger faculty, eager to justify their existence with strong enrollments, or simply more open to coeducation, welcomed women more readily than did their obstructionist dean.[96]

TOWARD A SEPARATE BARNARD FACULTY

Despite Seth Low's efforts, the difficulties of freeing enough Columbia instructors to teach Barnard students in their first three years continued to prove difficult, in part because the curricular needs of Barnard students were beginning to diverge from those of the male students at Columbia. This divergence stemmed not from the view, popular at some women's colleges, that women required a more "feminine" curriculum, one that emphasized art and music, as compared with the more typically "masculine" fare of Greek and Latin. Rather, Barnard officials sought a more varied curriculum in the sciences because of differences in the opportunities available to women, as compared with those open to men, after college.

In science, for example, professional opportunities for Barnard and Columbia students differed in significant ways. Although most scientists were hostile to the incursions of women, by the 1890s, women had made significant strides in botany, a poorly paid, marginal field. The United States Civil Service, which rigidly segregated employees by sex, preferred women as botany assistants. Developing an expertise in botany was one of the few ways in which a woman could support herself in science in the 1890s, so a strong botany curriculum at Barnard made a great deal of sense. Through the efforts of Emily Gregory, Barnard offered a much more extensive botany curriculum to undergraduates than did Columbia.

Barnard's curriculum diverged as well to meet the needs of young women who attended Barnard in the hope of preparing for careers in medicine. Columbia's medical school, which did not admit women, welcomed men, even those who had never attended college, with no preparation in science whatsoever. In contrast, the Johns Hopkins School of Medicine, which began admitting women in 1893, required a college degree and favored students with extensive scientific training. As a result, Smith had to ask special permission of Low to count toward the bachelor's degree courses in zoology, physics,

Barnard College Chemistry Laboratory
The chemistry laboratory at Barnard, when the college was at 343 Madison Avenue.
(Barnard College Archives)

chemistry, and calculus that were not part of the regular undergraduate curriculum at Columbia. In short, Barnard had to seek special permission to
offer a more demanding set of courses than Columbia then offered.[97]

The experience of Barnard students also diverged from that of Columbia
students, even when they were taking identical courses, because the Columbia faculty wrote the exams, even for courses taught by Barnard faculty
to Barnard students. One hapless student, who had excelled in the study of
Greek with Dean Smith, flunked the exam written by the Columbia professor who taught the same subject. When Smith looked into the matter, it
turned out that the exam was based on material added to the Columbia
course without notice to her.[98]

Even where the instructors were the same, problems emerged. Dean
Smith steadily complained that staffing a parallel set of courses at Barnard
was proving to be a logistical nightmare. She could never be sure until the
last minute which Columbia faculty would be available to her and at what
times. In theory, she could have hired extra faculty. But although Low had
insisted in 1890 that Barnard's by-laws be changed to make possible the hiring of non-Columbia faculty to teach Barnard courses when no Columbia
faculty member was available, in fact, he had authorized only two appoint-

ments (apart from Smith herself), both in botany. Intent on keeping Barnard as integrated into the Columbia academic structure as possible, he preferred to have Barnard classes offered at inconvenient times rather than to allow Smith to hire non-Columbia faculty. In Smith's view, however, making Barnard's course offerings dependent on the availability of individual Columbia professors was proving unworkable.[99] Columbia's set curriculum aggravated Smith's problems. Whereas Harvard's elective system gave administrators at Radcliffe considerable freedom in putting together an array of courses for their students, Columbia's more traditional approach forced Dean Smith to duplicate the courses offered at Columbia. She could not easily substitute a course in French literature for a course in Latin when the Columbia Latin teacher was otherwise engaged.

At Columbia College, the dean shared with various faculty committees the work of scheduling classes, admitting students, awarding scholarships and honors, and deciding the innumerable academic questions that presented themselves each year. At Barnard, all such decisions fell to the dean alone, since the Columbia faculty who taught at Barnard had no institutional responsibility beyond the individual courses to which they were assigned. Barnard could hire more administrators to fulfill these duties, but when academic decisions were to be made, Smith believed, faculty should make them to protect the value of the Columbia degree.[100]

Having to rely on Columbia faculty seemed unfair in another way. Of the more than eighty faculty who taught Barnard students in the 1890s, there appears to have been only three who were not members of the Columbia faculty. All were women. Emily James Smith taught Greek; Emily Gregory taught botany; and Louise Brisban Dunn served briefly as an assistant in botany, following the death of Gregory.[101] In other words, the only way that Barnard could provide its students with female faculty was to seek special dispensation from Low. As a man with political ambitions, who had once served as mayor of Brooklyn and seemed likely to return to politics in the near future, Low's services as an advocate of women could not be counted on indefinitely. It was not a happy situation for Barnard's founders, whose goal in establishing the women's college was, at least in part, to enlarge opportunities for women. As Smith commented following Gregory's untimely death in 1897, "The fact that our instruction is given by officers of Columbia, though it is one of our chief advantages, deprives our students of the object-lesson afforded by women of first-rate mental capacity and training."[102] As an undergraduate at Bryn Mawr, Smith had studied with both women and men, and she thought it important that her students have the same advantage.[103] Given the prejudice of so many of the Columbia faculty against hiring women, however, she concluded that Barnard would have to win the right to hire its own professors for women to teach there.

MOVING TO MORNINGSIDE

Those problems were irritating, but there was another difficulty that threatened to sink the women's college before it got fully under way. By the early 1890s, Columbia had outgrown its site on Forty-ninth Street. Some trustees wanted to move to Westchester County, north of the city; but what made Columbia unique, in Low's mind, was its position in and commitment to the city of New York. When he learned of the availability of land on Morningside Heights, therefore, he jumped at the opportunity, even though it would mean the outlay of $5 million. Columbia's decision to move created a crisis for Barnard College. It must move or perish. The Barnard trustees themselves were not, for the most part, wealthy individuals. But through their professional and social contacts, they reached out to wealthy New Yorkers. In 1893, Frederick Waite, a lawyer who succeeded Hamilton Mabie as secretary to the board of trustees, persuaded his client Mary (Mrs.Van Wyck) Brinkerhoff to give $100,000 for a new building if the trustees could acquire land on Morningside Heights so that Barnard could move with Columbia. Annie Nathan Meyer organized a publicity campaign in the local press to advertise Barnard's virtues and needs. Treasurer George Plimpton secured gifts ranging in size from John D. Rockefeller's $25,000 to just a few dollars. In 1896, Plimpton bought land at 120th Street and Broadway for $160,000. And the board chairman, Arthur Brooks, persuaded his parishioner Elizabeth (Mrs. A. A.) Anderson, heir to the Bordens Condensed Milk fortune, to give $170,000 for Milbank Hall, in memory of her parents, Mr. and Mrs. Jeremiah Milbank. In October 1896, the cornerstone of Milbank was laid at 120th Street, and in 1897 a procession of students, alumnae, Barnard and Columbia faculty, and trustees—including the Reverend Dr. Dix—celebrated the completion of the work. The same year, Martha (Mrs. Josiah) Fiske gave $140,000 in memory of her husband for Fiske Hall. Although intended as a science building, Fiske Hall opened as a dormitory in 1898 for almost a hundred women. Three buildings, all made possible by gifts from New York City women, provided space for five hundred students.[104]

Barnard's first commencement in 1893 was conducted on the stage of Carnegie Hall. Of the original fourteen students enrolled in 1889, eight graduated four years later. Seated discreetly apart from the Columbia graduates, they were dressed in light summer dresses and straw hats. At Barnard, as at Radcliffe, academic caps and gowns were thought too masculine for women to wear. The men's names were read; the women were told that they could pick up their diplomas at 343 Madison Avenue the next day. The first commencement uptown, in 1898, was different. A band played "Stars and Stripes Forever" on the steps of the new Abriel Abbot Low Memorial Library (named for Seth Low's father), and Barnard seniors, dressed now in caps and gowns, joined the procession with all the other divisions of the university. The difference between women's and men's cultures at the university was beginning to lessen.[105]

TEACHERS COLLEGE

When Butler resigned from the presidency of the New York Training School for Teachers in 1891 to devote himself full time to his new position as dean of the Faculty of Philosophy at Columbia, Grace Dodge felt abandoned, but Butler's position in the new graduate faculty gave Dodge valuable leverage at the university. The following year, she chartered the training school as Teachers College. Faced with mounting costs and plummeting resources, as she tried to build a new school at a time when the economy was sliding toward a major depression, Dodge, in consultation with Butler, proposed that the Columbia trustees take over the new school in 1892.[106]

The prospects for incorporation looked favorable. The Columbia trustees had eagerly absorbed the College of Physicians and Surgeons (P&S) the year before. Like Teachers College, P&S admitted students directly from high school. In that regard, it resembled most professional schools of the time. Although both Seth Low and Nicholas Murray Butler were striving to raise the admissions requirements of professional schools at Columbia so that they would occupy a place in the academic hierarchy equivalent to the graduate faculties, they had a long way to go. Law did not require a college degree until 1903; medicine would not do so until the 1920s. Not until after World War II could all Columbia's professional schools claim graduate-level status.[107] As of the 1890s, professional training in medicine, like professional training in teaching, offered an alternative to college, rather than a sequel to it.

In addition to asking no more than a high-school education for admission, Teachers College resembled the College of Physicians and Surgeons in several other respects. Both provided training in the skills of a particular craft: teaching at the one, and doctoring at the other. Both provided practical experience as part of their education: Teachers College through its laboratory school, and P&S with its clinical activities. Both traced their intellectual roots to the ancient Greeks: the teachers to Plato, and the doctors to Hippocrates. Both were moving away from rote learning in favor of a more individualized, experimental approach. Both regarded affiliation with the university as a way of enhancing the scientific education of their students. And both were experiencing financial difficulties. They differed, however, in one important respect. Physicians and Surgeons admitted men only; Teachers College accepted women as well. This last fact proved decisive in the thinking of the Columbia deans and trustees. They rejected the application from Teachers College on the explicit grounds that the college would "introduce co-education into Columbia in a most pronounced form" and, as the University Council warned, would jeopardize the "reputation" of the fledgling university system.[108]

Wanting to keep the hope of incorporation alive, Seth Low worked out an "alliance" with Teachers College. Under the agreement, Teachers College would retain its separate organization and control its nondegree programs, but the Faculty of Philosophy would supervise all work at Teachers College leading to the B.S., M.A., and Ph.D. degrees. In addition, Columbia promised to offer courses each year at Teachers College in the history of education, philosophy, psychology, and ethics. Butler, for his part, quietly let Dodge know of Columbia's plans to move to Morningside Heights, and Dodge was able to acquire the property at 120th Street on which Teachers College was then built. In 1894, Teachers College moved to 120th Street, thanks to a $100,000 gift from George Vanderbilt (whose brother William had given P&S money for its building), which enabled Dodge to begin building a new facility.[109]

In 1894, even before Barnard College moved from Forty-fourth Street to its new quarters on Broadway at 120th Street, a massive brownstone and red-brick structure took shape diagonally across Broadway to house Teachers College. The building represented a huge gamble on Dodge's part; it was not clear that it would be possible to attract enough students of sufficiently high standing to satisfy Columbia administrators. If she could not produce a school that held the promise of becoming a graduate training center, even physical proximity to Columbia would not guarantee continued affiliation. Fortunately, in 1897, Dodge, Butler, and Low were able to recruit James Earl Russell to lead the new college. A survivor of the "deadly drudgery" of New York's public-school system, Russell had discovered the joy of learning only after going to Cornell, where he earned his B.A. in philosophy in 1887. Joining the American exodus to Germany, he made an intensive study of secondary schools in Germany, France, and England; studied psychology and pedagogy with Germany's foremost savants; earned a Ph.D. in Leipzig in

1894; and returned to the United States fired with the desire to put the theories he had learned into action. He intended to teach teachers to teach. In the process, he threw off conventional shibboleths about what was natural for women and men to do.[110]

He thought that there was a growing public need for "women capable of assuming leadership positions in educational affairs." And he thought that that leadership might be exercised in a variety of ways. "I cannot see," he wrote in 1913, "any inherent differences in college men and women. Some women, whom I know, are spiritually stronger, intellectually keener, and physically more robust than some men of my acquaintance." Given that, he added, "I doubt whether there is any profession or even manual vocation that might not be better served by certain women than by many men." Conversely, he noted, "there are men who are essentially more feminine than some women. Even the maternal instinct," he suggested, "is better developed in some men, than in some women."[111] True to his principles, Russell hired a mix of women and men. Edward Thorndike in psychology, Patty Smith Hill in kindergarten and nursery-school education, Adelaide Nutting in nursing, and Mary Schwartz Rose in nutrition were among the pioneers.[112] In the beginning, Teachers College's female faculty were located exclusively in the Domestic Arts Division of the college, which was the direct outgrowth of Grace Dodge's Kitchen Garden experiment in 1880. But as more women earned Ph.D.'s, they won appointments throughout the college; by the 1950s one-third of the faculty was female.[113]

At the turn of the twentieth century, as Barnard College struggled to secure its place on the western flank of the university, the founders of Teachers College worked along similar lines on the university's northern border. Like siblings, the two colleges enjoyed a close but often tense relationship. Laura Gill, dean of Barnard from 1901 to 1907, refused to give credit at Barnard for domestic-science courses taken at Teachers College and complained that Teachers College students enrolled in Barnard courses frequently lacked the necessary training. An irritated Russell responded, "Your imputation of inferior standards to Teachers College is not likely to weigh heavily upon us, but I do resent the charge, indirectly made, that we are . . . indifferent to University regulations." To Felix Warburg, a Teachers College trustee, Russell wrote that the students whom Gill complained about were "practically all of them licensed teachers." Many were enrolled in general lecture courses, where, sitting "quietly," they could "not disturb anyone else"; others were enrolled "in gymnasium work, where I suppose the only danger can be *personal* contamination, certainly not intellectual." Russell suspected the Barnard dean of snobbery, pure and simple, and was unhappy that Gill not only complained about the presence of Teachers College students in Barnard classes but also seemed to be steering students away from all but secondary-school teaching, a practice guaranteed to ensure that primary-school teachers would continue to be regarded as second-class citizens within the academic world.[114]

For all that Barnard and Teachers College quarreled, they shared a great deal. Both were financially independent of Columbia and yet linked to it (and to each other) by complex agreements. Both had been founded, and were largely funded, by women. Both provided an intellectual home to large numbers of female students and increasing numbers of female faculty. And both served as academic beachheads from which women would make incursions into the larger university and the wider society over the course of the twentieth century. The trustees and faculty of Columbia never felt completely comfortable with either one.

THE INTERCORPORATE AGREEMENTS

The move of Barnard and Teachers College to Morningside saved the nascent institutions from an early demise, but it did not resolve lingering questions about their place within the university structure. Gradually, Low came to accept the need to grant Barnard greater autonomy, while tying Teachers College more securely to Columbia.[115] In 1900, the boards of trustees of Barnard and Columbia signed an intercorporate agreement that granted Barnard the right not simply to hire instructors on a per-course basis, but also to maintain its own separate faculty, subject only to the approval of the university president. At the same time, the college gained the corresponding right to design its own curriculum, subject only to the approval of the Columbia College faculty, and to give its own exams. Female students would continue to receive Columbia diplomas. As part of this shift toward greater autonomy for Barnard, the women's college would assume complete responsibility for the three professorships that it had bestowed on Columbia in 1895 and add such others as it deemed necessary.[116]

For the male faculty, this bureaucratic shift had little practical significance. Professor James Harvey Robinson, newly appointed a Barnard professor, continued to teach advanced history courses in the graduate school at Columbia, while Professor Franz Boas of Columbia continued to teach anthropology to undergraduates at Barnard.[117] For women, however, the agreement signified a momentous change. Anticipating the time (only a year off) when Seth Low would leave Columbia, the new agreement provided explicitly that "Members of the Faculty at Barnard College may be either men or women." By the fall of 1900, Barnard had hired nineteen professors and twenty-eight instructors. Ten of the instructors were women. This faculty, many of whom divided their time between Barnard and Columbia, taught 424 students at Barnard. In gaining responsibility for hiring its own faculty and devising its own curriculum, Barnard College gained greater independence than any other affiliated women's college in the country could claim, while reserving the right, nowhere else granted, for its students to be awarded the university degree.[118]

The 1900 agreement was a defeat for those who sought coeducation. Indeed, the agreement included a partial retreat in that Barnard agreed to provide faculty not only for the first three years of college instruction but, as of 1904, for the senior year as well. Seniors would still have the right to take Columbia courses if their equivalent did not exist at Barnard, but Burgess could rest assured that the pressure on Columbia faculty would abate. Even with this concession to the Burgess faction, however, the new agreement produced advantages for women that the advocates of coeducation at Harvard were never able to achieve.[119]

President Eliot and the Harvard Board of Overseers followed closely the developments at Columbia and took care not to repeat what they viewed as their colleagues' missteps. When they agreed to the transformation of the Harvard Annex into Radcliffe College in 1894, they refused to award Harvard degrees to the new college's female graduates. Radcliffe would have to grant its own degrees. Moreover, in explicit contrast to Columbia, the Harvard Board of Overseers refused to admit women to the Harvard graduate schools. Reluctantly, they permitted women registered as graduate students at Radcliffe to audit Harvard classes, but they refused to award them a degree for their work. If those auditors wanted a Ph.D., Radcliffe would have to provide it. If they wanted jobs, they would have to seek them elsewhere.[120]

Caroline Shaw Sherer, a Radcliffe graduate of the class of 1901, regretted the difference in the two institutions' fates. At Radcliffe, "there seems little opportunity for women graduates to advance in administrative work such as grows out of even minor teaching experience in the colleges where women are on the Faculty. . . . This seems unfortunate, for it means lack of full incentive to achievement of its own alumnae."[121] An investigation of life at Radcliffe in the early 1970s echoed that regret by lamenting the absence of female faculty at Radcliffe who might serve as mentors to women undergraduates.[122]

From virtually the beginning, in contrast, Barnard students encountered female professors and interacted with female graduate students who offered encouragement and models of female adulthood very different from the standard choices then open to young women. Taking classes from men and women who had chosen to teach women students, often living near women who were pursuing graduate work, able to explore special interests in Columbia's graduate schools before graduation—all these experiences oriented Barnard undergraduates in disproportionate numbers toward graduate and professional work. Partially as a result, no school in the country sent as large a proportion of its women students on to advanced study. Ironically, the efforts of John W. Burgess and Morgan Dix to protect Columbia from what they feared would be the disruptive tendencies of women, succeeded, instead, in giving women a base from which they could more easily enter the larger university.[123]

At the same time that the Columbia trustees signed the new affiliation agreement with Barnard College, they signed a parallel agreement with the trustees at Teachers College. Like Barnard, Teachers College would remain economically separate. Columbia's president would become president ex officio, and a dean would administer the school and sit on the University Council. The agreement said nothing about whether the faculty might be female as well as male, but that may not have seemed necessary. The college's original 1889 charter had provided for a "lady principal," and the staff already included a number of women teachers in its domestic-arts division.[124] Like Barnard, Teachers College also won control of the curriculum leading to its bachelor's degree, which at Teachers College was the B.S., a degree that required training in science but not in Latin or Greek; Columbia's Faculty of Philosophy continued to supervise all work at Teachers College leading to graduate degrees.[125]

The intercorporate agreements of 1900 represented a compromise. The Columbia trustees managed to keep Barnard and Teachers College, and the women they harbored, at one remove. Alone among Columbia's schools, they were required to be financially independent, and, together, they shared responsibility for all undergraduate women on Morningside Heights. But pressure from women and the men who supported them forced the university trustees to concede to both schools a partial integration into the larger university system. Students could take courses at other schools within the university; faculty, though appointed at one school, frequently taught at others within the system. The trustees erected walls between the different schools, but those walls proved highly permeable.

As Seth Low turned Columbia College into a research university over the course of the 1890s, he never tired of warning the deans of the graduate and professional schools that they would ignore women students at the city's peril. The former mayor of Brooklyn, who would leave Columbia to become mayor of New York City in 1901, believed that the problems of the metropolis—the corruption and inefficiency of city government, the poverty and crime of urban life, and the near collapse of the city's public-school system and health services—could be overcome only by defeating the machine politicians of Tammany Hall. But he also understood the basis of Tammany's popularity: its ability to deliver services to its constituents. The reformers would never defeat the political machine until they could provide better municipal services than those Tammany offered; honest administration, by itself, would attract little support. Low also knew that a significant expansion of municipal services would create a demand for trained personnel that males alone could not supply. Appealing to his colleague's institutional pride, he cautioned that if Columbia did not admit women as well as men to its graduate and professional schools, the city would have to look elsewhere to meet its growing needs.[126] As of 1900, his message did not seem to be getting through; Columbia had produced a mere eight female doctorates—compared with Yale's thirty-six, Cornell's twenty-eight, and Chicago's twenty-five—and women were barred from all but one of its professional schools. A worried Dean Emily Smith, who became Emily James Putnam upon her marriage in 1899 to the noted publisher George H. Putnam, tried to secure a promise from Columbia's trustees that the graduate and professional schools would accept women on the same terms as men. Failing that guarantee, she demanded that Barnard have the right to enroll female graduate students, as it had since 1890, and to provide training for them itself, if necessary.[127] She won neither concession. Even so, the next three decades witnessed a dramatic increase in women's presence on campus. By 1930, female enrollments in the professional and graduate schools outpaced men's by 7,810 to 6,277.[128] No other university in the country claimed so dramatic a surplus of women. The explanation has much to do with the story of reform-minded women and their success in exploiting New York City's distinctive demography and Columbia's particular organization for their own advantage.

Symbolic of the female presence Seth and Annie Low sought to encourage at Columbia was the statue that Seth Low persuaded the Columbia University Board of Trustees in 1901 to install on the Morningside Heights campus: the goddess Columbia, better known as Alma Mater (Latin for "nourishing mother"). Created at the time of the American Revolution to represent both freedom and wisdom, the goddess Columbia loomed large in the early republic. Topped by a liberty cap, she appeared in countless political cartoons. Accompanied by an eagle, she graced early United States coins. Wrapped in classical robes, she dominated the seal of the college (formerly known as King's College) that New York State rechartered in her honor in 1784. But she had been all but forgotten over the course of the nineteenth century. Low sought to restore her to a central place in the university. He chose the sculptor Daniel Chester French on the advice of Charles McKim (whose firm had designed the Morningside campus). One of the country's foremost sculptors, French later carved the marble statue of Abraham Lincoln for the Lincoln Memorial in Washington, D.C. In sharp contrast to the typical public statue of the day, in which a male figure is positioned to convey aloofness and emotional distance, French created a seated female whose arms extend in a gesture that is both authoritative and welcoming. Placed in front of Low Library, Alma Mater faces south, toward the city. In her lap rests an open Bible, and in her right arm is a scepter that ends in four heads of wheat holding a crown (part of the original seal of King's College). Each of the arms of the chair on which she sits bears a lamp, one symbolizing Sapienta (Wisdom), and the other Doctrina (Teaching). Paid for by Harriette W. Goelet as a memorial to her husband, Robert Goelet, who graduated from Columbia in 1860, Alma Mater was unveiled in 1903. From that date, she presided over a campus where, the Lows hoped, women would one day feel as welcome as men.[129]

THREE

CITY OF WOMEN

THE POPULATION of New York City more than doubled in the final third of the nineteenth century, reaching 3.5 million in 1898 with the consolidation of the five boroughs. In the process, Gotham became the American capital of female workers. One in every three women over sixteen years of age—344,509 women in all—qualified as a breadwinner. Chicago, New York's nearest competitor, provided employment to fewer than half as many. New York's largest industry was garment manufacturing, which employed 70,000 women. Book, newspaper, and magazine publishing engaged thousands more. The banking houses, corporate towers, and dazzling emporiums that radiated from Lower Manhattan demanded armies of clerks, growing numbers of them women, to manage the flow of goods and paper. Schools, hospitals, small shops, restaurants, theaters, and individual families employed most of the rest. New York reigned supreme, in part, because of its sheer size, but the structure of its economy also made a difference. Gotham lacked the heavy industry—steel production, meatpacking, and auto manufacturing—that fueled the growth of Chicago, Pittsburgh, and Detroit. This very absence created opportunities for women. New York became the capital of the female worker precisely because it could not satisfy its labor needs with men, whose best opportunities lay in the big industries that New York did not have. New York was the center of America's consumer culture; the country's productive life lay elsewhere. As a result, almost one-third of all women in New York worked, compared with one in five in the country at large, and they worked at a greater variety of occupations than existed anywhere else in the world.[1]

Opportunity pulled women into the city's economy, while cramped quarters, which rendered housekeeping a significantly less time-consuming occupation than it was in suburban or rural settings, and the city's high cost of living, which placed a premium on maximizing family income at all but the highest economic levels, pushed women out. The great majority of the women who entered the city's economy were the semiskilled daughters of immigrants from eastern and southern Europe and migrants from America's declining farm regions. They worked as domestic servants, garment workers, and retail clerks. But the demand for educated women expanded dramatically as the economy grew more complex. Indeed, the more education a woman had, the more likely she was to be employed. Nearly half of the women who graduated from Barnard College in 1900 joined the workforce and were still there fifteen years later.[2]

Not that the jobs available, even to the well trained, were particularly desirable. The biggest employer of educated women was the New York City public-school system, which, according to Brooklyn superintendent William H. Maxwell, was "the most antiquated and the worst in the United States." The city's lack of a secondary-school system had forced the City College of New York and the Female Normal School to become glorified high schools. Even at the grammar-school level, the city fell far short of a need that soared under the pressure of massive immigration. Thousands of children were turned away every year, making it impossible to enforce the 1874 compulsory school law. At the turn of the century, 13,000 teachers, nine out of ten of them women, struggled with limited training and insufficient resources to educate the city's children. The effort to find a solution to the crisis turned New York City into a laboratory for social reform and, inadvertently, into a laboratory for rethinking the meaning of politics in America.[3]

If there was one part of Columbia's graduate program that remained a masculine preserve at the turn of the century, it was the study of political science. Women were making their way in literature, sociology, history, and even science. But political science, under the supervision of John W. Burgess, remained a society of men. Burgess stood unrivaled, at the turn of the century, as the country's foremost producer of Ph.D.'s in political science, men poised to save the American state from the waste, corruption, and thievery of the political machine through their knowledge of law and political theory and their training in public administration. Burgess's students were not just administrators, but scientists whose principal laboratory was the city of New York and whose goal was the development of techniques and procedures of governance that would lead to peak efficiency: water delivered reliably and cheaply, and schools adequate to the needs of an expanding population. Through the work of these experts, the state might be drawn to that pinnacle of administrative efficiency that his professors in Berlin and Paris had promised nearly three decades before.[4] For Burgess, 1901 was a banner year for the reform he envisioned. Nicholas Murray Butler, his most prized student, assumed the leadership of Columbia University as acting president (he would become president the following year). Seth Low, his longtime ally in university building (if not on the woman question), defeated the Tammany machine to become mayor of New York City. And Theodore Roosevelt, his former student at the Law School, succeeded the slain William McKinley to become president of the United States. In the game of state building, to which he had dedicated his life, this was a rare and satisfying trifecta.

Burgess continued to believe that women had no aptitude for, and therefore no legitimate place in, this enterprise, but while he succeeded in keeping women out of his classroom and managed to limit their access to the Graduate Faculty of Political Science more generally, women in other parts of the university and in the city itself were beginning to challenge his vision of politics. They succeeded, in part, because of their large and active presence in the city and, in part, because some of the very administrative reforms that he championed, especially the administrative reform of the New York City school system, redounded to women's political advantage in ways that he could not foresee.

CONSOLIDATING THE NEW YORK CITY SCHOOLS

While Grace Dodge built Teachers College and tried to organize it to serve the teachers of New York, Nicholas Murray Butler launched a major campaign to wrest control of the city's schools from the "boodlers" and "ringsters" of Tammany Hall and centralize administration in the hands of professional educators. He began in 1891 by founding the *Educational Review*, in which he lambasted the "piratical" bosses who were destroying public education.[5] He ghosted articles for local newspapers on the need for school reform, drafted bills for the state legislature in Albany (dominated by upstate Republicans) to consolidate the New York City schools, worked to establish the College Entrance Examination Board to set a common standard for public-school achievement, and organized civic groups to lobby for change. Not everyone who opposed Butler's reforms was self-seeking and corrupt. The ethnic communities of New York and many teachers supported the status quo out of fear that a centralized board, dominated by white Anglo-Saxon Protestants like Butler, would ignore their concerns. Butler outmaneuvered them all.[6]

In 1896, the state legislature gave the New York Board of Education the power to set standards for teachers, establish a common curriculum, build schools, and increase salaries. The board immediately opened three new high schools and began to incorporate the "new education" pioneered at

Teachers College into the public-school curriculum. In 1898, the Board of Education took the further step of requiring that teachers who sought higher licenses present evidence of having taken appropriate courses in both subject matter and method. In 1901, consolidation became complete, as the legislature passed a charter that concentrated power in a professional bureaucracy under the control of the Board of Superintendents. This new, highly centralized school system was the biggest of any city in the country, and bigger than the school systems of most states. Enrollment at Teachers College soared as the Board of Education struggled to keep up with rising levels of immigration by building new schools and hiring thousands of new teachers and administrators to run them. By the end of the 1920s, the college was enrolling more than five thousand students a year and had become the largest professional school in the world. No other college of education in the country had as much influence. Harvard did not open its school of education until 1920. Chicago, which was Columbia's closest competitor, granted only one-tenth as many doctorates. By the 1920s, the college was seeding the city, the country, and even the world with thousands of professionally trained teachers and administrators, the majority of them women, every year. For women, the added training brought not just greater responsibility but a dramatic boost in pay.[7]

James Earl Russell, dean of Teachers College from 1898 to 1927, did not stop with simple expansion; he experimented with new educational ventures. Extension Teaching (which became University Extension in 1920 and the School of General Studies in 1947), along with the Summer School (1900), the Dental School (1919), and the Business School (1917), all had their start at Teachers College, and all admitted women from the start. They provided remedial courses to those not yet ready for college, practical training to those seeking to advance within a specific occupation, room for experimentation in fields that were ultimately incorporated into the university, and teaching opportunities for graduate students and faculty in search of added income.[8] The Summer School and Extension Teaching generated so much surplus revenue that the university took over the first in 1904 and the second in 1910. To staff the hundreds of additional classes that this experiment required, the university trustees agreed in 1904 to allow the appointment to the faculty of both "men and women not otherwise in service to the university." For the first time, women gained the formal right to teach, not just at Barnard and Teachers College, but also at Columbia itself.[9] By 1920, enrollment at Teachers College and all its spin-offs was generating 21,000 of Columbia's 27,000 annual registrations. The majority were women.[10]

The economic success of Teachers College and its curricular progeny brought in significant income but also gave rise to disagreements over the value of courses offered, the quality of the students who took them, and the growing presence of women on campus. As a sign of the growing tension, misogynists took to calling 120th Street "hairpin alley." In 1914, Butler decided that it was time to merge Teachers College into the university and so "simplify all our financial and academic problems forever." In Butler's view, the future prestige of Teachers College depended on raising the standards of admission and reducing the number of students, as the College of Physicians and Surgeons had done when it was incorporated into Columbia in 1891. The "history of higher education shows clearly," Butler warned Grace Dodge, "that there is no place outside the university for a high grade professional school."[11]

In 1892, Dodge and the other Teachers College trustees had been eager to be absorbed into Columbia. After a couple of decades on Columbia's border, however, they resisted the idea of losing their autonomy. As far as one Teachers College trustee, Felix Warburg, was concerned, Butler's proposal was of a piece with Columbia's long-standing pattern of taking none of the risks while claiming all the financial benefits of Teachers College's experimentation. He favored cutting off relations with the university entirely.[12] Dodge took a more conciliatory position. Fearing that the merger would threaten the college's independence (especially the domestic-arts program she had fought to establish), as well as the legacies she had worked so long to secure, she opposed it. Mindful of the value of the Columbia connection, however, she resisted divorce.[13] The battle between the Teachers College trustees and Butler revealed a basic philosophical disagreement. Butler wanted to train an elite corps of teachers and administrators. Dean Russell and the Teachers College Board of Trustees, by contrast, saw their enterprise in more inclusive terms, as a vehicle for spreading pedagogical training as widely as possible.[14] After extended negotiations, the boards of Teachers College and the university finally agreed to the middle course that Dodge sought. Under a new financial arrangement, students would pay for all courses on a point system, and the university secured its right to fees generated by courses taught by Columbia faculty. Teachers College, for its part, gained the right to grant doctorates in its Faculty of Practical Arts, the division known elsewhere in the country as Home Economics.[15]

THE TEACHER AS SOCIAL WORKER

Butler's principal interest in reform was in fighting political corruption, making school administration more efficient, and delivering education more effectively. Dodge was driven more by religious principles and a deep sense of social justice to want to improve the lives of the city's poor. Both felt

frustration at the terrible state of New York City's schools and their inability
to offer even a basic education to all children, much less the enrichment in
art, music, crafts, books, and physical education that they thought children
needed to develop to their fullest potential. Increasingly, they looked to the
settlement houses that were springing up in poor neighborhoods to help in
that effort. So interconnected did the work of the school and settlement become at the turn of the century that the terms "teacher" and "settlement
worker" became nearly interchangeable.

Settlement work began in New York in 1886, when Seth Low helped
found a settlement house, modeled on London's Toynbee Hall (and named
University Settlement in 1891), on the Lower East Side. Women's involve-
ment began the following year, when a group of teachers from Wellesley
College, led by Vida Scudder, founded the College Settlements Association. In 1889, they opened College Settlement (a few months before Jane
Addams opened Hull House in Chicago) on Rivington Street. Lillian Wald's
Nurses Settlement, the forerunner of the Henry Street Settlement, soon fol-
lowed. Together, University Settlement, College Settlement, and Nurses
Settlement created the nucleus for early efforts to find new ways of address-
ing the problems of the immigrant poor who were crowding into the city.

Surrounded by desperately poor Jewish refugees, who were fleeing from
persecution in eastern Europe, settlement workers, who were themselves
often seeking to escape from the suffocating shelter of the Victorian middle
class, found intense excitement in the raucous shouting, the strange foods,
the Yiddish newspapers, the crowded tenements and sweatshops, and the
cafés where residents heatedly debated anarchism and socialism. A College
Settlement resident, Mary Kingsbury, later recalled, "In the long period of
my education, this was the most exciting chapter, for here everything was
tested."[16] As New York City grew, so did opportunities for women to question their assumptions. By 1911, nearly a hundred settlement houses, most
run by women and most connected to schools, stretched out from the Lower
East Side to Brooklyn and up both the East and West Sides of Manhattan.
In these settlement houses, they tested the lessons being taught in college
classrooms.[17]

Elsie Clews was a Barnard College student who discovered the settlement-
house movement through a course in sociology with Professor Franklin Giddings in 1894. The daughter of wealthy and socially prominent parents, Clews
had come to Barnard to avoid becoming a woman who did nothing but
"bathe, curl, anoint, powder, manicure, etc., and think about dress all day
long."[18] A fervent admirer of Lillie Devereux Blake, Clews wrote to her Harvard boyfriend, Sam Dexter, following the 1894 meeting of the New York

State Woman's Suffrage Association, "According to my idea of the family there should be two heads and then the woman should have a part in the representing too."[19] Dexter's sudden death of a fever later that summer saved Clews from an early marriage. She returned to Barnard that fall and found a vehicle for self-fulfillment in the new discipline of sociology.

Students loved Giddings's enthusiasm and informality, if not his rambling style. He liked to shock his students, as the political scientist Charles Mirriam later remembered, "by drawing them up either to the edge of atheism or immorality or what not, and pressing them hard."[20] The mother of one of his students once complained to Nicholas Murray Butler that he was teaching atheism, to which Butler responded, "I'm glad you told me, madam, we aim to teach everything at the University."[21] Giddings's *Principles of Sociology* (1896), widely regarded as the most important volume in the field, argued that advanced societies developed out of what he called a "consciousness of kind"—that is, a person's ability to identify with others. In its most elevated form, "consciousness of kind" produced "self-realization" by giving one perspective on oneself. Inspired by Giddings and his field trips to the Lower East Side to see sociology in action, Clews founded a chapter of the College Settlements Association at Barnard in February 1895.

Giddings's ideal of self-realization appealed to his strong-minded women students, who saw in that concept a weapon against the constraints that Victorian society imposed on female achievement, but Giddings never intended his evolutionary scheme to support the women's movement. Insistent on the interdependent relationship of individual freedom and social cohesion, he believed that each "individual must have a definite part in the division of labor, and in the common life of the nation, the local community and the family." Full self-realization, Giddings argued, could be achieved only by evolution's highest product—the mature, rational, Anglo-Saxon male—and only if he found support in a social order in which everyone else faithfully performed his or her own duties. Giddings believed that women's tendency to "subordinate judgment to emotion" must restrict them to private rather than public duties. As Clews came to understand the full implications of Giddings's thought, she shifted her allegiance to the French sociologist Gabriel Tarde, whose work stressed the importance of individual freedom, creativity, and the accident of genius—not social evolution—as the igniter of change.[22]

In 1896, Clews took Butler's course on the history and philosophy of education. Butler sparked her interest in school reform and the role of settlements in it. In 1896/1897, she wrote her thesis under Giddings's supervision on poor relief in New York City. A brief stint of "friendly visiting" with the

Charities Organization Society persuaded her that settlement-house work and the "new" education were a better way of helping the poor. Through the City History Club, she led children on outings to give them a firsthand experience of the city's diversity. Butler introduced her to Julia Richman, New York City's first female superintendent of schools, who advanced the idea that the teacher was society's natural social worker.[23]

Inspired by Richman, Clews made plans to help found a combination settlement house and school that would be affiliated with Teachers College and dedicated to the study of "all forms of public education and social service." The result was the Speyer School (1898), named for Teachers College trustee James Speyer. The new settlement house and school worked directly with poor families, mostly immigrant Jews from eastern Europe who were beginning to migrate to the neighborhood just north of Columbia.[24] Although Clews was twenty-three years old, her parents refused to allow her to leave home to direct a settlement house, and the Speyer School carried on without her. Each year, it appointed two social workers from University Settlement to live at the school and work with members of the community. It opened its library to the public and served as a drop-off place for mothers who needed help in looking after their children. The teachers lived above the school with the social workers and kept the building open from 8:00 A.M. to 10:00 P.M. Inspired by the settlement houses of the Lower East Side, the Speyer School, in turn, served as a model for public schools throughout the city.[25]

Barred from directing the Speyer School, Elsie Clews agreed to stay at home for another two years, but only if her parents allowed her to pursue a doctorate. In 1897, she enrolled in the Faculty of Philosophy to begin a doctorate in education under the direction of Nicholas Murray Butler. Over the next two years, she divided her time between settlement-house work and library research for her dissertation on education in the American colonies. She received her Ph.D. in 1899. The same year, the city appointed her as school inspector.[26]

Clews's closest friend in graduate school was Mary Kingsbury, whom she had met at College Settlement. Kingsbury, a graduate of Boston University, was eight years Clews's senior and had been working in settlements for several years. Moreover, she had studied in Berlin and attended the Socialist International in London. She began graduate school with Clews in 1896 but left after only a year, convinced that she needed wider experience in settlement-house work before the sociology, economics, and history she was studying could have more relevance for her. Kingsbury departed sharply from the vision of reform advanced by professors like Butler and Burgess. She saw the settlement's main role as empowering the community by encouraging local leadership, and thought that if one class tried to make improvements for another through the kind of administrative reforms championed in Columbia's Fayerweather Hall, no permanent change was likely. She joined in the campaign to make local schools neighborhood centers, supported neighborhood theaters, helped establish a music school, and worked to improve housing and to restore old buildings.[27]

The link between Morningside Heights and the Lower East Side led to other developments as well. In 1898, the Charities Organization Society, founded by Josephine Shaw Lowell, tried to do for social workers what Teachers College was doing for teachers. It created the Summer School of Philanthropy to train social workers to deal more effectively with the problems of poverty that had threatened to overwhelm the city in the depression of the 1890s. Lowell had begun her career as a staunch opponent of "gratuitous charity" on the grounds that it undermined the work ethic among the poor. But she began to rethink her view of poverty in the 1880s, after an Episcopal minister condemned the Charities Organization Society as "the meanest humbug in the city of New York." Leonora O'Reilly, a young cap maker and labor organizer, contributed further to Lowell's transformation by opening her eyes to the appalling conditions under which women worked in sweatshops and department stores. Gradually, Lowell came to see poverty as a result of social and economic conditions more than personal failing. In 1891, she helped found the Consumers League of New York City. In order to circumvent court rulings against "blacklists" as an illegal boycott, the league came up with the idea of a "white list"—a list of those businesses that treated workers fairly. Lowell continued to oppose direct aid to the poor as an "evil," but the grounds changed. She now believed that it allowed employers to underpay workers, thus making it harder for workers to earn a better wage. She believed in the importance of training social workers to understand the structural roots of poverty and to help them win better pay and working conditions.[28]

The Summer School for Philanthropy grew into the New York School of Philanthropy in 1904 with a one-year course, which was extended to a two-year course in 1910. Students at Columbia were allowed to earn social-work certificates at the school, and students at the school could enroll for free and earn an M.A. in a field related to their work at Columbia. The school changed its name to the New York School of Social Work in 1917. It maintained continuous academic connections with Columbia University from the beginning, but, even more than Barnard or Teachers College, it remained on the university's periphery. Located downtown, on Twenty-second Street, it did not become formally affiliated with the university until 1940 and did not move to Morningside Heights until 1950. Then, in 1959, the university absorbed the school into its corporate structure, and in 1963 it became the Columbia School of Social Work.[29]

The peripheral existence of Barnard, Teachers College, and the School of Social Work had its benefits. While those who taught there often felt marginalized, they also experienced a freedom to experiment, collaborate, and debate that may have been more robust than would otherwise have been possible. In fact, many of the faculty and students at these institutions delighted in lambasting their more conservative colleagues on the graduate faculties. For those pioneering scholars, the early years of the twentieth century were a time of intense intellectual ferment and political engagement, as well as iconoclastic thinking about gender roles. Elsie Clews began her academic career as a teacher at Horace Mann, the coeducational model school that Teachers College maintained at 120th Street and Broadway, where the staff defied gender norms by teaching boys to sew. After earning her Ph.D. in 1899, Clews assisted Franklin Giddings in his classes in sociology at Barnard. While he gave lectures, she supervised fieldwork in the city's settlement houses and pioneered methods of family ethnography—the observation of beliefs, ideals, interests, amusements, and superstitions (rather than just economic facts)—that would later be used by anthropologists to study gender roles.[30] Mary Kingsbury never finished her Ph.D., but her extensive research on unemployment, racism, housing, and the assimilation of immigrant groups made her a valuable resource to social scientists on Morningside Heights. She taught classes at Barnard, Teachers College, and Extension Teaching from 1907 to 1913. Mary Adelaide Nutting, who started the country's first training school for teachers of nursing at Teachers College, worked collaboratively with Lillian Wald at the Henry Street Settlement to place nurses in the schools, develop public-health initiatives in poor communities, and create the Visiting Nurses Association. Mary Van Kleeck, a 1904 graduate of Smith College, lived and worked at College Settlement on Rivington Street while pursuing research on women workers and teaching at the New York School of Philanthropy. Crystal Eastman, a 1903 graduate of Vassar, earned an M.A. in sociology from Columbia in 1904 and became a settlement-house worker, before receiving a law degree from New York University (Columbia Law School did not yet admit women) and taking part in the Pittsburgh Survey, out of which came her book *Work Accidents and the Law* (1910). On the strength of that work, she was appointed to the New York State Employers' Liability Commission and helped secure passage of the state's first workers' compensation law. Frances Perkins, a 1902 graduate of Mount Holyoke, earned her M.A. in economics and sociology from Columbia in 1910 with a study of Hell's Kitchen that focused on the malnutrition of children. She worked at the Henry Street Settlement and campaigned for protective labor legislation for the National Consumers League, before embarking on a government career that culminated in her appointment as Secretary of Labor during the New Deal.[31]

MARRIAGE AND MOTHERHOOD

To many women at Columbia, the reform of society could not be separated from the reform of the family. In their own lives, family reform meant combining marriage, motherhood, and careers. New York offered a handful of prominent role models of women who had managed such a combination. The journalist Jennie June Croly was one; Lillie Devereux Blake, another. Dr. Mary Putnam Jacobi, the wife of Dr. Abraham Jacobi and the mother of three, was particularly influential in academic circles. The author of an early and effective rebuttal of Dr. Edward Clarke's theory that women could not withstand the physical rigors of higher education, she was one of the founders of the Consumers League and an aunt, by marriage, of the anthropologist Franz Boas. Inspired by the example of these pioneers and by a sense of possibility brought by a new century, a growing number of academic women resolved to embark on family life without abandoning their careers. In 1899, Dean Emily James Smith of Barnard married the publisher George Haven Putnam, Mary Putnam Jacobi's brother. After some debate, the Barnard trustees accepted the idea that marriage should not preclude their dean from continuing in her position. When she became pregnant, however, they insisted that she resign. She did so in April 1900, just as Elsie Clews announced her engagement to Herbert Parsons.

Parsons, a young Republican lawyer from a wealthy family, shared Clews's commitment to bringing about social reform and to using their wealth to help others. Parsons was active in the same reform circles as Butler, Low, and Roosevelt and was an ally in trying to overthrow Tammany Hall. But he found competing with Clews's academic ambitions difficult. Their courtship dragged on, as she pursued graduate work and fretted about the effect that marriage might have on her career. Determinedly a "new woman," she insisted on being a woman "not classified, perhaps not classifiable," and she set herself the task of destroying existing systems of values—especially where women were concerned.[32]

Clews made continuing to teach at Barnard a condition of her marriage to Parsons in 1900. Within months, however, she was pregnant and worrying about whether the trustees would force her to resign. To her surprise,

Elsie Clews Parsons (1875–1941)
Graduate of Barnard College (1896) and Columbia
University (M.A. 1897, Ph.D. 1899), sociologist
and anthropologist, and lecturer at Barnard College
(1902–1906), as photographed, with her daughter
Lissa, in 1900. (American Philosophical Society,
Philadelphia)

they did not. Annie Nathan Meyer, who had insisted on Putnam's resignation, wrote, "I heartily congratulate you that marriage may mean a going on
without a giving up. . . . Your work . . . need not—I should think—present
any problems, certainly not for a while. A Fellow or an Instructor or even a
Professor is different from a Dean."[33] Giddings at first pretended not to notice her condition and wrote in June 1901, when she was eight months pregnant, that he and his wife were "greatly interested in the news of yourself. . . .
I am very glad that you did not think it necessary to cut short the work at
Barnard, and I congratulate you on your good sense." [34]

Clews's friend Alice Duer, the great-great-granddaughter of William
Alexander Duer (president of Columbia College from 1829 to 1849), was another Barnard woman who struggled to find a way to combine family with a
career. Duer entered Barnard in 1895, following her family's disastrous economic reverses in the crash of 1893. To help pay expenses, she tutored other
students and wrote short stories and essays for *Harper's* and *Scribner's* magazines. In 1899, she graduated, having concentrated in mathematics and astronomy, and married Henry Wise Miller. To Clews's disappointment,
Miller took his wife to Costa Rica, where he expected to make a fortune in
land speculation. Duer kept on writing, however, "amid the venomous hardships of bungalow life." In 1901, she returned briefly to New York to give
birth to a son. Then, to her great relief, Miller agreed to return to New York
for good in 1903, his real-estate ventures not having panned out. Alice Duer

Miller taught composition at a girls' school and taught mathematics at Barnard until she began to write full time.[35]

Elsie Clews Parsons was back at Barnard by early November 1901. In addition to her teaching, she embarked on an unsuccessful campaign to persuade Seth Low, newly elected mayor of New York, to appoint women, herself in particular, to the new Greater New York Board of Education. Low's female supporters took him at his word that they were to play a central role in the business of the city. He quickly took advantage of experiments women were conducting through the settlement houses, accepting Lillian Wald's suggestion, for instance, that all schools employ nurses to deliver basic medical care to immigrant children. But he was slower to appoint women to key positions in his administration and seems to have decided that the best way to stay in touch with their concerns was to appoint James B. Reynolds, directory of University Settlement, as his private secretary. Low had a better record of appointing Italian, Jewish, and African American men, who had also been underrepresented under Tammany leadership, than he did of appointing women.[36]

At Barnard College, Parsons taught a course on the family from 1902 to 1905 and worked on a textbook, *The Family*, published in 1906. It provided an encyclopedic account of the ethnographic and psychological literature on family relations and sexual practices. Sparing in commentary, Parsons nonetheless made clear her disdain for evolutionary thinking. "[T]he habit of evolutionary thought is almost too readily acquired by the embryonic scientist," she warned in her preface. To counteract such tendencies, she offered comparisons between New York society and so-called primitive peoples. The "coming out party," for example, was just a variation on the initiation ceremony found in most cultures, while the rule against pregnant women's appearing in public was simply a variation on the pregnancy taboos that existed among many peoples. In giving students a comparative perspective on their own lives, Parsons believed, she would encourage them to think critically about their experience.[37]

For her own part, Parsons came to believe that the aspect of women's lives that most needed reform was the tabooed subject of sexuality. With the establishment of the Socialist Party in 1900 and the founding of the National Women's Trade Union League in 1903, it had become possible to talk about work and economic exploitation, but discussion of sexuality remained unacceptable. As Parsons prepared *The Family* for publication, she therefore wrote a series of articles in which she addressed that problem. She castigated women's colleges for failing to develop a curriculum that included the frank investigation of sexuality. That failure meant, among other things, perpetuating the idea of prostitution as a "necessary evil" without discussing candidly why it was "necessary" and what the consequences were of its being "evil." As a result, college women who entered settlement-house work did more harm than good as they imposed their own blinkered views in place of the community initiatives the settlements were designed to foster. Echoing Lillie Devereux Blake, Parsons went on to attack the New York City Board of Education for "mere Rip Van Winkleism" in outlawing married women teachers rather than studying the conditions under which women can work best. Such a study would entail confronting questions of sexuality and childbearing and dealing openly with matters of birth control and maternity leaves.[38]

By the time she published *The Family*, Parsons had reached the conclusion that society had to do more than deal frankly with sexual matters. It had to come up with a way for young people to find a healthy outlet for their sexual impulses without having to assume premature responsibility for children. She recommended a period of "trial marriage," during which young couples could determine their personal compatibility before formalizing their relationship and becoming parents. Society would simply have to provide them with "certain and innocuous methods of preventing conception" so that they were not saddled with children before they were ready.[39]

Herbert Parsons later confessed that, sensing he would not like its message, he never read *The Family*.[40] But others did. The day the book appeared, the *New York Herald* declared, "no more radical declaration from the pen of an author relating to matrimony has been published"; the following day, the newspaper went on to condemn the book's ethics as "the morality of the barnyard," an epithet that has stuck with Barnard students ever since. No one was more outraged than the Reverend Dr. Morgan Dix. Having made his peace with the higher education of women over a decade before with the founding of Barnard and Teachers College, he must have had second thoughts in 1906, when this first major publication by a Barnard College faculty member took the country by storm. On Thanksgiving, he devoted his sermon to condemning it.[41]

By the time *The Family* appeared, Elsie Clews Parsons had reluctantly resigned her post at Barnard to move her family to Washington, D.C., following her husband's election to Congress in 1904. She would never again teach at Columbia (though she would play a key role in the development of anthropology in later years). More immediately, her departure left women faculty at Barnard who sought to marry at the mercy of a new, more conservative regime. When the Barnard trustees forced Emily Smith Putnam to resign in 1900, they replaced her as dean with Laura Gill, a graduate of

Smith. Gill held to the traditional view that women who married made a choice to abandon their careers. In 1906, Harriet Brooks, a tutor in the physics department, wrote to inform Dean Gill that she intended to marry Bergen Davis, a Columbia physicist. Brooks indicated that she had discussed her plans with Professor Margaret Maltby, the chair of the Barnard physics department, and that Maltby had no objections. Brooks wanted to know whether marriage would prevent her from keeping her position. Gill replied that marriage would indeed end her career at Barnard. Maltby came to Brooks's defense, but Gill remained adamant. Ignoring the example set by Elsie Clews Parsons (or, perhaps, given Parsons's growing notoriety, taking her example into account), she announced, "The College cannot afford to have women on the staff to whom the college work is secondary."[42]

Mary Kingsbury encountered similar difficulties at the Friendly Aid House, the settlement where she went to work following her year of graduate study in 1896/1897. In 1899, she married Vladimir Simkhovitch, a Russian-born professor of economics at Columbia, whom she had met in Berlin in 1899, and in 1902 she gave birth to their first child. The board of the Friendly Aid House objected to her bringing up their baby in the settlement house and forced her to resign. Elsie Clews Parsons—with the support of a group of reformers, churchmen, academics, and bankers—raised money for a new settlement, Greenwich House, where Mary Kingsbury Simkhovitch could carry out her desire to combine motherhood with settlement work. At the same time, Parsons set about writing essays on the sexual taboos that made the experiment of combining work with motherhood so difficult. Pregnant women were expected to hide their pregnancy and nursing, especially from young people. Given the fact that teaching and social work were the two most likely sources of employment for college-educated women of childbearing age at the turn of the century, those taboos created powerful barriers to their success. The pregnancy taboo, Parsons wrote in 1904, "is both hurtful to the pride and a serious handicap to the productive activity of child-bearing women."[43] This concern affected Parsons especially, for, between 1901 and 1911, she gave birth to six children, four of whom survived infancy, while determinedly pursuing an active life of work and athletics.

Another Columbia woman who struggled to combine marriage, motherhood, and work was Mary Ritter Beard, who came to Columbia in 1902 with her husband, Charles, to pursue graduate work in the Faculty of Political Science. Mary and Charles Beard came from well-to-do midwestern, Republican families. They met as undergraduates at DePauw University in Indiana. Following her graduation in 1897, Mary Ritter stayed nearby, teaching German at a public school. Charles Beard graduated the following year and left alone for graduate study in history at Oxford University. The separation proved so painful, however, that he returned after only a year. They married in 1900, when she was twenty-four and he twenty-six, and spent their first two years together back in England, where Charles directed an extension school for workers in Manchester and pursued research on a history of the office of justice of the peace, which later became his doctoral dissertation. While in Manchester, Mary Beard encountered the "ghastly deprivations" of working-class life in an industrial city for the first time and became a "devoted friend" of the socialist Emmeline Pankhurst, who, with her three daughters, would soon achieve international fame for her militant actions on behalf of votes for women. While in England, Mary Beard also gave birth to the couple's first child, Miriam, in 1901 and began her career as a historian, publishing an article that deplored historians' blindness to women's contributions: "The volumes which record the history of the human race are filled with the deeds and the words of great men . . . [but] The Twentieth Century Woman . . . questions the completeness of the story." In 1902, the Beards returned with their daughter to the United States, and both enrolled in Columbia's graduate school of political science.[44]

THE "NEW HISTORY"

At Columbia, Charles and Mary Beard encountered an increasingly divided faculty. One group gravitated toward John W. Burgess, who had just published a constitutional history of Reconstruction. In Burgess's view, Reconstruction presented a "soul-sickening spectacle," one in which radicals in Congress had exceeded their constitutional authority by taking power away from an "intelligent and virtuous" southern elite and handing it over to "ignorant" and "vicious" carpetbaggers, scalawags, and freedmen. The result was the rapid destruction of "all that was left of prosperity, civilization, morality and decency."[45] Another faction in the graduate faculty gathered around James Harvey Robinson, who had just returned to teaching, following a term as acting dean of the new Barnard College faculty, made necessary by the forced retirement of Emily Smith Putnam.

Robinson was, like the Beards, a Midwesterner from a well-to-do family. He received his undergraduate degree from Harvard, where he studied with Ephraim Emerton, who introduced him to the newest scientific methods of historical research, and with William James, who inspired him to see the human mind as part of a larger natural order. Deciding to be a historian, Robinson joined the scholarly migration to Germany, where he earned his Ph.D. under the direction of Hermann von Holst, a leading specialist in American political history. When Burgess hired Robinson in 1895, with the funds made possible by Seth Low's anonymous gift to Barnard, Robinson appeared to be a safe choice. But no sooner had he arrived in New York and begun associating with social scientists like Franklin Giddings than he had begun to distance himself from the narrowly political approach of the historians with whom he had trained. Looking back on his education later, Robinson recalled that it had been the psychologist and philosopher William James, rather than the historians Emerton and von Holst, who had been the more enduring influence in his intellectual development. Gradually, Robinson reconceived his pedagogic goal and started to train students to understand the "new history," as it would later be known, from the bottom up. As he did so, he came to see the past as worthy of study only insofar as it could be exploited "in the interests of advance."[46]

Robinson continued to value the patient skills of scholarship, but he came to believe that scholars spent too much time on political events and abstract ideas, divorced from social and economic context. He was fundamentally an evolutionist, who conceived of human beings as part of a larger, natural environment. To understand change, he believed that scholars should seek not the dramatic or the unusual but rather the stories of everyday life. In studying the French Revolution, for instance, he avoided the horrors of the guillotine in favor of the daily lives of ordinary men and women—how they

James Harvey Robinson (1863–1936)
Professor of history at Columbia University
(1895–1900) and Barnard College (1900–1919),
as photographed in 1900. (Barnard College
Archives)

lived and thought and felt. He wanted his students to know more about bread, and less about Marie Antoinette.[47]

Robinson soon began to argue that a "new history" would enable the public to escape "from the limitations formerly imposed upon the study of the past. It will come in time consciously to meet our daily needs; it will avail itself of all those discoveries that are being made about mankind by anthropologists, economists, psychologists, and sociologists—discoveries which during the past fifty years have served to revolutionize our ideas of the origin, progress, and prospects of our race."[48]

Robinson seems to have been happy to teach at Barnard for the very reasons that Burgess refused to; he regarded the education of young women as part of a larger project of progressive reform. Barnard students later recalled Robinson as a small, kindly man with bright-blue eyes who taught them to be tolerant and to think independently. There had evidently been too many preachers in his family for him to complete the transition he often seemed to want to make to European cosmopolitanism. But he did his best to rebel against the pieties and respectability of his midwestern upbringing. One Barnard student recalled, "His last advice to us was to look at things with an open mind—not to accept blindly the godly and respectable—to be just and honest. As a result of his teaching I have been free and uneasy all my life." Robinson made the conservative Burgess uneasy, too, though for a different reason. Burgess aimed at training future leaders of the republic, an endeavor, he believed, in which women had no legitimate role. Using the tumultuous period that followed the American Civil War as a warning of the damage reformers could wreak, Burgess routinely warned young men of the dangers of institutional innovation, whether in the family or in the state.

Robinson took issue with Burgess on two grounds, one methodological, and the other political. In Robinson's opinion, Burgess paid too little attention to social and economic context. This methodological narrowness, Robinson believed, caused Burgess to hang on to outworn shibboleths like the inherent superiority of elites. Moreover, it prevented him from seeing that the world was changing, and that the very social groups he dismissed as "ignorant" and "vicious" were part of that forward progress.

Graduate students at Columbia, like undergraduates at Barnard, found Robinson a riveting teacher. Years later, the noted historian Arthur M. Schlesinger Sr. remembered Robinson as far more interesting than his other graduate professors, "who confined themselves to a wholly traditional subject matter." Schlesinger found Robinson's graduate course in European intellectual history, developed first at Barnard and popularly known as "The

Downfall of Christianity," as "the most provocative that I took at Columbia and the source of endless argument among the students."[49]

The Burgess faction disagreed with the students' positive assessment of Robinson. When William Sloane retired as chairman of the Columbia history department in 1915, he complained to President Nicholas Murray Butler that Robinson had strayed so far from historical norms that he had come close "to the creation of a new department." Sloane objected in particular to Robinson's "modernist point of view," which had led him to teach everything "except history as [his] colleagues understand it." He was not "expert in any one of the subjects as discursively treated." Moreover, the departments of economics and sociology "have been disturbed by the trespass."[50]

Robinson was the ringleader of a group of scholars who were engaged in vigorous "trespass" on the accepted forms of scholarly specialization. The group included Franz Boas in anthropology, Franklin Giddings in sociology, Vladimir Simkhovitch in economics, Harry Hollingworth and Edward L. Thorndike in psychology, and John Dewey in philosophy—all faculty who either held their appointments at Barnard or Teachers College, or spent a significant portion of their teaching time there. They were all committed to interdisciplinary study and social reform and were involved in the settlement movement. Dewey, a close friend of Jane Addams, became a key member when Butler recruited him from Chicago in 1904.[51]

Dewey had begun, like Butler, as a devotee of German idealism, but Butler soon realized that Dewey was headed in a very different direction. As one Columbia graduate, Randolph Bourne, later put it, Butler liked to preach the "absolute idealism" of the Good, the True and the Beautiful.[52] Dewey, in contrast, had abandoned the search for absolutes. He argued that truth existed only provisionally and only as it was revealed in the particular circumstances of a given time. That belief prompted Dewey to regard education as a process that properly began with the student, a view that horrified the Columbia president. In Butler's view, Dewey's "new education" turned the world upside down, placing responsibility into the hands of the learner, rather than keeping it where it belonged, in the hands of the learned. Butler revealed his disdain for progressive ideas in education when he recalled appreciatively the training he had received as a child in the Paterson, New Jersey, public schools. The young women who had taught him, he recalled, were "still old-fashioned enough to believe in discipline for the purpose of conveying facts which human experience had taught were of value." For him, the "present-day notion, that an infant must be permitted and encouraged to explore the universe around himself as if everything were at its beginning and there had been no human experience whatever, had, fortunately, not yet raised its preposterous head."[53] This was a caricature of Dewey's views, but it grasped his basic point that education was about questioning, exploring, and being open to new ways of seeing the world. For Butler, the point of educational reform was to wrest power from Tammany Hall, train administrators to run the schools more efficiently, and prepare teachers to teach more effectively. He supported manual training as a pedagogical technique, because he thought that the ability to draw enhanced a child's ability to learn subjects like geography.[54] He never doubted that the point of it all was to convey the accumulated wisdom of Western civilization. He joked about wanting to teach everything at Columbia, even atheism, but, in common with John W. Burgess, he found himself increasingly disenchanted by those like Dewey who gravitated toward James Harvey Robinson and his "modernist ideas." Butler saw Morningside Heights as an academic Olympus, where specialists refined knowledge that had been harvested from the urban laboratory in order to bestow it on the less able, while Robinson and Dewey viewed the university as part of the urban laboratory and thought that ideas should be tested and revised in light of the shifting experience. They saw women as an essential element, even the driving element, in this reform, and they were generally supportive of women's efforts. Mary and Charles Beard became active members of this intellectual circle, as they sought to integrate their interest in social reform with their scholarship.

Charles Beard completed his Ph.D. in 1904, having studied with both Burgess and Robinson, and won an appointment to the faculty. He published widely in academic journals and magazines of opinion, and in 1913 produced his pathbreaking *Economic Interpretation of the Constitution of the United States*, which argued, to the dismay of Burgess, that economic concerns motivated the framers of the Constitution. Mary Beard, in contrast, dropped out without earning a degree.[55] She left no record of her reasons. It was still uncommon for a married woman to tackle graduate study. For a mother to do so was unheard of. Elsie Clews Parsons offered the closest model, but she had completed her Ph.D. before marrying. Mary Beard undertook the rigors of graduate work with a one-year-old baby at home. As Charles Beard wrote to a friend in 1917, "I know how you feel about the restrictions of young motherhood as well as any mere man can know, for Mrs. Beard had everything fall on her young shoulders simultaneously."[56]

The pressures of motherhood, alone, could easily explain Mary Beard's departure. But the atmosphere in Fayerweather Hall likely played a part as well. Fired, even more than her husband, with a passion for political activism, Mary Beard shared with Mary Kingsbury Simkhovitch an impatience with piling fact on tedious fact, when so much needed doing in the world around her. Moreover, the hostility of John W. Burgess to the presence of

Mary Ritter Beard (1876–1958)
Graduate student in history and political
science at Columbia University (1902–1903)
and pioneer women's historian, as photo-
gaphed around 1910. (Detlev F. Vagts)

women, especially married women interested in history and political science, cannot have been lost on her. Franklin Giddings, at least, offered classes that had immediate relevance to social reform. Graduate work in history
and political science, however, promised only to prepare students for work
in political administration or universities, where women, as yet, were not
being hired. How could a young woman easily find a place in a discipline
defined so completely according to prevailing masculine norms?

Mary Beard left graduate school, but she did not abandon history or engagement in the outside world. Inspired by the Pankhursts in England, she
turned her energies to the problems of the working women of New York City
and to winning the vote as a way to overcome them. Engagement in labor
organizing and the suffrage struggle had one further benefit. It helped her
redefine the subject of political science and history so that women could
more easily be seen as a legitimate part of it.

ORGANIZING THE CITY'S TEACHERS

As a former schoolteacher, Mary Beard felt a special sympathy for the city's
women teachers, who at about the time she left graduate school were embarking on a campaign to protest their low wages. In 1900, the state had
passed a law setting maximum and minimum salaries for the city's schoolteachers. As a result, female teachers gained clear evidence that they were

paid less than their male colleagues for doing the same work. Katherine Devereux Blake, for example, who had risen through the ranks to become principal of the girls' department of P.S. 6 in Manhattan, made the maximum
salary allowed a woman: $2,500. Her male counterpart, the principal of the
boys' department, made the maximum for a man: $3,500. That pattern re-
peated itself throughout the city.[57] Pay differentials were actually greater
elsewhere in the state, but New York City offered a particularly conducive
climate for reform. As Butler and others sought to professionalize teaching
and to base hiring on academic achievement rather than patronage, non-
merit-based salary differences proved harder to justify. Blake, active since
childhood in the New York State suffrage movement, added salary discrimination to her list of grievances against the state and helped build a movement to end it. In 1906, she joined Grace Strachan, a district superintendent of schools from Brooklyn, in organizing the Interborough Association of
Women Teachers. Equal pay became the group's chief goal.[58]

Those who opposed equal pay for women insisted that men should be
paid more because they had families to support. This argument did not sit
well with Blake, who was by that time supporting her mother, Lillie. Male
teachers argued further that if women were paid the same as men, then men
would leave the profession. The result would be the feminization of boys,
who needed male models to achieve adult masculinity. Blake and Strachan
appealed to the male professors at Teachers College to combat that claim,
and John Dewey quickly obliged. "The notion that our splendid women
teachers were making mollycoddles of their boy students is utterly absurd,"
Dewey declared, to which the Teachers College psychologist Edward
Thorndike added that the "manly" influence of male teachers on boys was
"very slight."[59] Most of New York City's male-dominated unions supported
the women teachers, probably out of a desire to reverse what they saw as the
dangerous trend of employers taking advantage of women's willingness to
work for less to cut wages generally. In 1911, the state legislature finally relented and passed an equal-pay law.[60]

By 1910, the movement for equal pay had become part of a larger battle,
when Katherine Blake and Grace Strachan conspired with Margaret Haley
of Chicago to take over the National Education Association (NEA).
Nicholas Murray Butler, a past president and current trustee of the NEA,
was "shocked by the exhibitions of office-seeking, wire-pulling, and petty
politics" that preceded the election of Ella Flagg Young, Chicago's superintendent of schools, as president of the NEA. In the future, Butler glumly
concluded, it would be impossible "to secure the consent of any of the real
education leaders of the country to use their names in connection with the

presidency." Part of what bothered Butler was that Haley was a pioneer in the unionization of teachers. She had helped found the Chicago Federation of Teachers and had affiliated it with the American Federation of Teachers. Butler believed unionization to be unprofessional, and he saw the election of Ella Flagg Young to the presidency of the NEA as a defeat—a driving out of "genuine educational leaders." Butler was "a patrician at heart," as Richard Wittemore has noted. "[H]e envisioned the profession as a gigantic and benevolent trust administered by philosopher kings." The female teachers, whose professionalism he had done so much to foster, conceived of the profession in more democratic terms.[61]

Their conception of democracy, it should be noted, had its limits. Almost all female teachers were single, and most, including Grace Strachan, supported the Board of Education's ban on employing married women. Strachan believed that wives' domestic responsibilities prevented them from being effective in the classroom.[62] But a growing number of younger women disagreed. Ironically, Butler's success in centralizing the New York City schools made it easier to challenge traditional rules regarding marriage and motherhood by encouraging female teachers to take themselves seriously as professionals who conceived of their work as something they might pursue throughout their lives, not merely for a few years before marriage. Moreover, Butler's success in helping Columbia become a resource for teachers meant that the experiments (both pedagogical and personal) carried out there quickly spread throughout the city. Columbia women, such as Emily Smith Putnam and Elsie Clews Parsons, offered models, much discussed in the newspapers, for those who believed that women should be granted the right to continue their careers when they married.[63]

Kate M. Murphy, a teacher with eleven years of experience in the Brooklyn public schools, followed their example. Fired when she married in 1902, she took the Board of Education to court and in 1904 won a ruling that marriage, by itself, did not constitute "gross misconduct, insubordination, neglect of duty, or general inefficiency," the sole grounds provided for dismissal under state law.[64] The court ordered Murphy reinstated, but it could not erase the general prejudice against married women teachers, nor did its ruling affect hiring decisions. The board continued to bar the hiring or promotion of any married woman, "unless her husband is incapacitated from physical or mental disease, or has continuously abandoned her."[65] Facing so hostile a climate, newly married female teachers tended to keep their status secret, unless they became visibly pregnant, at which time they usually resigned.[66]

Over the next decade, however, a few pregnant teachers began to request a leave of absence so that they might return to work after giving birth. The

Board of Education resolutely refused, and when the teachers left to have their babies, they were fired for "neglect of duty." In 1914, Henrietta Rodman, a Teachers College graduate who had married while teaching at Wadleigh High School but had kept her status secret, launched a campaign on behalf of "teacher mothers." She organized meetings to rally support, lobbied the mayor, wrote articles for the *New York Tribune*, and sent one especially spirited letter to the editor in which she lambasted the board for "mother baiting."[67] The board promptly suspended her for "gross misconduct and insubordination," an action that won her even greater attention in the press. In 1915, Bridget Peixotto, a schoolteacher fired on charges of neglect of duty for being absent for three months owing to childbirth, appealed the board's decision to the state commissioner of education. She won a ruling that married women teachers had the legal right to the benefit of an unpaid leave of absence in case of childbirth. The commissioner further enjoined the schools from filling a position vacated by a teacher on maternity leave with a new employee.[68] The board had to employ a substitute and keep the position open for the teacher until the expiration of her leave. Pressured by Rodman's campaign and Pleixotto's legal action, the board grudgingly accepted the right of teachers to take maternity leaves in 1915. But it required women to notify the board as soon as they were aware that they were pregnant, and then promptly apply for and immediately accept a two-year leave of absence. Failure to do so would be regarded as "insubordination" and "neglect of duty" and therefore grounds for being fired under state law.[69] Mandatory leave was reduced to eighteen months in 1937, and there it stayed until the 1960s, when Columbia Law School graduate Ruth Bader Ginsburg challenged the board's restrictions on pregnant teachers in the courts and secured a ruling that made the length of leave a matter of the mother's discretion. New York City teachers' achievements were only partial, but, compared with the protections won elsewhere, they were notable. Because of New York City's acceptance, however grudging, of married women's right to work and their guarantee that they could return to their jobs after giving birth, wives made up half of all women teachers, compared with about one-quarter nationwide.[70]

THE NEW MEANING OF POLITICS

Whatever their position on marriage, teachers came increasingly to agree that they needed the suffrage to advance their interests in Albany. In 1907, Katherine Devereux Blake, together with her childhood friend Harriet Stanton Blatch, a daughter of Elizabeth Cady Stanton, formed the Equality League for Self-Supporting Women. Daughters of women who had been battling for the vote for sixty years, Katie Blake and Harriet Blatch enjoyed an advantage that their mothers had not: a rapidly growing constituency of working women who could see in the vote a tool for improving their own lives in immediate and concrete ways. Over the next decade, the campaign for women's suffrage and the struggle to improve the lives of working women proceeded together, with college-educated women working alongside grade-school teachers and uneducated factory workers to advance the cause of women. Mary Beard joined the Equality League in 1909 and worked close-ly with Blake and Blatch on a campaign against the election of an assem-blyman hostile to women's suffrage. The following year, she joined the Women's Trade Union League, where she worked with a garment worker, Leonora O'Reilly, to help young women involved in massive strikes. Beard served briefly as editor of the *Woman Voter*, the newspaper of the New York State Woman Suffrage Association, headed by Carrie Chapman Catt, and helped organize the Wage Earners' Suffrage League, in which O'Reilly be-came a leader.[71] As editor, Beard published essays by both O'Reilly and Co-lumbia professor Henry Rogers Seager. Beard wanted to publish "the work-ing girl and professorial views together," she told O'Reilly, as a way of making the point that the experience of a worker and that of an academic deserved equal consideration. Beard and O'Reilly put on a play as a fund-raiser, organized parades with an "army of banners," planned mass meetings with "stirring speakers," set up booths on sidewalks, and scheduled testimo-ny before the state legislature. Beard thought working-class speakers like O'Reilly were the most effective advocates of women's suffrage, because they had the most to gain from the vote and could most effectively rebut the leg-islators' myopic view of women as ladies of leisure. In reply to male legisla-tors' claim that the suffrage would destroy women's "incentive to mother-hood," Beard urged O'Reilly to reply: "What is the incentive to motherhood to-day among the working women?"[72]

Besides writing and organizing and raising money, Beard canvassed door to door, mostly in working-class areas. The work could be discouraging. One woman told her that she opposed suffrage because "the Mother of God did not vote." The woman then "slammed the door against further annoyance." No one seems to have been sufficiently hostile actually to harm any of the canvassers. As Beard later recalled, "The real danger to many of us was that our legs would give away with exhaustion from the countless flights of stairs we had to climb in the workers' quarters."[73]

Charles and Mary Beard worked tirelessly for municipal reform in the sec-ond decade of the twentieth century. They marched along sidewalks, climbed stairs, and rang doorbells for workers' causes and reform candidates.

Charles even joined Mary in the great suffrage parades down Fifth Avenue, though only after "some strenuous and noisy arguments" brought about his conversion to the suffragists' cause.[74] They also began writing, separately and together, on municipal government and American history. In 1914, they published a high-school civics text, at Mary Beard's suggestion, that boldly declared, "Civics concerns the whole community, and women constitute half that community."[75]

The following year, in *Woman's Work in Municipalities* (1915), Mary Beard filled in all that her Columbia professors had left out of their courses in political science. She wrote, as she said in her introduction, to encourage other women to take their place in public life, but also to ensure "that more men may realize that women have contributions of value to make to public welfare in all its forms and phases, and come to regard the entrance of women into public life with confidence and cordiality."[76] In doing so, she called attention to the dramatic expansion of governmental functions brought about by women's active intervention. Women had traditionally been responsible for their family's health, but under urban conditions they had learned that "to swat disease they must swat poor housing, evil labor conditions, ignorance, and vicious interests."[77] Women had led the way in conducting housing surveys because of "the greater readiness of women to admit women into the secrets of their homes." Women had been the first to call for kindergartens, which had fostered, in turn, such innovations as playgrounds, social centers, vacation schools, public libraries, and mothers' clubs. Women had initiated the campaign for mothers' pensions, minimum-wage legislation, and maximum-hour laws. They had also broken the code of silence that surrounded sexuality and had been the first to speak frankly about the dangers of venereal disease. Finally, women's public-health activities had carried them into "the municipal government itself," where they had mastered taxation and budget issues.[78]

Women already occupied administrative posts in education, as principals and superintendents, but that was just the beginning, she predicted: "The hour must come when women will occupy in proportion all these high municipal posts. They will be found ready as soon as men are found ready to give them their opportunity. It is not contended that they will be better or wiser, but that they will take a more intelligent and lasting interest and that there will always be certain things where children are concerned which they will know more and care more about than men."[79]

Soon after publishing her book, Beard gave a speech before the National Municipal League in which she castigated Woodrow Wilson for never once mentioning women in his five-volume history of the United States.[80] Although she never held an academic position—indeed, refused all professional identification—Mary Beard influenced a generation of readers through the six books she wrote on her own and the seven she wrote with her husband. From the monumentally influential *Rise of American Civilization* (1927–1942), which the couple wrote together, to her own *Woman as Force in History* (1946), Mary Beard insisted that women had exercised a very real, though unrecognized influence on the past. What male scholars called history was in fact, nothing more than the history of men, told from a masculine perspective.[81]

AT COLUMBIA: A NEW ASSAULT ON THE PROFESSIONAL SCHOOLS

Women's success as urban reformers in the early twentieth century inspired a renewed assault on male privilege at Columbia in the second decade of the twentieth century. The field marshal of this operation was Virginia Crocheron Gildersleeve, who became dean of Barnard College in 1911. Gildersleeve assumed office just as the women's movement in New York was shifting into a new phase, one that spoke more forthrightly about claiming the rights and privileges of men, rather than being satisfied with expanding the traditional role of women. Many of the women in this new generation called themselves feminists, and they demanded entry into all the political, economic, and professional realms traditionally reserved to men. In 1912, a group of them founded a club called Heterodoxy. The group met for lunch on Saturdays twice a month to talk about the burning issues of the day. Starting with talks about suffrage and how best to fight for it, they quickly moved on to discuss sexuality, birth control, and careers. Heterodoxy included a large number of women who had studied at Columbia, including Elsie Clews Parsons, Alice Duer Miller, Crystal Eastman, Henrietta Rodman, and Frances Perkins. The club carried on the tradition of Sorosis from the 1870s, while anticipating the more radical views of the consciousness-raising groups of the 1970s. "All feminists are suffragists, but not all suffragists are feminists," explained one participant. To feminists, she continued, the vote was merely a tool. The real goal was "complete social revolution." Feminists wanted to win for women the same sexual freedom claimed by men. They wanted to put an end to all the structural and psychological handicaps that limited women's economic independence. They wanted access to every civic and professional opportunity. As a former Unitarian minister, Marie Jennings Howe, put it, "We intend simply to be ourselves, not just our little female selves but our whole, big human selves."[82]

Parsons, who published nothing while her husband was in Congress, in deference to his political career, resumed writing with new vigor when he left politics in 1911. Her years as a congressman's wife had not been happy. As she strove to be a supportive spouse, she came to realize that she craved new ideas, adventure, and physical challenge. Her husband, in contrast, longed for the conventional routines of married life. In 1910, they visited the Southwest on government business. As he traveled with a forestry official, she explored the wild beauty of the desert canyons on horseback, camped in dwellings carved out of the cliffs, and discovered Indian cultures that fascinated her. Hooked on the adventure and physical challenge of her explorations, she resolved to turn herself into an anthropologist, not just a reader of ethnology, but an active researcher in the field. Armed with her findings, she could educate people to think critically about their assumptions and their experiences.[83]

Elsie Parsons quickly emerged as feminism's foremost propagandist. In a torrent of articles and books written between 1912 and 1917, she posed as a "native informant" and took aim at all the crippling fears and conventionalities that kept even the most privileged American women in their place. In *The Old-Fashioned Woman* (1913), she attacked evolutionary ideas on sex and race, arguing that the modern Anglo-Saxon woman was not the pinnacle of the Nordic race's accomplishment but an outmoded idea kept alive by bizarre rituals of the elders. In *Fear and Conventionality* (1914), she poked fun at the ceremonials that impeded open relations between strangers, parents and children, and men and women. And in *Social Freedom* (1915) and *Social Rule* (1916), she extended her analysis to the "primitive" thinking that dominated discussions of ethnicity, race, and nationality. Increasingly, she emphasized what Friedrich Nietzsche called the "will to power," an impulse rooted in fear of difference, which prompted white men to classify and exclude all women, as well as men from minority groups. For Parsons, the main object of feminism was "the declassification of women as women, the recognition of women as human beings or personalities."[84]

In April 1914, Parsons attended a talk by Dr. Oscar Riddle, of the Carnegie Institution's laboratory at Cold Spring Harbor, New York, at the "Columbia Feminist Forum." In response to Riddle's lecture, in which he suggested that sex might not be the immutable characteristic it was widely assumed to be, she wrote in her unpublished "Journal of a Feminist": "The day will come when the individual . . . [will not] have to pretend to be possessed of a given quota of femaleness or maleness. . . . This morning perhaps I feel like a male; let me act like one. This afternoon I may feel like a female; let me act like one. At midday or at midnight I may feel sexless; let me therefore act

sexlessly. . . . It is such a confounded bore to have to act one part endlessly."
Men, too, she added hopefully, "may rebel some time against the attribute
of maleness—The taboo on a man acting like a woman has ever been
stronger than the taboo on a woman acting like a man." She looked forward
to the day when there would be a "masculinism" movement that would encourage men to act "like women."[85]

Virginia Gildersleeve never claimed the term "feminist" herself; she
found it too threatening a term to embrace in the mostly male administrative environment in which she worked. But in demanding full economic
and political independence for women and the right to be included in every
undertaking of the male-dominated modern university, she embodied much
of feminism's core spirit. Born in 1877, the daughter of Judge Henry Alger
Gildersleeve and Virginia Crocheron, the future Barnard dean grew up in a
town house on West Forty-eighth Street near Fifth Avenue. "We . . . were not
'in society' exactly," Gildersleeve later recalled. "We were professional people." She prepared for college at the Brearley School and, upon graduation
in 1895, thought of attending Bryn Mawr, but her mother preferred that she
stay closer to home. Her father had attended Columbia Law School; her
older brother, Harry, had attended Columbia College; and she had once accompanied Harry to the library that Melvil Dewey had created on Forty-
ninth Street, where the shaded green lights and rows of books had deeply
impressed her. So she enrolled at Barnard, which had recently opened
around the corner from Brearley on Madison Avenue.[86]

Gildersleeve followed the college when it moved uptown to its elegant
new quarters alongside Columbia on Morningside Heights, and there she
studied European history with James Harvey Robinson, sociology with
Franklin Giddings, and history of philosophy with Nicholas Murray Butler. When she graduated first in her class in 1899, the offer of a graduate
fellowship prompted her to stay at Columbia, where she earned an M.A.
in history in 1900. After five years of teaching first-year composition at
Barnard, she returned to Columbia for a Ph.D. in English, which she
earned in 1908. Her dissertation, "Government Regulation of Elizabethan
Drama," signaled a lifelong interest in interdisciplinary studies. Not wanting to leave home, she turned down an associate professorship in English
at the University of Wisconsin, despite being warned that academic advancement required a willingness to move from school to school at the beginning of one's career. Instead, she pieced together teaching assignments
at Barnard and in Columbia's graduate program in English until an assistant professorship in English opened at Barnard in 1910. Continuing to
live at home, she commuted each day to her job, even after assuming the

Virginia Crocheron Gildersleeve
(1877–1965)
Graduate of Barnard College (1899) and
Columbia University (M.A. [history] 1900,
Ph.D. [English] 1908) and dean of Barnard
College (1911–1947), as photographed in 1912.
(Barnard College Archives)

position of dean of Barnard College and adviser to women graduate students at Columbia in 1911.[87]

Gildersleeve did not enjoy an auspicious start to her tenure as dean. The office had been vacant for almost four years, as Butler had searched in vain for a suitable replacement for Laura Gill, who seems to have alienated almost everyone in her six years at Barnard. Gildersleeve later credited her with "executive ability," but faulted her lack of "tact" and her misguided attempt to "mother" her students. James Harvey Robinson, who served as acting dean before her appointment, once observed, "Poor Miss Gill! She never had the slightest idea of what we were trying to do here!"[88] Nicholas Murray Butler, in particular, disliked Gill. When English professor William Brewster replaced Gill as acting dean, Butler found him a congenial administrator and concluded that he would prefer to work with a man. The Barnard trustees, however, insisted that a woman lead the college. Butler proposed a compromise. The trustees would change the college's statutes to provide for a second administrative officer, a provost, who would be in charge of the educational and financial administration of the college. The dean would represent the college to the outside world and have responsibility for the students. Refusing to sanction the idea of a dean as figurehead, the trustees said no. Butler appointed Brewster as provost, anyway. Moreover, he announced the changes as though they had been adopted by the trustees and kept Brewster on as acting dean until he could find a new dean.

Parsons, who was about to become a Barnard trustee, recommended her friends Mary Kingsbury Simkhovitch, Emily Smith Putnam, and Alice Duer Miller for the job in the hope that Butler and the Barnard trustees would take a stand on behalf of mothers.[89] But Butler settled on Gildersleeve, his former student, for the post. Refusing to be "chaperone to the students," Gildersleeve declared that she would accept only if the full powers of the dean were restored. Butler finally relented. The next day, he asked the Barnard trustees to change the statutes to give the dean responsibility for education and finance and reduce the role of provost to that of consultant to the dean. Gildersleeve accepted, assuming that Butler would announce the agreed-on terms to the press. He refused. Deciding that it would be a mistake for her to insist on a correction that would cause Butler to lose face, and after assuring herself that she had the full support of the Barnard trustees, Gildersleeve swallowed her indignation.[90]

The new dean had an opportunity to test the Barnard trustees' support almost immediately. When she took over the stewardship of Barnard College, the women's movement was in full flower and many parents were anxious about the movement's possible corrupting effects on young women. Gildersleeve had barely settled into her new office when the distraught mother of one student arrived at her door. The mother implored her to forbid Barnard students to participate in a planned suffrage parade down Fifth Avenue. To "march in a parade would be a shocking and shameful thing" for the students to do and would "injure the college greatly," the distressed mother warned.[91] Nor was this mother alone in opposing student support for women's suffrage. At Vassar College, administrators so feared adverse publicity should their students become involved in the unladylike world of political activism that student supporters of the suffrage movement had to hold organizational meetings in the local graveyard to avoid detection.[92] And at Barnard itself, many members of the board of trustees, including Annie Nathan Meyer, opposed Barnard students having anything to do with women's suffrage, on the grounds that it was unladylike and fostered sex antagonism.[93] Notwithstanding Meyer's outspoken views, Gildersleeve refused to interfere with student suffragists; indeed, she encouraged faculty and students to engage freely, not only in the fight for suffrage, but in all the political movements of the day. In contrast to Vassar, with its ban on all suffrage activity, Gildersleeve's Barnard boasted a chapter of the New York State Woman Suffrage League and an openly acknowledged Socialist League. And in the area of campus known as The Jungle (a space now occupied by parts of Lehman Library and the Lehman lawn), many a stump speaker defended a controversial cause.[94]

For all Gildersleeve's openness to heterodox political views, however, she had ambivalent feelings toward feminism. She rejected the confrontational tactics of those like Alice Paul and her followers, who, following the example of the Pankhursts in England, courted arrest as they castigated public officials for not supporting women's right to vote. Gildersleeve preferred "boring from within," an approach that she pursued with great delicacy, for, as she later recalled, "most of my colleagues outside of Barnard had to be handled rather gently."[95]

New York in the second decade of the twentieth century fairly burst with political, cultural, and economic energy. For women, this energy produced unprecedented opportunities in journalism, publishing, education, retailing, law, medicine, and social work. Determined that her students should be prepared to take advantage of whatever chance might become available, Gildersleeve organized the Committee on Women Graduate Students, to which she recruited Barnard professor of geology Ida H. Ogilvie and two male colleagues, James Harvey Robinson, whose appointment was at Barnard but who also taught at Columbia, and John Dewey, who also taught at Teachers College. Together they worked to protect women's interests in the graduate departments and open Columbia's professional schools. Between 1900, when the trustees forced Emily Smith Putnam to resign, and 1911, when they appointed Gildersleeve as dean, only one professional school—the School of Architecture—had agreed to accept women.[96]

As a college dean, Gildersleeve sat on the University Council, a position that gave her regular access to the deans of all the schools that made up the university. Whenever Butler raised the issue of some new educational venture, she raised the question of women's place. Some battles were easily won. Gildersleeve secured a place for women in the Business School, when it opened in 1916, because it grew out of Extension Teaching, in which women were already taking classes and even teaching. Winning access to the journalism and medical schools, however, proved more difficult: the first because it was an entirely new program, and the second because it had such a long history of turning aside women's assaults. As she lobbied, Gildersleeve played off the progressive themes that Mary Beard and others were working so hard to develop. She pointed to the work that women were already performing as investigative journalists and in the emerging field of public health to support her claim that neither journalism nor medicine could be viewed any longer as masculine preserves.

When Columbia announced that a $2.5 million bequest from Joseph Pulitzer, publisher of the *St. Louis Post-Dispatch* and the *New York World*, would allow it to open the Pulitzer School of Journalism in 1912, she immediately called for the admission of women. Since the impulse behind opening a school of journalism was, in part, to raise the moral standards of the field, admitting women (so often stereotyped as agents of morality) seemed only fitting, Gildersleeve argued. She proposed that Barnard students who wanted a career in journalism would take two years of college courses at Barnard and then finish up at the School of Journalism. Columbia College students would do the same. One of the required courses would be in government, a discipline that Barnard did not then offer, in part because Burgess, as the dean of the Graduate Faculty of Political Science, had long insisted that government was a subject suitable only for male students. Until 1912, the Barnard trustees had seen no reason to contradict Burgess on that point. Gildersleeve seized the opportunity, offered by the chance to gain a place for her students in the School of Journalism, to change that. On James Harvey Robinson's suggestion, she hired Charles Beard to teach Barnard's first course in American government.[97]

One of the first students to take advantage of this new opportunity was Iphigene Ochs, the only child of the publisher of the *New York Times*, Adolph Ochs, a resolute opponent of women's suffrage, not to mention more adventurous feminist goals. Iphigene Ochs had almost not gone to college. Dyslexic, she had floundered in school, but patient tutoring, along with her high intelligence, got her to Barnard in 1910, where she delighted in the students, the classes, the professors, and the bracing atmosphere of free inquiry, so different from the conservative atmosphere her father imposed at home. Her first-year English teacher, Claire Howard, later recalled that Iphigene's "inability to be what a son would have been to [Adolphe Ochs] made her inclined to underestimate herself."[98] But at Barnard, she began to shake free from her father's rule. She became a suffragist, volunteered at the Henry Street Settlement and at a home for unwed mothers, participated in school plays, and converted to socialism under the tutelage of Vladimir G. Simkhovitch. A history major, she also studied with James Harvey Robinson, who one day teasingly announced to a class in which Ochs was enrolled, "I am going to show you a perfect example of the workings of the Medieval mind." He proceeded to read from a *New York Times* editorial. Inspired by Charles Beard's courses in government, Ochs began taking journalism classes in her senior year with the intention of becoming a journalist.[99]

Adolph Ochs had never been entirely clear about his expectations for his only child. In a letter to her when she was ten, he greeted her as "My Ownest Daughter and Onliest Son," a label that neatly captured his conflicted emotions and expectations. He was too much the Victorian father to

Iphigene Ochs Sulzberger (1892–1990)
Graduate of Barnard College (1914) and member
of the Barnard College Board of Trustees
(1937–1959, 1963–1968), as photographed in 1914.
(Barnard College Archives)

imagine his little girl as his successor, but too dynastic in his impulses to en-
vision anyone else in that role. So he took her with him when he called on
Daniel Guggenheim, Jacob Schiff, and Andrew Carnegie; when she was
fourteen, he introduced her to Mark Twain as "the future publisher of *The
New York Times*"; and, ignoring the dyslexia that made grammar school a
nightmare for her, he praised her intelligence and industry and insisted that
she secure the college education he never had. But when his daughter
talked the *Times* managing editor, Carr Van Anda, into granting her an
entry-level job, Adolph Ochs was "enraged," Iphigene later recalled, "and
nearly murdered both of us." She shifted her ambitions, embarking on graduate work in history with the goal of becoming a professor, but her father put
a stop to that as well. Adolph Ochs did name his daughter to the board of
the *Times*, but she exercised her greatest influence through her husband,
Arthur Hays Sulzberger, who became publisher in her place after her father's death in 1935, and through her son, Arthur Ochs Sulzberger, who re-
portedly never made a decision as publisher without consulting her first.
Through conversations, letters, and memorandums, she goaded her husband to pursue stories on education, social welfare, the city's parks, and
other issues she deemed matters of conscience. She insisted that the *Times*
add a section that dealt directly with issues of concern to women; she pep-
pered editors with letters (signed by deceased members of the family); and
she fought to make a place at the *Times* for women journalists. She was the
liberal voice of the conservative paper.[100]

She was not alone. Helen Rogers (Barnard 1903) married into the Reid family and became a vice president of the *New York Herald Tribune*. From the 1920s on, she promoted the interests of women, both in the newspaper's coverage and in the appointment of reporters. By the 1940s, the *Herald Tribune* had more women staff members than any other daily paper in the country.[101] Among her writers was Alice Duer Miller (Barnard 1899), who wrote a popular column for the *Herald Tribune* called "Are Women People?" Another Barnard graduate, Freda Kirchwey (Barnard 1915), became a writer for the *Nation* following graduation and quickly rose to the position of managing editor. Throughout her tenure, from 1918 to 1955, the *Nation* ran stories on women's changing roles.[102]

Gildersleeve won women a place at Columbia's medical school with the same kinds of arguments that had worked in journalism. Through their settlement-house work, women doctors and nurses had become a vital part of the public-health movement, a fact that most medical schools had long since come to realize. The University of Michigan had been admitting women to its medical school ever since 1870. Both Johns Hopkins and Stanford admitted women when they opened in 1892; Cornell admitted women when it opened in 1899; six schools in Chicago admitted women in 1899. By 1916, New York University, Yale, and the University of Pennsylvania medical schools were all on the verge of following suit.[103] In this context, Columbia's resistance seemed increasingly unreasonable. The dean of the College of Physicians and Surgeons (P&S) when Gildersleeve became dean of Barnard was Dr. Samuel Lambert. More research-minded than his predecessors, Lambert also seemed more sympathetic to the idea of coeducation, but he insisted that the change must await the school's move from West Fifty-ninth Street to larger quarters in Washington Heights.[104]

In 1917, with the war in Europe placing heightened demands on medical services, Gildersleeve renewed her plea. She told Lambert that "a brilliant young Swedish woman, Gulli Lindh," was about to graduate from Barnard and attend Johns Hopkins Medical School, but that she would rather stay in New York. The dean responded that he would be happy to have her and others, but that, at a minimum he had to provide additional laboratory space and a woman's restroom. Assisted by the American Women's Medical Association and an "old gentleman from Texas," Gildersleeve raised the $50,000 needed for the project, but even before she had the money, Lambert agreed to take Gulli Lindh, as well as nine others to keep her company. Four years later, Lindh graduated first in the class, and two of the other women graduated third and fifth. After her internship at Presbyterian Hospital (also a first for a woman), Lindh, who had since married, was made an instructor at P&S. At the beginning of what promised to be a distinguished career, Lindh resigned to follow her husband to Harvard, where he was appointed to a professorship at the Divinity School. Slow though Columbia was to accept women to its medical school, Harvard held off until 1944. The only research opportunity available to Lindh was work as a researcher in a series of hospitals in the Boston area. She never held another academic appointment.[105]

In the same year that Gildersleeve succeeded in opening the medical school, the suffrage campaign finally achieved victory in New York. That success in 1917 represented the first breakthrough in the East, after decades of defeats. The following year, even Woodrow Wilson, eager to win women's support for the United States war effort, joined the suffrage campaign. Appearing before Congress, he asked that the House and Senate pass a constitutional amendment granting the vote to women as a war measure.[106] With women's contribution to the polity highlighted so dramatically, Gildersleeve assumed that she would easily add the Columbia Law School to the roster of Columbia professional schools open to women. But even though John W. Burgess had retired in 1912, his influence lingered. The Faculty of Political Science favored the appointment of Frank Goodnow to replace Burgess as the Ruggles Professor of Constitutional Law, but Burgess objected to Goodnow's "state socialist" point of view. Apparently, Goodnow's crime was that he thought the Supreme Court should defer to Congress in matters of economic policy. Insistent that his successor accept his constitutional vision, Burgess persuaded the board of trustees to appoint the ultraconservative William D. Guthrie.[107]

Prospects for change brightened briefly in 1915, when President Butler called a meeting at his home of the Educational Committee of the Columbia University Board of Trustees and several of the more senior members of the Law School faculty to discuss with Gildersleeve the matter of women's admission. But Butler failed to broker an agreement. Fearful that admitting women would cause their best male students to flee to all-male Harvard, a majority of the law faculty rejected coeducation. Gildersleeve's wry suggestion that the two law schools hold hands and take the dangerous step toward coeducation together did not receive a favorable reply. Indeed, in a letter the following week, Dean Harlan Stone advised her that a majority of his faculty viewed coeducation as "unwise" and warned that further "agitation" on the matter would not be helpful.[108] Although Yale Law School's decision to admit women in 1917 drew favorable notices from the press, and although Fordham Law School admitted women the following year, Columbia, in common with Harvard, refused to follow their example.[109] Among the most vigorous objectors to coeducation was William Guthrie, whose attention to Law School policy was otherwise fairly casual. Guthrie attended only four of sixty-two faculty meetings between 1909 and 1922: one in 1909, two in 1910, and one in 1917, to vote against the admission of women.[110]

John W. Burgess won the Law School battle, but he failed to arrest the expansion of women's influence in the university and in thinking about the nature of politics and history. His steadfast opposition to coeducation had, ironically, already helped ensure the founding of Barnard and Teachers College as self-consciously autonomous institutions for women. As those schools pressed the university to open its graduate faculties to their students, and as the women who gained entry took seriously their professors' exhortation to treat the city like a laboratory, they helped formulate a conception of political life that directly threatened the approach to reform that Burgess had long championed. The urban laboratory that attracted Mary Ritter Beard and Elsie Clews Parsons, among many other women, inspired a conception of public life centered on the problems of women workers and the families under their care, rather than one that looked to the training of the few administrative "supermen" as the rightful leaders of the American republic.[111]

FOUR

PATTERNS OF CULTURE

EARLY IN 1917, as the entry of the United States into the war in Europe began to look inevitable, Elsie Clews Parsons drafted an article entitled "Patterns for Peace or War." Why was it, she wondered, that a country dominated by a pacifist mood in 1914 could so quickly swing to militarism? Taking her cue from anthropology, she suggested that America, like all cultures, was composed of fairly stable patterns into which alien beliefs and practices are incorporated only if they fit within prevailing systems. Many reformers, she noted, and particularly feminists, had struggled over the previous two decades to advance the principles of toleration of minorities, freedom of speech, and equality for all. But those principles were "dropped with a facility amazing to many," because they had never fit comfortably within the "militarist pattern" that had long distinguished American life. "The theory of militarism that physical compulsion should be the preferred way out of a social misunderstanding or incompatibility has been fairly well acculturated throughout the country," she grimly observed. Over the past generation, as traditional male elites had felt the pressure of intensifying social and economic change, this militarist pattern had grown more entrenched. In the process, it had led to the disenfranchisement of African Americans, segregation, and lynching. Moreover, this militarist pattern had led to discrimination against immigrants from southern and eastern Europe, to resistance against feminist demands, and to the shibboleth that war was a natural guarantor of freedom.[1]

Events at Columbia in the spring of 1917 reinforced Parsons's pessimism. Even as she sat drafting her article in February, the university trustees were inviting students to report the unpatriotic statements of Columbia faculty, and Nicholas Murray Butler was wiring President Woodrow Wilson to pledge Columbia "to the service of the nation whenever the call shall come." Anticipating that call, Butler published a plan, *The Organization of Columbia University for National Service*, in which he informed the faculty and students that, in case of war, the normal functions of the university would be interrupted and the institution would be reorganized along military lines.[2]

Not all Columbia faculty rallied around their trustees and president. The anthropologist Franz Boas, for one, marched into his classes and read a statement in which he supported the faculty's right to dissent from the university's growing militarism. A German-born Jew, with relatives still in Germany, Boas believed that the entry of the United States into the war would be a disaster for all concerned. He urged his students to examine critically the reasons being given for intervening in the European conflict and to protect "nonconformist thought."[3]

Parsons defended Boas in a letter to the *New York Times*. "It has been popular in recent months to draw a picture of what would happen to New York given a German invasion," she wrote, "but even the most imaginative of our futuristic artists have never pictured the University as efficiently 'prussianized' as the Columbia trustees now propose." That the trustees "should seek to check in the university the kind of . . . discussion which may occur in any legislature, in any newspaper, at any public meeting," was, in Parsons's view, "a bit of almost incredible buffoonery."[4]

Her protest fell on deaf ears. When Congress declared war in April, President Butler commanded his faculty to support the military effort, and when the psychologist James McKeen Cattell and the English professor Henry Wadsworth Longfellow Dana continued to protest, Butler fired them. A few weeks later, Charles Beard, assigned under Butler's table of military organization to the "Civics Division" of the "Economics and Social Service Corps," walked into his classes and announced that the day's lecture would be his last. Although Beard supported the war, he resigned in protest over Butler's assault on academic freedom. A year later, James Harvey Robinson also quit. Looking for a new academic home, Robinson, along with Beard, John Dewey, and Barnard's first dean, Emily Smith Putnam, founded the New School for Social Research in Greenwich Village. Butler dismissed the whole enterprise as "a little bunch of disgruntled liberals setting up a tiny fly-by-night radical counterfeit education," but the alternative university endured as a refuge for scholars, many of them women, who believed that the war had revealed the elitist, antidemocratic, repressive heart of Butler's vision of reform.[5]

Butler believed that the future of America depended on the ability of Anglo-Saxon leaders to assimilate immigrant groups. Those who founded the New School, in contrast, were pluralists, who believed that the country's greatness stemmed from its openness to fresh talent, new ideas, and alternative perspectives. They wanted to save the cultures of other peoples from Americanizing efforts. The tension between the Americanizers and the pluralists reached the breaking point as war approached. Hunter College, formerly the Female Normal School, and since 1914 the city's public college for women (many of them immigrants), had asked Parsons to give a commencement address on Americanization in 1916. She angrily declined, declaring that she was "for practical and definite pacifism in nursery and school and for democratic tolerance for all nationalities as against the melting pot propaganda."[6]

The threat of war placed even greater strains on feminism. For several years, conflict had been building over issues of sexuality. In the view of older feminists, like Charlotte Perkins Gilman, female autonomy depended on eradicating the double standard by teaching men to hold themselves to the same exacting standard of sexual restraint that middle-class Victorian culture demanded of women. A new generation of women, including Parsons, agreed with Emma Goldman and Margaret Sanger that women would never be truly free until they could control their fertility and thereby embrace sexual expression, as men did. The coming of war, with its heightened concern over the threat of venereal disease, gave new power to those who favored sexual purity over those who championed sexual freedom. Parsons realized how weak her position was in 1916, when she called a group of fifty feminist friends together in support of Margaret Sanger. Asking those assembled to sign a petition testifying to the fact that they used birth control, she watched in dismay as only three stepped forward.[7]

By early 1917, the audience for Parsons's polemical writings on pluralism and feminism had disappeared. At the New Republic, which she had helped found, Walter Lippmann had praised Fear and Conventionality when it appeared in 1914. But when war came, he used its Nietzschean theme of the will to power not as she intended it—as a warning against the human impulse to classify others in order to dominate them—but as a justification for American entry into war. Among her close friends, only the Columbia alumnus and New Republic writer Randolph Bourne and the anthropologist Franz Boas opposed America's drift toward militarism.[8]

Butler did his best to turn Columbia into a well-oiled military machine, and Parsons worried that he would succeed. But the university and the city of which it was a part proved too heterogeneous to sustain either Butler's aspirations or Parsons's fears. Indeed, one of the most important consequences of World War I at Columbia was the opportunity the war provided to consider how varied cultural patterns could be—and how subject to change. In shaping that opportunity, Parsons and Boas became partners in an academic enterprise that opened new opportunities to women and, in the process, challenged traditional thinking about masculinity, femininity, and sexuality, as well as race and ethnicity.

FRANZ BOAS

Born in Germany in 1858 to a Jewish family, Franz Boas grew up in an atmosphere suffused with "the ideals of the revolution of 1848." His father was a merchant; his mother, the founder of the kindergarten that he attended as a child. Trained as a scientist, Boas held a Ph.D. in physics, with a minor in geography. He also bore facial scars sustained, rumor had it, in a duel fought over an anti-Semitic slur. Following graduate school, he embarked on a series of field trips to survey the Arctic and examine the influence of the harsh surroundings on the peoples of the region. To his "complete disillusionment," he found that those he studied were molded less by their terrain and climate than by their particular historical experiences. Gradually, he came to question the narrow materialism of his training, and, inspired by the example of "an artistically gifted elder sister," he became more interested in psychology and culture.[9]

In the course of his field trips, Boas frequently passed through New York City, where his uncle and aunt, the doctors Abraham and Mary Putnam Jacobi, took him in. In 1887, he came to the United States permanently, taking a position first at Clark University in Worcester, Massachusetts; then at the Field Museum in Chicago; and finally, in 1896, at the American Museum of Natural History in New York. At the same time, he accepted a lectureship in physical anthropology at Columbia, paid for (without his knowledge) by his uncle, Abraham Jacobi. Seth Low promoted Boas to professor in 1899, with the understanding that he would split his time between Columbia and Barnard, where Emily Smith Putnam, the new sister-in-law of Abraham and Mary Putnam Jacobi, presided as dean. Over the next two decades, Boas became the dominant force in American anthropology with the help of an unusually talented group of graduate students, a mix of gentiles and Jews, mostly men from Columbia and City College.[10]

When World War I came, Boas stayed at Columbia, while Cattell suffered dismissal and Robinson and Beard resigned in protest. Not that Boas was any less opposed to the militarizing of the university to which he had devoted two decades of his life. But in 1915, he had been treated for a cancerous growth on his cheek. Fearing a recurrence, he concentrated on trying to finish his own work, while continuing to supervise the projects of graduate students who had not yet completed their degrees. There was also his family to consider. Of his six children, the oldest were grown, but Gertrude was still at Barnard and Franzeska was two years from entering. The time for picking up stakes and starting anew seemed well past.[11]

Boas stayed, but the war soured his relations with university administrators, as well as with members of other organizations in which he was involved. He had not been on good terms with Henry Fairfield Osborn, director of the American Museum of Natural History, for some time. Nor did he get on well with the museum's most prominent trustee, Madison Grant. Both men were eugenicists, and Grant, a lawyer and zoologist, was widely known for his belief in Nordic superiority. In 1916, Grant published *The Passing of the Great Race*, in which he argued that the intermarriage of Nordics and lesser Alpines or, worse, Mediterraneans was leading to a debilitating "mongrelization."[12] Boas regarded Grant's theories as "Nordic nonsense," but they were widely influential and threatened to encourage a movement toward immigration restriction in Congress. Still more troubling to Boas were events taking place inside anthropology. After the war, Boas discovered that a group of anthropologists had gone on a secret mission to Mexico and Central America for the United States government. In "Scientists as Spies," a letter to the *Nation*, he deplored what he saw as the wholesale abandonment of scientific neutrality. In 1919, with conservatives in the ascendancy, the American Anthropological Association censured Boas, expelled him from its executive council, and pressured him into resigning as liaison with the National Research Council, an important source of funds.[13]

Nicholas Murray Butler compounded Boas's problems by limiting the financial resources he needed to run his department. Anthropology had never been a big operation. Squeezed into three tiny rooms at the top of the journalism building, Boas carried out his mission far removed from the academic center of the university and with the assistance of a single instructor, Alexander Goldenweiser. Eager to expand the department's work and encourage interdisciplinary inquiry at Columbia College, Boas suggested to Butler in November 1917 that anthropology mount a new introductory course. To "make the course more valuable," he proposed "an affiliation between anthropology and other departments [history, economics/sociology, and psychology], in the same way as is being done in Barnard at the present time." Saddled as he was with an eight-course teaching load, plus nine office hours a week, Boas had not found time for such a course in many years and would need additional faculty to teach it. Butler not only denied Boas additional faculty, but fired Goldenweiser.[14]

The son of a prominent lawyer in Kiev, Goldenweiser had grown up in a secular Jewish milieu and was steeped in literature, art, and music. His peers

Franz Boas (1858–1942)
Lecturer in and professor of anthropology at
Columbia University (1896–1936), as photographed
around 1930. (Columbia University
Archives–Columbiana Library)

and students admired him for his brilliance, erudition, and generosity. He lent his books freely and organized informal seminars to discuss the philosophical and psychological theories that Boas assumed students either knew or would learn on their own. Butler's justification for firing Goldenweiser was lack of funds, but his reasons were likely more complicated. It surely did not help that Goldenweiser had failed to return books to the library, had neglected to pay his bill at the Faculty Club, had once been jailed for nonsupport of his wife, and, as even his friends admitted, had lived a life in which "peccadilloes hung like a fringe around his loins."[15] But those failings might have been overlooked had Goldenweiser not exemplified a trend Butler found troubling: the growing number of Jews, especially Russian Jews, coming to the university. At a moment of war-induced preoccupation with Americanization, the presence of a group that seemed particularly resistant to assimilation provoked heightened concern among university officials.

THE "JEWISH PROBLEM"

When the Columbia trustees decided to move to Morningside Heights in 1891, the surrounding neighborhood was, in the words of one newspaper, "the rural retreat of the aristocratic New Yorker." Plans to build the Cathedral Church of St. John the Divine at 110th Street and to relocate St. Luke's Hospital to 113th Street, both on Amsterdam Avenue, guaranteed a strong Episcopalian presence in the immediate vicinity, while Harlem, stretching to the north and east, offered an attractive mix of townhouses, cultural institutions, and open fields to wealthy New Yorkers in search of homes away from the bustle of downtown. Stanford White, whom Seth Low had in mind as the architect of the new campus, was designing what would later be called Strivers Row, on 139th Street; Oscar Hammerstein was building an opera house; and dozens of theaters, churches, clubhouses, and banks were beginning to dot the landscape. A few pockets of poor Irish and black settlements remained, left over from less favored times, but on the whole, an air of comfortable European elegance prevailed.[16]

Then came the announcement of plans for new subway lines, which set off a wave of speculation in Harlem land at the turn of the twentieth century. Eastern European Jews, fleeing the congestion of the Lower East Side, and, in smaller numbers, Italians escaping similar conditions in Little Italy streamed north to find better housing. The well-heeled moved into spacious new apartments that developers were building in central Harlem. Those less privileged crowded into tenements to the east, farther from the anticipated transportation lines. By World War I, more than 170,000 Jews lived in the immediate area of Columbia University, and many of their children were knocking at Columbia's door.[17]

In fact, a large number of Jewish daughters had been knocking at the door of Barnard College for some time. In June 1906, Mrs. N. W. Liggett, Barnard's bursar, made what appears to be the first official reference to Jews as a problem in a worried letter to George A. Plimpton, treasurer of the Barnard College Board of Trustees. "Personally I am discouraged. Considerably discouraged," Liggett confided. Barnard was "drawing a very large percentage of Hebrews, and others of foreign extraction." The situation might not be so serious if "we had plenty of the children of well-to-do New York families also, for the affiliation would do much to neutralize race limitations," but Barnard's reliance on the public schools had grown so dramatically in the past few years that students who had prepared for college either with tutors or in private academies now constituted a mere 20 percent of the total student body. Liggett enclosed with her letter a list of those admitted to the class of 1910. Helpfully, she had ticked off the name of every Jewish student in red ink, 40 out of 102. Eleven came from New York City private schools, the largest number from Teachers College's Horace Mann School. Most of the rest came from New York City's newly established public schools, the largest number from Wadleigh High School in Harlem.[18] Nicholas Murray Butler's campaign to build a first-class public secondary-school system in New York City had succeeded all too well.

It is doubtful that the percentage of Jews at Columbia College was ever that high. A national census of Jewish college students, done by a Jewish or-

ganization in 1918, put Jews at Columbia University as a whole at only 21 percent. John W. Burgess may have been right in worrying that Jewish women
posed a greater threat to Columbia's Anglo-Saxon traditions than did their
brothers. Well-to-do Jewish families, he believed, were more likely to send
their sons away to college, while keeping their daughters close to home.[19]
Whatever the number of Jews at Columbia College (and there do not appear to be any official figures for the college itself), the university trustees
worried that it threatened the school's standing as the college of choice for
the city's Anglo-Saxon elite. The fact that four out of five students at City
College were Jews suggested that pressure from Jewish applicants and the
consequent danger of Protestant flight was likely to grow.[20]

Mindful of that risk, Columbia administrators did what they could to keep
the number of Jews as low as possible. In 1909, the trustees appointed a
university-wide undergraduate admissions committee, chaired by a Barnard
professor of philosophy, Adam Leroy Jones. Jones's charge was to regularize
admissions practices and ensure that those admitted were not only academically prepared, but also socially acceptable. In 1911, Jones reassured Butler
that the committee was admitting only half of those who applied and that he
was "personally acquainted with at least four-fifths of the students who entered this autumn."[21] Yet the level of Jewish enrollment remained a concern, until a solution suggested itself during World War I.

In 1917, President Butler, in fulfillment of his pledge to make Columbia
available for war work, transformed the university into a branch of the Student Army Training Corps (SATC) to train officers for the military. Under
the army's rules, applicants for the SATC need only have completed high
school and passed a medical exam. As a result, Columbia found itself deluged with applications, and the admissions committee was frantic for some
means of sorting through them. Assistance came in the form of an intelligence test developed by Edward L. Thorndike at Teachers College. Only
eight pages long, the exam—a mix of fill-in-the-blanks, mathematical word
problems, and tests of general information—purported to measure innate
ability but included a number of questions that betrayed the small-town
American origins of its creator.[22] One section asked, "What joint is situated
between the transmission and the differentials of an auto?" and "What is the
name for the pointed end of an anvil?" Immigrant children growing up on
the congested streets of New York City, with little occasion to tinker with
cars or hammer on anvils, were at a distinct disadvantage in responding to
such questions.[23]

To Franz Boas, this test and others created during the war were nothing
more than old wine in new bottles. In The Mind of Primitive Man (1911), he

had argued against the belief that some peoples are more intelligent than others. The human mind was not a particularly inventive organ, Boas contended. Groups that seemed to be more intelligent had simply had the accidental benefit of more human contacts in the course of migration and therefore had more ideas with which to work. In the end, a person who did well on a test demonstrated nothing more than proficiency in what the test tested.[24]

President Butler disagreed. He and his deans believed that Thorndike's test offered a way of distinguishing the innately intelligent from the merely studious, a type they believed to be over-represented among immigrant children and especially the children of Jews. As Dean Herbert E. Hawkes explained to a Columbia colleague, "It is a fact that boys of foreign parentage who have no background in many cases attempt to educate themselves beyond their intelligence. Their accomplishment is well over 100 percent of their ability on account of their tremendous energy and ambition. I do not believe however that a College would do well to admit too many men of low mentality who have ambition but not brains." The tests seemed to be guarding against that danger, for, as Hawkes went on to report, "during the administration of our mental tests the percentage of Jews has been cut down."[25]

According to evolutionary theory, the Thorndike test, in identifying the most intelligent students, should also generate a homogeneously Nordic student body. But, despite initially encouraging signs that the tests were doing just that, Hawkes and Butler obviously harbored doubts. In addition to approving the use of the test, they authorized the development of a detailed admissions application that, for the first time, included questions about family background and religious affiliation. For good measure, the admissions office required school principals to rank candidates according to their leadership qualities and social skills.[26] By these various means, the administration attempted to keep Jewish enrollment within the 15 to 20 percent range that Hawkes thought the college could assimilate. A story in the *Columbia Spectator* in October 1921 suggested that he was succeeding. Of those freshmen who reported religious affiliation, only 18 percent were Jews.[27]

Word of Columbia's efforts eventually reached the press, and in an unsigned editorial for the *Nation*, entitled "May Jews Go to College?" the managing editor, Freda Kirchwey, denounced Columbia for its exclusionary practices. A 1915 graduate of Barnard College and the daughter of George Washington Kirchwey, a prison reformer and Columbia Law School professor, she had an intimate knowledge of both Barnard and Columbia Colleges. Having served as a junior-class president at Barnard, she had won election to the presidency of the undergraduate association by one vote against President Butler's daughter Sarah. Sarah had voted for Freda, because, as she put it, "You can't vote for yourself," while Freda had voted for herself, since, in her words, "If I didn't think I was the best person for the office, I wouldn't be running."[28]

A defiantly modern woman, Kirchwey declared next to her yearbook picture, "I dare do all that would become a man." She abhorred bigotry and particularly despised the exclusionary policies of the fraternities and sororities that flourished on Morningside Heights. In 1915, she organized a campaign with her classmate Margaret Meyer, the only child of Annie Nathan Meyer, to eliminate sororities at Barnard. Meyer and Kirchwey objected to their undemocratic spirit, secrecy, and "attitude toward Hebrew members."[29] A student of James Harvey Robinson and Franz Boas, Kirchwey considered an academic career but settled on journalism instead. By 1922, she had married, given birth to a son, and worked her way up to the position of managing editor at the *Nation*.

In her editorial, Kirchwey condemned the use of psychological tests at Columbia. "It is widely charged that the psychological tests have been used to discriminate against Jews," she announced. "[C]ertainly the drop in percentage of Jews which has frequently followed their application is extremely suspicious in view of the previous complaint that the Jews ran away with all the prizes and scholarships." Kirchwey went on to deplore Columbia's new emphasis on "outside" school activities and its requirement that principals mark candidates according to their "fair play," "public spirit," "interest in fellows," and "leadership." These were all traits, she insisted, in which "a school principal of old American stock is likely to rank low the boy from an immigrant home who is excluded from some of the social life of his fellows by prejudice and the need of earning his own way from more."[30]

Kirchwey made no mention of Barnard, but the Barnard administration was doing its share in trying to hold on to Columbia University's traditional clientele. In November 1920, Dean Virginia Gildersleeve wrote to Butler that she would like to see Barnard adopt the tests already in use at Columbia as a way of improving "the elasticity" of the admissions process. She added, however, that she might have difficulty persuading her faculty to make the change.[31] Proud and protective of their independence, Barnard professors could never be counted on to follow the university's lead.

Gildersleeve weighed her words carefully at the next Barnard faculty meeting. The college, she explained, was finding it increasingly difficult to attract "conventional middle-class" students from New York City because of the widespread perception "that we have a large proportion of Jews and of radicals." During the Red Scare that followed World War I, Judaism and Bolshevism became synonymous in the minds of many. Gildersleeve did not hesitate to play on that link. The college needed students "of every creed, group, and race," she assured the democratically minded among her listeners, "but not too many of any one" kind, she quickly added, so that "all may be assimilated." Anticipating that the faculty would be more open to enlarging opportunity than to restricting it, she celebrated the tests as a way of casting the admissions net more widely. Barnard, she believed, would find it easier to recruit students from beyond the metropolitan area if they were given the chance to take a short intelligence test, for which they need not study, rather than having to prepare for the traditional entrance exam. At first, a doubtful faculty was willing only to make the tests optional, but after a year's debate it finally voted to adopt the "psychological exam in use by Columbia" on a trial basis. That trial persisted for another decade.[32]

Gildersleeve invented an additional way of reorienting Barnard College away from New York City's Jews and radicals by forming what came to be known as the "Seven Sisters," an association of Barnard, Bryn Mawr, Mount Holyoke, Radcliffe, Smith, Vassar, and Wellesley. Gildersleeve's stated aim was to give a higher profile to women's colleges as a way of raising endowment for them all. Barnard and Radcliffe, in particular, suffered financially from living in the shadow of the far more famous universities with which they were affiliated. These two colleges shared another concern, as well: large Jewish enrollments. Radcliffe's Jewish enrollment rose to 20 percent in the years between the wars, compared with about 6 percent at Bryn Mawr and Mount Holyoke, and about 10 percent at Smith, Vassar, and Wellesley. For Radcliffe, as for Barnard, cooperation with the other women's colleges reoriented them away from their urban settings toward a more genteel and gentile image.[33] Gildersleeve's various strategies of detailed application forms, interviews, tests, and identification of Barnard as one of the "Seven Sisters" seem to have succeeded; the proportion of Jews in Barnard classes from 1933 through 1935, for instance, ranged from a low of 17 to a high of 22 percent, the same range as at Columbia College in those years, and well below the 40 percent mark reached early in the twentieth century.[34]

As Robert A. McCaughey has shown in his history of Columbia University, the efforts of Columbia and Barnard at keeping a lid on the number of Jews on Morningside Heights did not, as administrators had hoped, allow them to hold on to their traditional WASP clientele. Instead, their efforts simply opened the door to an expanding number of Catholics. Columbia had always included a small number of Catholics, but as second-generation Italian and Irish students increasingly began seeking admission, admissions officials seemed to find them the lesser of two evils—different, yes, but at least Christian and easier to assimilate than their Jewish peers. The same

Spectator article of October 1921 that put Jews at 18 percent of the first-year class at Columbia College, put Catholics at 22 percent. By the early 1930s, despite the administration's best efforts, Columbia had ceased to be a predominantly Protestant institution.[35]

THE "NEGRO INVASION"

While ceasing to be a predominantly Protestant institution by the early 1930s, Columbia remained a bastion of whiteness—even though the surrounding neighborhood, which had been largely Jewish in 1920, became largely black by 1930. Blacks had always lived in Harlem. Whites had brought them as slaves in the seventeenth and early eighteenth centuries, and many had stayed as squatters when the farmland became depleted and white owners abandoned it. When Seth Low came to survey Morningside Heights in 1890, two apartment houses for blacks, the Garrison and the Sumner, stood next to each other just north of the university, at 125th Street and Broadway.[36] In 1898, according to a Columbia master's essay on the neighborhood, black families could be found "clear across the city from river to river."[37] The number of blacks increased sharply, however, after a collapse of the real-estate market in 1904, which left landlords with a glut of high-priced apartments on their hands. Although white realtors tried to keep blacks out, the financial pressures proved too great. Long discriminated against in the housing market, middle-class blacks were willing to pay higher rents than whites, and desperate sellers quickly began to break ranks. In 1911, the *Harlem Home News* exhorted its readers, "The Negro invasion . . . must be valiantly fought . . . before it is too late to repel the black hordes."[38] By 1917, there were seventy thousand blacks in Harlem, roughly one-fifth of the population. In the next decade, that number more than doubled, as Jews, Irish, and Italians moved to newer developments in the Bronx, Brooklyn, and Queens and blacks replaced them.[39]

Even as blacks came to dominate Harlem, however, the university on the heights overlooking them offered, at best, a mixed reception. John W. Burgess had established a hostile climate in the Graduate Faculty of Political Science in the late nineteenth century, one that was perpetuated by his student William Dunning, whose work, together with that of his students, was dedicated to proving that blacks had been largely responsible for the political and economic problems that plagued the South after the Civil War.[40]

The reception of blacks into Columbia's undergraduate colleges was no friendlier. Although Harvard and Yale had been admitting black students since the middle of the nineteenth century, Columbia College did not admit its first black student, a young man from South Africa who went on to found the African National Congress, until 1902.[41] And, although Wellesley, Radcliffe, and Smith had been admitting black women since the late nineteenth century, Barnard did not do so until the 1920s.[42]

Despite that exclusionary pattern, Columbia was never united in its hostility to blacks. As in the matter of religion, so in the matter of race, there were pockets of resistance. Teachers College and its spin-offs, Extension Teaching and the Summer School, welcomed blacks from the start. This relative openness was largely a product of the liberal and entrepreneurial design of Dean James Earl Russell. In contrast to the racist tone set by John W. Burgess in the Graduate Faculty of Political Science, Russell established a welcoming atmosphere by actively recruiting blacks not only from Harlem but also from the South, especially from Hampton Institute, St. Augustine's School, and Tuskegee Institute, where Seth Low served as president of the board of trustees from 1907 until his death in 1916. As early as the academic year 1900/1901, Russell traveled throughout the South, visiting black colleges and encouraging students to come to Teachers College. At a time when Booker T. Washington was under steady fire from W. E. B. Du Bois for stressing vocational training at Tuskegee, instead of a classical liberal-arts curriculum, Washington sought Russell's advice on how to upgrade his school. Russell praised the industrial work, but told him that his academic work definitely needed improvement. Washington sent three students, at least one of them a woman, to Teachers College in 1901 with the help of full scholarships provided by the Teachers College trustee V. Everett Macy. According to college records, between 1903 and 1907, Teachers College awarded scholarships to six students from Tuskegee, four of them women.[43]

In the years that followed, Teachers College attracted hundreds of southern black teachers, who rented rooms in Harlem and took post-baccalaureate courses (often in the Summer School). The training they received not only raised the educational level among African Americans in the South, but also improved public health, for the courses in chemistry and nutrition they took at Columbia allowed them to teach others how to avoid pellagra and other diseases rooted in nutritional deficits.[44]

Three of the black women who came to Teachers College after World War I were Sadie and Bessie Delany and May Chinn. The Delany sisters' father was the head of St. Augustine's School in Raleigh, North Carolina, as well as the first African American bishop of the Episcopal Church. Sadie Delany earned her B.S. from Teachers College in 1920 and her M.S. in 1925 and went on to teach home economics in the New York City high-school system. After graduating from St. Augustine's (a school that gave the equivalent of a high-school education), she taught in the segregated schools of the South for several years. Although Teachers College was by World War I a graduate school, it accepted teaching experience as a substitute for college preparation, and it was under that provision that many southern blacks were able to gain admission. Bessie Delany was the first black woman to attend Columbia's dental school (Dental School 1923). There were 170 students in her class, including 11 women, and 6 black men; she was the only black woman. Dentistry appealed to students who could not afford the time or the money to take the full sequence of science courses required of regular medical students. She later recalled that most of her classmates at Columbia were "self-assured city folk and their families were paying their tuition," but she had worked for half a dozen years as a teacher in the rural schools of the South to earn enough money to take science courses at the all-black Shaw University required to enter dental school. Both sisters had to work during the summer breaks as movie-theater ushers and factory workers back home to save enough money to make it through the program. They credited their greater maturity (Bessie was twenty-six and Sadie twenty-eight when they came to Columbia), their family support, and the encouragement of a few white friends, deans, and teachers for their success. May Chinn, the daughter of an escaped Virginia slave, arrived at Teachers College with the intention of teaching music, but discovered science and became a doctor. Graduating from Teachers College in 1921, she became the first black woman to obtain a medical degree from Bellevue Hospital Medical College, in 1926. For decades, she was the only black woman doctor in Harlem.[45]

After James Earl Russell, the person most responsible for recruiting black students to Columbia was Professor Mabel Carney. Born in Missouri in 1885, Carney came to Teachers College as a student in 1909 at the age of twenty-four and joined the faculty in 1917. She founded a program in rural education at Teachers College, devoted in part to the study of "Negro life" in the South, and introduced courses on African American education, in which students did fieldwork in Harlem. Wanting to teach those courses in a broader context, Carney traveled and conducted research in South Africa and Latin America, bringing back more students with each visit. Always, she emphasized the need for interracial work.[46] Teachers College prepared more black leaders of higher education than any other institution in the United States. As of 1938, Teachers College had granted 121 advanced degrees to blacks, compared with 81 for the University of Chicago, and 66 for Howard University. A third of those Teachers College degrees went to women.[47]

There were pockets of resistance to racism, too, in Teachers College's spin-off, Columbia's Summer School. In the Summer School, not only

African Americans, but also a number of liberal white Southerners, found spaces where, as Georgia-born Katharine Du Pre Lumpkin later recalled, "fresh, free air circulated." Lumpkin initially came to Columbia in 1918 to study sociology in the graduate school. She "sat in the classrooms of some of its best known men," Franklin Giddings, among them. But she seems to have encountered the same difficulties that Mary Kingsbury and Mary Beard had before her. Giddings's "dry categories were like dust in my throat," she later recalled. She envisaged "scholarship as something moving and breathing"; instead she discovered learning treated "as a corpse on which men of learning performed a continuing autopsy" and left students with the evolutionary message that "mores" were so deeply embedded in human social habits "as to make it nearly impossible to alter them."[48]

Lumpkin did not finally find "fresh air" until she enrolled in the Summer School, where, among her fellow students, she encountered "three Negroes, one man and two women." One of the women, Lumpkin reported, "was Georgia-born, even as I was. The course browsed in the field of race relations." To her surprise, the black woman spoke with directness and bluntness she could not have expressed in Georgia about the realities of segregation in their home state: "She confronted me with truths as to what southern Negroes wished for in education, citizenship, job opportunities, equality before the law, and what in fact they had." At the end of the term, "our professor invited his seminar to tea." Lumpkin went, fully aware that she was breaking one of the most sacred of southern white taboos: "This was 'eating with Negroes' . . . this was 'social equality.'" She survived, having concluded that the "mores" she had read and heard about in Giddings's sociology lectures were not so intractable after all, that the taboo against "eating with Negroes" was simply one of a hundred rules that served the useful purpose of keeping blacks in their place.[49]

The "fresh air" of Teachers College and the Summer School, together with the explosion of literary firepower produced by the Harlem Renaissance, finally began to affect Columbia's other schools. In 1921, Langston Hughes enrolled in the School of Mines, under pressure from his father, but he left after a year to dedicate himself to his writing. Four years later, Zora Neale Hurston enrolled at Barnard College. Hurston came to Barnard with the help of Annie Nathan Meyer, who, in addition to being a founder and a trustee at the college, was also a novelist interested in the Harlem Renaissance. In May 1925, Meyer attended an awards dinner arranged by Charles Johnson, editor of the Urban League's magazine *Opportunity: A Journal of Urban Life*, to introduce young black writers to three hundred of New York's literary elite. There she encountered Hurston, who won four separate prizes that evening for her short stories and plays. Meyer introduced herself and promptly offered Hurston a place at Barnard. But powerful though Meyer was, she did not have the authority to admit students on her own. Virginia Gildersleeve would have the final say.[50]

Hurston, a native of Eatonville, Florida, had left home as a teenager and had picked up what education she could, while supporting herself at odd jobs. She had spent some time at Howard University, where she had earned "a few high marks," but her record was on the whole not good. "Ordinarily we would not admit a transfer with this record," Gildersleeve told Meyer after reviewing Hurston's transcript. But the dean was willing to make an exception in Hurston's case, on the strength of the prize-winning short story she had submitted.[51] Hurston won admission, but Gildersleeve did not think that her academic record warranted a scholarship. Undeterred, Meyer raised the $300 needed for tuition and helped Hurston find work as a secretary in exchange for room and board with the famous novelist Fanny Hurst.[52]

Hurston was not only Barnard's first black student, but also probably the oldest student Barnard had ever enrolled. She admitted to twenty-six years, but in fact was thirty-three. Blessed with a youthful appearance and abetted by a peripatetic past, she had successfully shaved seven years off her real age by the time she reached New York City.[53] It says much about how difficult it was for a black woman to win admission to Barnard that the first one to succeed was an award-winning author, with the maturity and confidence of someone more than a decade older than the typical student. Even so, Barnard proved tough going. Given her weak educational background, heavy course load, and need to work to pay for living expenses, Hurston found Barnard's academic demands daunting. As she confided to Annie Nathan Meyer, she missed exams, flunked a French test, and got into trouble at the registrar's office for not following proper procedures in registering for classes. And yet she reveled in the academic challenges she faced. Taking seven courses her first semester, she managed to earn three B's, and C's in everything else—including French. "You see," she wrote Meyer, "being at Barnard and measuring arms with others known to be strong increases my self love and stiffens my spine."[54]

Hurston's experience at Barnard reveals a great deal about the mixture of liberal good intentions and sexual/racial anxieties that marked the college in the 1920s. In a letter to Meyer, Hurston reported that the Barnard students "are perfectly wonderful to me. They literally drag me to the teas on Wednesday and then behave as if I am the guest of honor—so eager are they to assure me that I am desired there." They even invited her to the Junior Prom and "offered to exchange dances with me if I will bring a man as light as myself," Hurston reported. Rather than object to the color bias this offer reflected, Hurston—at least to Meyer—joked about it: "Their frankness on that score is amusing, but not offensive in that dancing is such an intimate thing that it is not unreasonable for a girl to say who she wishes to do it with." Meyer counseled Hurston not to attend the prom, and Hurston agreed. Interracial tea was one thing; interracial dancing, another.[55]

And then there was interracial living. The majority of students who attended Barnard commuted from home, while those who came from a distance lived in the college residences. Hurston, a student who came from a greater distance than most, would seem to have been a candidate for the dormitories, but she ended up living, after a brief period with Fannie Hurst, in a room in Harlem. Dean Gildersleeve was no doubt relieved by this resolution of Hurston's housing needs. Johnson Hall, the graduate residence for women, was integrated, but the graduate dormitory, Gildersleeve believed, was "somewhat different than the undergraduate residences." The problem she anticipated seems not to have been unease among the women so much as the awkwardness that she imagined might occur were young black men to come calling. Not until 1929 was she willing to consider the "experiment" of integrating the undergraduate residences.[56]

Following Hurston's admission to Barnard, other black women followed, including a librarian, Jean Blackwell Hutson, who graduated from Barnard in 1935 and went on to be curator of the Schomberg Collection of Negro Literature and History at the New York Public Library, and the poet June Jordan of the Barnard class of 1958. Their numbers were small, however, only one or two a year until after World War II, about the same number as at Columbia College and the other Seven Sisters.[57] Few potential black applicants could hurdle the academic and financial barriers that stood in the way of admission to Barnard. Pauli Murray, who would go on to become a pioneering civil rights lawyer, feminist leader, poet, and Episcopal priest, was turned away in 1927 for want of funds and the inadequate preparation that she had received in the segregated schools of Durham, North Carolina. After repeating her senior year in the New York City public-school system, Murray won entry to Hunter College and lived with relatives in Brooklyn. But even a northern education and an Elks scholarship did not get future civil rights leader Dorothy I. Height into Barnard in 1929. Two other black students, she was told, had already been admitted.[58] By the 1930s, civil rights activists, including the Reverend James Robinson (whose church was at Morningside Avenue and 122nd Street), apparently persuaded Gildersleeve of the need both to recruit talented black students and to provide full scholarships to enable them to attend. Pressed by students in the early 1940s to do more, the dean paid for the full scholarship of at least one black student from Harlem out of her own pocket. But by the time Gildersleeve retired in 1947, Barnard still had only eight black students in its student body of fourteen hundred.[59]

THE WOMAN QUESTION REVISITED

As an African American, Zora Neale Hurston represented a small shift in Columbia's demography, but as a woman, she was part of a sea change. The Columbia registrar's reports for the 1920s show female topping male enrollment by the mid-1920s, just as Hurston was arriving. In the Summer School, Barnard College, and Teachers College, especially, but increasingly in the graduate faculties as well, women were making progress, with consequences for the intellectual work of the university that have not been fully appreciated. Nowhere did women's presence make a bigger difference than in anthropology, where debates over the "Jewish problem," the "Negro invasion," and the woman question sparked a flurry of new studies.

Boas took a particular interest in challenging the prejudice that war had heightened, and he resolved to counter the bold claims of his adversaries. But he was hampered in that effort by what the historian George Stocking has called the "mutual inhibition" of his scientific caution and his compulsion to assemble all available evidence. A dearth of funding further impeded his work. Boas appealed successfully to James C. Egbert, the director of Columbia's Extension Teaching, to hire the occasional adjunct professor, but he could not wangle funds from President Butler for even a secretary, much less for additional faculty positions, research, or publishing. Given his estrangement from the American Anthropological Association and the National Research Council, he could not count on money from those sources either, at least in the short term. The only alternative was to raise money privately or to look elsewhere in the university for support.[60]

Into the breach strode Elise Clews Parsons, who saw in anthropology a refuge from the politics of war. Committing her personal wealth to Boas's work, Parsons paid Boas's secretary, covered deficits for the publication of the *Journal of American Folklore,* provided money for summer field trips, and sponsored the compilation of a concordance of southwestern folklore. Her financial assistance not only contributed significantly to Boas's success in rebuilding anthropology at Columbia after the war, but also helped create a haven for female scholars.

In common with other fields, anthropology lost male students to the war, but the loss in Boas's department was exacerbated by the chairman's outspoken antimilitarism. When Ralph Linton, who had left the department to join the army in 1917, returned in full military attire in 1919, Boas made him feel so uncomfortable that he left to finish his training at Harvard. Boas's antimilitarism had profound implications for the gendering of anthropology. "I have had a curious experience in graduate work in the last few years," a bemused Boas wrote a colleague at the Field Museum in 1920. "All my best students are women." In fact, his only remaining graduate students were women. Erna Gunther and Gladys Reichard, who were completing their doctoral degrees in 1920, became the core of a new group of scholars who, with the scholarly inspiration and financial help of Elsie Clews Parsons, expanded Boas's work on race to include research related to masculinity, femininity, and sexuality.[61] The department's most important new recruit came from the fledgling New School for Social Research. In 1919, Emily Smith Putnam asked Parsons to teach a class there. Having learned that Boas could no longer keep Alexander Goldenweiser at Columbia, Parsons persuaded Putnam to hire the unemployed instructor as well, and the two scholars formed the core of the New School's offerings in anthropology. Among their first students was an unhappy suburban housewife, Ruth Fulton Benedict.

Born in 1887 in New York City, the daughter of a doctor and a Vassar-trained teacher, Ruth Fulton grew up within a privileged community of white Anglo-Saxon Protestants whose roots stretched back to the American Revolution. But she never enjoyed the sense of belonging that privilege should have brought. Her father died of a fever when she was only twenty-one months old, and she spent her early years on her maternal grandparents' farm near Norwich, New York, with her mother; her younger sister, Margaret; and her mother's sisters. Her family regarded her as a moody child who would not answer when called and was given to violent tantrums. Benedict later attributed her behavior to the loss of her father and the deep conflict she felt between her memory of him, composed and serene in death, and the memory of her mother, explosively emotional in her grief for years thereafter. She also remembered being deeply troubled by the quarreling among her aunts that punctuated day-to-day life on the farm. Her withdrawal from family life and her tantrums, as well as a lifelong tendency to stammer, may have stemmed from those childhood experiences, but they may also have been the result of partial deafness, the product of a bout of measles when she was three years old and discovered only when she entered school.[62] Whatever the reason, she experienced life as an outsider. Preoccupied by death and frequently depressed, she retreated into an imaginary world and, as she grew older, sought refuge in literature and writing.

Ruth Fulton's mother supported her daughters, first as a teacher and later as a librarian, and sent them both to Vassar, where the sisters entered an intensely intellectual community populated by strong, ambitious women. Suffrage was a major issue on campus when they arrived in 1905, and the sisters greatly admired their classmate Inez Milholland, who defied college rules against political organizing on campus by holding a suffrage rally in a nearby graveyard and inviting Charlotte Perkins Gilman, Harriet Stanton Blatch, and Rose Schneiderman to speak. Fulton supported suffrage, but her hearing made political work difficult, and she resolved to make her mark as an intellectual (rather than a political) radical.[63]

In her mother's day, Vassar had imposed a fixed curriculum on its students, but the college adopted a system of electives in 1903, patterned on a plan pioneered at Harvard, and Fulton pursued interests in philosophy, history, and literature. Vassar teachers included many strong-minded, dangerous women, who impressed on their students the lesson that mental activism could be a worthy alternative to political activism. Through them she discovered William James, who taught her to celebrate the creative energy of the soul; George Santayana, who opened her eyes to the power of ideas; and Friedrich Nietzsche, in whose *Birth of Tragedy* she discovered a metaphor for the war within her: the Apollonian order she associated with her father and the Dionysian emotionalism she identified with her mother.[64] Majoring in English, she immersed herself in Shakespeare and the vast body of literary criticism that had grown up around his work. She was especially drawn to the writings of the literary critic Walter Pater, which helped her overcome her frequent feelings of "blank despair," by impressing on her "the power of conceiving humanity in a new and striking way . . . selecting, transforming, recombining images." By the time she graduated in 1909, the essential vocabulary of her later career was largely in place.[65]

Following college, Fulton became, briefly, a social worker and then a teacher. Finding satisfaction in neither vocation, she accepted, with some misgivings, the marriage proposal of a young chemist, Stanley Benedict, and sought, without success, to have children. Tensions grew between them. Stanley did not like to discuss problems; Ruth wanted to talk them out. Stanley wanted his wife to take care of him; Ruth needed meaningful work of her own. What this work should be was not at first clear to her. She applauded the achievements of the suffrage movement and agreed with Charlotte Perkins Gilman on the importance of economic independence for all women. But neither political engagement nor a job, by itself, satisfied Ruth Benedict's need for personal fulfillment. True liberation, she came to believe, must be "an inward affair, a matter of attitude." She wanted to be, in Olive Schreiner's words, a fighter "in the depths of the individual consciousness, that primal battle-ground, in which all questions of reform and human advance must ultimately be fought."[66] She began to draft a biographical study of three feminists: Mary Wollstonecraft (1759–1797), Margaret Fuller (1810–1850), and Olive Schreiner (1850–1920). But World War I greatly diminished interest in stories of restless women, and she failed to find a publisher. At thirty-one, the age at which her father had died, she resolved to return to school. She learned of the New School, enrolled in Elsie Clews Parsons's course "Sex in Ethnology," and discovered her calling. In her examination of women's lives in cultures throughout the world, Parsons offered a framework for understanding how social convention inhibited self-expression. Following up her work with Parsons, Benedict took a series of courses taught by Goldenweiser, who helped her see the relevance of her literary training to the understanding of other cultures. Recognizing Benedict's brilliance, Parsons and Goldenweiser urged her to continue her graduate studies at Columbia, and Parsons personally escorted her to an interview with Boas.[67]

In many ways. Parsons saw her mirror image in Benedict. Here was an intensely intellectual woman, a younger version of herself, in search of meaningful work and a way of understanding how societies inhibit human—and especially female—freedom. But the two women's relations were strained from the start. For all Parsons's advanced views, she struck Benedict as inaccessible by virtue of her age and wealth. She was always Mrs. Parsons, never Elsie. Benedict also chafed under Parsons's relentless empiricism. Anthropology married art and science, but for Parsons, trained just as sociology was

Ruth Benedict (1887–1948)
Graduate of Vassar College (1909) and Columbia University (Ph.D. 1923), anthropologist, and assistant professor (1931–1937), associate professor (1937–1948), and professor (1948) at Columbia University, as photographed around 1933.
(Columbia University Archives–Columbiana Library)

establishing its empirical bona fides, science was always the more important; indeed, the longer she lived and worked, and the more disillusioned she became over the prospect of political and social reform, the more narrowly empirical her scholarship became. What the world needed, she believed, was the careful, scientific recording of cultural practices while there was still time. Benedict, steeped in literary criticism, viewed art as more significant. For Benedict, cultures, like literary works, had themes, larger meanings. Long intrigued by irrational, dissonant, seemingly dysfunctional ideas, she resolved to specialize in the study of mythology as a way of understanding culture, how it worked, and how it changed. In her first published paper, "The Vision in Plains Culture" (1921), and then in her dissertation, "The Concept of the Guardian Spirit in America" (1923), Benedict brought her interpretive vision to the center of the anthropological enterprise at Columbia. Even as she dutifully catalogued the diffusion of stories from one people to the next, according to Baosian precepts, she began to emphasize the ways in which individuals create the world they live in according to definite patterns and themes. Individuals were products of culture but also creators of it, as myth tellers and visionaries. Until that was understood, we would "be unable to see our cultural life objectively, or control its manifestations."[68]

THE FEMALE PROFESSOR

The arrival of Benedict and other female students helped reinvigorate and redirect anthropology at Columbia, but it also created a problem. Boas had enjoyed stunning success in winning appointments for his male students at colleges and universities around the country. By the mid-1920s, Alfred Kroeber and Robert Lowie were teaching at Berkeley, Leslie Spier was at the University of Washington, Alexander Goldenweiser was holding forth at the New School, Melville Herskovits was on his way to Howard University, and Edward Sapir was about to move from Ottawa to Chicago. Placing female students in academic positions proved far more difficult. Apart from Erna Gunther, who married her classmate Leslie Spier in 1921 and taught with him at Washington, Boas's female students looked unemployable. At a time when male educational leaders were worrying publicly over the effect on American masculinity of an increasingly female teaching force in the public high schools, all-male colleges were without exception committed to protecting their students from what they feared would be the feminizing tendencies of female teachers. Columbia's rapidly expanding graduate school hired a few women, but only at the subfaculty ranks of assistant, lecturer, and instructor. Even the famous psychologist Christine Ladd-Franklin, who won a position at Columbia in 1914 as a nonsalaried lecturer, never rose above that rank. The only women to reach the faculty ranks before 1920 did so at Barnard and Teachers Colleges.[69]

Their numbers were small—a couple at Teachers College, a dozen at Barnard—but even that limited success worried male administrators. In a 1921 memorandum to Virginia Gildersleeve, the Barnard English professor and provost William Brewster agonized over the "feminization" of Barnard's teaching staff and what it meant for Barnard's affiliation with Columbia.[70] When Barnard won the right to hire its own faculty in 1900, most of its professors were accorded the privilege of offering courses in Columbia's graduate school. In exchange, an equivalent number of Columbia faculty taught at Barnard. But as male faculty at Barnard retired, Brewster warned Gildersleeve, the sorry state of the Barnard endowment was making it increasingly difficult to replace them with men of comparable stature. Instruction was therefore coming more and more to be "in the hands of women." As a consequence, Brewster feared, Barnard would soon "lose its privilege of exchanging instruction with Columbia men," because only in cases of "very rare distinction" would women be accepted as teachers in the graduate faculty, and under no condition would they be accepted as teachers in Columbia College. "At the present rate of progress," Brewster grimly predicted, "80 percent of our instruction will, within fifteen years, be in the hands of women, to the ruin of our plan of exchanges with Columbia, from which we get substantially no more than we did twenty years ago."[71]

Far from faulting his Columbia colleagues for their unwillingness to accept female faculty, he accepted it as altogether reasonable. "I believe that at present and probably for many years to come," he continued, "women will display much less intellectual enterprise and initiative than men, and I believe them to be much less productive of what a sound college should stand for." Reiterating the well-worn shibboleths of social Darwinist thinking, he continued, "My observation is that they reach their maturity faster than men, that their decline is more rapid, and that they have lost much of their value at an age when a man is at the fullness of his powers and has many years to go." Shifting from biology to the marketplace, he concluded, "Surely the majority of college and university students prefer, for various reasons, the instruction of men to that of women. They associate the higher intellectual reaches and the real sources of knowledge with the masculine rather than the feminine mind."[72]

Gildersleeve readily conceded the need to increase faculty salaries to maintain parity with Columbia and to ensure the quality of her faculty. She also accepted Brewster's argument that she was going to have to pay more to hire men with families. Indeed, she was willing to pay single women less than single men, knowing that there was a surfeit of talented, underemployed academic women in New York City.[73]

Gildersleeve disagreed, however, with Brewster's argument that the increase of women on the faculty by itself signaled a decline in quality or that it need jeopardize the faculty exchange with Columbia. For one thing, bigotry against women was not as universal as Brewster seemed to believe, since at least some Columbia men were willing to include female faculty in the Barnard–Columbia exchange. As early as 1910, Gildersleeve had become the first Barnard woman to teach a graduate course at Columbia. And in the academic year 1921/1922, the graduate school at Columbia asked a Barnard associate professor, Ida H. Ogilvie, to teach glacial geology; Assistant Professor Louise Hoyt Gregory to teach general physiology; and Helen Parkhurst, though still only an instructor, to teach philosophy.[74]

Inspired by this early sign that male faculty at Columbia might be willing to relax their chauvinism, and clearly worried about Brewster's jaundiced view of female prospects, Gildersleeve set about negotiating an agreement with Nicholas Murray Butler that would address mutual concerns. She agreed that Columbia departments would have the right to guarantee the quality of Barnard faculty who taught Columbia graduate courses by gaining a veto over the promotion of any Barnard faculty—female or male—to the rank of associate professor. Columbia's acceptance of that right would carry with it the understanding that anyone who had gained Columbia approval would be deemed qualified to teach on the graduate faculty. Moreover, Gildersleeve and Butler agreed to abolish the old system of faculty exchange in favor of a fee-based arrangement, whereby the fees of Barnard students enrolled in courses taught by Columbia faculty would be remitted to Columbia and the fees of Columbia students enrolled in the Columbia graduate courses taught by Barnard professors would go to Barnard. As a practical matter, the fees went mostly from Barnard to Columbia, since many more Barnard students took courses with Columbia faculty than vice versa, but both schools benefited. Barnard students gained access to a far richer array of courses than their small college could offer. Barnard and Columbia administrators alike won the prospect of cutting costs by virtue of the greater efficiency that closer cooperation would provide. Columbia faculty gained greater control over the quality of the Barnard faculty who taught in the graduate school. Barnard women professors gained, at least in theory, the right—if they were deemed sufficiently eminent—to join the men as professors in the Columbia graduate faculty. And the few Columbia women who were beginning to teach as assistants, lecturers, and instructors in the graduate faculties gained the prospect that, in time, they too might rise to professorial rank at the university.. Gildersleeve hoped that as Barnard students were more thoroughly integrated into Columbia, first as upper-level students and eventually as graduate students and instructors, they would more often qualify as Barnard faculty able to teach in the Columbia graduate schools and, perhaps, in time, gain full acceptance as graduate professors at Columbia. At a time when no women were teaching on the graduate faculties of Harvard and Yale, and a mere handful were teaching in state universities (mostly in departments of home economics), the 1922 agreement represented a significant step forward.[75]

Franz Boas was the first Columbia faculty member to capitalize on Gildersleeve's efforts. Promising to grant anyone hired at Barnard the right to teach graduate courses in the anthropology department at Columbia, he persuaded Gildersleeve in 1922 to add a position in anthropology. Barnard became the first liberal-arts college in the country to provide a permanent position in anthropology. On Boas's recommendation, Gildersleeve appointed Gladys Reichard in 1923 to the rank of instructor. With Boas's backing, Reichard won promotion to assistant professor in 1928.[76]

Winning women professorial rank at Columbia took more than the example set by Barnard. Having found a position for Gladys Reichard, Boas next turned to the task of finding work for Ruth Benedict. Unable to secure a faculty position from the Columbia administration, Boas pieced together a job made up of editorial work for Elsie Clews Parsons and the various journals he controlled, a few classes in University Extension and in the Summer School, and a visiting position at Barnard when Reichard won a Guggenheim Fellowship for the academic year 1925/1926. By 1927, the contrast between Benedict (subsisting from year to year on temporary appointments) and Reichard (due for promotion the following year to assistant professor at Barnard) seems to have inspired him to renew his campaign to Columbia's administration for an additional position in anthropology. He wanted to hire Benedict at Columbia as an assistant professor. But while at Barnard he was dealing with Virginia Gildersleeve, at Columbia he faced Frederick J. E. Woodbridge, the resistant dean of the graduate faculties.[77]

Woodbridge had studied theology at Union Theological Seminary but had decided against entering the ministry. When later asked why, he responded, "The Church had moved from the worship of God to the worship of welfare."[78] The social gospel, with its reformist and feminine overtones, did not appeal to the would-be cleric. Instead, he entered academe. At Columbia, he rose to the rank of professor of philosophy and in 1912 became dean of the Graduate Faculties of Political Science, Philosophy, and Pure Science. Repeatedly Woodbridge rebuffed Boas's efforts to win a position for Ruth Benedict. Only when Howard McBain, the Ruggles Professor of Constitutional Law, replaced Woodbridge as dean in 1929 did Boas's efforts meet with success.

McBain, whose interest in municipal reform had prompted Charles Beard to bring him to Columbia in 1913, had succeeded to the Ruggles professorship (established originally for John W. Burgess) in 1923. In contrast to Woodbridge, McBain supported female ambition. In 1926, for instance, when the faculty of Columbia Law School finally succumbed to Virginia Gildersleeve's decade-long campaign to open the Law School to women, one of McBain's students, Margaret Spahr, was among the first to seize the opportunity for legal training.[79] Having just earned her Ph.D. in constitutional law under McBain's direction, Spahr raced through the Law School in only two years, becoming the first woman to serve as an editor of the *Columbia Law Review* in the process. Upon graduation she accepted a position on the faculty of Hunter College, where she trained a generation of young women in political science and law.[80]

Editors of *Columbia Law Review*

Margaret Spahr (*standing, third from right*), first woman to graduate from Columbia Law School (1929) and teacher of constitutional law at Hunter College (1926–1959), as photographed in 1929. (Columbia Law School Special Collections)

When McBain became dean in 1929, Boas finally found the support he needed for his campaign to make Ruth Benedict an assistant professor.[81] In the end, Boas was not the first faculty member to advance a female protégé into the professorial ranks. That honor went to the chemist Henry C. Sherman, whose student Mary L. Caldwell, with a B.A. (1913) from Western Reserve and an M.A. (1919) and a Ph.D. (1921) from Columbia, specialized in nutrition. After earning her Ph.D. in chemistry, she began work as an instructor in 1922. In 1929, the year Henry Sherman became chairman of the chemistry department, he recommended that Caldwell be promoted to the rank of assistant professor in the graduate school. He succeeded, in large part, because of the critical role that Caldwell played in mentoring chemistry's large number of graduate students in nutrition, a field that had already become a female-dominated subdiscipline.[82] Ruth Benedict was next. The number of advanced-degree candidates in anthropology was small compared with chemistry, but, with women playing an increasingly important role in the field, the idea of promoting a woman to a professorship struck McBain as overdue. In 1931, he did so, more than doubling Benedict's salary to $3,600.[83]

THE DEBATE OVER THE CURRICULUM

A few strategic hires made anthropology more welcoming to female students in the 1920s, but just as important to their growing numbers in the field was an ongoing debate on Morningside Heights over how to structure the undergraduate curriculum. While at Columbia College the faculty devised a core curriculum aimed at giving all students a common experience, at Barnard professors voted to eliminate required courses altogether. The difference in approach had much to do with the history of the two undergraduate colleges' relations with each other and the relation of each, in turn, with the graduate faculties. Ever since the 1880s, when Columbia trustees had sided with the university faction in its battle with defenders of the college, the undergraduate faculty at Columbia (officially organized as a separate body in the 1890s, with thirty-three members) had felt insecure about its place in the university's academic firmament. Especially with the creation of Columbia's accelerated program, in which students on their way to professional school could lop off a fourth year of college in order to go straight to law or medical school, the Columbia College faculty felt increasingly marginalized. Faculty concern during World War I that the future officers they were training were woefully ignorant of the political and economic issues over which the war was being fought, together with an increasing desire to assimilate the sons of foreigners to a common intellectual tradition, made a core curriculum seem increasingly attractive as a way to secure the college's independent identity.[84]

The Barnard faculty might have been assumed to feel much the same way, overshadowed as they also were by the graduate school and uneasy about the heterogeneity of their student body. But the very fact of having agreed to teach young women made Barnard professors more skeptical of tradition and less concerned than their colleagues at Columbia College with maintaining it. The Barnard sociologist William Ogburn, who was beginning to make a name for himself with his theory of "cultural lag"—that in rapidly developing societies technological change tends to outstrip cultural attitudes—led the campaign at Barnard to eliminate requirements. At a 1923 faculty meeting, he ridiculed the notion of a required curriculum as intellectually outmoded. It "cannot be shown," he declared, "that one course is necessary and another is not."[85]

Although Dean Gildersleeve initially hesitated, she ultimately endorsed the prevailing view "that it did not matter greatly which subjects a student studied" as long as the teachers were good and the methods of study sound. Gildersleeve always emphasized that Barnard differed from other colleges for women in being a "university" college, with close (though always precarious) ties to the graduate faculty at Columbia.[86] While Columbia College faculty were busy distinguishing their mission from that of the graduate faculty, the Barnard faculty sought to emphasize their common interest with the graduate school. Their job, as they saw it, was to prepare students for the graduate training that they had fought so hard to open up to them. They enjoyed remarkable success in that effort. From 1920 to 1974, tiny Barnard College, which admitted only a couple of hundred students a year, sent more women on to Ph.D. programs than any other school in the country, except the much larger Hunter College and the University of California at Berkeley.[87]

Ironically, the discrimination that women faced in the professional worlds of law and medicine made them all the more eager to take advantage of their professors' special interests. Comparing the experience of teaching anthropology at both Barnard and Columbia, Franz Boas reported to President Butler, "The Barnard students are interested in the subject, intelligent, and take hold of it in a satisfactory way; while the quality of the Columbia students is on the whole not as good as I should like to see it." The reason," he continued, was that "a large percentage of the Columbia students prepare for professional work, and very few of the better class find time for an isolated subject such as anthropology." Those like Boas with "isolated" subjects to teach frowned on a curriculum that left no time for experimentation.[88]

The Barnard faculty's insistence that women be encouraged to take responsibility for their own intellectual development clashed not only with the idea of a common curriculum but also with prevailing ideas about women's place in the university. No one at Columbia gave more vivid voice to these ideas than John Erskine, a professor of English. A member of New York's Episcopal elite, Erskine graduated from Columbia College in the same year that Virginia Gildersleeve graduated from Barnard. Together they served on the editorial board of the Columbia literary magazine, the *Morningside*, and studied Elizabethan literature in Columbia's graduate school. Erskine earned his Ph.D. from Columbia in 1903. By 1910, both had decided to commit themselves to undergraduates, Gildersleeve as dean at Barnard, and Erskine as a professor of English, first at Amherst and then at Columbia. Gildersleeve and Erskine shared one other connection: Erskine's younger sister, Helen (Barnard 1904), served for many years as Gildersleeve's public-relations assistant.[89]

Despite their shared background and common interests, however, Gildersleeve and Erskine parted company on how to educate undergraduates. While Gildersleeve came to support the elective system, Erskine became a passionate advocate of a core curriculum. Like many of his colleagues, Erskine worried about the "literary ignorance of the younger generation," which could no longer be assumed to have read Homer, Dante, Shakespeare, or even Melville. He urged that a course be offered on "great books," read in translation and discussed in small groups, to help redress the situation.[90] In a lecture entitled "The Moral Obligation to Be Intelligent," which he began giving during World War I, Erskine explained why he advocated his "great books" approach. Education, at its best, he argued, should be a force for unifying humanity through the development of intellectual faculties. "It is a mistake to think that men are united by elemental affections," he declared. "Our affections divide us. We strike roots in immediate time and space, and fall in love with our locality, the customs and language in which we are brought up. Intelligence unites us with mankind, by leading us in sympathy to other times, other places, other customs." There was a hint of relativism in Erskine's reference to intelligence "leading us in sympathy to other times, other places, other customs," but he shared with most academics of his day a belief that some cultures were better than others and that the Anglo-American culture that was his specialty had reached the point of highest development. The purpose of education should be to liberate a student from the inferior custom of his background and expose him to other, better customs of the intellectual elite. Ultimately, a proper education would lead the "human spirit" to "one unifying mind, wherein the human race shall know its destiny and proceed to it with satisfaction, as an idea moves to its proper conclusion."[91] The "great books" course that he began to teach at this time was intended to contribute to this "one unifying mind" at Columbia by providing an opportunity for the college's increasingly diverse student body to gain the basis for "an intellectual life in common." By the mid-1920s, Erskine's course had become the center of Columbia's core curriculum.[92]

Just as important as the subject taught, Erskine insisted, was the person who taught it. In America, that person should be male and preferably white, Anglo-Saxon, and Protestant. He defended that position in *The Influence of Women, and Its Cure* (1936), in which he deplored the growing presence of women, as well as of immigrant men, in American academic life. Erskine called for a concerted effort to restrict the influence of both for the sake of maintaining WASP masculine cultural traditions. Warning that over the previous generation "the women have gradually taken control" and "in the mass are now busy reducing men to slaves," he declared that "the mass drive of the women toward their new opportunities has the effect not of educating the men to a civilized equality, but of dislodging them altogether." The "cure" for that evil, as he saw it, was for men like himself to take up the responsibility of teaching the next generation: "Let the boys be taught by men, and encouraged to be masculine—not to imitate the manners of the cave dweller, but to cultivate initiative, persistence, backbone. . . . [I]f the older American stocks won't pass on their tradition, the youth of the country will be taught by the children of later immigrants, and the path of our ideas will rapidly be changed. OR, if the men won't teach and the women will, the balance of the sexes will be upset, and ours will be a feminine civilization." A feminine civilization would quickly become, he warned, a homosexual civilization. "I find nothing happy in a program," he declared, "which is sympathetic and encouraging toward the lesbian and the fairy." As far as Erskine was concerned, schools in which women were given a prominent place and encouraged to think for themselves inevitably threatened traditional standards of femininity and masculinity, and in so doing, undermined heterosexuality.[93]

To the extent that members of the Barnard faculty gave the matter any thought, they appear to have been ready to assume that risk. Their goal was to prepare their students for making intellectual advances rather than trying to preserve intellectual traditions. To that end, they not only scorned requirements but also championed interdisciplinary study as a way to ensure innovation. Students were expected to major in a particular subject but also explore other fields of knowledge in the hope that a kind of intellectual cross-fertilization might take place.[94] In 1925, Gildersleeve presented the proposed Barnard curriculum to the University Council for approval. It passed, but not, as she later recalled, without Dean Herbert Hawkes's withering comment: "The proposed curriculum is certainly not one which I should wish to have in any college of which I was Dean. But if the Barnard Faculty wants it, then, on behalf of Columbia College, I have no objection."[95]

THE INTERDISCIPLINARY APPROACH IN PRACTICE

The program that the future anthropologist Margaret Mead (Barnard 1923) fashioned for herself typified the interdisciplinary approach that the Barnard faculty was working to encourage. Mead, who had just completed a miserable year at her father's alma mater, DePauw University—where she had arrived with the wrong dress and had been rejected by the sorority she wanted to join—arrived at Barnard in 1920 with the hope of becoming a poet.[96] The stiff competition she met from her roommate, Leonie Adams, who began publishing her poetry when they were still undergraduates, took the wind out of Mead's literary sails. A hardworking, ambitious young woman who had grown up in a family of academics—her mother was a sociologist, her father an economist—she resolved to redirect her talent toward work in social science.[97]

She began with a course in sociology with William Ogburn on the psychological aspects of culture, in which the work of Sigmund Freud was treated respectfully. For a generation, Freud had been challenging the image of the highly sexed male and the less passionate female of evolutionary theory with the argument that women, like men, have sexual needs that must be met to ensure health. Not that Freud abandoned the belief that women are more passive than men. But whereas medical science viewed psychology as a direct expression of physiology, Freud regarded it as shaped by children's social history within the family. According to Freud, children are born bisexual. Only as they confront the Oedipus complex, through which boys resolve their fears of castration and girls come to terms with the fact that castration has already occurred, do their adult personalities take form, and do passivity in women and aggression in men gain an all-but-universal ascendance.[98] For Mead, Ogburn's course was a revelation that started her thinking about sexuality as an intellectual, as well as a personal, issue.[99]

Mead also took a course in psychology with Harry Hollingworth, from whom she learned of work being done by his wife, Leta. A graduate student of Edward Thorndike at Teachers College, Leta Hollingworth had achieved recognition for her research on sex differences. Having earned her B.A. and

Margaret Mead (1901–1978)
Graduate of Barnard College (1923) and
Columbia University (M.A. [psychology]
1924, Ph.D. [anthropology] 1929), anthropologist, curator at American Museum of Natural
History (1934–1935, 1941–1942, 1948–1953),
and adjunct professor at Columbia University
(1948–1978), as photographed in 1923.
(Barnard College Archives)

certificate in teaching from the University of Nebraska in 1906 and having taught for two years, she married Henry Hollingworth in 1908 and moved to New York, where he had accepted a fellowship with the Columbia psychologist James McKeen Cattell. She planned to teach in the public schools. Discovering to her dismay that New York City still did not hire married women, she tried to work as a writer but could not sell her stories. She then applied for a graduate fellowship to study psychology but found few awards open to women. Only when her husband completed his own degree and became an assistant professor at Barnard in 1910 did the couple have enough money to enable Leta Hollingsworth to pursue graduate work in educational psychology at Teachers College.[100]

To make extra money for his wife's education, Harry Hollingsworth taught a course in Extension Teaching for business students, which led him to think about how psychology might be applied in business. In 1911, the Coca-Cola Company, under attack from the Food and Drug Administration, hired him to study the effect of caffeine on mental and motor performance. Controlling for as many variables as possible, Hollingworth asked his female subjects to keep track of their menses. When he reported his results, which included the finding that caffeine was a transient, nonhazardous stimulant, he made no mention of the influence of menstruation on the female subjects. Curious at this oversight, Leta Hollingsworth examined the data and found that menstruation had no effect. While her husband saw no significance in this non-finding, she immediately recognized that it flew in the face of the widespread belief that menstruation was a major impediment to women's participation in public life. Designing her own study, she examined the effect of menstruation on women's mental performance for her doctoral dissertation and found that over the course of a month, her female subjects varied no more in their mental performance than her control group of males. If menstruation did not interfere with women's performance on standard mental tests, then a major justification for barring them from professional careers could be challenged.[101] In the years that followed, she devised a series of studies that provided powerful ammunition for the feminist belief that men and women did not differ in their mental endowment.[102] By 1927, she had effectively made her case. As a male reviewer of the psychological literature on sex differences reported, "few, if any, of the so-called 'sex-differences' are due solely to sex." The "social training of the two sexes," not biology, he concluded, accounts for the differences in women and women's interests and abilities.[103]

Inspired by the Hollingworths, Mead decided to major in psychology and pursue graduate work in that field. In the end, however, the subject did not fully engage her, and a course on mental testing at Teachers College put her off entirely.[104] An anthropology class with Franz Boas and Ruth Benedict, though, captured her imagination. Benedict attracted students like Mead, who were interested in both social science and literature. Here was a discipline that seemed more open to the insights of the poet and literary critic than either psychology or sociology. Benedict and Mead shared their poems with each other and with Edward Sapir, another Boas student then teaching at Ottawa but a frequent visitor to New York. In anthropology, the vision of the artist mattered. Moreover, as Benedict insisted, anthropology had to be "done now" since "primitive" cultures all over the world were disappearing under the assault of Western expansion.[105]

Turning to anthropology did not mean abandoning psychology. Indeed, psychology assumed a much more important place within anthropological research in the 1920s than it had previously enjoyed. Franz Boas, outraged over what he believed to be the misuse of psychological tests in the admissions process and in the debate over immigration, encouraged his students to conduct research in psychology as well as anthropology to challenge prevailing prejudices and policies. Ignoring department boundaries, Boas assigned Mead a topic for her master's essay in psychology. She was to administer standard psychological tests to Italian American children in the New Jersey community where her family spent its summers, and where her mother had been conducting research for her dissertation in sociology for many years. Believing that these tests discriminated in particular against those whose first language was not English, Boas set as many of his students as he could to testing children in cross-cultural settings to see whether performance varied, depending on how long their families had lived in the United States. As predicted, Mead found that the children she tested varied in their performance, depending on the social status of their families, how long they had been in this country, and how much English was spoken in the home.[106]

Mead employed psychological tests in fieldwork throughout the remainder of her career, and psychoanalytic concepts informed much of her writing, especially in the 1950s. But the psychological approach that most influenced her was that offered by Kurt Koffka, whose work on Gestalt psychology, *The Growth of the Mind*, appeared in English as she was completing her study of Italian American children. Excitedly passing the new book along to Ruth Benedict, as well as to Edward Sapir, she knew immediately that this was what they needed to make sense of culture. Testing was useful, but limited. Psychoanalysis was fascinating, but universalizing. Koffka wrote about psychological configurations—the notion that people respond to some stimuli and not to others, depending on the particular patterns to which they have become accustomed. The world would be a meaningless blur to anyone who had not learned from infancy to organize visual, auditory, and other stimuli into meaningful patterns.[107]

Ruth Benedict was the first to make use of Gestalt psychology in her work. For years, Boas had urged his students to study the diffusion of practices and beliefs from one culture to the next, as a way of critiquing the evolutionists' belief that all societies evolve by going through a fixed series of cultural stages. What distinguished the Native Americans from the Europeans, according to a nineteenth-century evolutionist like Lewis Morgan, was that they were less fully evolved. Boas and his students destroyed that belief through their diffusion studies, which showed that people did not invent ideas according to their particular cultural stage, but simply borrowed them from neighboring peoples. The attention given to diffusion tended to blind investigators, however, to evidence of sharp differences between adjacent cultures. On a trip to the Southwest in 1925, Benedict noticed something that had escaped earlier researchers. Two adjacent peoples, the Zuñi and the Pima, while sharing much, were, as cultural totalities, strikingly different. The Zuñi were methodical, orderly, controlled, rational—Apollonian—in their approach to life. The neighboring Pima were emotional, violent, irrational—Dionysian—in theirs. Culture was more than a dispersion of ideas and behaviors across time and place, it occurred as a pattern—what later came to be known as a personality writ large.[108]

The notion of cultural patterning was not new. Boas, Parsons, and others had used it for some time as an idea that referred to a set of specific patterns of behavior, the pattern of American militarism, for instance, that Parsons saw so deeply entrenched in 1917. But Benedict was the first to see a culture as having a distinctive perspective or psychological mind set. This approach set her off not only from the diffusionists, but also from the functionalists— anthropologists like the British scholars A. R. Radcliffe-Brown and Bronislaw Malinowski—who tried to understand how the different elements of each culture made up a functioning whole. Benedict appreciated the interest of the functionalist in trying to explain the interrelationship of cultural elements, but she objected—as did most American anthropologists—to what she saw as the functionalists' inability to deal with dysfunction and change.[109]

Benedict's deafness and her training in linguistics gave her an additional insight. Borrowing from phonology—the study of sound—she posited that culture was much like hearing. Just as any individual can pick up on only a limited range of auditory stimuli, so any culture, to be coherent, must limit the possible range of psychological types that it honors. Benedict invented the metaphor of the "arc" of human potential, only part of which any given culture could incorporate.[110]

Benedict put those ideas together in a paper, "Psychological Types in the Cultures of the Southwest" (1928), which caused a stir at the Twenty-third International Congress of Americanists, in New York. Contrasting the Apollonian Zuñi and the Dionysian Plains Indians, she posited that a culture's particular personality gave it direction and purpose; the basic pattern of the culture served as an ideal, providing a standard or norm of acceptable thought and behavior, and mediating change. "The fundamental psychological set," she concluded, produced "an intricate cultural pattern to express its own preferences." Those preferences fundamentally shaped individual development.[111]

The preoccupation of the Columbia anthropologists with culture and its ability to shape individual development was intensified by the transformation of the neighborhood around Columbia University from a predominantly Jewish neighborhood to one almost entirely black. Determined to challenge prevailing beliefs about black inferiority, Boas sent his students into Harlem to administer psychological exams.[112] One of those investigators, Otto Klineberg, the grandson of Austrian Jewish immigrants to Canada, proved through extensive studies, both in Harlem and in parts of the South from which African Americans were migrating, that the scores of blacks in the North rose as they had longer contact with northern culture, suggesting that intelligence was by no means fixed.[113]

All of Boas's testers were white, until the arrival of Zora Neale Hurston. Intent on developing as a writer, Hurston majored in English at Barnard, but her adviser urged her to round out her education by exploring the social sciences. Intrigued by the idea of studying anthropology, she took an introductory course with Gladys Reichard and signed up for independent study with her in anthropometry, the study of human body measurements for use in anthropological classification and comparison. Standing on Lenox Avenue with a pair of calipers, Hurston set about measuring heads. "Almost nobody else could stop the average Harlemite on Lenox Avenue," Langston Hughes later remembered, "and measure his head with a strange-looking anthropological device and not get bawled out for the attempt, except Zora, who used to stop anyone whose head looked interesting, and measure it." Hurston studied with Ruth Benedict the following year, when Reichard received a Guggenheim Fellowship and Benedict took over her courses at Barnard. Reichard and Benedict brought Hurston to Boas's attention. Recognizing Hurston's intelligence and ability to relate to the black community, Boas immediately swept her up into his campaign to transform the way Americans thought about race He admitted her to graduate work, taught her the methods of anthropological fieldwork, and sent her to Florida to collect folklore for her doctoral dissertation. Like Boas's other students, Hurston revered her mentor and adopted the female students' nickname for him. One day she burst into his office, asking for "Papa Franz," and Boas's secretary told her she had better not let the professor hear her say that. "Of course, I knew better," Hurston later recalled, "but at a social gathering of the department of anthropology at his house a few nights later, I brought it up. 'Of course Zora is my daughter. Certainly!' he said with a smile, 'Just one of my missteps, that's all.'"[114]

Although Hurston never completed a dissertation, she made important contributions to anthropology through her study of folklore, both in the vast material she collected and in the methodological insights she provided. She credited her academic training with Franz Boas, Gladys Reichard, and Ruth Benedict with giving her the perspective to "see my people as they really are." At the same time, however, she worried that her attempt to be objective entailed risks. "I found that it did not do to be too detached as I stepped aside to study them. I had to go back and dress as they did, talk as they did, live their life, so that I could get into my stories the world I knew as a child."[115] Of all the Columbia anthropologists, Hurston was the most experimental in her writing, the most self-conscious about the role of the anthropologist, and the most sensitive to the power of the investigator. In *Mules and Men* (1935), she has a female character try to kill her; that is, the

Zora Neale Hurston (1891–1960)
First African American graduate of Barnard
College (1928) and writer, anthropologist,
and folklorist, as photographed by Carl Van
Vechten, 1934. (Yale Collection of American
Literature, Beinecke Rare Book and Manuscript
Library. Courtesy of the estate of Zora Neale
Hurston)

informant tries to kill the observer who is trying to abscond with folk knowledge "before it is too late." Hurston's point was that the observer changes
conditions by her very presence. The perspective she brought to anthropology from her own experience as a poor southern black woman, together with
the insights she brought from anthropology to literature, had a profound influence on later generations. As the literary critic Graziela Hernandez has
observed, "by calling her own interpretive power into question," Hurston insisted that researchers and writers alike "recognize the imitations of their
representational strategies." In doing so, Hurston urged investigators to be
aware that their very presence threatened the cultures they sought to save.[116]

SEXUAL TABOOS

Boas's female students were interested in psychology because it gave them a
way of questioning negative assumptions about female intelligence and personality. It interested them, too, because it challenged Victorian assumptions about sex. They read Sigmund Freud, Havelock Ellis, and Magnus
Hirschfeld and debated the relevance of their theories to their own lives—
lives that they lived in the same experimental spirit they directed toward
their studies. Elsie Clews Parsons set the standard. In the 1920s, one of the
greatest impediments to women working in the field was the taboo against
women and men traveling together, a taboo based, in turn, on men's diffi-

culty in seeing women except through the lens of sex. The School of Engineering, which faced a similar problem when it sent geologists into the field, had settled the matter in the 1890s by asking the trustees to bar women from the school, a decision that was not reversed until World War II.[117] Anthropology took a different approach. Parsons and others argued that anthropology needed women in the field, for women could more easily gain the confidence of other women and children than could men. To facilitate fieldwork, some women married their co-workers, but for most women, marriage to another anthropologist was not an option. Parsons traveled with a number of men, with whom she had very different levels of intimacy. Her point was that she traveled for the sake of fieldwork in which they had common interests. In some cases, a sexual relation was involved; in other cases, not. She insisted that sex was a private matter that should not be confused with work. With considerable difficulty, and amid raised eyebrows, she resolutely set about making it possible for women and men to work in the field as colleagues.[118]

Creating greater freedom of movement for heterosexual researchers was one thing; creating freedom for homosexual researchers was another matter entirely. Homosexuality was so strongly tabooed that knowledge of such a relationship could destroy a career. Tabooed or not, homosexuality, as well as bisexuality, flourished at Columbia in the 1920s and 1930s. When Margaret Mead arrived at Barnard in 1920, she immediately set about organizing a group of undergraduates who embraced both political and sexual radicalism. Drawn to the grand gesture, they sang the Communist "Internationale" in the school dining room on May Day, joined the Intercollegiate Socialist League, marched on picket lines, and, in response to a conservative commencement speaker's insult, adopted the name Communist Morons. In Mead's memoir, she recalled that the group, half Jewish and half gentile, were linked also by a common love of poetry and a sense of being part of the cultural avant-garde. Together they explored Greenwich Village, paid homage to Edna St. Vincent Millay, and studied theater with Barnard's "contemporary-minded Minor W. Latham," who dubbed them the Ash Can Cats after a group of painters they admired. According to Mead, the Barnard group debated the theories of Freud and "learned about the existence of homosexuality . . . mainly through the occasional covert stories that drifted down to us through our more sophisticated friends and through upper classmen who were close to some members of the faculty."[119] In fact, Mead quickly became a sophisticate herself, embracing free love with women and men alike.[120]

The course of anthropology was most greatly influenced by Mead's relationship with Benedict, who lived near Columbia in a rented room during the week and returned to Bedford Hills, New York, to her husband, from whom she was increasingly estranged, on the weekends. Mead awakened in Benedict sexual possibilities she seems to have been struggling against much of her life. For Mead, the relationship proved to be one in a series of love affairs with women and men she engaged in throughout her life. Married three times, she later reported finding greater physical fulfillment with men, but greater spiritual fulfillment with women, most especially Benedict.[121] Mead had affairs with lesbians, but did not think of herself as one. Nor did she regard herself as bisexual; she preferred the more fluid and, she thought, less biological term "mixed type." For Benedict, the affair with Mead had a different meaning—not a revelation of "mixed type" tendencies, but an acceptance of homosexual feelings she had long denied. Fundamentally monogamous, she was deeply hurt by Mead's inconstancy. And yet the relationship with Mead helped her separate from her husband in 1930 and find love with another woman, Natalie Raymond, the following year.[122]

Mead's and Benedict's sexual experimentation carried real risks. Even in the Columbia anthropology department, where the valuing of human difference was a point of honor, tolerance did not extend to include the concept—much less the reality—of homosexuality. Boas characterized homosexuality as one of the "abnormal sexual habits." Edward Sapir, among Mead and Benedict's closest friends, judged homosexuality to be "unnatural," adding "the cult of the 'naturalness' of homosexuality fools no one but those who need a rationalization of their personal sex problems."[123] Although there were other lesbians in anthropology, including Gladys Reichard at Barnard, their sexual identity remained carefully concealed. So anxious was Mead about the danger her personal life posed to her career that she never revealed her many-sided love life even to the daughter, Mary Catherine Bateson, she bore in 1939. In fact, once when her daughter confessed to a brief lesbian encounter, Mead upbraided her for not having considered the damage to her mother's career the relationship might have caused if news of it had become public.[124] In the 1890s, women who loved one another raised few suspicions; women were expected to love one another spiritually, not physically. But as the work of Havelock Ellis and Sigmund Freud gained greater currency, female attachments, if discovered, invited trouble.

In 1922, Sholem Asch's Yiddish drama *The God of Vengeance* featured a lesbian character. When the play moved uptown from Greenwich Village, the police closed it down and arrested the entire cast. Four years later, Edouard Bourdet's play *The Captive*, about the breakup of a marriage by the wife's lesbian lover, opened on Broadway and attracted hundreds of female couples to each performance. The police shut it down, too. The following year, the New York legislature passed a law banning any play that depicted "sex perversion." And in 1929, a complaint from the New York Society for the Suppression of Vice prompted the police to remove Radclyffe Hall's *The Well of Loneliness* from all bookstores. The fear of harassment by the police and even arrest discouraged open displays of affection between women. Under such circumstances, Barnard's female environment offered a cover for a good deal of discreet experimentation, both physical and intellectual. Mead's theater teacher, Minor Latham, was a well-known lesbian; so, too, were many of her Barnard friends, including the poet Leonie Adams.[125]

Virginia Gildersleeve approached the thorny matter of sex at Barnard in an aloof and determinedly evenhanded way. From the moment she assumed the position of dean at Barnard, she supported women who wanted to marry. When a young assistant in physics announced her plans to marry in 1912, Gildersleeve responded, "How nice, I wish you much happiness." When the physics teacher inquired whether marrying would jeopardize her career, as had been the case with her predecessor, Gildersleeve responded, "As long as you do your work here satisfactorily, your marriage seems to me entirely your own business." In her memoir, Gildersleeve professed not to have given the matter any thought, but she was almost certainly affected by the citywide campaign then being conducted by Elsie Clews Parsons and Henrietta Rodman to guarantee married schoolteachers the right to continue working. Gildersleeve did not limit her support to faculty women's right to marry. In 1931, with the help of two Barnard alumnae who were staunch feminists and married career women—Helen Rogers Reid of the class of 1903 and Alice Duer Miller of the class of 1899—and with the example of the French government (whose policies she knew well as part of her work with the International Federation of University Women), Gildersleeve persuaded the Barnard College Board of Trustees to enact a maternity policy that provided one semester off at full pay or a year off at half pay for all new faculty mothers. In the first year, three women took advantage of the new policy. Gildersleeve also wrote many articles and gave more speeches about the importance of encouraging women to prepare for and pursue careers whether or not they married.[126]

Married women were not always as supportive of her as she was of them. In her 1954 memoir, Gildersleeve poignantly protested the "particularly cruel and unwholesome discrimination against *unmarried* women," like herself, who chose to spend their lives living with other women. She attributed this trend to "the less responsible psychologists and psychiatrists of the day," who voiced "disrespect for spinsters in the teaching profession as 'inhibited'

Honoring Virginia Crocheron
Gildersleeve

Helen Rogers Reid (Barnard 1903), chair of the
Barnard College Board of Trustees; Virginia
Crocheron Gildersleeve (Barnard 1899); and
Nicholas Murray Butler (Columbia College
1882), president of Columbia University, at the
celebration of Gildersleeve's twenty-five years
as dean of Barnard College, in 1936. (Barnard
College Archives)

and 'frustrated.'" Gildersleeve never identified herself as a lesbian, preferring
instead the adjective "celibate," but celibacy did not mean loneliness or a
lack of intimacy.[127] At the end of World War I, she met the English professor Caroline Spurgeon, the first British woman to hold a university chair,
whose work on Shakespeare's imagery provided inspiration for Benedict's
work on culture, and the two English scholars lived together until Spurgeon's death in 1943. Thereafter, the central person in Gildersleeve's life was
a Barnard English professor, Elizabeth Reynard, with whom she lived until
her death. Those long-term relationships may or may not have had a physical dimension, but they were clearly de facto marriages in all other respects.
The example of those relationships conveyed the message, however oblique-
ly, that in Gildersleeve's view one's private life was one's own business. This
opinion held not only for faculty but also for students, at least for those who
were discreet. As a result, and despite the clear danger involved, some of the
most interesting writing coming out of Barnard and Columbia in the 1920s
and 1930s dealt with sexual themes, as scholars tried to create a more open
world for sexual expression.

In 1925, Margaret Mead embarked on a trip to Samoa to investigate a
question that Boas had long wanted studied: Were the stresses of adolescence, so common in the West, universal? This trip, which resulted in
Mead's first book, the hugely successful Coming of Age in Samoa (1928), answered Boas's question with a clear no. In almost every way, the passage to

adulthood in Samoa was easier than it was in the West. Not that conflict was unknown. Indeed, one chapter, "The Girl in Conflict," deals explicitly with the place of misfits in Samoa, and provided Mead with an opportunity to consider a topic that she had discussed with Benedict at length: how different societies treat their deviants. The deviant was a popular topic among social scientists in the 1920s. Typically the word "deviant" had negative implications, and the task was to try to help the person—a wayward girl or a delinquent boy—meet social expectations. But Mead defined deviance simply as a type not capitalized on by the dominant society, and she chose to look at deviance as a potentially positive response to social constraint. The delinquent girl, someone who might be too heterosexually expressive or who, perhaps, gave evidence of homosexuality, could be considered delinquent if she behaved with shame, Mead believed; but a girl who was an advocate of free love, who protested convention, ought to be seen as responding in a positive way to social control. Mead was suggesting that lesbianism should be considered harmful only when it was accompanied by the internalization of society's negative judgment through drinking or self-hating.[128]

Benedict picked up that theme a few years later, shortly after falling in love with Natalie Raymond, in "Anthropology and the Abnormal," an article that became the foundation for *Patterns of Culture*. She began by taking the example of a trance as an abnormal state in Western societies, but one that in certain Native American societies was viewed as a door to prestige when exhibited by a tribal leader. She proceeded to homosexuality—an aberrant condition in Western cultures—and pointed to its acceptance in some other cultures. In ancient Greece, for instance, homosexuality was regarded as a "major means to the good life." Among the Plains Indians in America, as a further example, the institution of the *berdache*—men who took the dress and occupations of women—was also honored. Benedict believed that in a society that institutionalized homosexuality, most people would be homosexuals, but in America such a person could participate in the dominant culture "only by doing violence to his whole personality"; the alternative was to be branded as abnormal because he has "betrayed his culture." Only if psychiatrists learned to encourage tolerance and appreciation toward less usual types would society be able to benefit from a fuller range of talents and would those deemed abnormal be able to flourish. Reading Benedict's article today, one is struck by the timidity of her remarks about homosexuality. Given the hostile climate in which she wrote, however, it constituted a call to arms.[129]

Zora Neale Hurston was just as secretive about her sexual liaisons as Mead and Benedict, but she was far more open in her celebration of female sexual freedom. Hurston had a reputation for being very much a part of Harlem's sexually experimental culture, with its nightclubs and "buffet flats," which catered to sexually diverse crowds. While lesbianism was regarded as deviant in Harlem, bisexuality suggested an abundant sexuality, and Hurston was nothing if not abundant where sex was concerned. "Zora would go anywhere, you know—one time at least," her friend Arna Bontemps observed. She seems not, however, to have had any lesbian love affairs, unless one counts her friendship with the singer Ethel Waters, who was widely known to be bisexual. They became so close that Hurston believed they could speak for each other. "I am her friend and her tongue is in my mouth," was the way Hurson described their friendship, in classic double entendre. At the same time that she was making her way in sexually emancipated Harlem, Hurston was conducting a long-distance relationship with Herbert Sheen, a man she had met at Howard. In 1927, on a field trip to Florida, she married him, but the marriage proved short-lived. She left him a few days later and divorced him in 1931. Four years later, she fell in love with Percy Punter, a Columbia graduate student twenty years her junior. Punter was "the real love affair of my life." But Punter wanted her to give up her career, which she could not do, and so the relationship ended, too. Self-sufficiency was her lodestar.[130]

PATTERNS OF CULTURE

Benedict, Mead, and Hurston's preoccupation with issues of gender, sexuality, and race culminated in the mid-1930s in the publication of three of their most important books: Benedict's *Patterns of Culture* (1934), Mead's *Sex and Temperament in Three Primitive Societies* (1935), and Hurston's *Their Eyes Were Watching God* (1937). The authors' careers had diverged by then. Only Benedict remained at Columbia. Boas secured Mead a position as curator at the American Museum of Natural History in 1928, and she divided her time between the museum and fieldwork. Mead would later teach the occasional course in fieldwork methods at Columbia, but she never held a full-time position there. Hurston supported herself through her writing and the occasional fellowship. Intellectually, however, the three women remained remarkably close. Indeed, so similar were the works that they published in the mid-1930s, in their structure and themes, that they constituted a three-way conversation.

Each author adopted a tripartite structure. Benedict and Mead chose three tribes; Hurston imagined three differently situated African American communities. In each case, two of the cultures were either violent or oppressive to women; the third was peaceful and egalitarian. Benedict's chapters on the Dobu and the Kwakiutl in *Patterns of Culture*, like Mead's chapters on the Mundugumor and the Tchambuli in *Sex and Temperament*, caricatured aspects of American life—the cutthroat individualism and conspicuous consumption that had assumed central importance in American capitalism. The Zuñi and Arapesh, in pointed contrast, accorded women significant authority.[131]

Hurston adopted a similar strategy in *Their Eyes Were Watching God*, by following the development of Janie, her black protagonist, through three communities. The first is the racially violent community of Janie's grandmother, Nanny, a woman raped as a slave by her white owner. The female mulatto offspring of this union, Janie's mother, grows up to be raped, in turn, by a white schoolteacher and to produce Janie, whom she abandons to Nanny's care. In an effort to halt the cycle of rape and abandonment, Nanny marries Janie off to an older black farmer, whom Janie detests. Badly treated, Janie flees to the all-black town of Eatonville, Florida, to become the wife of the town's mayor. While Janie's husband gains a powerful voice in a culture removed from the dominant white society, Janie must settle for life on a pedestal, a mute trophy of male achievement—reminiscent of a Kwakiutl woman. Only by escaping to the more egalitarian world of black migrant laborers does she discover true love and gender equality. But even there, violence intrudes, brought by nature and a hostile white world. Her lover turns violent, and Janie kills him in self-defense. Sad but free, she returns to Eatonville, where, among the women of the town, she discovers her own voice. Telling her tale to her best friend, Janie authorizes her to speak to the others: "Dat's just de same as me, 'cause mah tongue is in mah friend's mouf."[132]

Mead, Benedict, and Hurston all portrayed gender as socially constructed, and each concluded her book with a chapter celebrating individual (especially female) autonomy. But in their treatment of sexuality and race, they differed from one another, and they did so in ways that continue to mark scholarly debates to this day. Mead argued explicitly, and Hurston implied, that sexual attraction was highly fluid; only one's temperament was biologically fixed. Homosexuality, in Mead's view, was not innate, but the result of social pressure. In America, she believed, many men with passive temperaments were pushed into a homosexual identity because society would not accept their submissive natures. In Hurston's telling, same-sex love was a choice that could free one from gender oppression. Benedict disagreed. In her view, homosexuality was the product of "congenial drives." Societies that honored sexual difference benefited from the talents of their "deviants"; those that allowed prejudice to triumph did not.[133]

The authors differed, too, in their treatment of race. Although all advanced the case for cultural relativism, only Hurston examined the ways in which gender relations varied, depending on one's position within a larger racial hierarchy. To Mead and Benedict, race was a category that people of goodwill should ignore once anthropologists could demonstrate that it was socially constructed. To Hurston, race was an embodied and historically potent reality, something that must stand at the center of any analysis of gender or sexuality. Only by examining the dominance of whites over blacks in American society, could one understand the sexual oppression of women, especially black women.

THE ANTHROPOLOGIST AS WRITER

Benedict, Mead, and Hurston deserve to be remembered not only as key contributors to modern debates about race, gender, and sex, but also as innovative writers. Part of the modernist literary tradition pioneered by Gertrude Stein, HD, Marianne Moore, and others, they sought to move beyond the image of the sentimental female writer of the Victorian era, without accepting the elitist and antiwoman overtones of such male modernists as T. S. Eliot and Ezra Pound.[134] They owed much to Virginia Woolf, whose most experimental work, *The Waves*, was about characters trying (and failing) to make connections. Benedict read *The Waves* when it came out in 1931 and immediately wrote to Mead, "Did you like *The Waves*?" she asked, and "did you keep thinking how you'd set down everybody you knew in a similar fashion? I did." Benedict was then working on *Patterns of Culture*, and she structured her narrative according to the pattern adopted by Woolf. Her "way of setting people down seemed very exciting to me," she confessed to Mead, "and I wish a whole crop of authors would try it; then there'd be lots of different sorts of people included." The point that Benedict sought to emphasize, and the one she thought that Woolf conveyed so effectively through her parallel narratives, was the difficulty of gaining perspective on one's own situation. "To me of course," Benedict wrote, Woolf's literary masterpiece was fundamentally "about life's being a wrapping and wrapping oneself in one's own cocoon. What you can spin is all you have to work with, and the result is altogether dependent on that. Don't you think, given the limited types she allows herself, she's done it beautifully?"[135] To Benedict, how one wrote was as important as what one wrote. It was Benedict's rhetorical strategy of conveying radically different perspectives in a way that made them seem connected that was most innovative in her work, and most important in shaping the work of Mead and Hurston. For all three authors, multiple perspectives were a goal to be achieved, not, as with John Erskine, a defect to be overcome.

Many male colleagues criticized the literary efforts of Columbia's most widely read female anthropologists, their "wind in the palm-trees style of writing," as Evans Pritchard once complained of Mead's prose.[136] Female readers were not necessarily more appreciative. Although Hurston went on to write nine books, win two Guggenheim Fellowships, and achieve considerable critical success, Virginia Gildersleeve, for one, found the dialect that she used in her novels extremely off-putting. But more recently, the approaches pioneered by Columbia's female anthropologists have gained a more appreciative audience, not only among the public, but also in academe.[137] Clifford Geertz sums up this more recent view in his writing about Ruth Benedict. Calling Benedict the "founder of discursivity," he likens her rhetorical strategy to that employed by Jonathan Swift in *Gulliver's Travels*: "the juxtaposition of the all-too-familiar and the wildly exotic in such a way that they change places."[138]

Benedict summed up her dual debt to empirical research and literary criticism in her presidential address, "Anthropology and the Humanities," at the 1947 meeting of the American Anthropological Association. She began by acknowledging anthropology's roots in science and emphasized that those roots were secure. Anthropology's relationship to the humanities, however, needed defense. For centuries, the study of the humanities, especially the study of the Greeks, had given intellectuals their principal cross-cultural insights. Then, in the mid-nineteenth century, the sciences began to take leadership away. Science and the humanities were not mutually exclusive, she insisted: "modern anthropology handicaps itself in method and insight by neglecting the work of the great humanists." She praised, in particular, the value of literary criticism as practiced by A. C. Bradley in his work on Shakespeare, and urged her listeners to follow the "core of his method"—that is, to "surrender to the text itself," to pay close attention "to what was said," but, just as important, "to what is not said." In the same way, students had to examine not only "what was done," but also what was "not done." She recommended, as well, the work of Caroline Spurgeon, whose study of Shakespeare's imagery offered a "technique useful in the study of comparative cultures," one that "can reveal symbolism and free association which fall into patterns and show processes congenial to the human mind in different cultures." Once "anthropologists include the mind of man in their subject matter," Benedict concluded hopefully, "the methods of science and the methods of the humanities complement each other. Any commitment to methods which exclude either approach is self-defeating."[139]

When Elsie Clews Parsons wrote her article "Patterns for Peace or War" in 1917, she concluded that culture was so powerful a force that reform efforts amounted to little more than tilting at windmills. Benedict, Mead, and Hurston took a more optimistic and a more individualistic view. Although all people were the product of their cultures, they argued, no culture could exercise perfect control. Inevitably, creative individuals, especially those who lived on cultural boundaries, would foster change. The most likely agents of change under those conditions were those with special insights into a given culture's unspoken assumptions: the myth tellers, the recounters of folktales, and the creative writers. Those were the people who took new cultural elements and used them to reshape tales to fit within the expectations of their culture. Those agents could serve as cultural stabilizers, but they could also deconstruct the foundational beliefs of a given culture by bringing unconscious fears and aspirations to the surface and subjecting them to scrutiny.[140] Neither Benedict, Mead, nor Hurston ever developed a theory about how, given their belief in cultural determinism, they thought an individual would be able to alter the direction of a given culture, but they embraced this deconstructing role for themselves and their students. It was not a role that most Columbia administrators welcomed.

VICTORY AND DEFEAT

In 1936, Benedict was assigned a seat in the Graduate Faculty of Philosophy, in anticipation of her promotion, at long last, to the rank of associate professor. Interestingly, this decision, though a long time in coming, seems to have been hurried along by the actions of Adolf Hitler. With Hitler's policies driving Jewish scholars from their academic posts in Germany, Columbia gained the opportunity to acquire some extraordinarily distinguished faculty. In 1934, Gildersleeve learned of the possibility of hiring the renowned archaeologist Margarete Bieber. In keeping with Bieber's academic stature, Gildersleeve inquired of Dean Howard McBain whether Bieber might be granted a tenured position at Columbia as well. McBain demurred on the grounds that, while he had no objection to breaking with tradition, he would rather that the first tenured appointment go to "some member of our own staff. . . . Assistant Professor Benedict for example." Pressure to hire a Jew, in short, helped McBain make the case to Butler for giving due recognition to Benedict.[141] Benedict's case was further helped by the declining health of Franz Boas, whom Butler forced into retirement, at the age of seventy-eight, in 1936. McBain named Benedict as acting executive director from 1936 to 1937, and apparently intended to make her permanent head thereafter, but

Butler insisted on appointing an ad hoc committee, chaired by the Columbia College dean, Herbert Hawkes, to look into the department's future. McBain died before the committee finished its work. The final report called for the appointment of Ralph Linton, then a professor at the University of Wisconsin, to be the permanent executive head.[142]

Boas was furious. Linton was the graduate student who had famously returned to Columbia after World War I dressed in uniform, only to be snubbed by the angry department chairman. Linton had gone on to complete his Ph.D. at Harvard. Although a dynamic teacher, he was not particularly known as a scholar. His book *The Study of Man* (1936) included only one footnote and no references. When Boas learned indirectly that the ad hoc committee had selected Linton, he wrote to the new dean, George B. Pegram, that Linton was good enough "in his place in Madison" but that he was a "mediocre man without any original ideas who would go on in a routine way" rather than offer genuine leadership.[143]

As a sop to Boas and Benedict, the Committee on Anthropology also recommended that Benedict be promoted to associate professor with tenure. In 1937, Benedict thus became the first woman ever to be promoted to tenure at Columbia. Achieving a tenured associate professorship on the graduate faculty required exceptional talent and absolute dedication. But even women who possessed those qualities only rarely received further recognition. Having risen through the Columbia ranks, Benedict had little leverage with the administration, despite the fact that the Committee on Anthropology had conceded that she was a "scholar of no less distinction than any of those whom we might have recommended for the position of executive head of the Department."[144] Benedict was not promoted to the position of full professor until 1948, a few months before her death. Mary Caldwell won promotion to full professor in chemistry at the same time.[145]

The first woman to reach the rank of full professor at Columbia was an outsider. In 1940, the Department of English hired Marjorie Hope Nicolson, then dean of the faculty at Smith College and newly elected national head of Phi Beta Kappa. A brilliant scholar of seventeenth-century literature, Nicolson succeeded far better than most other academic women of her day in winning the acceptance of male colleagues. Careful to avoid political controversy, she emphasized to an interviewer upon her appointment to Columbia, "I am no feminist."[146]

Although Benedict was denied both promotion to full professor and the chairmanship of anthropology in 1937, she continued to attract students, especially women, until her untimely death from heart disease at the age of sixty-one in 1948. At that point, women, who had come to constitute 50 percent of the graduate students in anthropology under her leadership, quickly lost ground.[147] No other woman won tenure in anthropology until the 1970s. In the meantime, the bridge that Benedict had struggled to build between the humanities and the sciences was badly damaged. Cultural studies went into eclipse in anthropology and elsewhere in the university, as World War II and the Cold War gave science a new importance in university life. In the social sciences, historical materialism, functionalism, and empiricism competed for control. In the humanities, a new emphasis on structure eclipsed earlier interest in cultural context. Over them all, science reigned supreme. The women who succeeded at Columbia during World War II and in the postwar era did so on the terms established by those—all men—in charge of science.

FIVE

WOMANPOWER

THE BATTLE of Britain, the desperate aerial clash that saved the British from Nazi invasion in 1940, forced the British, and later the Americans, to reconsider some of their most settled assumptions about women's place in public life. As the struggle to defend the island nation exhausted all available sources of "manpower," government officials began to speak of the need to press "womanpower" into service. Exploiting their leverage to the fullest, British feminist leaders warned that the country could count on its women only if the government promised to grant them better pay and more responsible positions than it had been willing to offer in the past.[1] Within two years, the idea of "womanpower" had caught on at the United States Women's Bureau, where officials were fighting their own battle to improve opportunities for women. As the American female labor force ballooned from 12 to 18 million under the pressure of wartime demand, women entered fields long reserved exclusively for men and secured wages that doubled, even tripled, their previous earnings. In most quarters, those gains proved short-lived. Following the war, concern for "womanpower" faded as a celebration of domesticity enveloped the country. But among a small group of scholars at Columbia, the idea persisted, inspiring scores of studies that culminated in the book *Womanpower* (1957). At the height of what Betty Friedan would later dub the "feminine mystique," *Womanpower* called on the country to encourage all women—including mothers—to participate in the workforce and urged policy makers to reform American laws and expand social services to make that participation possible.

TRAINED BRAINS

No one worked harder to advance women's interests during World War II than Barnard College's dean, Virginia Gildersleeve. In articles, radio broadcasts, and speeches, she hammered away at her favorite theme: to win the war, the nation needed "trained brains"; to have enough, the country would have to turn to its women. Gildersleeve did everything she could to keep her students in school, to dissuade them from quitting to take a job in a factory—no matter how glamorous wartime propaganda made the job seem. She even did what she could to keep from losing her students to marriage. Accepting the fact that, given wartime pressures, marriage to departing soldiers would occur, she drew the line at students following their new husbands to wherever they might be sent. In her view, young wives were better off at Barnard, completing their education, than they were staying near some military camp.[2]

The war offered Barnard students an unprecedented chance to find work as physicists, chemists, mathematicians, and social scientists. Gildersleeve was aware of the Manhattan Project at Columbia, just across Broadway from Barnard, and she pressed to have women hired there. She knew that there was a need for engineers, and she used that knowledge to win women admission to Columbia's School of Engineering in 1942—the last professional school to hold out against women.[3] She housed one of the country's foremost code-breaking programs at Barnard. She established one of the nation's first programs in international relations, to prepare women for the Foreign Service. And she won a place for women in the armed forces by helping to found the WAVES (Women Accepted for Voluntary Emergency Service), the navy's female reserve officers' corps. The WAVES, under Gildersleeve's leadership as president of its advisory board, became a military branch of the Seven Sisters. Its highest-ranking officer was the president of Wellesley, Mildred McAfee; its second-in-command was Gildersleeve's close friend, the Barnard English professor Elizabeth Reynard; its officers—8,500, at one time—were college graduates or had at least two years of college with two more years of professional or business experience.[4]

Gildersleeve had no illusions about what would happen to women's opportunities after the war: they would almost certainly shrink, perhaps drastically. But, she insisted, where opportunity remained, her students were going to have as big a competitive advantage as she and the educational resources at her command could ensure. More than a decade before the publication of *Womanpower*, Gildersleeve was leading the way.

WOMEN AND THE RISE OF BIG SCIENCE

The rapid expansion of the sciences at Columbia following World War I had already created greater opportunity for women at the university than existed anywhere else in the country. As of 1938, the graduate faculties employed twenty-two female scientists in fields ranging from chemistry to psychology. Together with Barnard, which employed twelve more, the university led the country, though it bears noting that a number of the women's colleges were close behind: Wellesley employed thirty-three female scientists; Vassar, twenty-six; Mount Holyoke, twenty-five; and Hunter, twenty-five.[5] Departments in the Graduate Faculty of Pure Science and the College of Physicians and Surgeons routinely hired women as technicians, librarians, research associates, and instructors. In 1929, in a display of the dual importance of growing enrollments and effective patronage, the chairman of the chemistry department, Henry C. Sherman, opened the professorial ranks to women when he advanced his protégé, Mary Letitia Caldwell, from instructor to assistant professor.[6] Aleita Hopping followed at Physicians and Surgeons in 1930, when she rose to the rank of assistant professor of physiology. Virginia Apgar (creator of the "Apgar Score," a measure of newborn well-being) was the first woman to reach the rank of full professor at the medical school, when she won promotion in 1949, the year after Caldwell reached that rank in chemistry.[7]

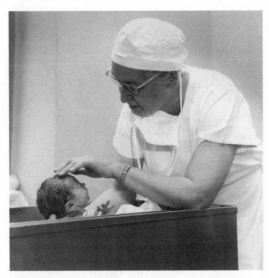

Virginia Apgar (1909–1974)
Graduate of Mount Holyoke College (1929) and Columbia University College of Physicians and Surgeons (1933), anesthesiologist and obstetrician, creator of the "Apgar Score," and first woman full professor at Physicians and Surgeons (1949), as photographed by Elizabeth Wilcox. (Columbia University Health Sciences Library Archives)

Opportunities for women expanded in other science departments, because Columbia tended to hire its own, and female graduate students therefore enjoyed an advantage as insiders. Even married women were able to find work at Columbia, because the university did not apply nepotism rules as systematically as most other universities did.[8] This liberality was due in part to Columbia's balkanized structure. A husband might work at Barnard College and a wife at Teachers College, or a wife might work in the graduate faculty and her husband at the medical school. By World War II, the demand for scientific talent grew so acute that a wife and husband might even work in the same division. More typically, job opportunities elsewhere in the city—in other colleges and universities and in the city's myriad laboratories—made it possible for a wife to accept a position at Columbia with the assurance that her husband would be able to find an acceptable job nearby. And yet, despite the relative flexibility that Columbia and New York City afforded academic couples, married women faced limited opportunity. In most cases, they worked in off-ladder positions, not as regular faculty.

Even in biology, where women and men earned M.A. and Ph.D. degrees in equal numbers, Columbia hired women as research associates only. The embryologist Salome Waelsch, who received her Ph.D. in Freiburg in 1925 and immigrated to the United States with her husband in 1933, remained stuck at the level of research associate in L.C. Dunn's biology lab in Schermerhorn Hall for seventeen years. Her husband, the Nobel Prize–winner Hans Spemann, was on the faculty of the College of Physicians and Surgeons. Only by leaving Columbia for the newly opened Albert Einstein College of Medicine in the late 1950s was Salome Waelsch able to achieve faculty rank.[9]

In physics, where, as in chemistry, one-third of the students were women, no woman advanced beyond the rank of instructor until after World War II. Not that physics lacked able women. One of the best students produced in the 1920s was Lucy Hayner, born in 1898, who graduated Phi Beta Kappa from Barnard in 1919 and went on to earn her Ph.D. in physics at Columbia in 1925. In recognition of her outstanding promise, the physics faculty awarded her the F. A. P. Barnard Fellowship for postdoctoral work in England and Germany and feted her at the University Club on the eve of her departure for Europe, where she worked at the Cavendish Laboratory at Cambridge University and then at the University of Göttingen in Germany. At Göttingen, she met another American fellowship holder, Dr. Bernhard Kurrelmeyer, of Johns Hopkins, whom she married in 1927. She had returned to the United States in 1925, whereupon she won a position on the research staff at General Electric, a rare accomplishment for a woman at that time. Kurrelmeyer, in the meantime, accepted work as an instructor at Columbia.

Following their marriage in 1927, Hayner continued at GE until the birth of the couple's son in 1928. She then moved back to New York City, where, in 1930, she accepted a part-time position as an assistant to her former adviser, Harold Webb, in his physics laboratory. When he retired, she assumed responsibility for what came to be known as "Lucy Lab." Hayner remained an instructor for the remainder of the decade. In 1939, the physics chairman, George Braxton Pegram, made Hayner an associate in the department. Having worked at Columbia for eight years as an instructor, she had exceeded the time the university allowed its faculty to work at that rank without promotion—a regulation that was designed to protect instructors from being exploited but that often led to their being fired. Pegram apparently wanted to keep Hayner but did not want to advance her to the rank of assistant professor, which, in time, would require either advancement to yet higher ranks or dismissal. He therefore moved her to the off-ladder position of associate. Although disappointed, Hayner never seems to have sought out other women to protest, and while she considered leaving Columbia, she ultimately stayed out of loyalty when war came.[10]

It is not clear how much of the delay in advancement was due to prejudice and how much was a function of Hayner's limited engagement in work outside her laboratory teaching, either in the work of the department or in the profession. Her mentor at Barnard, Margaret Maltby, believed that marriage was largely to blame. "Alas! Marriage makes a tremendous change among women in such an absorbing time and energy consuming science as physics," Maltby lamented. While Hayner's husband left Columbia for the newly opened Brooklyn College, where he built a career in teaching and research that won him the status of fellow in the American Physical Society, she dedicated herself to full-time teaching in the physics laboratory at Columbia and to raising their son. The responsibilities of motherhood may have slowed Hayner's research, but it does not entirely explain her career path. Several of the men with whom she had studied in graduate school whose publication record was delayed, as was hers, by heavy teaching duties were promoted to the position of assistant professor ahead of her. Dana Paul Mitchell, for instance, who, like Hayner, graduated from college in 1919, but did not complete his Ph.D. until 1936 (eleven years after she did), was promoted to assistant professor in 1940. Not until I. I. Rabi assumed the chairmanship of the physics department, after World War II, did Hayner's fortunes change. Rabi, the son of Jewish immigrants and the recipient of the

F. A. P. Barnard Fellowship at Columbia two years after Hayner, promoted Hayner to assistant professor in 1946.[11]

The acute labor shortage created by World War II brought other women into the department in those years, as Columbia expanded its research facilities under the government-financed Manhattan Project. Two scientists, in particular—Maria Goeppert-Mayer and Chien-Shiung Wu—both immigrants and both mothers, would build on the opportunity they found there to achieve international fame in the postwar years. Both physicists faced prejudice as women and experienced delays to their careers as a result of the responsibilities they assumed as mothers. But their background and timing gave them an advantage that had eluded Hayner and others in the interwar years. Both Goeppert-Mayer, born and raised in Germany, and Wu, born and raised in China, came from elite families in which professional accomplishment for women was accepted to a degree that was still unusual in the United States. Moreover, both came to Columbia at a critical moment, one in which some of the world's leading physicists had converged to work on the central problems of the day. From that opportunity, each was able to move on to make important contributions.

Goeppert-Mayer was born in 1906, the only child of a distinguished academic family. She trained as a mathematician and physicist at the University of Göttingen, where she studied with several of the greatest physicists of the day. Her Ph.D. thesis on the theory of double emission and absorption of light quanta was regarded as a fundamental contribution to the field. At Göttingen, she met and married an American chemist, Joseph Mayer, who had come to study on a Rockefeller Fellowship. In 1930, the couple left for Baltimore, where Mayer joined the physics department at Johns Hopkins. Normally, a physics department in this country would have been delighted to hire a scientist of Goeppert-Mayer's accomplishments, but rules preventing nepotism precluded that possibility at Hopkins. She turned, instead, to research, collaborating with her husband and other male scientists without holding a university post. By World War II, Joseph Mayer had accepted a professorship in chemistry at Columbia. Goeppert-Mayer joined the Manhattan Project, on which she worked with Harold Urey and Enrico Fermi. Hiring an English nanny to care for her two young children, she worked part time throughout the war. In 1946, the Mayers followed Urey and Fermi to the University of Chicago, he as a full professor, and she as an associate professor. Because of nepotism rules at Chicago, Goeppert-Mayer worked without salary, but she did so to be able to continue her research, which led to the development of a theory for the movement of electrons in the atom. Not having had a conventional scientific career, she hesitated to publish. When, on the urging of her husband, she finally did so, other physicists were publishing the same results. In 1963, she shared the Nobel Prize in Physics with them.[12]

Wu was born in 1912 in Nanking, where her parents were part of the reform movement that brought the Republic of China into being. Committed to sexual equality, her father founded a girls' school and her mother organized other mothers to send their daughters to it. Wu expected to be a schoolteacher, but her father, struck by her precocious talent for mathematics and science, encouraged her to become a physicist. Graduating first in her class from the local normal school, she won admission to National Central University, from which she graduated with a degree in physics in 1936. Immigrating to the United States, she earned her Ph.D. in physics at the University of California at Berkeley in 1940 under J. Robert Oppenheimer and the 1939 Nobel Prize–winner Ernest Lawrence. Married to a fellow Chinese physicist (Luke C. L. Yuan, the son of the second president of the Republic of China) in 1942, she came east to teach at Smith College. Lawrence believed that Wu was wasting her talent at Smith, which did not have the resources for her to continue her research. Urging her to move, he wrote to several institutions on her behalf, and she received offers from them all, but as a research associate, not as a professor. She moved first to Princeton and then to Columbia, where she joined the Manhattan Project in 1944 to work on uranium 235. After the war, she built on that work to become part of a three-person research team that in 1956 shattered the principle of parity in physics,

Chien-Shiung Wu (1913–1997)
Graduate of University of California at
Berkeley (Ph.D. 1940), physicist, and senior
scientist (1942–1952), associate professor
(1952–1958), and professor (1958–1980) at
Columbia University. (Columbia University
Archives–Columbiana Library)

an achievement for which the two men—both theorists—won the Noble Prize. Wu, an experimentalist rather than a theorist, was passed over, though many have since argued that she deserved it as much as the men did.[13]

TAKING ON THE WORLD

The accomplishments of women during World War II, at Columbia and across the country, prompted President Franklin Roosevelt to include a woman in the United States delegation to the conference to write the United Nations Charter in 1945. He appointed Virginia Gildersleeve. The only woman named to the delegation, Gildersleeve won her spot through both her work in support of the war and her reputation as an internationalist. That reputation dated back to World War I, when, influenced by Nicholas Murray Butler, Gildersleeve had begun speaking to Barnard students in 1916, even before America entered the war, about establishing an international organization. A "league to enforce peace," she called it. She thought that it should include an international court, but she also advocated establishing an organization that would foster contact among nations, even when there were no outstanding disputes. Many women leaders of her day—including, most notably, Jane Addams—were pacifists. Gildersleeve was not. She strongly supported the League of Nations, however, and worked on postwar committees to lobby the American public on its behalf. That work failed, but Gildersleeve enjoyed greater success within academe. When the war ended, a delegation of British educators came to the United States in search of innovations that might be usefully transplanted to England. One of those educators was Caroline Spurgeon. Meeting Spurgeon allowed Gildersleeve to broach the topic most on her mind: the need to establish an association that would foster international cooperation among like-minded academic women. Gildersleeve imagined an organization built on the model of the American Association of Collegiate Alumnae; Spurgeon had in mind her own British Federation of University Women. In 1919, they created the International Federation of University Women (IFUW), basing it in London with a second home in Paris at Reid Hall (made available by the publisher and Barnard College trustee Helen Rogers Reid). For two decades, between World War I and World War II, Gildersleeve worked through the IFUW to keep alive the spirit of international understanding, even as isolationism gripped her country. She twice served as president of the IFUW, became a trustee of the American College for Girls in Turkey and of the Near East College Association, and traveled throughout Europe and the Middle East. When war came again, Gildersleeve joined the Commission to Study the Organization of the Peace, headed by the Barnard history professor James T. Shotwell. Longtime colleagues and friends, both Shotwell and Gildersleeve had taken the seminar on medieval Europe taught by James Harvey Robinson in 1900. During World War II, they met once a month with fellow commissioners to plan America's participation in a world organization following the war. The group included Owen Lattimore, an Asia specialist for the Office of War Information who would later be falsely charged by Joseph McCarthy as a Russian spy; John Foster Dulles, a Wall Street lawyer who would go on to be Dwight D. Eisenhower's secretary of state; and Max Lerner, a syndicated columnist for the *New York Post*. The committee's recommendations influenced the work undertaken at Dumbarton Oaks in 1944, which, in turn, became the basis of the United Nations Charter proposals that Gildersleeve and the world's delegates took up in 1945.[14]

Shortly before Gildersleeve was to leave for San Francisco, a celebration was held in her honor at the Commodore Hotel. There she was feted by, among others, William Allan Neilson, who had been her dissertation adviser at Columbia. Neilson noted that Gildersleeve's appointment gave recognition to two important facts: first, the increasing importance of academically trained experts in politics, and, second, the increasing influence of women in world affairs. Neilson regretted that Gildersleeve would be the only woman in the United States delegation, "but that will not matter," he concluded, "if only the men will listen."[15]

Founding the United Nations
Virginia Crocheron Gildersleeve at the United Nations Charter Convention, 1945. (Barnard College Archives)

When the delegates from around the world assembled in San Francisco a couple of months later, they accepted the instructions worked out for them the previous year at Dumbarton Oaks and reaffirmed at Yalta in February 1945. They were to write a charter that addressed two issues. The first was the need to prevent future wars, which they were to accomplish through the creation of a security council. The second issue was the need to enhance human welfare, which they were to accomplish through the establishment of an economic and social council. Gildersleeve sought and received assignment to the committee responsible for creating this second council—the one, as she put it, in charge of doing things rather than preventing things from being done.[16] She took particular pride in helping insert into the charter's statement of purpose the following goals for people around the world: "higher standards of living, full employment, and conditions of economic and social progress and development." Moreover, she persuaded the delegates to adopt the following aim for the United Nations: "universal respect for human rights and fundamental freedoms for all without distinction as to race, sex, language, or religion."[17] Gildersleeve endorsed those goals not only because of their importance to the enhancement of human welfare, but also because she saw them as providing job opportunities for all the women who had been training to be health professionals, research scientists, lawyers, teachers, and social workers. She advocated nothing less than an international Works Progress Administration for educated women. To carry out its work, the council was given the power to appoint whatever commissions it deemed necessary, but Gildersleeve insisted that the charter require the appointment of one in particular: the Commission on Human Rights. This was the commission that, under the direction of Eleanor Roosevelt, would write the Universal Declaration of Human Rights three years later. That declaration, in turn, was to serve as the basis for all of the United Nations work on behalf of women throughout the world over the next two generations.[18]

Gildersleeve's work for the United Nations ensured that, when Columbia opened its newest professional school, the School of International Affairs, in 1946, women would have the opportunity to train for the foreign service, which grew enormously after the war.

MILLICENT MCINTOSH AND THE THEORY
OF THE BASQUE PAELLA

The end of World War II brought a tremendous backlash against the advances made by women during the war. Economists worried about the possibility of a recession unless women withdrew from the workforce. Psychoanalysts warned that women's growing careerism threatened their emotional health as well as that of their families.[19] Educators attacked colleges for treating women like men and urged curricular reform that would prepare women to be more effective homemakers and mothers. Women, argued Mills College's male president, Lynn White, would get far more from a course in the theory of the Basque paella than from a course in the philosophy of Immanuel Kant.[20]

Those words provoked a spirited counterattack at Barnard College, where Millicent Carey McIntosh took over from Virginia Gildersleeve in 1947. The niece of Bryn Mawr's president, M. Carey Thomas, and the daughter of Anthony Morris and Margaret Cheston (Thomas) Carey, McIntosh was born in Baltimore in 1898, one of six children, into a family of Quakers actively committed to women's suffrage, racial equality, and prison reform. Graduating from Bryn Mawr in 1920, she studied for a time in Cambridge, England, taught briefly, and then returned to Baltimore, where she earned a Ph.D. in English at Johns Hopkins in 1926. At her aunt Carey's insistence, she took a position as an instructor at Bryn Mawr and dean of freshman. Grooming her niece to succeed her, President Thomas named her as acting dean of the college, only to be disappointed when she accepted the post of headmistress of the Brearley School in New York City in 1930. Founded in 1884 by Caroline Choate and Samuel Brearley, following Columbia's refusal to admit women in 1883, Brearley had become New York City's most academically demanding, as well as one of its most traditional, schools for girls. Millicent Carey introduced progressive ideas about education and child development. She hired young Dr. Benjamin Spock to be the school physician, and he introduced a number of new ideas, including the notion that efforts to thwart homosexual attachments among students would cause psychological harm.[21]

Two years after assuming the leadership of Brearley, at the age of thirty-four, Millicent Carey surprised her colleagues and family by deciding to marry. Her aunt Carey had assumed, as had those who had hired her at Brearley and as had Millicent herself, that she had made the decision, which most professional women still felt compelled to make in the 1930s, to remain single. But Rustin McIntosh, Carpentier Professor of Pediatrics at Columbia University's College of Physicians and Surgeons, persuaded her otherwise. Over the course of the next half-dozen years, the McIntoshes made up for lost time by having five children, four boys (including a set of twins) and one girl. M. Carey Thomas, famous for saying that at Bryn Mawr "our failures only marry," discouraged her from retiring. "You can have your babies in August," Thomas told her. McIntosh took to wearing academic

Millicent Carey McIntosh (1898–2001)
Graduate of Bryn Mawr College (1920) and
Johns Hopkins University (Ph.D. 1926) and
dean (1947–1952) and president (1952–1962) of
Barnard College. (Barnard College Archives)

robes to conceal her pregnancies and hired governesses, cooks, and maids to
care for her growing family while she continued to work.[22] Looking for a
leader who could maintain Barnard's academic excellence while appealing
to the postwar celebration of maternity, the search committee settled on
McIntosh to succeed Gildersleeve as dean.

MIRRA KOMAROVSKY TAKES ON THE FUNCTIONALISTS

One of McIntosh's first acts as dean was to appoint a committee to address
the challenges raised by Lynn White and others. To chair it, she turned to the
sociologist Mirra Komarovsky, a Jewish immigrant who had been associated
with Barnard College since the age of eighteen, first as a student and later,
following graduate school at Columbia, as a faculty member. Komarovsky
was born in 1905 in Akkerman, Russia, the first of two children of Mendel
and Anna (Steinberg) Komarovsky. Jews and ardent Zionists, the Komarovskys fled Akkerman following a pogrom in 1905 and settled in the more
cosmopolitan city of Baku, on the Caspian Sea, where Mendel became a
banker. Anna Komarovsky was a practical woman, with little education.
Mendel, in contrast, revered the life of the mind and instilled in their daughter Mirra a passion for learning. Educated, for the most part, by tutors, Mirra
studied Hebrew, Latin, French, and English, in addition to her native Russ-

ian; steeped herself in art, literature, religion, and economics; and played the piano two to three hours a day.[23]

This privileged existence vanished at the end of World War I, as Turkish, British, and Russian troops converged on Baku and battled for control of the city's rich oil fields. By 1919, the family had lost everything; only Anna's success in selling pirogi on the street and the money sent by her relatives who had emigrated to the United States kept them going. In 1920, the Russian Revolution reached Baku, and in November 1921—amid growing anti-Semitism, dwindling food rations, and Bolshevik persecution of the middle class—the Komarovskys fled to Wichita, Kansas, where several members of Anna's family had settled.

Mirra entered Wichita High School in the middle of the 1921/1922 academic year and graduated at the head of her class after only one semester. Ambitious for her, and convinced that Kansas held little opportunity, Mendel Komarovsky persuaded his wife to move once more, this time to Brooklyn, to live with another of her siblings. Mendel supported the family by working as a translator and writer for Hebrew journals (he later found work in a bank), while Mirra tried, at first unsuccessfully, to enroll at Barnard College. Told in the fall of 1922 that she would have to demonstrate her ability to handle college-level work by taking courses in Columbia's University Extension program for a semester before she would be allowed to take the college's entrance exams, Mirra took the required courses, reapplied, passed the entrance exams, and enrolled at Barnard in the spring term. She did so well in her first semester that she won a scholarship for her remaining three years. Mirra Komarovsky always believed that Barnard delayed her entry simply because she was Jewish, and she may have been right. The Barnard student body had more Jews than any other elite women's college in America, and the influx of Russian Jewish refugees following the Russian Revolution threatened to drive the number still higher. In Komarovsky's case, administrators may also have been concerned that, as a student who had completed only one semester of formal schooling in the United States, and had done so in a school with which they likely had no experience, she might not be able to handle the rigors of a Barnard liberal arts education. Komarovsky proved them wrong.[24]

Although drawn at first to chemistry by the economic security it seemed to offer, she soon shifted to the Department of Economics and Sociology. No college in the country, including Columbia, provided better training in the social sciences than did Barnard in the 1920s, and Komarovsky took full advantage. Drawn to the classes of the sociologist William Ogburn, the psychologist Henry Hollingworth, and the anthropologists Ruth Benedict and

Franz Boas, she came under the influence of Margaret Mead, four years her senior, when Mead served as a teaching assistant in one of the courses she took in sociology.

Komarovsky always praised Barnard for its academic rigor and the engagement of its faculty in the key issues of the day. In the Department of Economics and Sociology, Elizabeth Baker and Emilie J. Hutchinson were trying to persuade economists that the classical concept of "Economic Man" rendered invisible the experience of women workers. Baker studied protective labor legislation for women, while Hutchinson studied women's wages and employment discrimination. In an extended study of women scholars, Hutchinson laid out the particularly grim prospects for women's employment in academe. Both economists insisted that public policy should be made with the life experience of women explicitly in mind. At a time when neither political scientists nor historians gave much attention to the experience of women, both taught courses on the history of women. The only other Columbia scholar to do so was Willystine Goodsell at Teachers College.[25] From William Ogburn, Komarovsky learned about psychoanalysis, statistics, and the empirical method. She also learned about Ogburn's theory of cultural lag, the idea that culture has a tendency to trail behind technological change. It was an idea around which she would build much of her later work on women.

For all her praise of her professors, Komarovsky regularly criticized Barnard's placement office, which, under the direction of Katherine Doty,

Mirra Komarovsky (1905–1999) Graduate of Barnard College (1925) and Columbia University (M.A. 1927, Ph.D. 1940), sociologist, and lecturer (1934–1938), instructor (1938–1948), associate professor (1948–1954), and professor (1954–1970) at Barnard College, as photographed around 1950. (Barnard College Archives)

"viewed its function as that of dispelling youthful illusions." Rather than helping students explore possible opportunities, Doty preferred giving them a "chilling reminder of discrimination and other limits to women's professional aspirations." Komarovsky's aspirations were further deflated when, in her senior year, Ogburn asked what she intended to do following college and she responded that she wanted to teach college sociology. "Not a realistic plan," he responded. "You are a woman, foreign born and Jewish. I would recommend some other occupation."[26]

Ogburn did not limit his deflating remarks to Jews or to women; he discouraged anyone who came to sociology with reformist ambitions. Sociology was a science, he insisted, and the successful student had to accept it as such. Komarovsky bowed to that injunction. For his part, Ogburn recommended Komarovsky for a one-year Caroline Durer Graduate Fellowship, which she used at Columbia to earn an M.A. in 1927, with a thesis, "Invention: A Step in a Process," written under Ogburn's direction. When Ogburn left for the University of Chicago at the end of the year, however, Komarovsky faced a professional crisis: she needed funding and a new adviser to complete her graduate studies. For two years, she taught at Skidmore College, until a University Fellowship made it possible to return to Columbia to complete course work for her Ph.D. (1929–1930). Finding additional financial support and a suitable mentor for her dissertation, however, remained a problem. Robert MacIver, a social theorist who replaced Ogburn at Barnard and Columbia and later became her colleague, disdained the empirical approach that Ogburn had taught her to admire. Frank Hankins, with whom she also studied, emphasized biological determinism, which Komarovsky rejected. In 1930, she accepted a position as a research assistant to Dorothy S. Thomas, another Ogburn protégé, who had graduated from Barnard in 1922. As director of the Yale Institute of Human Relations, Thomas was conducting quantitative studies on child development. Quickly bored by following children around with a stopwatch, Komarovsky returned to New York for the academic year 1931/1932 to take a job as a research associate with George Lundberg, director of research for the Westchester Leisure Project. With Lundberg, she coauthored *Leisure, a Suburban Study* (1934). Like Ogburn, Lundberg believed in "the vision of a positivistic social science," but he did so, Komarovsky later recalled, "without doing any himself."[27]

In 1933, Komarovsky married Leo Horney, a dentist, and joined a growing number of New York City professional women determined to combine work with marriage.[28] Almost immediately, she realized that she had made a terrible mistake. Leo wanted a housewife who would cater to him, not a woman bent on a career. They quickly divorced. Komarovsky continued her work as a researcher, first as an associate for the Columbia Council for Research in the Social Sciences, and then with the Institute for Social Research, where she finally found the mentor she had been seeking. Paul Lazarsfeld, a mathematician and pioneer in social-research methodology, who with Robert Merton would lead the Columbia sociology department to prominence in the 1940s and 1950s, had just emigrated from Vienna. Collaborating with Lazarsfeld, she produced *The Unemployed Man and His Family* (1939), a study of fifty-nine families modeled on work that Lazarsfeld had just completed in Europe. Columbia awarded Komarovsky a Ph.D. in 1940.

Komarovsky's dissertation, like all her later work, was built on Ogburn's theory of "cultural lag." Komarovsky believed that traditional expectations created deep contradictions, especially in gender relations, which, in turn, had negative effects on society. The Great Depression of the 1930s hit blue-collar occupations, where men predominated, harder than the service sector, where women were concentrated; as a consequence, it was often harder for men than for women to find work. And yet, traditional expectations made it impossible for many married men to conceive of surrendering their breadwinning responsibilities to their wives: "I'd rather turn on the gas than let my wife work!" one unemployed man told her.[29]

Komarovsky began her teaching career at Barnard College as an unpaid part-time lecturer in sociology in 1934. In 1936, she advanced to a full-time, paid post, and in 1938 she became an instructor. By 1940, Komarovsky was an experienced sociologist, but reaching her full potential took the inspiration of two people: her second husband, Marcus A. Heyman, whom she married in 1940, and her second dean, Millicent McIntosh. Heyman, a businessman fifteen years Komarovsky's senior, respected her ambition and helped her resolve what had been a deep ambivalence about her career. McIntosh, for her part, quickly identified Komarovsky as a key resource in her effort to retain Barnard's reputation for intellectual achievement at a time when many educators were calling for a more domestically oriented education for women. She promoted Komarovsky to associate professor in 1948, named her chair of the Department of Sociology in 1949, and advanced her to full professor in 1954.[30]

Komarovsky entered the most productive years of her professional life at a time of unusual ferment at Columbia in sociology. In 1928, Nicholas Murray Butler had come close to abolishing the department, which had fallen on hard times after World War I, as Franklin Giddings, who had grown increasingly conservative and withdrawn, held on to his position as chairman. In frustration, the one active member of the department, Barnard College's

William Ogburn, left for the University of Chicago, then home to the leading sociology department in the country. In response, Butler called together a group of interested faculty to decide what to do. The Columbia historians were united in wanting to throw out sociology, but John Dewey and the newly hired political and social theorist Robert MacIver defended the field as having a distinct content and method. MacIver took over the department in 1928 and tried to build it up.[31]

MacIver's most important, and unconventional, hire was Robert Lynd, who, with his wife, Helen, had just published *Middletown* (1929), their community study of Muncie, Indiana, to widespread acclaim. Helen Lynd had earned an M.A. in history at Columbia in 1922; Robert Lynd's graduate education had been in divinity. Neither had formal training in sociology. Moreover, Robert's only major publication was the one that he had coauthored with his wife. MacIver dealt with Robert's educational deficiency by awarding him a Ph.D. on the basis of the book that he had written with Helen, after asking that Robert cross out those parts of the book that his wife had written in the copy of the book submitted as his dissertation. The Lynds complied, but Helen found the task impossible; the work had been collaborative. Helen Lynd went on to earn a Ph.D. in the Columbia history department in 1944, with an innovative dissertation on the roots of modern social-welfare policy in Britain in the 1880s, and to teach at Sarah Lawrence College.[32]

MacIver hoped that Robert Lynd would undertake the kind of investigative urban sociology on the basis of which Robert Park had made the sociology department at the University of Chicago the best in the country. Instead, Lynd tried to turn sociology in a more practical and reformist direction. By the late 1930s, he and MacIver were so much at odds that they could not agree on whom to hire when a vacancy in the department provided them with the chance of bringing in a new faculty member.[33]

MacIver wanted to hire Robert Merton, a young theorist from Harvard whose work on the sociology of science seemed particularly relevant at the moment that war threatened to engulf all of Europe. Lynd favored Paul Lazarsfeld, the mathematician and psychologist from Vienna who had already made a name for himself as an empiricist. Deadlocked, Merton and Lynd turned to President Butler, who allowed them to hire both.[34] Merton and Lazarsfeld could hardly have been more different, either in temperament or in intellectual approach. Yet they managed to work together to take a department that had been on the verge of extinction to a position of eminence within the profession.

The joint hiring of Robert Merton and Paul Lazarsfeld in 1940 signaled an important shift within the field, even as it recapitulated a lingering division.

Both conceived of themselves as scientists, whose job was to investigate the workings of society. But Merton approached his task principally as a theorist; Lazarsfeld, primarily as an empiricist. Merton was one of the pioneers in functionalism, a theoretical approach inspired by two British anthropologists, Alfred R. Radcliffe-Brown and Bronislaw Malinowski, and developed at Harvard by Merton's teacher, the sociologist Talcott Parsons. Functionalists looked at societies as organic systems and strove to understand how they achieved equilibrium. Not wanting to be confused with social workers (Merton married one), they strove to be scientists, to examine society as it is, not as it ought to be. They tried to explain stasis and equilibrium, not change. Merton's distinctive contribution was what he called "theories of the middle range"—that is, theories halfway between the working hypotheses of routine research and the master conceptual scheme of such pioneers as Auguste Comte, Herbert Spencer, and Franklin Giddings. He set students to studying the workings of "manifest" and "latent" functions, "opportunity structures," "relative deprivation," and the "self-fulfilling prophecy." In the process, he helped scholars understand why machine politics and gangs were functional in urban America and how the mere expectation that members of a particular group would fail helped to ensure that they would. To that scientific project, Lazarsfeld brought his skills as a mathematician, making important contributions to the study of mass communications, marketing, and political polling.

The one topic that neither Merton nor Lazarsfeld had any interest in pursuing was the role of women in modern society. When Merton began his dissertation on seventeenth-century British scientists, he later recalled, most of his peers were wrestling with the "problems of urban life, family and community," as could be seen from the "abundance of monographs [that] dealt with the juvenile delinquent, the hobo and the sales lady." But of all the studies being done, "not one dealt with the professional scientist."[35]

The rise of Adolf Hitler changed that. As many of Europe's leading scientists fled to the United States to escape persecution, the importance of science to defeating fascism became increasingly apparent. Nowhere was this more evident than at Columbia, where two émigrés—Leo Szilard, a Hungarian Jew, and Enrico Fermi, an Italian married to a Jew—split the atom in the basement of Pupin Hall in 1939, thereby establishing the possibility that the United States might build an atom bomb before Germany could do so. That achievement secured science's standing as the ultimate arbiter of academic status throughout the university. The good sociologist was a scientist, a member of a brotherhood that shared a capacity to transcend the particularities of life—religion, ethnic background, family relations, and politics—in order to look at society objectively. Women were welcome to join this brotherhood, only insofar as they were able to transcend the accident of being female. To write about women and the family was to regress to the period in which sociology was concerned with reform, and the sociologist (male) was often confused with the social worker (female). The important questions were about society as a whole and the way it functioned, not about reform, women's lives, or the examination of power in private relations. Directly and indirectly, professors signaled to their female students that work on women was not interesting and therefore not worthy of the sustained research required for the doctorate.

For some female graduate students, that signal delayed progress toward the degree by many years. Helen Mayer Hacker, the adopted daughter of middle-class Jews, grew up in Minnesota, graduated from the University of Chicago, and entered Columbia's graduate school at the outbreak of World War II. For years, she struggled to identify an acceptable dissertation topic. At one point, she came across material on a group of two hundred women ministers: "I hoped that Merton might agree that such a study would make a valuable contribution to the sociology of occupations in exploring the paradox that the ministry, stereotyped as the most feminine of male occupations, was most closed to women. He did not, however, find the suggestion interesting."[36] Discouraged, Hacker started taking courses at Teachers College, in the hope of finding a more congenial atmosphere. And she did: "It was at Teachers College that I decided that every term paper should explore some theoretical problem in relation to women in the hope that these papers in combination might constitute a dissertation." For Professor Goodwin Watson, a social psychologist and civil rights advocate, she wrote a paper entitled "Women as a Minority Group" in 1951, and then another, called "Marx, Weber, and Pareto on the Changing Status of Women," in 1953. By that time, Hacker was teaching as an adjunct at Hunter College, where she unsuccessfully proposed a course called "Conflicts of Modern Women." When her husband, afflicted with schizophrenia, required hospitalization, she took a job in advertising to earn more money and almost by accident hit on a topic acceptable to the Columbia sociology department. Employed by Young & Rubicam to supervise a series of special market studies on "Negroes, farmers, and adolescents, and most significantly, working wives," she won permission to add a page of her own questions on working wives to the agency's consumer poll. She wanted to discover why married women's rapidly increasing participation in the workforce had not seemed to change relations between men and women. Hacker's dissertation, "A Functional Approach to the Gainful Employment of Married Women," finally completed in 1961, argued that "women's attitudes toward work served to obviate any potential conflict between their jobs and the primacy of their family roles." She found that "the majority of working wives did not seek to compete for jobs on an equal basis with men, but were satisfied with the connotations attached to merely holding a job."[37] While this work did not initially attract much attention, within a few years it would be regarded as a pioneering study in the sociology of gender.

Alice Rossi, the daughter of working-class Protestant parents, grew up in Brooklyn, attended Brooklyn College, and entered graduate school in sociology following World War II. Although she would go on to be a leading figure in the study of women in the 1960s and 1970s, she accepted more readily than Hacker had the directives of the Columbia faculty in her years as a graduate student. Dutifully, she wrote her dissertation on generational differences in the Soviet Union. And yet, even she occasionally "stole across campus to listen to Ruth Benedict in anthropology, or to Mirra Komarovsky in sociology."[38]

That Rossi was willing to risk feeling like a "traitor" to her profession, as she later characterized her furtive visits, had much to do with the larger political context of the city in which she had grown up.[39] New York City from the 1930s through the early 1950s was a principal site of radical activity in the country, and that radicalism had a profound effect on many women who found in the perspective of class analysis a model for understanding not only their class position but also their status as women. Helen Hacker, a "convinced Marxist" from her high-school years and a sometime labor organizer; Alice Rossi, who had moved in a radical student subculture at Brooklyn College "that espoused some measure of equality between the sexes";[40] and Mirra Komarovsky, many of whose closest associates in the 1930s were Communists[41] all later reported being inspired by the Marxist debates that swirled around them. They were able to write about women in a period of antifeminism and about conflict in a period of consensus, because they lived and worked in a city that had nurtured a radical interest in women and sexuality for a century. Even in the midst of a conservative backlash in the post–World War II years, this radical interest in women persisted.

RED FEMINISM

Radicalism found wide support on Morningside Heights, despite the best efforts of administrators to discourage left-wing organizing.[42] The leading radical feminist of the late 1940s was Mirra Komarovsky's Barnard classmate Gene Weltfish. The granddaughter of Jewish immigrants to New York City, Weltfish lost her father when she was thirteen and had to start work the fol-

Gene Weltfish (1902–1980)
Graduate of Barnard College (1925) and
Columbia University (Ph.D. 1950),
anthropologist, and lecturer in University
Extension and School of General Studies
(1936–1953), as photographed around 1940.
(Columbia University Archives–Columbiana
Library)

lowing year as a clerical assistant to help support the family. She completed
high school by attending classes at night, entered Hunter College, and then
transferred to Barnard College, where she discovered anthropology in her
senior year. Following graduation from Barnard in 1925, Weltfish began
graduate work in anthropology and married a fellow anthropology student,
Alexander Lesser, with whom she had one child, a daughter. Working with
Boas and Benedict, she studied the language of the Pawnee Indians and the
technique and design of basket making among North American Indians.
She completed her dissertation in 1929, but financial pressures prevented
her from publishing it, then a requirement for the Ph.D. Even without the
degree, she taught a number of courses in University Extension, including
one on African anthropology, in which she considered the initial contact of
Africans with the Americas. Although Weltfish published some research
based on her fieldwork and in 1943 wrote a pamphlet with Ruth Benedict,
The Races of Mankind, an essay aimed at combating Nazi theories of racial
superiority (and distributed widely by the Office of War Information to promote racial tolerance in the United States and abroad), she did not receive
her doctorate until 1950, when the university began to accept dissertations as
bound typescripts.[43] During Weltfish's years as a graduate student and
teacher in University Extension, she was also active in more than a dozen
labor, civil rights, women's rights, and human rights organizations, including the Communist Party. In 1946, she assumed the presidency of the newly

formed Congress of American Women, the American branch of the Women's International Democratic Federation (WIDF), an interracial, pro-Soviet, and antifascist group that in the next four years came to have tens of millions of female members in forty-one nations.[44]

A number of Barnard students, besides Weltfish, turned to Communism in the 1930s and 1940s. Among them was the Texas-born writer Mary Patricia Highsmith, who entered Barnard in 1938 and joined the Young Communist League in 1939. Highsmith left the party two years later, however, when she concluded that its antimodernist dictates conflicted with her own artistic impulses. Her writings, filled with disturbing tales of alienation and anxiety, included *Strangers on a Train* (1947), in which two chance acquaintances "exchange" murders, and *The Talented Mr. Ripley* (1954), a story of a con man and murderer with whom she strongly identified. In between, she published *The Price of Salt* (1952), which in gender terms was the most radical of her writings. Written while Highsmith was undergoing psychotherapy to "cure" her homosexuality, *The Price of Salt* was a novel of lesbian love that defied both literary and psychotherapeutic convention by ending happily. Although the novel sold a million copies, suggesting that there was a huge market for positive stories of lesbianism, Highsmith was rare among radical feminists in broaching the topic of sexual orientation. For most of her peers, confronting heterosexual oppression was dangerous enough.[45]

The foremost analyst of heterosexual oppression in those years was a 1934 Barnard graduate, Betty Millard. Raised in the suburbs of Chicago in a Republican family, Millard was radicalized in the early 1930s at Barnard, where she majored in economics and sociology, and discovered the Communist Party. While still a student, she served as president of the Barnard Current Events Club and organized a protest on campus, despite efforts by Dean Gildersleeve to dissuade her. After graduation in 1934, she moved to Greenwich Village and went to work for *New Masses*, a left-wing literary magazine. In 1948, she joined the Congress of American Women (CAW) and, in celebration of the dual centenaries of the Women's Rights Convention in Seneca Falls, New York, and *The Communist Manifesto*, published *Women Against Myth*, a hard-hitting pamphlet meant to combat the antifeminism then on the rise.[46]

Inspired by the writings of Friedrich Engels and Karl Marx, Millard blamed the evolution of private property for the oppression of women, and credited capitalism with providing the ideas necessary for women's emancipation. By "undermining the rigid traditions of feudalism and substituting the concept of free contract for that of inherited right," she argued, capital-

ism had given rise to the idea of individual rights and had unwittingly undermined the tradition of patriarchy. In drawing women out of the home
and into the labor force, the industrial revolution, in turn, had created the
necessary conditions for women's economic independence.[47]

Millard parted with Marxism on one key point. She disagreed with Marx's
contention that the advent of large industry made women's emancipation inevitable. "Every inch of the gains women have made has had to be fought
for," whether it was the mill girls' demand for higher wages in Lowell, Massachusetts, or Elizabeth Cady Stanton and Susan B. Anthony's campaign for
suffrage.[48] The fight continued because women's subordination rested not
merely on economic conditions but also on a complex interplay of religious
doctrine, custom, laws, language, and, most recently, Freudian psychology.
Those influences were kept alive through "day-to-day attacks" on women in
"books, films, radio shows, and magazine articles."[49]

The battle for economic and racial justice posed a daunting challenge,
Millard freely granted, and one that the Communist Party was right to fight.
But "women's attempt to achieve equality with men," she wrote, involved
"an especially difficult, concealed and subtle struggle because women are
not isolated in ghettoes, but live in intimate daily relationships with the 'superior' sex."[50] So deeply entrenched was the belief in male superiority that
"many otherwise progressive men" accepted it uncritically and "many
women were so committed to the seeming security of their inferior yet 'protected' position" that they refused to see the need for change.[51] Struggling
against class and racial exploitation and for women's rights was necessary,
she concluded, but not enough. For real emancipation to occur, the party
had to wage a "serious attack on male chauvinism" in American society,
within the party, and in individual relations between men and women.[52]

Millard's audience within the Congress of American Women included
not only Gene Weltfish, but a roster of some of the most important feminists
of the next generation. The playwright and labor organizer Eleanor Flexner,
whom the party assigned to be secretary of the CAW, would go on to write
the pathbreaking history of suffrage, *Century of Struggle: The Woman's
Rights Movement in the United States* (1959). Betty Friedan, then working
for the Federated Press, a left-wing labor news service, would go on to write
The Feminine Mystique (1963).[53] Most important for the development of
feminist perspectives within academe, however, was Gerda Lerner.

An Austrian Jew who had fled to the United States in 1938 following the
Nazi seizure of Austria, Lerner had joined the Communist Party and the
CAW in 1946 while living in Los Angeles with her husband, Carl Lerner, a
film editor. In 1949, following Carl's blacklisting in Hollywood, the Lerners

returned to New York, where Gerda became increasingly interested in the theater and women's history.[54] In 1951, Flexner gave an enthusiastic review in the *Daily Worker* to Gerda Lerner's musical review *Singing of Women*, written with Eve Merriam and performed at the Cherry Lane Theater in New York. *Singing of Women* intended to "take the starch out of the theories and myths which depict women as the 'weaker and feebleminded' sex." The first act dramatized women's long-term militancy: their efforts to keep prices down during the American Revolution, their strikes in the early nineteenth century against working conditions in textile factories, their organization of the Women's Rights Convention of 1848, and their fight for women's suffrage. The second act explored the problem of "male supremacy, the dual exploitation of woman as housewife and worker, unequal pay, and women's role in the fight against fascism."[55]

The Congress of American Women might have sparked a rebirth of feminism in the late 1940s had not the Cold War intervened. In 1946, the CAW addressed a wide range of women's issues, including the ways in which sexism and racism reinforced each other. By 1948, the group had shifted its attention to an attack on the Truman Doctrine and the Marshall Plan and a defense of Communists threatened with deportation. When the House Un-American Activities Committee (HUAC) published a report charging that the CAW was less concerned with solving women's problems than with acting as an agent of the Soviet Union, the organization's days were numbered. In 1950, the Justice Department demanded that CAW officers and board members register under the Foreign Agents Registration Act. Rather than do so, they disbanded the organization.[56] At the same time, the FBI began to investigate left-wing activity on university campuses, and HUAC began to call faculty members suspected of being Communists to testify. A number of faculty members refused to do so, invoking the protection of the Fifth Amendment against self-incrimination. In response, university and college presidents throughout the country agreed that faculty had a responsibility to cooperate with federal officials and that anyone who refused to do so should be investigated. Rutgers dismissed the classicist M. I. Finley, following such an investigation; Michigan fired the mathematician Chandler Davis (the husband of the European historian Natalie Zemon Davis) and the pharmacologist Mark Nickerson; Harvard withdrew an appointment as counselor to foreign students from the young historian Sigmund Diamond.[57] In some ways, Columbia behaved better than most academic institutions. The sociology department hired Sigmund Diamond after Harvard fired him, and when the Columbia sociologist Bernard Stern refused to testify before HUAC, the faculty committee assigned to investigate him found no grounds

for dismissal.[58] But in the matter of Gene Weltfish, the university succumbed to the anti-Communist hysteria of the time.

Weltfish had been a source of concern among Columbia administrators
for many years. Alumni regularly complained about her very public left-
wing associations and pronouncements. They complained, in particular,
about her leadership of the Congress of American Women. To criticize the
treatment of women in the United States and to suggest, through its affiliation with the Soviet-sponsored Women's International Democratic Federation, that the position of women under Communism was to be preferred
seemed particularly dangerous to those who regarded the nuclear family,
and women's supportive role within it, as the very foundation of the country's security. For years, Columbia's administrators, including Dwight D.
Eisenhower, who succeeded Nicholas Murray Butler to the presidency of
Columbia in 1948, defended Weltfish against her critics. Then in 1952, as
pressure on the universities by HUAC intensified, as Senator Joseph Mc-
Carthy began his own investigations, and as the presidential campaign that
pitted Eisenhower against the Democrat Adlai E. Stevenson heated up, the
defense stopped. In a detailed memo to the Columbia University Board of
Trustees in June 1952, Grayson Kirk—a professor of international relations at
Columbia since 1940, the provost since 1949, and the acting head of the university since 1951 (when Eisenhower left to become commander of
NATO)—reported that it was time for Weltfish to go. In addition to her leadership of the CAW and her refusal to testify before HUAC, she had, according to news stories, accused the United States of employing germ war-
fare in the Korean War. Kirk called her in for a talk. Weltfish claimed that
she had been misquoted. Kirk did not believe her. Normally, he would have
turned her case over to a faculty committee for investigation, but he feared
that the committee would exonerate her unless the members discovered evidence that she was propagandizing in the classroom.[59] Having already conducted his own investigations of Weltfish's classroom teaching, Kirk knew
that no such evidence existed. In fact, students reported that she went out of
her way to ensure open and free discussions and to expose them to different
points of view. Kirk was convinced that the faculty committee would not be
willing to dismiss a faculty member for statements made outside the classroom, where there was no evidence that the classroom had been affected.[60]

Kirk had reason to worry. Earl Warren may have been exaggerating when,
as governor of California, he had sought to undermine Eisenhower's bid for
the presidency with the charge that there were more reds at Ike's Columbia
than at "any other [university] in the country." But it was certainly the case
that Columbia harbored few Republicans. When Eisenhower commenced

his run for the presidency, a group of 175 faculty, led by the historian Allan Nevins, placed an ad in the *New York Times* supporting Stevenson, his Democratic rival. Ike's supporters could round up only thirty-one faculty names for a counter-ad.[61]

Feeling pressure from conservative alumni and trustees to fire Weltfish, but fearing a firestorm of disapproval from faculty and students if he did so, Kirk devised a clever solution to his dilemma. He decided to fire Weltfish but to do so in the guise of an administrative reform. In October 1952, he notified the trustees of the need to review Columbia's policies with respect to faculty in non-tenure-track ranks. The university had long relied on off-ladder assistants and lecturers to meet its instructional needs. Many had been teaching for more than a decade. Kirk suggested that new rules be adopted that would limit lecturers to five years of service. If a lecturer had not been promoted to assistant professor in that time, he or she would have to leave. Duncan Strong, then chair of anthropology, tried to protect Weltfish by recommending that she be promoted to the position of assistant professor. Kirk refused. In November 1952, the board voted to adopt the new regulations governing off-ladder positions. According to those rules, the president had the right to retain a lecturer if he wished. In Weltfish's case, however, he declined. Although Kirk insisted publicly that Weltfish was not singled out, that she was one of twenty-five to thirty lecturers whose contracts would not be renewed, news stories made clear (and the minutes of the board of trustees confirm) that the rules had been rewritten with Weltfish specifically in mind.[62]

Shortly before news of Weltfish's dismissal became public in March 1953, the editors of the *Barnard Bulletin* asked faculty at Barnard and Columbia to respond to the administrative ruling that Communists would not be allowed to teach at the university. Weltfish's classmate Mirra Komarovsky was one of only four faculty members willing to speak publicly. In direct opposition to the positions taken by Presidents McIntosh and Kirk, she rejected the firing of a professor simply because he or she was a Communist.[63] Several months later, the Columbia faculty met to appoint a committee to draft a statement on academic freedom. The committee, chaired by the noted English professor Lionel Trilling, endorsed Komarovsky's position. Although never a member of the Communist Party, Trilling had worked briefly with his wife, Diana, on the party's fringes. Close experience with party discipline, however, soon turned both Trillings into anti-Communists, and by World War II, even Marxism had come to seem limiting to them as a tool of intellectual analysis. Nonetheless, Lionel Trilling's commitment to academic freedom made him suspicious of any political test. Accordingly, on behalf of his committee he declared that the only test of unfitness that could legitimately be applied to a faculty member would be that of competence and personal integrity. Political affiliation, he warned the administration, would not weigh in his committee's thinking if an investigation were demanded.[64]

WOMEN IN THE MODERN WORLD

In the politically troubled climate of the early 1950s, dissent of any kind required courage. In that context, Mirra Komarovsky's decision to continue her work on women and the family was almost as remarkable as her decision to speak out against the firing of Communists. Her one concession to the prevailing intellectual climate was to work within the functionalist framework, which dominated sociology at that time. To her early (basically historical) training in Ogburn's theory of cultural lag, Komarovsky added the language of functionalism, but her purpose was different from that of other researchers of the day. In contrast to Merton's fascination with equilibrium, she looked for dysfunction, discordance, and change. And in contrast to Lazarsfeld's gravitation toward the large-scale survey, she maintained a preference for the intensive case-study method—believing that it was better suited to her goal of finding those points in the social structure where change was taking place.

Ever since she began teaching full time at Barnard, Komarovsky had been collecting data on Barnard students' and alumnae's attitudes toward family and work. First in "Cultural Contradictions and Sex Roles" (1946), then in "Functional Analysis of Sex Roles" (1950), and, most fully, in *Women in the Modern World* (1953), she criticized mainstream sociologists for underestimating the psychological conflicts that educated women felt as they "played dumb" to catch husbands and then asked, "What is wrong with me that home and family are not enough?" To Komarovsky, the married career woman was the norm; the postwar reaction, an aberration that had to be reversed. Pointing to the rise in women's workforce participation, the increase in the divorce rate, and the decline in the average number of years spent on full-time mothering, Komarovsky denounced as shortsighted the campaign to train women for domesticity. Instead, she urged that female students be prepared for "occupations which give full play to their abilities and ensure a comfortable standard of living," that "good nursery schools [be made] available to all," and that a "shift in men's duties within the home" be accepted. Invoking the theory of cultural lag, Komarovsky argued that technological change was drawing women into the workforce, that there was no turning back, and that the role of the college should be to provide students with the broader liberal education that would encourage the flexibility they would need to lead lives that were both professionally and personally fulfilling.[65]

Komarovsky wrote with conviction both because she was herself a married career woman and because, even in the midst of postwar conservatism, the women she taught were more liberal in their views, more determined to have careers, and luckier in their options (in terms of both higher education and employment prospects) than most other women of their time. When researchers in 1962 surveyed Barnard's twelve thousand alumnae (dating back to 1893), they discovered that 47 percent were currently in the workforce, compared with 35 percent in the country at large, and that another 10 percent were temporarily out of work, retired, or full-time students. When asked their profession or principal occupation (whether or not they were employed), a mere 14 percent of the respondents listed "housewife."[66] The remainder claimed a more diverse set of occupations than those reported by female graduates of colleges anywhere else in the country.[67] Most Barnard graduates, especially those who graduated following World War II, married and became mothers. But within a few years, most of them had entered the workforce. One of Komarovsky's students, Helene Lois Finkelstein, graduated from Barnard at the age of twenty and married her Columbia Law School boyfriend, Mark Kaplan, the year that Komarovsky published *Women in the Modern World*. She read the book a year later, just after giving birth to her first child, and wept at the thought that she would never be more than a mother. But after her two daughters reached school age, she went on to attend New York University's law school and to pursue a distinguished legal career. In 1973, as Helene L. Kaplan, she joined the Barnard College Board of Trustees and in 1984 became the board's chair.[68]

Women students' high aspirations and varied work experience stemmed most significantly from the university's location in New York. No city in the country had as broad an array of opportunities for college-educated, professionally trained women. While a study of college graduates in America conducted in 1952 found that 59 percent of employed alumnae were teachers, the Barnard figure was only 31 percent. Barnard graduates worked as secretaries, editors, journalists, advertisers, writers, business managers, statisticians, psychologists, lawyers, doctors, dentists, medical researchers, engineers, social workers, chemists, librarians, civil-service personnel, actresses, musicians, and artists.[69] They worked because the opportunity existed and because the city's high cost of living dictated that the women take advantage of available opportunities to support themselves and their families. They worked, too, because a group of pioneering women and supportive men had succeeded in opening gates to the graduate and professional schools that gave them a competitive advantage in a market prejudiced against them.

The separate existence of Barnard College was particularly important to its students' high aspirations. As mentioned earlier, if one looks at the baccalaureate origins of female Ph.D.'s, one finds that of all the colleges and universities in the country, only the University of California at Berkeley and Hunter College (New York City's college for women in the first half of the twentieth century) sent more women undergraduates on to graduate education. If one controls for enrollment, Barnard College was easily the largest producer of female Ph.D.'s in the country from 1920 to 1974.[70]

No doubt Barnard's part in this accomplishment had something to do with the fact that Barnard is a small liberal-arts college. Liberal-arts colleges have long been the biggest producers of doctorates in the United States. But studies suggest that women's colleges are more successful than other liberal-arts colleges in sending *women* on to earn Ph.D.'s, and no other women's college was as successful as Barnard in inspiring women students to pursue graduate study.[71] Barnard's success seems to have been due, in large part, to the combination of having its own liberal-arts faculty and the availability of Columbia's resources across Broadway, which meant that women students had access to graduate and professional training while still undergraduates and encouragement from their own professors to take advantage of it. Due in large measure to these factors, Columbia's graduate faculties produced more female Ph.D.'s than any other university in the country between 1920 and 1974, a period in which Columbia ranked sixth in doctoral production overall.[72]

Barnard's success depended, as well, on the college's unusually welcoming attitude toward transfer students, including those who were married. With land at a premium and endowment scarce, Barnard was a century old before it had the resources to house all its students. In the meantime, most students commuted from home, as Mirra Komarovsky had throughout her college years and even into graduate school. By the 1950s, as marriage rates soared and the average age of marriage plummeted, an increasing number of those commuters were married women who had been forced to leave schools that had a no-marriage policy. Accompanying their new husbands to New York, where jobs were plentiful, these women transferred to Barnard to complete their undergraduate studies. Whereas most women's colleges after the war lost large numbers of students to early marriage, Barnard kept married students in school, gained more as transfers, and exposed them all to the possibility of professional training across Broadway.[73]

Barnard's unusually high number of female faculty reinforced the college's message that students should pursue careers. Not that those faculty women enjoyed the same opportunities that their male colleagues did. Dean Gildersleeve had always been perfectly frank that she kept women relegated, disproportionately, to the lower ranks. To maintain close relations with Columbia, she had to be able to attract top-flight male scholars and pay them more. She knew that she would always have an ample pool of talented women to fill the lower ranks. Komarovsky had published two books before she could persuade Gildersleeve to promote her to the position of assistant professor in 1945. When McIntosh succeeded Gildersleeve, she made the promotion of deserving female faculty a priority.[74]

To make good on that aspiration, however, McIntosh had to find the money to do so. The new dean took two steps to accomplish this aim. First, she persuaded the Barnard College Board of Trustees that Barnard had to establish a more independent identity from Columbia to make clear its separate funding needs. Raising money for a college that was widely believed to be part of a large and wealthy university, and therefore not particularly needy, had posed an enormous problem for Barnard fund-raisers from the very beginning. To call attention to Barnard's institutional autonomy, the Barnard board resolved in 1952 to promote McIntosh to the newly created position of president of Barnard and to free her for fund-raising by dividing most of her administrative functions among a group of newly designated deans. She would thereafter assume the same institutional rank as the administrative heads of all the other Seven Sisters. It is not clear whether this titular change greatly enhanced Barnard's financial prospects. The college's endowment continued to lag badly behind those of its peers. To find the cash to increase the salaries of female faculty, McIntosh was forced to cut the budget elsewhere. Ironically, this mother of five slashed the faculty maternity benefits, which Gildersleeve had fought to provide in 1930, to come up with the money she needed.[75]

Barnard offered its students not only female faculty who could serve as role models but also a curriculum that made room for women's experience (without ever venturing as far as the theory of the Basque paella). During a period in which work on women at Columbia (and elsewhere) was suspect, students at Barnard found attention to the experience of women in their Barnard classes. In anthropology, Gladys Reichard taught the course "Social Life of Primitive People," which included, according to the catalog, "reflections on marriage customs" and discussion of the "position of women." In economics and sociology, Elizabeth Baker taught about women workers until her retirement in 1952, and Mirra Komarovsky taught about women and the family.

Barnard was not the only school on Morningside Heights to offer courses on women's experience. The School of General Studies, which, after Barnard and Teachers College, had the greatest number of female faculty on

Morningside Heights, also offered a few. Created in 1947 to accommodate the flood of veterans (virtually all male) who returned to school on a wave of funding under the GI Bill of Rights, General Studies replaced University Extension but inherited its coed faculty. Once the veterans graduated, General Studies became home to a growing number of older women who, having dropped out of school to raise children after World War II, found in the school for returning students a way of completing their undergraduate degrees. In General Studies, they could take classes with, among many others, Margaret Mead, who, as an adjunct professor, regularly taught a course on sex roles called "The Study of Cultural Character."[76]

Attention to women also occurred within the interdepartmental field of American Studies. In 1939, an instructor in the government department, Elspeth Rostow (Barnard 1938), had persuaded Gildersleeve and English professor Elizabeth Reynard to establish one of the country's first programs in American Studies. Students read Charles and Mary Beard's *The Rise of American Civilization*, among other texts, in the hope that doing so would help them "preserve [a] democratic culture against fascist attack." At the end of World War II, Henry Steele Commager proposed a program at Columbia modeled on the Barnard plan, one that would include not only an undergraduate program but also an institute and a Ph.D. degree. He hoped to present American culture as an integrated subject that would prepare students for careers in museums, foundations, and the State Department, as well as university faculties. But his colleagues remained too suspicious of interdisciplinary work to accept his proposal.[77]

Over the next two decades, Barnard's program came to provide a forum for a broad-ranging consideration of American culture, one that included low culture as well as high, the interests and needs of diplomats as well as housewives. At a time when most historians and teachers of government were focused narrowly on politics and most professors of English were concentrating on high culture, unconnected to social context, American Studies pursued a broader, more democratic mission. In the words of those who refashioned the endeavor as American Civilization in the early 1950s, their goal was to cultivate citizenship, not through narrow courses in the subject, but by "offering an opportunity to all within its reach to deepen and broaden understanding of the character of our civilization." Toward that end, the college secured funding from the Carnegie Foundation to support a program of public lectures, for which the audience included not just majors but also a wider audience of Barnard students, alumnae, and the general public—especially parents and friends, who were given a reading list and encouraged to set up discussion groups.

One of those who lectured was Dorothy Kenyon, an attorney and the first United States member of the United Nations Commission on the Status of Women, who presented "What Women Have Done" in November 1950. Eight months earlier, Joseph McCarthy had charged her with being a Communist, and she had been forced to testify in her own defense. Never a Communist, though a fighting feminist for decades, she had no trouble defending herself, but her political career was over. So, too, was the political career of a former Barnard undergraduate, Helen Gahagan Douglas; she was defeated in the 1950 California senatorial race by Richard Nixon, who charged her in the campaign with being, "pink, right down to her underwear." In that context, Kenyon's speech had special meaning. She began with an overview of United States women's history and went on to defend women from the charge that they had not accomplished much since winning the vote. Urging her young listeners to take up the torch of their foremothers, she concluded, "As people . . . in a democracy, we are struggling, learning slowly, to act like intelligent human beings."[78]

Those who sought to make good on that claim included a Barnard English professor, John A. Kouwenhoven. A graduate of Wesleyan, with a Ph.D. in English from Columbia, Kouwenhoven was always conscious of the fact that he was preparing young women for productive lives. When he taught freshman English, the obligatory Shakespeare play on his syllabus was not *Hamlet, Julius Caesar,* or *Macbeth,* but *Antony and Cleopatra,* which, as his student Linda Kerber (Barnard 1960) later recalled, "meant that the relationship of women and power, and of Europe and Africa, was central to our introduction to the western literary tradition." Kouwenhoven also taught a course called "American Vernacular Literature and Art," in which he focused on popular culture—dime novels, folktales, and comics—with attention to "their relationship to traditional forms and to dominant forces in American life."[79]

Annette Kar Baxter, a 1947 graduate of Barnard who went on to earn M.A.'s at Smith and Radcliffe before getting her Ph.D. at Brown in 1959, was another supporter of American Studies. Baxter returned to teach at Barnard in 1952, while still working on her dissertation on Henry Miller, whose erotic novels were then banned in the United States as obscene. In 1958, she published an insightful account of the significance of Elvis Presley's wildly popular song "Blue Suede Shoes." As chair of the program in American Studies throughout most of her three decades at Barnard, she carried on the tradition of teaching women's history begun by the Barnard economists Elizabeth Baker and Emilie J. Hutchinson, and through it helped legitimize the study of sexuality and the history of women among her undergraduates.[80]

Linda Kerber later credited American Studies, and both Kouwenhoven and Baxter especially, with inspiring the pathbreaking work she did in women's history. Although she recalled that the subtext of Professor Basil Rauch's history seminar was essentialist, "stressing what we now call American exceptionalism," she remembered Kouwenhoven and Baxter differently. Kouwenhoven "displayed for us the authentically *interdisciplinary* mind and the unpredictable angles of vision that distinguished American Studies." In his view, what was American about America was "the grid plan of cities, jazz, the Constitution, soap operas. Grids could be endlessly expanded; jazz admits infinite varieties and entrances. In his vision democracy was composed of components without prescribed limits or closure. And that meant that there was space for us. . . . Somehow we understood that the maverick, the outsider, is what the intellectual is *supposed* to be."[81] For Kerber, the granddaughter of Jewish immigrants, whose mother had grown up on the Lower East Side, Kouwenhoven's affirmation of outsider status as a fundamentally important element of the good scholar and Baxter's attention to women's history were both reassuring and inspiring.[82]

Students did not have to major in American Studies to find encouragement for their rebellious spirits. Nancy Miller, who in 1981 would become the first full-time director of Women's Studies at the college, found inspiration from the avant-garde professors in English and French. A graduate of Hunter College High School, she arrived at Barnard in 1957, six years too late to meet Jack Kerouac, but still inspired by the idea of going "On the Road." One could not come of age between 1957 and 1967 in New York City, she later recalled, "without reading the Beats and hearing about the obscenity trials." Not ready to set off cross-country on her own, Miller transferred her desire for self-expression to French and made her way to feminism through reading—or trying to read—literary texts that were banned or newly unbanned. Henry Miller's *Tropic of Cancer*, published in Paris in 1934, and *Sexus*, published in Paris in 1949, did not reach the United States until the early 1960s. Reading French put one on the cutting edge of the sexual revolution, if only in one's head. "Barely past virginity," Miller later confessed, "I was floored by [Henry] Miller's descriptions—mainly of women's sexual appetite."[83]

WOMANPOWER

The Barnard faculty had allies at Columbia who supported their efforts to raise their students' aspirations in the face of social disapproval. Chief among them was Eli Ginzberg. An economist, Ginzberg spent much of his career directing research on human resources at the Business School. Perhaps because of its origins in University Extension and its even deeper roots in Teachers College, the Columbia Business School was a more heterodox place than such rival institutions as the Wharton School and the Harvard Business School (which did not admit women to its first-year class until 1963).[84] Not only did the Business School train large numbers of women for work in the business world, but it became, under Ginzberg, a center for research on the country's human capital, its characteristics, and what needed to be done to develop it further. From the beginning, Ginzberg made clear that he regarded women as an essential part of the human capital he was investigating.

Ginzberg's father was a professor of Talmudic studies at Jewish Theological Seminary (up the street from Columbia). His mother, though not college trained, "was a doer," active in women's organizations throughout the city and determined that her son would grow up to make a difference in peoples' lives. His decision to enter academe and study the problem of human resources was a rough compromise between his parents' very different influences. Growing up in Washington Heights and Morningside Heights, Ginzberg entered Columbia College in 1927, graduated in 1931, and went straight on to graduate school in economics and sociology. His teachers included several women, among them Ruth Benedict in anthropology and Evelyn Burns in economics. While still an undergraduate, he began taking courses with the economist Wesley Clair Mitchell, famous for his work on business cycles, and came to know Mitchell's wife, the outspoken feminist and founder of the Bank Street School, Lucy Sprague Mitchell. Ginzberg wrote his dissertation, "The Illusion of Economic Stability," under Wesley Mitchell's direction and earned his Ph.D. in 1934. He also worked with Robert MacIver and Paul Lazarsfeld in sociology. Interested in psychology but viewing the Columbia psychologists, with their growing emphasis on behaviorism, as "just hopeless," he studied with Karen Horney at the New School. The dean of the Business School cobbled together a job for him between University Extension and the Business School, where he displayed a genius for getting grants in the field of human resources.[85]

Ginzberg later dated his interest in "womanpower" to an experience in 1936 at the Business School, where he discovered that some of his best students were women, but that their undergraduate training in French and art had prepared them badly for the business world. Hectoring the administrators of women's colleges whenever he could, he insisted that women had to be steered into math and science courses so that they would be prepared to assume positions of leadership in the business world. During World War II, Ginzberg left the Business School to work on manpower issues in Washington, where he learned of the British use of women in the war effort. He

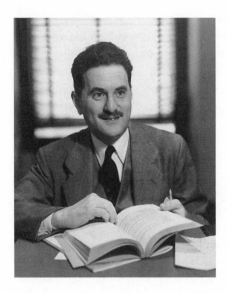

Eli Ginzberg (1911–2002)
Graduate of Columbia College (1931)
and Columbia University (M.A. 1932,
Ph.D. 1934), economist, and on faculty
of Business School (1935–1970), as photographed in 1948. (Columbia University
Archives–Columbiana Library)

urged that the United States government start registering women for the
draft, but "was laughed out of the room." Ginzberg's study *Womanpower*
(1957) came out of a decade-long study of human resources, funded by the
Ford Foundation. The decision to do a study of "womanpower," he later recalled, marked "the only time in the ten-year history of the Manpower
Council that a theme had to be voted on." It was adopted by only one vote.
Like Komarovsky, Ginzberg preferred in-depth investigations to the large
statistical studies that Lazarsfeld pushed at Columbia. Interviews were held
across the country in which specialists on women testified.[86]

Ginzberg and his team of mostly female researchers played a critical role
in the 1950s and early 1960s in persuading the American public of the need
to take advantage of the labor potential of women, especially educated
women. Ginzberg saw the potential in female workers because of his own
background and the simple fact that he worked in the city with the largest
female workforce and at a university with the largest number of female faculty and the largest number of female Ph.D.'s in the country, next to a
women's college that sent more students (per capita) on to advanced study
and careers than any other school in the country.[87]

Womanpower appeared in the fall of 1957, just as the Soviets launched
Sputnik, a 184-pound space satellite, carrying little more than a radio trans-
mitter to signal its position. The book recalled the importance of women
during World War II, emphasized "the extent to which [the] nation's

strength and security [depend] upon its manpower resources," deplored the nation's failure to utilize women's talents fully, called for training women in subjects long stereotyped as masculine, and responded to those who argued that education was wasted on wives and mothers. The "more education [a woman] has," the authors writing under Ginzberg's direction pointed out, "the more likely she is to work." Among women aged twenty-five to sixty-four in 1952, fewer than 30 percent of those who had no more than an elementary-school education were in the workforce, while 37 percent of those who were high-school graduates and 47 percent of those who were college graduates were in the labor force.[88] The clear message of *Womanpower* was that, if America was to win the Cold War, it would have to make the most of the available talent, even if it was female.

Ginzberg followed *Womanpower* with another study, *The Life Styles of Educated Women* (1966), which, despite its title, was not about educated women in general but about high-ranking female students at Columbia's graduate and professional schools in the years after World War II. The study began as a survey of educated men and women, an unusual decision in itself, since most social science studies at that time excluded women so as not to complicate any findings. When female respondents complained, however, that the questions posed did not speak to their concerns—especially the challenge of balancing work and home—Ginzberg and his team of associates drafted a special questionnaire for women only. With the help of university administrators, they sought out the university's best female graduate students—as demonstrated by their having held fellowships, ranked high in their class, or been elected to an honorary society. The survey looked specifically at those women who had attended Columbia on fellowships between 1945 and 1951.[89]

The group included 311 women (three-quarters of all the women approached). The investigators found no difference in field of study, marital status, number of children, or work history between those who responded and those who did not. One-third of the group either were born abroad or were the daughters of immigrants. Jews accounted for one-quarter of the group; Catholics, for one-tenth. Three-quarters were married or had been married. Three-quarters had mothers who had worked. In general, their parents encouraged their education and their careers, but the biggest influence on them were teachers in college; peers, husbands, and employers all played a minor role. One-third of the studied group earned doctorates. "Most pursued careers, some have settled for jobs." On discrimination, the researchers concluded that "any *close* competition is still between the exceptional woman and the average man." But there was also evidence of men who were determined to help women succeed: "A biologist reported that her employer had a conscious desire to show that a woman could have a family *and* a successful scientific career. His willingness to accept my leaves of absence and part-time work made all the difference to me."[90]

The study found little evidence "to support the widespread belief that most educated women are trapped in situations that create frustration and disappointment." In a triumph of hope over experience, the report reassured parental readers that "parents of the new generation of teenagers should know that their daughters will not experience much discrimination either in pursuing higher education or in finding suitable employment." Returning to his favorite mantra, Ginzberg urged guidance counselors to "steer women toward math and physical sciences," and, taking up the topic of the older woman returning to the workforce, Ginzberg lamented that "most academic institutions remain hidebound and do not make the major modifications required to meet the special needs of adults with interrupted education or careers, among whom women predominate." Employers had to understand that women were in the workforce to stay.[91]

What distinguished the women's from the men's questionnaires was the women's propensity to write at length about their experiences. The men were following a path determined for them by their elders; women were forging a new life, and they were intensely conscious both of the effort and of the obstacles they faced. They complained about employers who would not hire women for fear that they would quit to care for their families or would put in less effort because of the burden of domestic responsibilities. They lamented their experience with husbands who moved to follow career opportunities and expected them to follow, even if no opportunities existed for them. And they regretted never being able to find a man willing to be a wife. Men had the tremendous advantage of the expectation that they would succeed; women faced the daunting obstacle of the expectation that they would fail. One of Ginzberg's most important contributions was his insistence that expectations were changing and that parents should set their daughters' sights higher.

"MIXED SIGNALS"

In the fall of 1959, Millicent McIntosh devoted her convocation address to the theme of rising aspirations. She urged Barnard students to prepare themselves for a career, whose demands they should never "discard" at "their own convenience." And yet, in the next breath she counseled her students to "adjust" themselves without "resentment" to the most rewarding of all jobs, their families. She did not explain how her listeners were supposed to do this, and many students later looked back on her address as a classic example of what Rosellen Brown Hoffman (Barnard 1960) later recalled as "mixed signals" and "incomplete feminism." But those who sought encouragement in her address for the belief that they would not have to make the choice between family and career—a choice that society seemed so ready to force on them—found McIntosh's address inspirational.[92]

McIntosh's encouragement was all the more striking in the context of Barnard's relationship with Columbia, where top administrators discouraged even men from taking on family responsibilities. In 1957, Columbia's provost, the noted historian Jacques Barzun, published a handbook for Columbia graduate students that explicitly advised them against marriage. "The combining of the student life with the married state is rather recent anywhere," he noted, "and the innovators are often unprepared for the obstacles they run into." Quoting the head of one of Columbia's science departments, he cautioned that "a candidate for a fellowship or other form of assistance should be reminded that the University, while sympathetic with his problems, is justified in asking itself whether its funds are more wisely spent in helping a man who will shortly join the company of independent scholars and teachers or one who has allowed circumstances (or has been in collusion with circumstances) to force him into a long series of lean years before he can possibly reach the degree."[93]

The messages of President McIntosh and Provost Barzun could hardly have clashed more sharply. A school that openly championed the educational aspirations of its female students and encouraged them to start taking courses "across the street" in Columbia's graduate departments and professional schools while still seniors, even if married, was challenging an institution that conceived of graduate training as an undertaking that could not be successfully combined with family life under current circumstances and that did not conceive its responsibility as including any effort to change those circumstances. But the growing presence of women at Columbia, together with the larger social changes taking place in the 1960s, meant that the institution's responsibility with respect to women would not long go unchallenged.

SIX

SEXUAL POLITICS

FOR WOMEN at Columbia, the 1960s seemed filled with promise. The Soviet Union's launching of *Sputnik* led both the federal government and private foundations to fund higher education as never before and in the process made unprecedented levels of fellowship money available. Moreover, the demographic bulge produced by the baby boom guaranteed that student demand would soon outstrip the available supply of male faculty.[1] This Cold War combination of political and demographic pressures seemed to ensure that Columbia's women would strengthen their position in the years ahead. And they did. In 1960, women at the university earned 40 (11 percent) of the 358 Ph.D.'s granted. By 1970, they had more than doubled their percentage and tripled their absolute number, as Columbia awarded them 124 (24 percent) of the 511 Ph.D.'s earned.[2] Employment opportunities followed, not only at schools elsewhere but also at Columbia. By the end of the 1960s, women held nearly one in five faculty positions at the university, the highest rate for any major institution in the country.[3]

And then came the crash. In 1969, just as doctoral production hit a historic high, faculty hiring plummeted. The result was a glut of Ph.D.'s. Columbia felt the full force of the excess first. Unusually dependent on federal and foundation funding, compared with its peers, it suffered disproportionately when those funds disappeared or were redirected, in the face of the Vietnam War and urban riots, to other, more pressing, needs.[4] Because women were so large a part of the academic life at Columbia, both as graduate students and as faculty, they felt the impact of this reversal of fortune more sharply than women elsewhere. If ever there was a revolution of rising, and summarily dashed, expectations, it happened on Morningside Heights at the end of the 1960s.

Women had suffered through reverses before—most seriously in the aftermath of World War II, when women's share of academic appointments at Columbia (as elsewhere) actually declined. But the 1960s were different. A decade that produced not only historic numbers of female Ph.D.'s, the 1960s also witnessed a wave of social protests that encouraged a growing number of students and faculty, especially in English and history, to investigate the question of women's place in society. By the end of the decade, this work would collide with narrowing opportunities to produce a confrontation unlike anything seen since the days of John W. Burgess, a confrontation that produced ripple effects throughout the city and across the country.

"THE BEST MAN AT COLUMBIA"

No department in the 1960s saw greater change in research about women than the Columbia Department of English and Comparative Literature. In 1961, when Marjorie Hope Nicolson became the first woman to chair the department, the topic attracted virtually no attention. In 1970, by contrast, a dissertation entitled "Sexual Politics" opened a whole new field of literary criticism. Nicolson would never have predicted or even approved that shift. A full professor since her appointment in 1940 at the age of forty-eight, widely respected for her brilliant lectures and insightful scholarship on seventeenth-century science and literature, Nicolson was widely known as "the best man at Columbia."[5] And yet, although she never claimed to be a feminist, she played an important role in giving women a greater voice within academe generally, and in her department particularly.[6]

Marjorie Hope Nicolson (1894–1981) Graduate of University of Michigan (B.A. 1914, M.A. 1918) and Yale University (Ph.D. 1920), literary scholar, professor and dean of faculty at Smith College (1923–1941), and first woman full professor at Columbia University (1941–1962), as photographed around 1960. (Columbia University Archives–Columbiana Library)

Just before coming to Columbia in 1940, Nicolson took the nation's colleges and universities to task for not training or hiring female scholars in greater numbers. She conceded that part of the problem was women themselves. "Women bear the children," she noted, and one could not expect universities to provide women with expensive training just to make them better mothers. But, she added, there were women like herself who never married and others who married but whose marriages interfered with their professions no more than marriage interfered with the careers of their husbands.[7]

One such married woman was Susanne Howe Nobbe, an assistant professor of English at Columbia when Nicolson arrived. A 1917 graduate of Vassar, Nobbe had spent a number of years in social work and high-school teaching before earning her Ph.D. at Columbia in 1930. In 1933, she married George Nobbe, an English instructor at Columbia College. In 1934, she gave birth to twin boys, and in 1935 she bore her third son. The same year, she became the first woman in a humanities department to win promotion to the rank of assistant professor, following the publication of her second book, *Geraldine Jewsbury, Her Life and Errors*, a study of female literary friendship in nineteenth-century England. Promoted to the position of associate professor in 1945, following the publication of her third book, *Novels of Empire*, she still languished at that rank in 1961, when Nicolson took over formal control of the department as chair and promoted her, at long last, to full professor.[8]

Women like Nicolson and Nobbe made their contribution, as Nicolson was quick to point out, without the benefit of what most of their male colleagues took for granted: a wife. Not only could male colleagues look to their spouses to care for their everyday needs, but in addition, most could count on them for the steady encouragement so important to sustaining productivity in an otherwise lonely career. Nicolson never married, but she enjoyed the close friendship of the English department's administrative assistant, Adele Mendelsohn, who provided the kind of emotional support that Columbia's most powerful female faculty member recognized as essential to her continuing productivity. For Nobbe, having a husband and three sons constituted more of a drain on her professional energies than an enhancement of them. By the time she won promotion to full professor, Nobbe had lost much of her early effectiveness as a teacher and scholar. Classes packed at the beginning of each term with students eager to learn about nineteenth-century British literature had dwindled to a handful of committed young scholars by the end. Nicolson's decision to promote Nobbe in 1961 was more a recognition of past service than a reward for current achievement.[9]

That service had included efforts to make the English department a more welcoming place for all students, but most particularly for women, who made up one-third of the department's enrollment. Given the size of the graduate program, no student of English, male or female, could expect to secure much attention at Columbia. Faculty members in the more popular fields had responsibility for forty to fifty doctoral candidates at a time. The typical graduate lecture course, in which scores, even hundreds, of graduates might be enrolled, required no written work, not even a final exam. Students registered simply for "R" credit, indicating that they planned to attend the lectures; they received no grades. To compensate for the anonymity of such instruction, Nicolson developed a system of small "proseminars" for master's candidates and hired the faculty to teach them.[10]

Even with the addition of proseminars, no graduate student at Columbia could take success for granted. Women faced special obstacles. When Nicolson arrived at Columbia in 1940, there was an unwritten policy not to admit women over thirty to graduate study. She insisted that the policy end, but some of her male colleagues never reconciled themselves to the change. Lionel Trilling, for one, viewed older women, many of whom had spent years raising children, as dilettantes. "These women are just wasting our time," he complained. To which Nicolson tartly replied, "I don't know why you attract that kind of student, but the rest of us don't."[11] Susanne Nobbe had a similar encounter with Trilling in 1952, when he called to complain about one of her students, a woman on whose dissertation defense committee he had belatedly agreed to serve. Trilling and Nobbe met to discuss the student. Nobbe conceded that the student was not among the department's strongest but that her work had been approved, chapter by chapter, by her adviser (the man who had advised Trilling's dissertation, as it happens). If Trilling wished to see a better product, Nobbe suggested, he ought to spend more time engaged in the work of the department, rather than raising objections, as he had a distressing tendency to do, only at the eleventh hour.[12]

Trilling was famously unsympathetic to female graduate students, not just older women, but also those fresh from college. In part, his distaste stemmed from his dislike of graduate training in general. The Columbia College faculty prided themselves on being New York intellectuals who published in magazines like the *Partisan Review* for a general audience. Trilling vastly preferred the wide-ranging intellectual debates in his undergraduate courses to the narrower scholarly training required of future professors. But where women were concerned, something more than the requirements of graduate training was at work. Trilling's antipathy dated back to his own undergraduate years in Columbia's proudly all-male setting. A 1925 graduate of Columbia College, Trilling had enjoyed beyond every other experience his membership in John Erskine's honors colloquium (the forerunner of Literary Humanities), which he had taken with some of Columbia's most distinguished future scholars, Jacques Barzun and Meyer Schapiro among them.[13]

Trilling was just the kind of student for whom Erskine had organized his course: a son of immigrants, whose immersion in the great texts of Anglo-American literature, under the tutelage of a white Anglo-Saxon Protestant professor, would enable him to transcend the localism of his background and enter into the higher unity of mind and culture. The son of eastern European Jews, Trilling grew up in an observant home, studied Hebrew, and celebrated his bar mitzvah. By the time he was an adult, however, he had lost whatever religious feeling he had once had. Being a Jew, for him, became a matter of cultural tradition rather than faith or religious practice.[14]

Following graduation, Trilling entered Columbia's graduate program in English even though the department was not known for its openness to Jews—in fact, had never hired one. But his dazzling intellect impressed Ashley Thorndike, then the department chair, and perhaps in an attempt to test the waters, Thorndike appointed Trilling as an English instructor at Columbia College in 1932, without consulting anyone else. To his classes, Trilling brought not only a deep intellectual engagement, but also the insights of Marx and Freud. Troubled by the economic collapse of the early 1930s, Trilling, like most of his friends, found in Marxism a response to the despair he saw all around him. Watching Marxism being put into practice by the Communist Party soon cooled Trilling's faith in that theory's transformative power, but his engagement with Freudian ideas endured.[15]

As a Jew, a Marxist, and a Freudian, Trilling challenged the Anglo-Saxon traditions of the department. The ideas he introduced into his teaching struck his senior colleagues as at best irrelevant and at worst subversive of good pedagogy. Moreover, Trilling increasingly struck his colleagues as depressed and distant. He simply did not fit in. Trilling was, in fact, unhappy. His wife, Diana, whom he had married in 1929, had been seriously ill, first with a life-threatening thyroid condition and more recently with panic attacks—an affliction that, she gradually came to understand, owed much to the difficulty that a talented and ambitious woman of her generation faced in trying to live the self-abnegating role of a wife. In addition to his domestic travails, Lionel was not making progress on his dissertation. He gave the appearance of a passive, depressed figure, someone almost asking to be fired. In 1936, the department obliged.[16]

To everyone's surprise, not least of all his own, Trilling fought his dismissal. Meeting with each member of the department individually, he persuaded his senior colleagues that they had underestimated his talent and would not find a replacement as qualified. As Diana Trilling later recalled, her husband's ability to reverse his superiors' decision had a profound effect on him: "From this time forward he spoke and wrote differently, bore himself differently, and truly became a different man." He still had difficulty writing and still suffered from depressions, but this experience gave him "an authority appropriate to his capacities."[17]

Lionel Trilling came to "set great store by anger," Diana recalled. It "seemed to him a means of self-definition, an active as against a passive state." Entry into therapy and Trilling's study of Freud's writings reinforced this view and shaped the way he thought about women. Whereas Margaret Mead had discovered in Freud support for her belief that sexuality was a product of social circumstance, Trilling focused on those aspects of Freud's thinking that saw women destined for a life of passivity, the quality that he most feared in himself.[18]

Women's passivity, biologically determined and culturally reinforced, made them unlikely candidates for literary accomplishment, in Trilling's view. There were exceptions among the professional women of his acquaintance—Mary McCarthy, Hannah Arendt, Susan Sontag, and his own wife, Diana, who conquered her inner turmoil enough to become a leading writer for the *Nation*—but the exceptions were few. Trilling's lack of sympathy for female students reflected his indifference, even hostility, toward female authors, most particularly Virginia Woolf and Edith Wharton. Both failed to address the themes he thought central to literary analysis: conflict and moral agency—the hero in literature. Women were not heroes, and thus attention to women, whether as authors or as characters, was not a worthy use of a good student's time.[19]

Those who persisted as graduate students despite Trilling's lack of faith in them were, not surprisingly, a small and determined group. Cynthia Ozick, who went on to a distinguished career as a writer was one; Carolyn G. Heilbrun, who became a leading feminist literary critic, mystery writer, and Columbia professor, was another.

"WHEN MEN WERE THE ONLY MODELS WE HAD"

Born in 1926, the Jewish daughter of an accountant and a housewife, Carolyn Gold grew up on Manhattan's Upper West Side. She attended Wellesley College and, in 1945, while only a sophomore, married James Heilbrun on the eve of his departure for war in the Pacific. Following the war, the Heilbruns moved to New York City, and Carolyn entered the Columbia graduate program in English. Living in New York City "saved me," Heilbrun later recalled. In contrast to her friends from Wellesley, who "all ended up in the suburbs," she found that living in New York allowed her "to have a career." She found encouragement from Marjorie Hope Nicolson, "a brilliant lecturer," who recommended her for a Guggenheim Fellowship in 1966, at a time when it was still unusual for a woman to win one. Heilbrun found encouragement as well from Susanne Nobbe, "a woman who did much to soften what was otherwise an unwelcoming atmosphere." Determined to earn her Ph.D., Heilbrun at first held out against the postwar maternity craze, but in 1955 she bore a daughter and two years later twins (a boy and girl). Still two years shy of her doctorate, she had the care of three children under the age of three.[20]

Such a life pattern did not commend her to the support of Lionel Trilling, a man who was not sympathetic to the professional aspirations of women to begin with and certainly not to those of a woman who had saddled herself with three young children. And yet, even without Trilling's active encouragement, Heilbrun found inspiration in his work more than in that of any other mentor. He became a model, a writer whose insights and analytic techniques she learned to put to her own use. She learned first from his insistence that all literature was rooted in time and place. Although Trilling grew disillusioned with Marxism, he never lost his conviction that the best literature was grounded in social, historical context, and that the best criticism should be also. He refused to follow scholars in the 1950s who sought in literature an essential American spirit. To him, such a quest ignored life's complexity and variability, especially as it related to class and ethnicity. Heilbrun learned also from Trilling's use of Freudian theory, though she drew very different conclusions. To her, Freud's value was his insight into every person's original bisexuality. Masculinity and femininity were constructed through each person's life, she came to believe, not ordained at birth. Finally, Heilbrun found inspiration in Trilling's tortured efforts as a Jew to find a place within the Anglo-American literary tradition. He confessed to a feeling of in-betweenness as a result of his Jewish identity—a feeling of never fitting in, of living on the cultural margin. It was a feeling that was central to his critical insights and that provided a model to a student like Heilbrun, a Jew also, but more important, in her mind, a woman, for whom the in-betweenness of gender provided an analogy to the marginality he experienced as a Jew.[21]

Heilbrun took Trilling's idea of in-betweenness and used it to defy his advice, given one day after class, that she avoid spending too much time with women authors or characters. For her first published essay, she chose to study Hamlet's mother, Gertrude. While male scholars had accepted Hamlet's conclusion that his mother was frail—a passive, weak creature—Heilbrun discovered in Gertrude another person—frail, yes, but no fool. Having seen a side of Gertrude that male critics had missed, Heilbrun went on to discover sides of characters, both male and female, that had long escaped critical notice. That effort culminated in her book *Toward a Recognition of Androgyny* (1973). Despite Trilling's warnings against female authors in general and Virginia Woolf in particular, Heilbrun discovered in Woolf, as Ruth Benedict had before her, the view that "everyone is partly man and partly woman."[22]

The Columbia English department had a tradition of hiring its own, but the actual position that a successful student came to fill depended heavily on whether the candidate was a man or a woman. Men secured positions at the graduate school or Columbia College. In rare instances, a woman might win an appointment to the graduate school, but appointments to Barnard or the School of General Studies were more likely. An assistant professorship on the Columbia College faculty was out of the question. Not until Carl Woodring took over as chair of the college's department in 1967, did women begin to win regular faculty positions there. Lionel Trilling, for one, was dismayed by that reform. "This is not at all a good idea," a younger colleague recalled Trilling saying. "Older men should teach younger men, and younger men should then go out and encounter women as the Other." Carolyn Heilbrun and her colleagues Alice Fredman and Joan Ferrante were placed by their advisers in General Studies.[23]

"SEXUAL POLITICS"

Occupied with General Studies students in Lewisohn Hall, Carolyn Heilbrun had no contact with the graduate students who congregated across the campus in Philosophy Hall. As a consequence, she never encountered a young woman whose disenchantment with literary criticism as it was then being practiced mirrored her own. Kate Millett, born in 1934, grew up in St. Paul, Minnesota, the daughter of a Catholic family. Her father, an alcoholic, abandoned his wife and children, consigning them to a life of genteel poverty. Despite hardship at home, Millett excelled at parochial school and attended the University of Minnesota. After her graduation in 1956, a wealthy aunt sent her to study at Oxford, a gesture that had less to do with the aunt's respect for Kate's intellectual gifts than with the family's discovering that she was in love with another woman. After winning her master's degree with first-class honors in 1958, Millett returned to the United States, worked in the civil rights movement, and taught English for a year in North Carolina. In 1961, she moved to Japan, where she taught English, pursued an interest in sculpture, and met an artist, Fumio Yoshimura. She returned to the United States with Yoshimura in 1963, settled on the Bowery on New York City's Lower East Side, and married him to protect him from being deported in 1965. In the meantime, she entered Columbia's graduate program in English and comparative literature, taught English at Barnard College, and discovered feminism. In short order, she joined the National Organization for Women (NOW), Downtown Radical Women, and Radicalesbians.[24]

Millett adored teaching at Barnard. She loved the students and the challenge of opening their eyes to the world of ideas. But she found Barnard a difficult place to work. Her colleagues divided, roughly, into three groups. There was an aging group of old-style feminists who had begun their careers in the 1930s, impressive scholars but, in Millett's view, hopelessly dated in their outlook on the world; a middle group of post-feminist scholars from the 1950s, with whom she identified not at all; and a younger set—radical, untenured, and determined to bring the institution up to date. The radicals, whom Millett quickly joined, believed that Barnard was failing in its declared mission to provide an education *for* women. Summing up the group's view in *Token Learning* (1968), Millett blasted the college for giving its students an inferior "Jim Crow" education rather than providing them with critical tools necessary to understand their position in a patriarchal society.[25]

Her call to action found more extended exposition in the dissertation that she was struggling to write for the Department of English and Comparative

Kate Millet (b. 1934)
Graduate of University of Minnesota (1956), Oxford University (M.A. 1958), and Columbia University (Ph.D. 1970); writer, sculptor, and literary critic; and instructor at Barnard College (1964–1970), as photographed in 1968. (Barnard College Archives)

Literature. By the time Millett arrived at Columbia, Nicolson and Nobbe had retired; the only female professors who might have been sympathetic to her work were at Barnard, Teachers College, or General Studies. None taught in the graduate program. Millett asked George Stade (Columbia, B.A. 1955, Ph.D. 1965), an Americanist and the principal examiner on her doctoral orals, to supervise her dissertation. Years later, Stade remembered Millett's "brilliant" performance on her doctoral orals: her ease with difficult questions, and the responses she rendered in French. But he remembered just as clearly her tense demeanor, her appearance always of speaking through "clenched teeth." Stade agreed to serve on Millett's dissertation committee, but suggested that her dissertation adviser ought to be either Carolyn Heilbrun, because of her interest in women, or Steven Marcus (Columbia, B.A. 1948, Ph.D. 1961), because of his work on Engels, whose theory of the origins of patriarchy was central to Millett's analysis. Never having encountered Heilbrun, Millett chose Marcus, whose recent book *The Other Victorians*, a study of pornography in Victorian culture, was part of a new movement among critics to explore the theme of sexuality in literature. Millett's contribution was to reveal the masculine bias of that analysis and of the male-authored texts on which it relied. Much to Marcus's credit, he accepted the young radical as an advisee and gave every page, in Millett's words, a "most careful reading." As Millett appreciatively concluded in the acknowledgments of the book that followed, Marcus was an adviser who "could always find time and patience to insist rhetoric give way to reason."[26]

For several years, Millett's dissertation lay unfinished. Then in December 1968, the Barnard English department, pleading the need to cut its budget (but no doubt put off by Millett's stinging attack in *Token Learning* and vocal engagement in radical politics), did not reappoint her. Shocked, Millett fell into a deep depression, lifted only by the concerted efforts of feminist friends who persuaded her to turn her energies to completing her dissertation. In a productive fury, she hammered out "Sexual Politics" in a matter of months.[27]

An updated version of Simone de Beauvoir's *The Second Sex* (1952), "Sexual Politics" was part literary criticism, with biting attacks on some of the leading authors of the twentieth-century sexual revolution, and part cultural criticism, with extended analyses of anthropological, sociological, Marxist, and psychoanalytic theory. Millett opened her dissertation with an excerpt from Henry Miller's novel *Sexus*, set in a bathroom, with the narrator in the bathtub. A woman, dressed in only a silk robe and stockings, brings him towels. To begin a dissertation with a sexually explicit scene that features a woman's "muff" viewed at eye level was a bold move—even in the context of an English department located in cosmopolitan New York City. But Millet followed that excerpt with a critical move that was bolder still. She invoked the existence of a female reader, one who could respond not only to Miller's imaginative use of detail to evoke sexual excitation, but also to his assertion of male dominance over a weak, compliant, and unintelligent female. Here was sexual politics at the fundamental level of copulation. Henry Miller was a writer, Millett concluded, whose "ideal woman is a whore." Other male modernists fared no better. Millett denounced Norman Mailer as "a prisoner of the virility cult" and D. H. Lawrence as a believer in the "mystery of the phallus." The only major male author who came close to understanding women's position in society, Millett believed, was Jean Genet, a homosexual.[28]

Millett went on to build on the insights of the civil rights movement to draw an explicit link between racism and sexism. Just like racism, she argued, sexism permeated society. It was not simply a function of misguided public policy, as many of NOW's leaders seemed to believe, but part of a patriarchal system that affected every aspect of social relations. Sexism was institutionalized in the legal system, the government, the church, the schools, the family, and the sex act itself. It ensured that men and women would develop different personalities and play different social roles. "Male and female are really two cultures, and their life experiences are utterly different," Millett wrote. Sexism guaranteed that men would rule and that women would remain subordinate. Women would depend on men, define themselves in relation to men, and develop contempt for both themselves and other women in the process. Seeing women's personal relations with men as, at root, political, Millett dismissed the legislative lobbying of NOW as unequal to the task of dismantling the patriarchal order. Only a social revolution that brought about true democracy and the abolition of sex roles could hope to liberate all women.[29]

Candidates for the Ph.D. at Columbia must distribute copies of their dissertation to the five members of their committee a month before the defense. Millett stunned her examiners by distributing bound galleys from Doubleday. The examiners were three white men, George Stade, Steven Marcus, and Michael Rosenthal, from English; the first African American man to be tenured at Columbia, Elliott Skinner, from anthropology; and Annette Baxter of Barnard, from history. Speaking of his own experience in reading Millett's manuscript, Stade later told a reporter that it "was like sitting with your testicles in a nutcracker."[30] And yet the committee recognized the broad learning that had gone into the creation of the dissertation, not to mention its originality. After offering a number of suggestions for revision, they not only passed the dissertation but also awarded it "distinction." With her publisher's tight production schedule to meet, Millett never made any changes, and long passages remained unencumbered by the usual scholarly apparatus expected in Columbia dissertations. In a matter of months, *Sexual Politics* became something rare in academe: a runaway best-seller.[31]

A year later, Carolyn Heilbrun published a thoughtful consideration of *Sexual Politics* and the firestorm of controversy that followed. Still not having met Millett and having encountered *Sexual Politics* for the first time when it was presented to her as a gift from a friend visiting for the weekend, Heilbrun spoke not out of personal affection but from a sense of shared vision. She brushed aside criticisms from such reviewers as Irving Howe, Midge Decter, and Norman Mailer that the book was nothing more than a polemic, and praised Millett's achievement. Hers was a book, Heilbrun wrote, that "every woman this side of Mrs. Ronald Reagan has sometimes dreamed of writing, and though we may now feel that we would have done it otherwise or better, that feeling is a gift to us from Kate Millett. She had the guts and the brains and the talent to do it, and she did it at exactly the right time. Those of us who failed in her perilous task may now safely take up our own: the emendation and amelioration of her manifesto." One might recoil at the sexual explicitness of Millet's opening scene, and yet feel grateful for the gift included there: the idea of the female reader. For the first time, "we have been asked to look at literature as women; we, men, women and Ph.D.'s, have always read it as men."[32]

Heilbrun's point was not that females read differently from males, for, as she indicated, women can read, and have read, as men. She was simply asking that women avoid reading as men have done, that they learn to identify and correct the distortions of which men have so often been guilty. To read as a woman was not to assume some original, biologically ordained female state, but to seek to achieve the condition of critical reading that would enable a person, male or female, to identify male bias.[33] Heilbrun recognized Millett's book as the beginning of a transformation of literary criticism. Younger feminist scholars agreed. According to Nancy Miller, then a graduate student in French, Millett had succeeded in using "bad" sex—sex driven by male domination—to produce "good" feminism, or at least one strand of it, the one that focused on "the ideological critique of male authored literature."[34] Most of the graduate faculty in both French and English, however, regarded *Sexual Politics* as part of a political firestorm that would soon burn itself out.[35]

"WHERE ARE THE WOMEN?"

The English department's encouragement of its female students was warmly supportive compared with that of the history department. As of 1960, history had never employed a woman. When someone suggested that year that the department consider departing from that particular tradition, the sixty-year-old economic historian Shepard Bancroft Clough announced that the department would have to do so "over my dead body."[36] In history, the spirit of John W. Burgess had triumphed over that of James Harvey Robinson. And yet, there were murmurings of dissent. The social history that Robinson had pioneered at the turn of the twentieth century had gained a growing number of followers among younger historians. Richard Hofstadter, for one, who had been drawn to Marxism as a college student and joined the Communist Party in 1938, only to leave it the following year, believed that a consideration of social and economic forces was fundamental to any historical account. Even as Hofstadter abandoned the Marxism of his youth, his appreciation for social structure remained. It remained, as well, in the work of Hofstadter's students Eric McKitrick, Stanley Elkins, and Eric Foner. Social history became increasingly important in the Columbia history department over the course of the 1960s, and while the emphasis, even in the study of family history, tended to be on men—fathers and sons (never mothers and daughters)—the possibility of enlarging history's mission to include the experience of women was clear to those female students ready to take advantage of the opportunity.[37]

The first to do so in a sustained way was Gerda Lerner. Having decided that she had to have credentials for her work on women to be taken seriously, Lerner enrolled at the New School in 1958 at the age of thirty-eight to complete the credits she needed for a bachelor's degree. Early in her studies at the New School, she discovered Mary Beard's *Woman as Force in History* (1946). "Somehow," she later recalled," I was able to disregard her poor presentation, her fervent, and sometimes ill-tempered rhetoric and to connect with her central idea: that women have always been active and at the center of history." From her own experience organizing women, Lerner knew Beard's insight to be true, and she found comfort in the realization that Beard had arrived at this core idea in the same way, by organizing women to bring about social reform. Inspired by Beard, Lerner taught a pioneering course in women's history at the New School in the spring of 1963, which departed from Beard's approach to women's history only by focusing, as Beard never had, on the "structural, cultural, and sexual subordination of women and their exploitation." Although by this time Lerner had left the Communist Party, Marxist theory continued to inform her historical work, including a biography she wrote, while still a student at the New School, of Sarah and Angelina Grimké of South Carolina. Through the lives of the Grimké sisters, Lerner explored the link among race, class, and gender in the abolitionist movement.[38]

Determined to complete the work that Beard had begun more than a half-century before, Lerner decided, after earning her B.A. at the New School, to continue on to the Ph.D. Her daughter had just entered college, and her son was a senior in high school. Aged forty-three, she believed that she had twenty years left to make a career. Not wanting to lose any time, she shopped around for a program that would allow her to turn her Grimké biography into a dissertation. Columbia was the only place she could find where the department chair was willing to tailor the institutional regulations to meet the needs, in Lerner's words, "of this eager, somewhat superannuated, and certainly 'different' student." The chairman who proved sufficiently flexible was Robert Cross, an American history specialist, whose wife, Barbara, taught English at Barnard College and was at work on her second book, *The Educated Woman in America: Selected Writings of Catharine Beecher, Margaret Fuller, and M. Carey Thomas* (1965), when Lerner arrived for her initial interview. More than many of his colleagues, Cross understood the urgency that some women were beginning to feel about recovering women's past. Although he sometimes challenged younger female applicants to justify their decision to pursue a Ph.D., telling the future historian Carol Berkin (Barnard 1964), for instance, that "a pretty girl like you will be married and pregnant before you know it," he did not challenge Lerner. Here was a woman four years his senior, whose two children were now grown and whose determination and focus were readily apparent. When he asked her the standard question of why she wanted to study history, she quickly replied that she wanted "to complete the work begun by Mary Beard." Six decades after Mary Beard left Fayerweather Hall in some combination of disgust and despair over the hostile climate she had encountered, Gerda Lerner took up graduate work in a more hospitable, but still highly skeptical, department.[39]

In the brief three years that it took Lerner to complete her degree, the course she later recalled most vividly was one taught by Carl Degler. The son of a fireman, Degler was Lerner's contemporary, as were most of her professors. He had earned his doctorate at Columbia in 1952, with a dissertation on labor history. Taking a job at Vassar College, still an all-female school, he scoured the Vassar library stacks for works by women that he might include in his courses and came across Charlotte Perkins Gilman's *Women and Economics* (1898), then almost completely forgotten. He wrote an article on Gilman, submitted it to a journal edited by Marjorie Hope Nicolson, only to have it rejected on the grounds that Gilman, in Nicolson's tradition-bound opinion, was not a person of sufficient intellectual significance to merit inclusion in her journal. Besides teaching at Vassar, Degler taught a

Gerda Lerner (b. 1920)
Graduate of New School for Social
Research (1963) and Columbia University
(M.A. 1965, Ph.D. 1966) and writer and
historian. (Courtesy of Gerda Lerner)

graduate seminar in American social history at Columbia as a visiting professor during the 1963/1964 academic year. Including a section on women's history, he provoked a mixed response from the students. Several of the men dismissed the material as insignificant, but Lerner supported the inclusion passionately. That class began a lifelong friendship between Lerner and Degler, as they worked toward greater recognition for women scholars and women's history within the historical profession. The same year, Degler published an essay entitled "Revolution Without Ideology," in which he argued that women's surging participation in the workforce was nothing short of revolutionary, but that women had yet to formulate an ideology that could capitalize on the economic gains they were making in the way that Charlotte Perkins Gilman had done in the later nineteenth century. In the same volume in which his essay appeared, however, a Columbia-trained sociologist, Alice Rossi, published an essay on sexual equality that, in its demand for an androgynous conception of sex roles, went a significant distance toward laying out the ideology that Degler thought was needed.[40] Working with Degler and later with Eric McKitrick, who supervised the revision of Lerner's manuscript into a dissertation, Lerner learned the trade of the professional historian. But she never lost her crusading dedication to the proposition that historians had for too long failed to ask a central historical question: "Where are the women?"[41]

Others were beginning to ask the same question. In 1966, the year that Lerner received her Ph.D., three women on the Barnard faculty won permission from the Committee on Instruction to teach a new course in the college's American Studies program. Associate Professors Barbara Cross of the English department and Barbara Novak (Barnard 1950) from art history and Assistant Professor Annette Baxter (Barnard 1947) from history would offer "The History of American Women." According to Cross, the course would "illuminate an aspect of history which has been neglected, although half the population has been involved in it." She continued that it would "steer away from the conventional focus on women's rights in favor of a more complete study of the experience of women in America." Baxter added that the course, in placing women's experience at the center of the history of the United States, would likely challenge some of the most hallowed concepts of American historiography, most particularly "the Turner expansion thesis," which claimed that American institutions had taken on their distinctive form as a consequence of men's engagement with the frontier. Instead, she suggested, the course would consider an idea first proposed by the historian David Potter a few years before that the conquest of the West was less important to the development of the United States than the process of urbanization and immigration, an experience in which women had been central figures.[42]

Cross, Baxter, Novak, and Lerner represented the vanguard of a small army of scholars who would develop the field of women's history in the decades to come. Barnard College graduates Linda Kerber (1960), Carol Berkin (1964), Regina Morantz-Sanchez (1965), and Estelle B. Freedman (1969) all earned their Ph.D.'s at Columbia. There, they joined Carroll Smith-Rosenberg, Jacquelyn Dowd Hall, Lois W. Banner, and William Chafe. And those were just the Americanists. On the European side, Joan Kelly-Gadol, Renate Bridenthal, Bonnie S. Anderson, Mary Nolan, Paula Hyman, and Sarah B. Pomeroy all went on to distinguished careers in women's history.

Lerner, who would found a master's program in women's history at Sarah Lawrence College and a doctoral program at the University of Wisconsin, taught some of those future women's historians at Columbia's Summer School, the program in which the department's best graduate students often got their first experience as teachers. Freedman, who had missed out on the opportunity to take women's history at Barnard, because, as she later recalled, she had the "nerve" to tell her adviser, Annette Baxter, that she wanted to study "real" history, took both Lerner's undergraduate lecture course and her graduate research seminar on women's history in the early 1970s. Through Lerner, she learned "there was a field out there and the challenges of doing research in it." Most important, Lerner taught her that asking the question "Where are the women?" would allow her to change the way in which history was conceived, researched, and written.[43]

THE STUDENT BODY

As female graduate students and junior faculty grew increasingly critical of conventional thinking about women, undergraduates became more restive about constraints on their lives. The "Bermuda Shorts Affair" set the stage. In the spring of 1960, Columbia president Grayson Kirk complained to Barnard president Millicent McIntosh that Barnard students were parading across the Columbia campus in costumes unbefitting serious female scholars. They wore slacks and, worse, shorts. He called for a dress code; McIntosh agreed, and the Barnard student council reluctantly did as it was strongly encouraged to do. According to the revised dress code, Barnard students could wear shorts on the Barnard campus, as long as they revealed no more than two inches of leg above the knee, but whenever they crossed Broadway, they would have to cover themselves with a long coat.[44]

Although at first Barnard students bowed to administrative fiat, the revision of the dress code began a debate about the role of the college in their personal lives. In addition to rules about dress, which were soon relaxed but which did not disappear entirely until after 1970, Barnard students objected

"Bermuda Shorts Affair"
Barnard student reveals some leg, but
still within the dress code, as photographed
by John Orris, 1960. (*New York Times*
Pictures)

that they were required to submit to a far more restrictive set of housing rules than those that prevailed at Columbia College.[45]

In one respect, parietal rules at Barnard College were more liberal than those in force at Columbia. By 1961, McIntosh had agreed that students who lived in Barnard dormitories could entertain young men in their rooms from 2:00 to 5:00 P.M. every other Sunday afternoon, as long as their doors remained ajar by at least the width of a book—a rule that students quickly interpreted to include matchbooks.[46] Rosemary Park, the president of Connecticut College who succeeded McIntosh as president of Barnard in 1962, continued the "open house" policy. Columbia College, in contrast, and alone among Ivy League male schools, maintained an absolute ban on female visitors, except for students' mothers or visitors accompanied by a parent.[47] In 1962, Columbia students organized to protest those restrictive rules, and on March 20, 1963, Kirk agreed to an experiment. Columbia College students would be granted the same rights already in force at Barnard, but only if Columbia men abandoned their annual ritual of the spring panty raid at Barnard.[48] While editorialists for the Columbia Spectator objected to the condition imposed, Columbia adopted the Barnard open-house system.[49] Not everyone was pleased. Lionel Trilling, for one, objected to the reform on the grounds that, in seeming to encourage sexual activity in the dormitories, college officials were depriving students of an important chance to rebel and grow. But his was a minority view.[50]

While Barnard may have been a pioneer in initiating an open-house policy, rules governing housing remained much stricter than any that had ever existed at Columbia. Housing had always been a problem at Barnard. As late as the 1960s, the college could house only one-third of its students.[51] Columbia had a similar problem, which it solved by encouraging men to leave the dorms after their first year and find housing in the neighborhood. Barnard administrators, feeling a greater responsibility to protect the morals, as well as the physical safety, of its students, took a more restrictive approach to the housing crunch. Students who lived within commuting distance of the school had to live with their parents, a close relative, or (while still under twenty-one) a person (usually an elderly woman) over the age of twenty-five.[52] Students who lived too far away to commute had to live in the dormitories—unless they had a job that required them to live with a family. Students disliked what they viewed as outdated supervision, especially in the context of New York City, where the ideal, if not always the practice, of sexual freedom had flourished for decades. By 1962, Barnard students had persuaded administrators to loosen the rules a little. The two-thirds of the student body that commuted gained the right to live wherever they liked after their first year, as long as they had their parents' permission. But students who came from farther away remained subject to the old rules—living on campus and bound by sign-outs and curfews—unless they had a job as a live-in babysitter.[53] Barnard therefore had a set of housing rules that were as liberal as any in the country for the majority, but as restrictive as any then in force for the minority, who came from a distance. Those rules did not succeed in protecting women students from sex, of course. "The Paris Hotel [at West End Avenue and Ninety-seventh Street] did a brisk business," one Columbia student, Roger Lehecka, later recalled. Moreover, some dormitories were laxer than others in enforcing rules, and some women lived where they pleased and simply lied about it.[54]

The practice of living off campus in defiance of college rules became public in March 1968, when a story on cohabitation appeared on the "Family Page" of the New York Times. The article included an account of a Barnard student who was living off campus with her boyfriend, without the knowledge of either her parents or college officials.[55] Barnard graduate (1914), longtime liberal, and Times owner Iphigene Ochs Sulzberger was dismayed by the Times's story, which she denounced as "outrageous" and a virtual endorsement of "loose living" among college students. "What are those girls on the Women's Page trying to do to the reputation of The Times and Barnard College?" she angrily demanded of her son, Arthur Sulzberger Jr., who had succeeded his father as publisher of the newspaper. "Premarital affairs are nothing new, but they are not a desirable way of life. . . . If we have a family page, let's stick to the subject." As it happened, her grandson Stephen Golden, a student in General Studies, was then cohabiting with his girlfriend (later his wife), though that was a living arrangement that the older members of the Sulzberger family chose to ignore.[56]

According to the Times, the twenty-year-old Barnard student was from New Hampshire, a fact that enabled the Barnard dean of studies, Helen Bailey, to determine her identity immediately as Linda LeClair. LeClair was well known to administrators. She had performed poorly in her first year at the college, had become pregnant, and had taken a medical leave to go to Puerto Rico with her boyfriend, Peter Behr, to have an abortion. At a time when abortions were illegal in the United States and the college doctor would not prescribe birth-control pills, sexually active Barnard students were accustomed to having to fend for themselves by going "underground," as one student protested in a Barnard Bulletin editorial.[57] According to an informal poll conducted by students in the spring of 1967, 70 percent of the students who had grown up in New York City used some form of birth control. The figure for the college as a whole was 40 percent. Every student

"LeClair Affair"
Linda LeClair and Peter Behr, as
photographed in 1968. (AP/Wide World
Photos)

questioned said that she knew where to go to obtain birth-control services—
Planned Parenthood and World Planned Childhood were the two most
often mentioned—but not everyone did so. In the words of one student, "I
don't use any birth control devices, but I should."[58] As soon as Bailey identified LeClair, who, having returned to Barnard after a year's absence, was
now on academic probation, she demanded that the young woman come to
her office for a talk, not just about her violation of the college's housing rules
but, more seriously, about her having lied about her whereabouts.[59]

LeClair questioned the right of the college to determine where she lived.
A member, with her boyfriend, of Students for a Democratic Society, she
was part of a nationwide SDS campaign to challenge the undemocratic nature of American political and social institutions. Founded in 1960, SDS
championed the ideal of participatory democracy and rejected hierarchical
leadership based on race, class, age, or sex. By 1965, the year Columbia students organized an SDS chapter, the national organization had focused its
attention on the Vietnam War and resistance to the draft. A leader in this
protest, Peter Behr refused induction into the army on March 13, 1968, and
faced prosecution as a result.[60]

Less well known to later generations, opposition to parietals drew even
more student support than opposition to the war before 1968. In 1965, newly
energized SDS members were among the first to protest parietals at the University of Kansas, where Martha Peterson had been dean of women before

going on to be dean of students at the University of Wisconsin and then president of Barnard in 1968.[61] In March 1968, the week after the story on cohabitation appeared in the *Times,* LeClair joined the anti-parietal movement, by protesting Barnard's housing rules. Echoing Elsie Clews Parson's call for trial marriage back in 1906, LeClair announced that the time had come to legitimize cohabitation. The SDS challenge focused on discrimination against the young by their elders. But, as LeClair sought to stake out her own contribution to SDS, her challenge specifically addressed society's discrimination against women. Pointing out that "Barnard College was founded on the principle of equality between women and men," she implied that the college was guilty of hypocrisy. "If women are able, intelligent people, why must we be supervised and curfewed?" she asked.[62]

Barnard administrators disagreed that LeClair was being treated unfairly and sent her case for adjudication to the college's faculty–student judicial council, an organization that had long embraced the idea that students should have a role in college governance. Testifying before the council, LeClair accused the college of enforcing policies that discriminated "on the basis of sex, age, class in the College, and the distance one's family lives away from the school." Expanding on her theme, she declared, "Although I am old enough by law to marry without my parent's consent, support myself, which I am doing, live anywhere I want, without parental control, I am not old enough, according to Barnard, to live outside the dorm except as a

Martha Peterson (b. 1916)
Graduate of University of Kansas (B.A. 1937, M.A. 1943, Ph.D. 1959), instructor and dean at University of Kansas (1942–1956), dean of students at University of Wisconsin (1956–1968), and president of Barnard College (1968–1975), as photographed around 1968. (Barnard College Archives)

domestic."[63] Obliged to enforce college rules, the council sanctioned LeClair. At the same time, however, it signaled its dissent from those rules by merely banning her from the school cafeteria.[64]

Reports in the New York press were picked up all over the country, and Barnard's new president, Martha Peterson, found herself deluged with demands that she expel Barnard's wayward student. One writer referred to Barnard as "P.U.—Prostitute University" and voiced dismay that a women's college would countenance such behavior. But Barnard students seem to have been solidly on LeClair's side; in fact, seventy signed a statement affirming that they, too, had lived off campus with men. At first, Peterson rejected the council's ruling and considered expelling LeClair, but as the days passed and the furor over the LeClair affair mounted, she deferred her initial impulse and decided to wait and see how LeClair, already on academic probation, would do in her courses that term. As it turned out, neither LeClair nor many of her classmates did much academic work in the remainder of the spring semester of 1968. The events of the following weeks, which included the takeover of Low Library by, among many others, Linda LeClair and Peter Behr quickly eclipsed—though it did not end—the debate over whether college administrators should have the right to supervise the personal lives of their female students.[65]

COLUMBIA WOMEN'S LIBERATION

Even as Martha Peterson mulled over what to do about Linda LeClair, events across Broadway overtook concern with housing regulations at Barnard College. For several years, the civil rights movement and the antiwar movement had bred discontent among undergraduates with institutions in American society. In the spring of 1968, student leaders succeeded in focusing that discontent on Columbia University because of what they believed to be the university's complicity in the Vietnam War and its insensitivity to issues of race in the surrounding community.

African American students at Barnard and Columbia had been working in Harlem ever since Zora Neale Hurston and Langston Hughes arrived in the 1920s. In the 1930s, they participated in the boycotts of establishments that refused to hire black workers. "Don't Buy Where You Can't Work," the signs read. In the 1950s, they boycotted New York outlets of national chains like Woolworth's that discriminated against blacks in the South. Throughout those years, their numbers remained small, compared with the growing population of blacks in the surrounding community. Despite the efforts of students in the 1940s to persuade Dean Virginia Gildersleeve actively to recruit

African American students, there do not seem to have been more than five per class into the 1950s, only a little more than at other Seven Sisters colleges, where two black students per class remained the norm.[66] With the rise of the civil rights movement, however, the number began to increase, and following the summer of 1964, when students from Barnard and Columbia joined others from across the country to help with the voter-registration drive in Mississippi, both colleges stepped up their recruitment of African American students. Eight black students entered Barnard in the fall of 1964; the number jumped to eighteen in 1965 and rose to forty-four by 1969. That increase, which was paralleled at Columbia College, enabled African American students to begin to develop their own social life on campus for the first time. Black undergraduates at Columbia formed fraternities and in 1965 organized the Society of African American Students (SAS). Some members of SAS continued the tradition of working with black women students in Harlem: organizing rent strikes, protesting police brutality, and joining in civil rights protests. They did not turn their protest toward Columbia until the spring of 1968, when they sided with those in Harlem who opposed Columbia's decision to build a gymnasium in Morningside Park. For black male undergraduates, the gym became a symbol of Columbia's power as a white landlord in a predominantly black neighborhood. The black women of Barnard cared less about the gym, since it was to be restricted to Columbia College undergraduates.[67]

Nor was the gym a particular concern to the white men of SDS, whose attention was increasingly focused on the antiwar movement. But in the spring of 1968, Mark Rudd, a Columbia College junior, was elected chairman of the Columbia chapter of SDS on a platform entitled "How to Get the SDS Moving Again and Screw the University All in One Fell Swoop," and he saw the possibility of a cross-race alliance by including the proposed gym on the SDS agenda.[68]

In the space of a few hours on April 23, 1968, Rudd led a crowd to the site of the proposed gym in Morningside Park to protest the taking of parkland from Harlem for university purposes. When the police arrived, Rudd diverted the protesters to Hamilton Hall, where they held Dean Henry Coleman (Columbia College 1946) hostage. Evicted from Hamilton by members of SAS, Rudd led the remaining protesters to Low Library, where they took possession of President Grayson Kirk's office. Over the next four days, other protesters occupied Avery, Fayerweather, and Mathematics Halls before settling in for a siege.[69]

The immediate justifications for the takeover of university buildings were two: the university's alleged racism in building a gym in Morningside Park and in buying up property in the neighborhood, with the result that long-time residents, many of them black, were evicted; and the university's complicity in the Vietnam War through the Institute for Defense Analysis, which advised the government on research. In its own defense, the university responded that the community had endorsed the building of the gym many years before (and had only recently come to regard the gym as a racist gesture), that the buying of property was part of an effort to save buildings from ruin and to protect the neighborhood from further decline, and that the university's involvement with government defense work was modest, at most. The takeover, which paralyzed the university for a week, also launched a series of debates on campus that soon moved beyond the gym and defense research to include other issues: the faculty's responsibility for university governance, the university's responsibilities toward the community and toward minority students, and, most startling at the time, the place of women within the university and, more generally, in society.[70]

Ever since 1964, women in SDS had protested their male colleagues' failure to live up to their egalitarian beliefs where women were concerned. With the escalation of the Vietnam War and the increase in harassment by the FBI, the men turned increasingly militant and strident. Their conduct during the protests at Columbia made more evident than ever before the contradiction between their rhetoric and their behavior. Judging from later arrest records, about one-third of the protesters were women, mostly from Barnard, but SDS did not welcome women into the leadership ranks. Rusti (Carolyn) Eisenberg, a graduate student in history who earned an M.A. in 1969 and a Ph.D. in 1971, was the only woman on the strike coordinating committee during the occupation. Even she felt marginalized. Although older than most of the men and long accustomed to exercising leadership in left-wing causes, she later remembered how difficult it was to exert authority in the context of the occupation. Men on the committee, mostly undergraduates from Columbia College, began to engage in "very macho behavior," shouting down one another and taking increasingly more militant stances. "It was the first time as a political activist that I was aware of gender affecting debate," Eisenberg recalled. "If you didn't have a loud voice, you did not get heard." Eisenberg was not only shouted down by the men, but also shunned by their women. "A lot of the guys had girlfriends who were also SDS. The girlfriends were, from my point of view, not helpful and not friendly. They hung on to their guys and fed their egos."[71] In Fayerweather Hall, these were the women who assumed the housekeeping chores. They cooked three meals a day for three hundred people in a kitchen no bigger than a telephone booth.[72] Eisenberg was the most prominent female striker to resist the "macho man, clinging woman" polarization that occupation produced. But she was not alone. Sandwich shops in the neighborhood began to do a booming business when other women refused to perform their expected role.[73] A few went further than refusing to cook. They began to portray the call for sexual freedom, which had come to define their generation, as a male-inspired campaign to facilitate men's sexual conquest of women. An English professor, Robert Hanning, whose wife, Barbara Russano (Barnard 1960), was then completing her Ph.D. at Yale in musicology while mothering two children, was particularly alert to the changes taking place. He later recalled eating at John Jay Hall in that period and "picking up a daily supply of manifestos." One proclaimed, "Women Are Not in the Movement for Free Fucking." The takeover at Columbia ended, but the manifestos continued.[74]

Black women, disgruntled about being largely ignored by the male leaders of Columbia College's Society of African American Students, were among the first to break free from male control. They established their own organization, the Barnard Organization of Soul Sisters (BOSS), in the fall of 1968. The founders of BOSS came from the class of 1969, a class that entered with eighteen black women, and were quickly joined by younger, more numerous students. BOSS enabled black women at Barnard to focus on the issues that mattered most to them and to speak out with their own voices without being drowned out by the men of SAS. Although the women of BOSS were not as interested in the gym debate as the men, their demands were otherwise much the same. Feminism was not at that point an issue for them. As one black student asked, "How can I fight for white women to get jobs that black men still can't get?" They wanted more black women on campus. They wanted to read about blacks in their courses. Increasingly alienated from campus life, they demanded the right to live on an all-black floor in the dorm.[75]

Black students were not the only ones feeling alienated in 1968. Linda LeClair dropped out, as did many others—black and white, men and women—who were so estranged from academic life that continued participation in the university became impossible for them. But for the women who remained, the events of 1968 led to new ways of thinking about women's place in American society broadly and at Columbia in particular.[76]

The first public manifestation of that new thinking occurred in early 1969, when a hundred women—students, faculty, and staff—met in the main-floor lounge in Fayerweather Hall to form Columbia Women's Liberation (CWL). The immediate inspiration for founding the group came from an abortion rights demonstration held several weeks before. One of a number of states then considering reform of their highly restrictive abortion laws, New York announced that it would hold hearings in Manhattan on February 13, 1969, and that fourteen men and one woman—a nun—had been selected to give testimony as expert witnesses. Outraged by the choice of witnesses, feminists from NOW and the more radical Redstockings began recruiting women to disrupt the hearings. Harriet Zellner, a Columbia graduate student in economics who had learned of the protest from other women in her department, met Flo Kennedy (Law School 1951), one of Columbia Law School's first black graduates and a NOW leader, at the hearings and solicited her advice about starting a women's group at Columbia. Kennedy suggested that she contact Kate Millett, another NOW member. Zellner proposed the idea of creating CWL to Millett the following week, and together they made up flyers and posted them in women's bathroom stalls all over the campus.[77]

The easy communication between women's groups from downtown and women at Columbia followed a historical pattern. Columbia women had always been involved in the city, and their work regularly found a broader audience through their connections to the media and government. In 1963, Margaret Mead wrote the foreword to the *Report of the Presidential Commission on the Status of Women*, which had, in turn, been inspired by Eli Ginzberg's book *Womanpower* (1957). The same year, Betty Friedan published *The Feminine Mystique*, which drew heavily on the work of Mirra Komarovsky. Three years later, Columbians Friedan, Alice Rossi, Gerda Lerner, and Carl Degler became charter members of the National Organization for Women, and Muriel Fox (Barnard 1948) helped Friedan found the New York chapter of NOW, which counted among its early members Kate Millett. At the same time, a number of Columbia graduate students, including Millett, joined early radical groups like New York Radical Women and the Redstockings. To be a feminist at Columbia was to be a joiner.

In response to Millett and Zellner's leafleting on the Columbia campus, female staff members, graduate students, faculty, and a few Barnard students packed the first meeting of Columbia Women's Liberation in Fayerweather Hall. Millett, who had the more extensive speaking experience, made a few introductory remarks and then turned the meeting over to Zellner. Nervous before such a large audience, Zellner began by asking the assembled women to ensure the confidentiality of the discussions and then asked them to tell their stories. The floodgates opened. Graduate students testified that even in the midst of the largesse of governmental and foundation funding of graduate fellowships, they had been denied fellowships by professors who told them that the likelihood they would marry made them bad investments.

Those who had not been able to secure outside funding worked as secretaries in the university and thereby delayed their progress. Junior faculty noted the absence of promotion prospects for women and discrimination in salaries. Administrative staff complained of having to train men for promotions that they were denied.[78]

Some grievances came out only later, in whispered discussions with friends and in the consciousness-raising groups that quietly formed. In certain departments, male professors saw women only as sexual beings. A "casting couch" was widely rumored to be the only sure way to a graduate fellowship in one department. Even for those who succeeded in the sexual competition, that ritual carried risks. A soured relationship usually required a change of field, something that in a small department could greatly constrain one's progress. Relationships based on mutual affection had other hazards. As the sociologist Cynthia Epstein has written, academe "still supposes that the contributions of younger women who associate with established men are usually a reflection of the senior person's ideas." Those who did not catch a professor's eye or who, for reasons of sexual preference, had no interest in doing so found that winning academic support could be difficult. No one knows how much talent failed to develop because of the sexual hurdles that women, more than men, had to clear.[79]

Columbia Women's Liberation quickly fell into a pattern of weekly meetings. In addition to Kate Millett and Harriet Zellner, the group's regulars included Catharine Stimpson, an assistant professor of English at Barnard who had earned her Ph.D. from Columbia in 1967; Ann Sutherland Harris, an assistant professor of art history at Columbia; Barbara Buonchristiano (General Studies 1966), an administrative assistant at the Business School; Rachel Blau DuPlessis (Barnard 1963), a graduate student in English; Linda Edwards, a graduate student in economics; and Amy Hackett, a graduate student in history. "We had a rotating chair," Zellner later recalled. "We were serious feminists who started by working in our own backyard." Members divided themselves into committees to attack specific problems: the absence of gynecological care anywhere in the university, discrimination in pay against maids, the dearth of women among the university's security-guard staff. Members of CWL spoke at other college campuses, helped found women's caucuses at professional associations, set up consciousness-raising groups, and began organizing the university's clerical workers. Barnard and Columbia abandoned parietals. Barnard allowed students to live where they liked and ended its dress code. The Barnard College and Columbia University health services hired gynecologists and started prescribing birth-control pills. The work that was to have the most dramatic impact, however, was a report prepared by the Committee on Discrimination Against Women Faculty.[80]

The committee, organized by Harris and DuPlessis, sat down with the university catalog for the academic year 1968/1969, which listed every faculty member. They divided the list by gender and rank, and called those with ambiguous names to ask whether the person was male or female—a strategy that was not well received by some of the women they called, who objected to the disruptive potential of focusing attention on gender issues. They then calculated percentages and compared them with the percentage of women who had earned doctorates long enough before to be eligible to hold each of the ranks examined. "Ha!—my math anxiety disappeared," DuPlessis later exulted.[81]

In making its calculations, the committee excluded Barnard, where two-thirds of the faculty was female, but noted that even at that college for women, male faculty dominated the senior ranks. At Columbia, the disparities between women who earned doctorates and women who held faculty positions were in many cases dramatic. In the graduate faculties, Columbia employed not a single woman in a full-time faculty position in French, psychology, anthropology, and philosophy. One had to go to General Studies to find the only female professor teaching in any of those fields: Gita May, professor of French. And yet, between 1966 and 1968, the percentage of women doctorates produced in those departments was significant: 44 percent in French, 36 percent in psychology, 44 percent in anthropology, and 17 percent in philosophy. The Department of Art History, which awarded more than half of its doctorates—54 percent—to women, had the best record. It claimed three female full professors—Edith Porada, Evelyn Harrison, and Jane G. Mahler—out of a total of eleven, and two female assistant professors: Ann Sutherland Harris and Ann Farkas. No other department had as many women in its professorial ranks, but even so, the number of female faculty trailed significantly behind the pool of female Ph.D.'s that the department produced. The English department, which awarded 27 percent of its doctorates to women, had only one tenured female, Elizabeth Dunno. One had to go to General Studies to find Associate Professors Carolyn Heilbrun and Alice Fredman, and Assistant Professor Joan Ferrante. The history department, which awarded 17 percent of its doctorates to women, could claim only one assistant professor in African history, Marcia Wright, and one half-time professorial appointment in Middle Eastern history, Nina Garsoian; it had none in either European or American history, the fields that produced the largest number of Ph.D.'s.[82]

The university's record of hiring women was better for the lower ranks; the percentage of assistant professors had almost quadrupled from 1962 to

1967, rising from 4 to 15 percent in only five years. But the percentage of female full professors for the university as a whole was under 5 percent, in a country in which women had earned more than 10 percent of the doctorates for over twenty years.[83]

CALLING IN THE FEDS

Upon completing their study in December 1969, members of CWL hand-delivered a copy of their report, tied in a blue ribbon, to Andrew Cordier, who had become acting president of Columbia after Grayson Kirk's retirement following the uprisings of 1968 and president in August 1969. For good measure, they also sent copies to the newly created University Senate, the *Barnard Alumnae Magazine*, and the *New York Times*. An editor at the *Times* sent Linda Greenhouse, a young reporter who would later cover the Supreme Court for the newspaper, to speak to the report's authors. Greenhouse's story "Columbia Accused of Bias on Women" appeared in the *Times* on January 11, 1970, a Sunday, and caught the attention of Bernice Sandler in Maryland.[84]

Having raised two children and earned a Ph.D. in clinical psychology at the University of Maryland, Sandler had recently decided to return to full-time work. She had applied for a position at the university's Department of Counseling and Personnel Services, but even though the department had seven openings, she had been rejected. When she asked the reason, she was told that she "came on too strong for a woman." Sandler's husband, a lawyer, believed that she was a victim of blatant sex discrimination, but he counseled that there was not much she could do because federal legislation against employment discrimination exempted institutions of higher education.[85] She could not sue on her own behalf, but she might be able to bring pressure on the University of Maryland to treat women fairly because the university was a "government contractor." Sandler joined the Women's Equity Action League (WEAL), a 1968 spin-off of NOW, and gave herself a crash course in civil rights law.[86]

In 1965, President Lyndon Johnson had issued Executive Order 11246, under which all employers holding federal contracts, including educational institutions, must agree not only to refrain from discriminating in their employment practices but also to develop affirmative-action programs to rectify the effects of past discrimination. At first, the executive order covered race, but not sex discrimination. Under pressure from NOW, however, Johnson amended the original order in 1967. Executive Order 11375 banned discrimination against women and became effective in 1968. The executive branch had the power to enforce those orders through revoking the federal contracts of any business or educational institution that failed to demonstrate, through an acceptable affirmative-action plan, that it was not discriminating. The two government agencies that were authorized to monitor colleges and universities were the Department of Labor (DOL) and the Department of Health, Education, and Welfare (HEW).[87]

As of the winter of 1968/1969, Sandler discovered, the federal government had done little except put medical schools all across the country on notice that they would soon be subject to a compliance review, during which their hiring practices with respect to minorities would be examined. Women were not mentioned. Distressed that federal officials were ignoring sex discrimination, Sandler began to look into hiring practices, first at the University of Maryland and then elsewhere. If she could demonstrate that Maryland and other universities around the country were guilty of a pattern of sex discrimination in hiring, she reasoned, she could complain to both DOL and HEW and ask that they investigate. If the investigation found that a university was discriminating, or if the university merely failed to comply with federal investigators, the government could terminate the institution's federal contracts. Research universities had become increasingly dependent on government contracts during the Cold War, and losing those contracts could have a devastating effect on their budgets, certainly enough to get the attention of university administrators.[88]

Sandler was working on a blanket complaint against the nation's colleges and universities when she read Linda Greenhouse's story about the women at Columbia. She immediately contacted Ann Sutherland Harris, who provided her with a copy of the CWL report.[89] Sandler appended the report to her complaint, which she filed with the Department of Labor on January 31, 1970. The CWL report was especially helpful, Sandler later recalled, because it was more detailed than any other study then available. A few weeks later, she used the CWL report to file another complaint, specifically against Columbia, with Secretary of Labor George Shultz. Shultz, in turn, passed the complaint to J. Stanley Pottinger, the newly appointed general counsel of the Civil Rights Division of HEW.[90]

A 1965 graduate of Harvard Law School, Pottinger had spent his first five years as a lawyer working on the problems of prisoners and migrant farm workers in California. Appointed to the Civil Rights Division of HEW, he viewed his chief responsibility as improving the educational prospects of minorities. Bernice Sandler set out to broaden his thinking. She organized a letter-writing campaign to Congress to prompt representatives to pressure federal agencies to enforce their own guidelines.[91] She arranged meetings at

J. Stanley Pottinger
General counsel of Civil Rights Division,
United States Department of Health,
Education, and Welfare, as photographed by
Arnold Newman, 1972. (*New York Times*)

DOL and HEW. As Pottinger later recalled, he had barely moved in when women began descending on his office to ask why he was not enforcing regulations that banned discrimination against women.[92]

At the same time that Sandler tried to bring pressure on the executive branch to enforce its own regulation against sex discrimination, she worked on Congress to pass a law that would protect women more directly. Her chief ally was Edith Green, one of the highest-ranking members of the House Committee on Education and Labor. For years, Green had watched helplessly as various civil rights measures had exempted institutions of higher education from coverage. In 1970, her committee considered an omnibus educational reform bill, and she was determined that, this time, women would be protected against discrimination in education. She appointed Sandler to her staff and prepared for hearings on the bill in the summer of 1970.[93] Sandler went to Columbia to talk to the members of CWL. She suggested that they write to members of Congress, urging them to bring pressure on DOL and HEW to enforce regulations against sex discrimination and to support new federal legislation. She also recruited Ann Sutherland Harris to join academic women from around the country to testify at the summer legislative hearings.[94]

The mounting pressure from Congress and the women's movement gradually had an effect at HEW. Pottinger made a conscious decision to help women, as well as minorities. Not everyone on his overworked staff was eager to do so. Many were resistant to addressing sex discrimination against privileged, well-educated white women, Pottinger later recalled, while "there were still black kids in Alabama going to school under trees." Nonetheless, Pottinger forced a shift in direction.[95]

Columbia administrators were not at all prepared for what was about to happen. In the wake of the 1968 campus uprising, the top administrators had departed, leaving growing annual deficits that had placed the university in an extremely vulnerable position. In the late 1960s, fiscal pressures intensified further when, first, the Ford Foundation, on which Columbia had relied heavily, began redirecting funds to combat growing poverty and violence. Then, in 1969, President Richard Nixon, facing his own budgetary problems, terminated all National Defense Education Act Fellowships; Columbia suddenly lost more than two hundred of these fellowships. By the early 1970s, Columbia was running a deficit of $16.5 million on a budget of $170 million.[96] On top of those problems, Columbia had a history of terrible record keeping. Decentralized and thinly staffed, the university simply did not have the kind of employment records that the government required for compliance.[97]

Nor did the university have any generally agreed-on procedures for either hiring or promoting in its seventy-seven departments or schools. Some departments hired assistant professors from their own pool of graduate students; others proceeded informally. A faculty member simply placed a telephone call to one of a handful of professors known to be training students in a given field and asked who was available. Women did not fair well in that "old-boy network." Promotions could be just as informal. George Fraenkel, dean of the graduate faculties, later recalled a hastily convened university ad hoc committee granting tenure to a male professor on the basis of one very brief letter.[98] Moreover, Columbia did not have an accurate count of the number of women and men in its employ, or what their race might be, much less a comprehensive set of figures on how many were working in each job category and at what rank. While other universities, like Harvard and Chicago, with significantly fewer minorities and women in their professorial ranks (as subsequent research revealed), dutifully submitted hiring data to the federal government, Columbia struggled to identify who exactly was in its employ.[99]

Finally, on November 3, 1971, Pottinger acted. In a twelve-page letter, he laid out the history of his office's dealings with Columbia administrators. Beginning with the January 31, 1969, letter that alerted the College of Physicians and Surgeons to a forthcoming review, Pottinger detailed twenty-one separate efforts over thirty months to obtain information. Not that Columbia had failed entirely. It had proposed two affirmative-action plans. The second, submitted on July 30, 1971, committed the university "to intensify efforts to recruit females and minority individuals." But neither document provided any supporting data or a clear plan for recruiting more women and minorities. In the "absence of an analysis of existing hiring practices, including recruitment sources," Pottinger noted, "it is impossible to evaluate the intended or practical effect" of the university's good intentions. In closing, Pottinger announced that, since all efforts at bringing about compliance had failed, he was recommending that the federal government take steps "to terminate all existing Federal Contracts with Columbia University and all of its divisions, and to debar the University and all of its divisions from future participation in Federal contracts."[100] The government had suspended approval of individual contracts before, but no other institution had ever faced formal proceedings for blanket termination. Pottinger arranged for his letter to be hand-delivered to President William McGill the following day.

William McGill, born in East Harlem, New York City, in 1922, the son of Irish Catholics, was a 1943 graduate of Fordham with a Ph.D. in mathematical psychology that he earned in 1953 from Harvard. He first came to Columbia in 1956 as a professor of psychology, but, convinced that the department was not keeping up with new developments in the field, he left for the University of California at San Diego in 1965 to become head of the school's Department of Psychology. His success as an administrator catapulted him in 1968 to the position of university chancellor. Leading San Diego during a period of turmoil similar to that at Columbia, he drew on his experience as a scrappy Irish kid from the streets of New York to face down angry students, a performance that impressed Columbia trustees, who asked him to succeed Andrew Cordier as president in 1970. McGill was the first Catholic to serve in that position.[101]

Presented with Pottinger's report, the new president scrambled to respond. The federal government's decision to cut off federal funding meant that the university was about to lose $33 million in federal contracts. McGill announced the government's action to the Columbia community in a carefully worded letter. Emphasizing that the university did not discriminate and had not been charged with doing so, he conceded that its record keeping had been deficient and promised that it would be improved. McGill observed that he was operating in uncharted waters: "We are no longer in all respects an independent private university. Our access to federal and state resources depends on our ability to provide a level of accountability heretofore not practiced or even envisioned at Columbia University. . . . We simply must be prepared . . . to subject ourselves to an external scrutiny that makes us all occasionally uncomfortable. I see no other way."[102] According to one of his associates, McGill felt "blind-sided" by the government's charge of discrimination and "didn't give a damn about affirmative action." But he had to do something to keep Pottinger from making good on his threat to cancel government contracts. He turned therefore to his vice president for administration, Paul Carter, and gave him thirty days to solve the university's problems with the government.[103]

Four days later, the University Senate, formed in April 1969 in response to the student protests of 1968, created the Commission on the Status of Women. In one of its first meetings, the commission, co-chaired by Frances Hoffman, director of chemical laboratories at Columbia, and Ivar Berg of the Business School, condemned the administration for appearing to be more concerned with restoring contracts than with ending discrimination. The committee urged the administration to abandon its "isolationist" attitude and called on McGill to "seek active participation of concerned groups."[104]

In two gestures born of long experience, McGill met with members of Columbia Women's Liberation and formed an advisory board on which he asked some of the university's most respected female faculty to serve.[105] Unlike many men of his generation who had difficulty dealing with women outside a domestic role, McGill had been accustomed to the concept of the working woman from early childhood. His mother was a nurse; one of his sisters, a telephone operator. A female professor at Fordham, Dorothea McCarthy, had been the faculty member who first inspired him to study psychology. His wife, a nurse like his mother, had worked the evening shift at a nearby hospital when he was in graduate school, leaving their young daughter in his care every day at 4:00 P.M. And while there were as yet few women in his field when he came to Columbia as a psychologist in the 1950s, Rose Edith Sitgreaves, a statistician at Teachers College, became one of his collaborators. However, McGill never appointed a woman to a senior administrative position. Indeed, he allowed Marion Jemmott, who had worked her way up through the ranks from secretary of the philosophy department to "acting" secretary of the university, to languish in that position for seven years before granting her a regular appointment shortly before he left Columbia.[106] Moreover, he had a low opinion of feminists, as he once confided to Marjorie Hope Nicolson.[107] But when forced to confront injustice, he had the political savvy to reach out for help in addressing it.[108]

Reaching out to faculty from across the university, McGill tried to achieve ethnic and racial as well as gender balance on his twelve-member Faculty Affirmative Action Advisory Committee. He named five women: Patricia Graham, from Teachers College and Barnard; Frances Hoffman, director of the chemical laboratories at Columbia; Chien-Shiung Wu, professor of physics at Columbia; Nina Garsoian, professor of history and a member of the Middle East Institute; and Ann Hirsch, assistant dean of the graduate faculties. The women were joined by seven men: Eli Ginzberg from the Business School; Jonathan Cole from the sociology department at Barnard; Charles Hamilton, the committee's only black member, from the Columbia political science department; Herbert Robbins, a statistician from the Columbia math department; Ichiro I. Shirato from the department of Asian languages and cultures; Gerald Thompson from the medical school, and Robert Brookhart, associate provost. McGill asked for their advice in setting goals and developing programs to reach them.[109] Patricia Graham taught history and education at Barnard and Teachers College and had published in *Science* in September 1970 the article "Women in Academe," a detailed analysis of the discrimination women faced in the academy.[110] Graham came from an academic family. Her maternal grandfather was a classicist; her uncle, a president of the University of Oregon; and her mother, Marguerite Hall Albjerg, a historian with a Ph.D. from the University of Wisconsin, who gave up a full-time appointment when she married and taught only occasional courses in history and government at Purdue University, where her husband had a regular appointment. Prevailing nepotism rules precluded her from ever securing a professorial position, despite her publication of four books and more than thirty articles on history and education. Graham and her husband, Loren Graham, who was a professor of Russian history at Columbia, resolved that theirs would be a different academic partnership, one in which the wife would not have to sacrifice her ambition to the fulfillment of her husband's career. The balkanized structure of Columbia University, where the separate existence of Barnard and Teachers College offered opportunities to a number of Columbia faculty wives, made that goal possible.[111]

More than most men on the faculty, Loren Graham understood the pressures faced by women who sought to succeed within academe. At about the time the advisory committee was formed, the women graduate students in history called a meeting of the faculty in the same Fayerweather lounge in which CWL had first met. As Estelle Freedman later remembered the event, each woman had written out a "horror story" on a note card. The students had shuffled them, and then the "women read the stories anonymously, not of their own experience but from someone else in the department." One reported an experience on the first day of graduate school in which a professor had defended Columbia's continuing use of the M.A. degree, when other universities were beginning to phase the degree out, on the grounds that it was useful to the many women who would leave graduate school after the first year or two. Another described learning of a letter of recommendation that said she was not mobile because she was married. "At the end of the exposition, most faculty who spoke seemed shocked and disbelieved that any of these things could have happened in their department, which they assured us held no biases against women," Freedman recalled.

But then one ally spoke out, the Russian historian Loren Graham, who basically described the emperor's clothes. He recalled having been a graduate student in the department along with his wife, Patricia Graham, and then he compared the treatment he got with hers. That silenced the group, and I like to think that in the end we raised some consciousness. But, I note, only after a male faculty member broke ranks.[112]

In 1973/1974, the history department conducted searches that resulted in the hiring of three female assistant professors, two in European and one in American history. At the same time, Columbia adopted its first code of academic freedom, which included a section devoted to faculty parents. Any faculty member who was the principal caretaker of a child under the age of nine would have the option of teaching half time and slowing his or her tenure clock by half. With promotions to tenure largely frozen, this new policy had little immediate effect. But its appearance in the university's code represented an important first step toward taking account of the pressures that young parents, and especially mothers, faced as they sought to pursue academic careers. Patricia and Loren Graham played a critical role in bringing this change.

The chemist Frances Hoffman emphasized the problem of salary disparities. "We made a short list of the egregious examples of the women professors whose salaries needed adjustment," Hoffman recalled. McGill "put it into his pocket and said he would take care of it. He did; people got raises." Chien-Shiung Wu was one of those affected.[113] "What came out of this ad hoc committee was wonderful," Hoffman later recalled. "These women, who had all been scattered throughout the university, met in the presidents' office and became good friends. We got along so well. Wu had a beautiful home on Claremont Ave. She got women together so that they would know each other. She invited every woman at Columbia."[114]

The physicist Chien-Shiung Wu had come to feminism gradually, but with increasing emotion, over the course of the 1960s. Attending a conference on women in science and engineering at MIT in 1964 with, among others, Alice Rossi, she had listened in stunned disbelief to the comments of the psychoanalyst Bruno Bettleheim about the nature of women's contributions in science. Speaking of a young Russian woman, he said, "She loved her work with a womanly embracing of her tasks rather than a masculine conquering of them." He went on to say that a woman's point of view might be productive in some fields of education and the social sciences but not in physics or mathematics, where one strives for objectivity. "I doubt that the tiny atoms and nuclei or the mathematical symbols of the DNA molecules have any preference for either masculine or feminine treatment," Wu indignantly responded. Alice Rossi, in a lengthy address, blamed attitudes like those voiced by Bettlelheim—and widely shared in America—for women's low numbers in science. Everyone expected women to drop out, felt more comfortable when they did, and even encouraged them to do so. Following that conference, Wu became an increasingly active participant in discussions about women's place in science. As she told a meeting of the American Physics Society in February 1971, no one reading about the "recent women's liberation developments" could fail to see the "urgent needs of upgrading the woman's position in the academic profession." She set forth to do so by her participation on McGill's advisory committee.[115]

Another committee member, Eli Ginzberg, agreed that the need for change was obvious. He thought, moreover, that the university, as well as its women, would benefit from it. In a memorandum to President McGill, written two weeks after the Pottinger bombshell, Ginzberg urged that the university turn the government's intervention to the university's advantage. For too long the administration had allowed departments to operate without adequate supervision. As a consequence, "too many mediocre people have received tenure," there has been no effort "to improve the staffing in weak departments," it has been difficult to arrange joint appointments, and there is "duplication of staff teaching similar subjects in different divisions of the University with suboptimal numbers of students." Ginzberg conceded that compliance with the government could be both costly and destructive of academic standards, "but this need not happen." Indeed, he argued that the government was handing the administration the means to build a much better, more diverse, and higher quality institution.[116]

The sociologist Jonathan Cole agreed. A protégé of Robert Merton, Cole was an assistant professor at Barnard College at the time the committee was formed. McGill recruited him because of his skills in social-scientific data analysis, which he had developed while working on his dissertation on social stratification in the sciences. It fell largely to him, "working 24/7" as he later recalled, to amass the data without which no affirmative-action plan could exist. Raised in Queens, and a product of New York City's public schools, Cole had graduated from Columbia College in 1964. Continuing at Columbia for graduate school, he earned his Ph.D. in five years. Experience on McGill's advisory committee was to prove important to his later career. It helped him advance to tenure at the young age of thirty-one, inspired him to embark on a number of studies of women in science, and ultimately led to his appointment in 1989 as provost and dean of the faculty at Columbia, in which position he oversaw some seven hundred tenure reviews. Looking back from his position as provost on the ferment of the early 1970s, he identified women's rising aspirations, as well as their organizing efforts, as the most important factors in advancing women in the academy. But he credited affirmative action with giving women "a hammer to use against the university," particularly in promotion to tenure. "The chief problem in the early 1970s was the barrier to tenure," he remembered. "The evidence of discrimination was clear."[117]

While the president's advisory committee, and especially its female members, felt strongly that only the pressure of goals would produce change, many on the faculty decried what they saw as the government's abuse of power. In their view, the government's demand for hiring data and an affirmative-action plan was a blatant assault on academic standards, freedom, and privacy. They were appalled at the idea of having to work with government statisticians who seemed to think, for instance, that all historians were fungible and that a department looking for a specialist in twentieth-century central European history could just pluck one out of the general pool of Ph.D.'s in history. Concerned faculty were even more resistant to the idea of turning over confidential personnel files to government investigators.[118]

To many Jews, the entire project smacked of anti-Semitism. They saw the goals and timetables required by an affirmative-action plan as the equivalent of quotas. Having struggled for decades to eradicate the quotas that had limited the admission and hiring of Jews in the Ivy League, they denounced any policy that might lead to quotas being imposed once more, however noble the purpose might be. Lionel Trilling worried that affirmative action would lead to a decline in academic standards.[119] Not all Jews shared that view. Bernice Sandler, for one, scoffed, "Nonsense. They're upset because they have to compete against women."[120]

Faculty members' dependence on federal funding did not dictate their response. Some faculty at the medical school, who were most at risk of losing funding, were most resistant to change and took the dimmest view of government bureaucrats. Physically removed from the rest of the university, the College of Physicians and Surgeons differed from it in its administrative structure. Department chairs, for instance, did not rotate and thus were very powerful; many did not brook interference with their prerogatives. Others, however, both at the medical school and in the sciences "downtown," were eager to achieve a quick resolution, either for practical reasons or because they agreed that better administrative procedures were necessary.[121]

While the faculty debated, the administration went to work to produce an affirmative-action plan that the faculty could live with and that Pottinger would accept. Provost Jacques Barzun brought in Abe Jaffe, a demographer experienced in labor statistics, to work with government statisticians, most of whom had no experience with a university workforce. Ivar Berg, co-chair with Frances Hoffman of the University Senate's Commission on the Status of Women, came over from the Business School. Gradually the people at Columbia and those at HEW were able to agree on common goals.[122]

The university completed its affirmative-action plan on April 10, 1972, a month after Congress passed the Equal Employment Opportunity Act and the Equal Rights Amendment. As the university's lawyers reviewed the text one final time before submitting it, President McGill summoned Chien-Shiung Wu, Frances Hoffman, and Nina Garsoian to Low Library to read it and suggest any necessary revisions to the final text. The women worked through the evening in the Burden Room, ordering in Chinese food from the Moon Palace when they got hungry. By 11:30 P.M., they had finished the pages they had been given and went to the president's office to request the rest of the report. "A young lawyer came out—all full of himself," Hoffman later recalled, to go over the final pages with the women. "At one point he said, 'you can skip over that page because it has a lot of statistics.' Madame Wu responded to the poor fellow, 'I've forgotten more mathematics than you ever knew.'" In its final form, the plan ran to more than three hundred pages and included detailed data on employees sorted by race and gender. The plan included, as well, directions on how to advertise and conduct a proper search, five-year goals, and strategies for determining possible deficiencies. The university promised to make "every effort" to add almost nine hundred women and members of minority groups to its academic and nonacademic staffs by 1977. Pottinger accepted the plan and restored Columbia's federal contracts.[123]

Implementing the affirmative-action plan proved a daunting task. Dean Fraenkel, who had denied that discrimination existed at Columbia on the day that Pottinger's letter was made public, found evidence of bias as he implemented the plan, especially in salaries. Some administrators, even President Martha Peterson at Barnard, routinely favored men with families over women in dual-income families in setting salary scales. Fraenkel insisted on corrections. The most important outcome of the government's initiative, in

Fraenkel's view, was the creation of affirmative-action procedures in hiring, promotion, and compensation where none had previously existed. Recalling the efforts of four advisory committee members—Chien-Shiung Wu, Nina Garsoian, Patricia Graham, and Frances Hoffman—Fraenkel later recalled, "They really kept us on our toes."[124]

But progress was slow. According to the English professor Joan Ferrante, despite clear directives to follow affirmative-action procedures, and concerted efforts in some departments to do so, not all faculty took affirmative action seriously. To make matters worse for women, at the very moment that a new generation stood poised to assume faculty positions in the early 1970s, academic expansion in the country came to a virtual standstill. The crisis was especially severe at Columbia. As administrators told federal officials, they could not meet affirmative-action goals through an increase or even a "steady state" in their staff; "financial problems necessitate a *reduction* in staff." Between 1971 and 1973, women's share of the faculty increased by only three, as the university set about cutting fifty-four faculty members. For years, progress for women at Columbia, as throughout academe, remained frustratingly slow.[125]

Even as they advised McGill, Frances Hoffman and her colleagues sought to institutionalize their work through the Commission on the Status of Women. Over the course of the next four years, the commission came to comprise eight members, two observers, and six consultants—all but three of them women. Chien-Shiung Wu, Nina Garsoian, and Barbara Low (of the medical school) were the most senior. The women from the Columbia English department were there in force: Elizabeth Dunno, Joan Ferrante, Alice Fredman, and Carolyn Heilbrun. Catharine Stimpson represented Barnard. Frances Hoffman and Marion Jemmott represented women in the administration. In 1975, they released a report on the status of women on the faculty, calling for further action to bring women into the professoriate, promote them to senior positions, and pay them fairly. The report began with an excerpt from a speech that McGill had given at the University of Michigan (which also had been under fire from Pottinger) soon after completing Columbia's affirmative-action plan. In it, he suggested that he had come to endorse what the women were trying to accomplish. "For too long we have been content with appointment practices at faculty level that have produced relatively few women faculty members. . . . Thus we have no quarrel with affirmative action, or with its objectives," McGill declared. "Women, blacks, and Latins are crying out for their full rights in our society and there is no excuse for pious or sanctimonious explanations of why these rights cannot be granted." Immediately following the release of its report, the commission introduced a proposal from several faculty at the Law School, including Michael Sovern, Ruth Bader Ginsberg, and Harriet Rabb, which called for the establishment of an ad hoc committee to conduct a department-by-department salary review.[126] The commission's Committee on Salaries met from 1976 to 1980. Meeting with department chairs, they compared faculty résumés, teaching responsibilities, and community service. They scrutinized the different elements of each salary package (grant money or straight salary). Sometimes adjustments were made. Hoffman, who chaired the salary committee, later recalled, "McGill deserves a great deal of credit. His attitude was constructive. He did it for all the wrong reasons—not to lose grants—but he established a temporary and then a permanent salary committee" over the strong opposition of other administrators.[127] The women of Columbia had made a start. The university would never again be the same.

CHANGING THE FACE OF THE LAW SCHOOL

Asking questions about women's place in society occurred first at Barnard College and the graduate faculties and only later at Columbia's professional schools, in many of which women continued, even into the 1970s, to occupy a marginal place. As of 1970, female students in the Law School, for instance, counted for only 10 percent of the total enrollment, and the proportion of women on the Law School faculty was, and remained until 1972, zero. And yet, in the early 1970s, as a direct result of the efforts of Columbia Women's Liberation, Columbia suddenly became the leading center of sex-discrimination law in the country. One would not have predicted that outcome when women first entered the Law School in 1927.

A few men on the faculty went out of their way to encourage their female students, but others never adjusted to women's presence. One professor simply continued to address the class collectively as "Gentlemen"; another grilled women on the infamous "ladies day," while avoiding them for the rest of the year. Members of the faculty routinely posed demeaning hypotheticals that featured women as either gold diggers or dumb housewives. As late as the 1950s, Dean Young B. Smith addressed the entering class by saying, "The average capacity of our student body is very high and included among them are many young men of extraordinary ability." Women, lacking the support of a broader culture of protest, ignored slights and resigned themselves to the absence of female faculty. In the early 1950s, women did, however, form the Women's Law Society and invited speakers to advise them on law careers, a decision that at least signaled the recognition that women would likely encounter obstacles to their careers.[128]

And they did. As Nancy Fraenkel Wechsler (Barnard 1938, Law School 1940) recalled her first foray into the world of private practice, "At one firm, the receptionist told me they'd hired female stenographers only two years ago and they were not about to hire women lawyers." A few women won jobs in private firms, usually through family connections or with the understanding that they would practice in trusts and estates, where, as Edith Spivak (Barnard 1929, Law School 1932) once quipped, "all the clients were dead and no one would see you." Helen Hessin Robinson (Barnard 1927, Law School 1930), the first Barnard student to graduate from the Law School, went on to practice law at Lord, Day & Lord. Harriet Pilpel (Law School 1936) joined Greenbaum, Wolff & Ernst. Some women found jobs in academe. Margaret Spahr, the first woman to graduate from Columbia Law School, in 1929, secured an appointment as professor of political science at Hunter College, where she taught constitutional law for thirty years, publishing books, articles, and book reviews, and sent dozens of young women back to Columbia for legal training. The Columbia law faculty briefly considered hiring Sonia Mentschikoff (Law School 1937), one of the country's leading experts on the commercial code, for a position on the faculty following World War II, but decided that hiring a woman would be too big a break with tradition; Mentschikoff taught instead at Harvard and Chicago before becoming dean of the University of Miami School of Law. A number of female Columbia Law School graduates went into government, and a few became judges. Although the number of women remained low at Columbia, the 1950s and 1960s saw the training of women who would play an important role in challenging gender roles, not merely by their example, but also by the work they did—most particularly Ruth Bader Ginsburg (Law School 1959), who played a leading role in expanding the reach of the Fourteenth Amendment to cover sex, and Harriet Rabb (Barnard 1963, Law School 1966), who pioneered in the area of employment discrimination in the 1970s.[129]

The first to make her mark was Ginsburg. Born into a Jewish family in Brooklyn in 1933 and a product of Brooklyn's public schools, Ginsburg was an academic star from the start. Although close to her father, she was influenced more profoundly by her mother, a woman of great intellect and drive, who lived in a generation when most husbands still believed that having a working wife was a sign of personal failure. For all her academic brilliance and accomplishment, Ruth Bader was also fun-loving in a shy way, until she lost her mother to cancer the day before her high-school graduation in June 1950.[130]

In the fall, she left home for Cornell, where she met Martin Ginsburg, a year older than she. Ruth persuaded him to go to law school, with the expectation of attending herself, and married him in 1954. She had just graduated from Cornell, and he had completed his first year at Harvard Law School. The ebullient antithesis to Ruth's shy reserve, Marty, as his friends called him, completely supported his wife's desire to work. Both of their careers had to be deferred, however, when Martin, a reserve officer in the U.S. Army, was sent to Fort Sill, Oklahoma, in 1954. A relentless challenger of gender roles, he worked his way through *The Escoffier Cookbook* in his spare time and became an accomplished cook.[131] Ruth found work at the local office of the Social Security Administration as a manager, but when she revealed that she was pregnant, her boss decided that she could not be sent to Baltimore for training and demoted her to a clerical position. She did not consider protesting. "The only thought that occurred to me," Ginsburg later recalled, "was maybe it wasn't so smart of me to say anything about being pregnant." The job went to another woman, pregnant as well, but less forthcoming. When Ginsburg became pregnant a decade later with her son, James, she kept her condition a secret as long as she possibly could.[132]

In 1956, with her new baby, Jane, in tow, Ginsburg entered Harvard Law School, to which her husband had returned to take his place in the second-year class. After two years, during which time she served on the *Harvard Law Review* and helped her husband survive both an automobile accident and cancer, Ginsburg asked Harvard to allow her to complete work for her degree at Columbia Law School, so she could remain with her husband, who had secured a job in New York City. Harvard rejected her proposal, but Columbia willingly admitted the *Law Review* editor, elected her to its own *Law Review*, and watched her graduate tied for first in her class.[133]

After law school, Ginsburg looked in vain for a job with a large law firm — a position that any man with her credentials would easily have secured. "In the fifties," she reported, "the traditional law firms were just beginning to turn around on hiring Jews. But to be a woman, a Jew and a mother to boot—that combination was a bit too much." Instead of entering private practice, Ginsburg clerked for Federal District Judge Edmund L. Palmieri in Manhattan. A man with her credentials might have expected a Supreme Court clerkship, but no one on the Court would have considered hiring a woman. Having secured a clerkship finally opened the doors to private firms, but by then Ginsburg had decided to pursue an academic career.[134]

She began at Columbia, where Professor Hans Smit asked her to join his international procedures project as associate director in 1961. Ginsburg first began to think about her experiences as part of a larger pattern of sex discrimination, when, as part of the project, she visited Sweden to study its system of civil procedure. Attention to the issue of sex roles was then considerably more

Ruth Bader Ginsburg (b. 1933)
Graduate of Cornell University (1954)
and Columbia Law School (1959), lawyer,
professor at Law School (1972–1980), and
associate justice of United States Supreme
Court (1993–), as photographed around 1972.
(Columbia Law School Archives)

advanced in Sweden than it was in the United States, and the discussion there got her thinking about restrictions on women in American law.[135]

Upon completion of the project, Columbia failed to hire her as a faculty member, but Ginsburg found a position teaching at the Rutgers University School of Law. While there, she did some work for the New Jersey office of the American Civil Liberties Union (ACLU). By the end of the 1960s, women began coming in to complain of being fired because they were pregnant. Having only recently tried to hide her own pregnancy, Ginsburg asked herself, "How have people been putting up with such arbitrary distinctions? How have I been putting up with them?" Not only did she take on the cases of women who were being fired because they were pregnant, but she took the further step of insisting that her clients receive the benefits she had been denied. Moreover, she began writing briefs for Supreme Court cases that would transform the law of sex discrimination. Following the example of two feminist lawyers at the ACLU, Dorothy Kenyon and Pauli Murray, she argued successfully that sex, like race, was an unreasonable classification in the law and should not be used to limit a person's opportunities.[136]

Harriet Rabb, a decade younger than Ginsburg, came to political consciousness as well as gender consciousness much more quickly. Born in Houston to a Jewish family, Rabb came to Barnard in 1959 to escape the role of the southern belle. Most of her Barnard friends who wanted to be lawyers married lawyers instead. She was the unusual one. She entered Columbia

Law School, married, worked for the radical lawyer William Kunstler on civil rights cases in Mississippi, divorced, remarried, and moved with her new husband to Washington, D.C., where she had trouble getting a job, not only because she was a woman, but also because of her FBI file, which included references, in the words of a judge who was considering employing her, to "some pretty strange meetings." She and her husband moved to New York, and she began teaching at Rutgers.[137]

When Professor Michael Sovern (Columbia College 1953, Law School 1955), a specialist in labor law and employment discrimination, became the new dean at Columbia Law School in 1970, one of his first acts was to recruit Ginsburg and Rabb to come to Columbia. Sovern had played an important role in resolving disputes between the faculty and the administration during the 1968 student protests. Along with the political scientist Alan Westin, Sovern served as co-chair of the Executive Committee of the Faculty, a group created in the midst of the takeover of Columbia buildings to represent the faculty in negotiations with the administration. The committee's most significant achievement was the creation of the University Senate, through which the faculty reclaimed power in the governance of the university that they had long ago ceded to the administration. When Columbia Women's Liberation charged the university with sex discrimination, the University Senate sponsored a series of forums to hear testimony from women about their experiences.[138] That testimony led the senate to create the Commission on the Status of Women. Among the women's grievances was that Columbia Law School continued to be led, as late as 1970, by an all-male faculty that prided itself on preparing its overwhelmingly male student body for careers on Wall Street. When Sovern took over as dean, he resolved to bring change, an impulse stemming not only from recent protests but also from his early encounters with female lawyers.[139]

Sovern had entered law school in 1952, while still a Columbia College student, as part of an accelerated program that allowed students to combine their senior year of college with their first year of law school. Born into a Jewish family in the Bronx in 1931, Sovern attended the Bronx High School of Science, still an all-male bastion, before entering Columbia College in 1949. He never took an undergraduate class with women, though he once signed up for a Barnard course, only to see it canceled for lack of adequate enrollment. He encountered more women at law school, but the numbers were low, a mere 7 percent of his classmates. What he best remembered decades later, however, was how well those few women did. Six out of eighteen of the female law students were among his colleagues on the *Columbia Law Review*. Among them were Harriet Sturtevant Shapiro, the second woman at

Columbia to hold the position of editor in chief of the *Law Review*, and Barbara Aronstein, later dean of Columbia Law School "We were comfortable together," Sovern later recalled of the women and men in his class.[140]

Sovern began his tenure as dean of Columbia Law School by breaking the all-male monopoly on the faculty and expanding the school's clinical programs. A director of the NAACP Legal Defense Fund's training program, as well as a founder of the Mexican-American Legal Defense Fund and the Puerto Rican Legal Defense Fund, Sovern wanted to develop the Law School in the direction of public-interest law. Raiding the Rutgers University School of Law, he hired Ginsburg and Rabb. Becoming Columbia's first tenured female professor in 1972, Ginsburg split her time between teaching civil procedure and sex-discrimination law and directing the Women's Rights Project for the American Civil Liberties Union. Thirty-year-old Harriet Rabb, who came to the Law School in 1971 as an instructor and director of a clinic devoted to employment discrimination, became the school's first female administrator the following year, when she was named assistant dean for urban affairs. Sovern's hiring of Ginsburg and Rabb was one of the most consequential acts of his deanship.[141]

BEYOND THE IVORY TOWER

When Michael Sovern recruited Ruth Bader Ginsburg to Columbia, she had just persuaded the Supreme Court, in the pivotal case of *Reed v. Reed* (1971), that it was not reasonable to prefer men to women as executors of estates simply because they were male, even if assuming that men had greater financial experience saved the government the trouble and expense of holding an administrative hearing to determine whether that assumption was true. During the years that Ginsburg was at Columbia (1972–1980), she coauthored the first casebook on sex discrimination and wrote or co-wrote briefs for nine cases before the Supreme Court. Arguing six of those cases, she won five. She also wrote fifteen amicus briefs. Representing both female and male defendants (to the consternation of some feminists), she insisted that to discriminate against women inevitably meant discriminating against men as well. She argued that female military officers deserved the same right to benefits for their male dependents as their male colleagues collected automatically for their female dependents, that young men should have the right to drink at the same age as young women, and that widowers should be entitled to the same benefits as widows. Taken together, the cases to which she contributed laid the foundation for what gradually became known as gender-discrimination law.[142]

While Ginsburg taught civil procedure and worked on Fourteenth Amendment cases, her junior colleague Harriet Rabb battled employment discrimination under Title VII of the Civil Rights Act of 1964. Rabb handled some of the most important early class-action, sex-discrimination cases— cases that banded together large numbers of female employees with common complaints to challenge large corporate employers more effectively. She successfully represented women at Wall Street law firms, at New York Telephone, at *Reader's Digest*, and at *Newsweek*, and in each instance won settlements that included affirmative-action goals for advancing women into formerly male-dominated jobs and raising salaries. But Rabb's most important case was one in which a Barnard alumna became the name complainant in a class-action suit on behalf of six hundred female co-workers at the newspaper whose owners had provided trustees to both Barnard and Columbia from 1937 to 1968. The case was *Elizabeth Wade Boylan, et al. v. The New York Times Company*, and it pitted Betsy Wade (Barnard 1951, Journalism 1952) against the Sulzberger family.[143]

Betsy Wade, born in Manhattan in 1929 and raised in Bronxville, New York, showed an early facility for language, which her father nurtured through vocabulary-building games, and a strong sympathy for the downtrodden in Depression-era America. Following high school, she attended Carleton College and then Barnard, where she "learned something about the life of the mind." Graduating in 1951, she entered the Columbia School of Journalism and further honed her excellent verbal skills in courses on copyediting taught by newsmen who were supplementing their salaries at the *New York Times* by teaching as adjunct professors at Columbia. The "men who taught copyediting thought I was the berries," Wade later recalled. "They just fell out of their chairs with joy. I was a good editor and I wrote wonderful headlines. I would find messy copy and clean it up. All that reading of dictionaries, all that force-feeding of vocabulary from my father— it had peculiarly fitted me for this trade. I could see the other shore. I could see a job at *The Times*."[144]

Wade graduated in June 1952, at the top of her class in copyediting, but the men who were willing to take her tuition fees at the Columbia School of Journalism and award her top marks there were not yet ready to integrate the *Times's* all-male copy desk with a female copyeditor. Wade secured her first job, therefore, not at the *New York Times* but at the more liberal *New York Herald Tribune*, where she met her future husband, the journalist James Boylan. She thrived there until the Friday before Labor Day 1953, when she was fired because she announced that she was pregnant. "You couldn't get unemployment insurance in those days if you were pregnant," she later noted, confirming Ruth Bader Ginsburg's, and countless other working women's, experience. The Columbia School of Journalism took her back as a secretary, and while in that position she overheard Turner Catledge of the *Times* tell a mostly male audience of alumni that the newspaper was experiencing a terrible shortage of copyeditors. Taking advantage of the crisis, Wade finally won the job she had long coveted. In 1956, she became the first female copyeditor ever hired at the *New York Times*.[145]

The *Times* had been a male bastion longer than any other publication. But for Iphigene Ochs Sulzberger (Barnard 1914), it might have remained so even longer. It was she who in 1936, following her father's death, persuaded her husband, Arthur Hays Sulzberger, Adolph Ochs's successor as publisher, to hire her friend Anne O'Hare McCormick, one of the country's leading European correspondents. The following year, McCormick won a Pulitzer Prize for her reporting from Europe. Other protégés included Charlotte Curtis, who came to the *Times* in 1961 and transformed the "Women's Page" into the site at the paper where social and cultural change was investigated. She wrote or commissioned stories on the Black Panthers, urban affairs, black fashion models, politics, abortion, lesbians, drug abuse, incest, peace marches, protest at Barnard and Columbia, and cohabitation. It was Curtis who, to Iphigene Sulzberger's dismay, ran the story that touched off the Linda LeClair affair. Sulzberger also championed the art historian Ada Louise Huxtable. From childhood, Iphigene Sulzberger had been concerned with the urban landscape, and she believed that Huxtable would be the ideal person to broaden the newspaper's coverage of the "built environment." Hired in 1963, Huxtable seven years later won the newspaper another Pulitzer Prize for her distinguished architectural criticism. McCormick, Curtis, and Huxtable proved that, with the forceful backing of Iphigene Ochs Sulzberger, female stars could find a place at the *New York Times*. But for all the visibility and influence of those female celebrities, management remained securely in the hands of men. Women who were merely as good as their male colleagues had to make do with lower positions and poorer pay.[146]

And yet the women at the *Times* remained reluctant to agitate, even after they began covering stories about the women's movement and how the women at Columbia pressed the university for better treatment. It took not just academic women but fellow journalists and feminist litigators to push them to take action. The women at *Newsweek* showed the way, when they complained about the magazine's practice of confining women to research jobs and giving writing assignments only to men. For those women, the final indignity came when editors went outside *Newsweek* to find a woman to write a story about women's liberation, "Women in Revolt," which appeared in the magazine on March 23, 1970. In anger, the *Newsweek* women hired Harriet Rabb.[147]

Finally, the women at the *New York Times* took action, turning to Betsy Wade, as one of the most senior and most respected women at the *Times* as well as an active member of the Newspaper Guild, to help them form a women's caucus to protest indignities they faced: editors who refused to print the honorific "Ms.," the absence of women in top management positions, low pay, and promotions that went almost always to men. Wade got payroll records from the Guild and found that male reporters made $59 a week more than women, half of whom had been working longer. Education and experience accounted for part of the difference, but limits set on the jobs women could hold were more important. Wade wrote a letter to the *Times* publisher, Arthur Sulzberger Jr., reporting her findings:

The voices of women are being heard in greater numbers in this country. As a result of this pressure, some improvement has taken place in the status of women in . . . the professions. In other cases, as in the academic world [a reference to women at Columbia], women are being compelled to take remedial action to assert their rights. . . . We call your attention to the twenty-one names on the masthead—both editorial and business executives. Not one of them is a woman.[148]

Wade sent copies of the letter to Sulzberger's mother, Iphigene, and to his sisters. Iphigene Sulzberger was dismayed to find that women made less than men for the same work. Punch, as Arthur Sulzberger Jr. was known, promised relief, but little happened. So Wade turned to Harriet Rabb, who instructed the women to file charges with the New York Commission on Human Rights and the United States Equal Employment Opportunity Commission. Limited progress began to be made on the editorial side, but nothing happened on the business side. Finally, the women filed a class-action suit and prepared for trial. The women had statistics and personal testimony on their side, but the *New York Times* had editors willing to testify that the women were receiving no less than their due. In the end, both sides agreed that a trial would hurt everyone involved. The editors at the *Times* refused ever to concede any wrongdoing, but Rabb hammered out a settlement agreement with their lawyers in 1978 that established an affirmative-action plan for advancing women at the newspaper and that for the first time set goals for placing women at the highest levels of management. One in eight top corporate offices would have to be held by a woman by 1982. Over the

Coming to Terms with the *New York Times*
Harriet Rabb (Barnard 1963, Law School 1966, dean of urban affairs and professor of law at
Columbia 1972–1993) explaining the terms of settlement in the case of *Elizabeth Boylan,
et al. v. The New York Times Company* to members of the Women's Caucus and their
supporters. The name plaintiff, Betsy Wade (Barnard 1951, Journalism 1952), is seated fifth
from right in this drawing by Marilyn Church, 1978. (Courtesy of Elizabeth Wade Boylan)

next generation, the *Times* would become a far different place, a place more
open to women and to minorities, a more liberal place, a place where the
subjects of particular interest to women were regularly covered, and a place
where topics long assigned to men would finally be covered by women.

The innovative thinking about women's place in American society, pioneered by students and faculty at Columbia in the 1960s, which led, in turn,
to their bringing pressure on the university to promote women into more responsible and higher-paying positions, had far-reaching consequences. Columbia women were never alone, but they were among the earliest to
protest, and given their situation in the media capital of the country, their
protests were widely publicized. Protests in other cities often remained local,
while those in New York became national news and the inspiration for further critical thinking. Gerda Lerner's question, "Where are the women?" inspired new work in history. Carolyn Heilbrun's and Kate Millett's critique of
the leading male modernists inspired new work in literature. Columbia

Women's Liberation's challenge to the university inspired academic women everywhere to demand better pay and more responsible positions and brought immediate change to Columbia, including the hiring of two women who would pioneer the field of sex-discrimination law. Ruth Bader Ginsburg gave new meaning to the Equal Protection Clause of the Fourteenth Amendment. And Harriet Rabb, collaborating with Betsy Wade, advanced the interests of women at the *New York Times*. Working and studying in the heart of New York, the commercial, cultural, legal, and media capital of the country, and taking part in a city of striving, ambitious immigrants, inheritors of a radical feminist tradition dating back to the mid-nineteenth century, the women of Columbia challenged some of the nation's most powerful, male-dominated institutions. More than women anywhere else, they made themselves heard.

SEVEN

THE BATTLE OVER COEDUCATION RENEWED

A S WOMEN at Columbia demanded greater opportunity within the university, the question of Barnard's separate existence reemerged. The civil rights movement in the South, which had drawn many recruits from northern college campuses in the mid-1960s, already had brought the subject of single-sex education under heightened scrutiny. A century after the suffragist Lillie Devereux Blake found inspiration in the Civil War–era struggle for racial justice to demand equal rights for women, veterans of the modern civil rights movement renewed the question Blake that had so insistently posed: Was not the separate education of women, like the separate education of blacks, unjustified? The sexual revolution then sweeping the country, and given local emphasis by Linda LeClair, raised a related issue: Was not the segregation of female students into separate dormitories also discriminatory, a Victorian holdover that prolonged adolescence unnecessarily for both sexes? By the end of the decade, a consensus seemed to be emerging that in the case of gender, as in the case of race, separate was "inherently unequal."[1] Single-sex colleges began to act on that belief in 1969, when Yale and Princeton opened their doors to women, and Vassar and Connecticut Colleges opened theirs to men. Within the next decade, Williams, Wesleyan, Dartmouth, Amherst, and the University of Virginia all admitted women. At the same time, men's and women's colleges that had long existed side by side in a coordinate relationship began to merge: Radcliffe with Harvard, Pembroke with Brown, and Jackson with Tufts.

For a brief moment, it looked as though Barnard would merge with Columbia. As even a cursory perusal of the *Barnard Bulletin, Barnard Alumnae Magazine,* and *Columbia Spectator* reveals, a steady stream of articles signaling the apparent breakdown of single-sex education began to appear in 1967. That year, the *Barnard Alumnae Magazine* featured a five-page photo essay on the arrival of "The Class of 1971" to a "coed campus" filled with young men. The following year, the discovery that Linda LeClair was violating college rules by living off campus with her Columbia boyfriend fueled a campus backlash against parietal rules.[2] A few months later, in the midst of student protests at Columbia, the Barnard Ad Hoc Strike Committee attacked Barnard's separate curriculum, declaring that "any differentiation in courses offered to or required of Barnard students as opposed to Columbia College students can only be the result of an archaic male-chauvinist value system which is repugnant to every liberated person."[3] But though merger occurred at nearly every other university with an affiliated women's school in the following decade, Barnard never merged with Columbia.[4]

The key to Barnard's remaining independent was its separate faculty. As Ellen Futter (Barnard 1971) later observed, "Having a separate faculty made Barnard more than real estate and endowment. It gave Barnard an intellectual core that reinforced the college's sense of mission as an educator of women." The fact that two out of three Barnard teachers were women reinforced that commitment, as did the arrival of women's liberation.[5]

Many feminists challenged the widespread assumption that coeducation would benefit women. In their view, coeducation meant not greater equality, but submission to male power. Barnard had always been feminist, in a genteel way. Students had plenty of opportunity to study whatever topics might interest them, including topics related to women, but most faculty expected them to do so within a curriculum that remained overwhelmingly male-centered into the early 1970s.[6] With rare exceptions, courses in the English department included only the literary works of men; courses in history concentrated on male politicians, military figures, and intellectuals; courses in art history ignored the contribution of female artists. As members of the Barnard Organization of Soul Sisters (BOSS) were quick to point out, the curriculum was not only overwhelmingly male, but overwhelmingly white. Women's liberation challenged that curricular emphasis and, in the process, brought a more radical perspective to feminism at the college.

This challenge exacerbated tensions that had long existed between Barnard College and Columbia College, while also aggravating the troubled relation of each with the university's graduate schools. As a new generation of feminists challenged the Barnard curriculum as being too male-centered, the possibility of bridging curricular differences with Columbia became increasingly difficult. But tensions between Barnard and Columbia were as nothing compared with the tensions that each felt with respect to the graduate faculties, which had dominated the university for a century. To the leadership of both of the colleges, merger meant not just the prospect of coeducation, but also the danger of "submerger," in the words of one combatant, into the larger university system.[7] The separate faculties of Barnard and Columbia College viewed their respective educational missions, not to mention their very survival, in terms that dated back to the emergence of the graduate faculty in the 1890s as the dominant institutional force on Morningside Heights. By 1969, support for merger began to diminish at both Barnard and Columbia Colleges, but it gained new strength in the administrative offices of Columbia University in Low Library.

THE VIEW FROM LOW LIBRARY

No one liked the idea of merger better than George Fraenkel, dean of the graduate faculties. Combining the faculties of Columbia's different schools provided an attractive way of dealing with the crushing fiscal problems he faced. Trained at Harvard in the 1940s, Fraenkel came to the Columbia chemistry department in 1949 and was recruited by Columbia's president, Grayson Kirk, in February 1968 to administer the graduate faculties and to work toward merging Columbia's various schools. Fraenkel could not have taken up his new duties at a less propitious time. Within weeks of moving into his new office in Low Library, he began confronting a series of crises that would cripple the institution: student unrest, faculty discontent, administrative disarray, and, most troubling of all, a massive financial shortfall in the arts and sciences. To a man faced with such problems, merger—not just of Barnard and Columbia Colleges but of other divisions as well—offered a way to reduce the costly waste and inefficiency that plagued the university.[8]

When Dean Fraenkel assumed office in 1968, he discovered specialized classes with tiny enrollments that were being taught two, three, even four times in the same term—once at Columbia College, again at Barnard, again at the School of General Studies, and sometimes even in the graduate school. In 1971, in response to an order from Columbia's president, William McGill, to present a five-year plan that would eliminate the university's deficit, Fraenkel called for admitting more students to Columbia College, increasing the size of classes, freezing tenure, eliminating duplicate courses, and, in general, ensuring that the faculties of General Studies, the graduate schools, the School of International Affairs, Columbia College, and Barnard College cooperate more fully in hiring and curricular planning. Over the next decade, Fraenkel worked steadily to reduce redundancy at the university, through greater cooperation if possible, or through absorption if necessary.[9]

What made Barnard especially attractive to Fraenkel was its bargain faculty. Paid less than their Columbia colleagues, accustomed to a heavier teaching load, more likely to be untenured (and thus expendable), and more heavily female, the Barnard faculty had much to recommend to a cost-conscious administrator, who also happened to be facing scrutiny over the university's hiring of women. Moreover, Barnard, while small, was still solvent. It regularly made between two and three tenure appointments a year. Fraenkel saw in Barnard a vehicle for increased flexibility. Columbia could save money by using Barnard faculty to teach courses that Columbia wanted taught while using openings at Barnard to hire scholars in specialties that Columbia wanted covered.[10]

Many administrators in Low Library had one further reason for wanting to merge with Barnard. From their perspective, an independent Barnard represented a financial drain on Columbia resources. In theory, Barnard had been financially independent of Columbia from its founding in 1889. It paid its own faculty, maintained its own buildings, and collected its own tuition. To the extent that it used Columbia steam or telephone service, it paid for it on a pro rata basis. And yet there was a growing financial imbalance between the two schools as a result of cross-registration. As late as the 1950s, relatively few Barnard students took Columbia classes, but over the course of the 1960s, a growing number began to do so. In those same years, Barnard students, as well as faculty, came increasingly to rely on Columbia's library system. In McGill's judgment, as he told his trustees on December 7, 1970, "Columbia in effect subsidizes Barnard." If Columbia were to absorb Barnard, it could offset its instructional and library costs with Barnard tuition.[11]

The prospect of merger did raise one concern for Columbia administrators. In their view, the Barnard faculty did not meet Columbia standards. In 1922, Virginia Gildersleeve had sought to address Columbia's skeptical view of the increasingly female Barnard faculty by proposing that no faculty member be granted tenure without winning the endorsement not only of his or her Barnard department but also of the counterpart Columbia department. This policy had worked reasonably well until the end of World War II. The majority of Barnard's faculty was well known at Columbia, most having trained there. With the coming of Millicent McIntosh, however, Barnard became significantly more autonomous from Columbia. Faculty were more likely to be trained elsewhere and to have fewer contacts with Columbia colleagues. This was especially true in the sciences, where the growth of "big science" in the Cold War years tended to reinforce distinctions between university scientists, with their access to graduate students and increasingly well-equipped research laboratories, and college scientists, with their more limited resources and greater emphasis on undergraduate teaching. Under these conditions, the science faculty at Barnard was seldom in a position to compete on equal terms with that at Columbia. Disparities between Barnard and Columbia faculty were smaller in the humanities and social sciences. Especially in small departments, like classics and Russian, which worked closely with their counterpart departments at Columbia, quality was known. But in some of the larger departments, such as English and psychology, consultation with Columbia on hiring and tenure was minimal at best.[12]

As a step on the way to possible merger, Columbia administrators decided that they had to have greater control over who got tenure at Barnard. The most direct means of doing so would be to require Barnard faculty to go through the same ad hoc process imposed on all faculty in the arts and sciences, as well as some professional-school faculty. Under this system, a five-person faculty committee, advisory to the president, reviewed each candidate's scholarly credentials. For professional-school faculty, the ad hoc committee was composed of three professors from the arts and sciences and two from the candidate's own school. If Barnard faculty could be screened according to the professional-school model, Barnard would have a say in who gained tenure, but Columbia would have the deciding vote. Vetting Barnard faculty in this way would, in the short run, ensure greater quality control and, in the long run, pave the way for absorbing Barnard college — and its faculty — altogether.[13]

THE VIEW FROM HAMILTON HALL

George Fraenkel began his teaching career at Columbia in 1949, but it was not until 1964, when he was assigned a seat on the Committee on Instruction, that he first found his way to Hamilton Hall.[14] That a long-term member of the graduate faculty could have avoided, for the first fifteen years of his professional life, the building that housed Columbia College speaks volumes about the institutional culture on Morningside Heights. The "college" rarely crossed the radar screen of most professors on the graduate faculty. This attitude helps explain why the idea of merger, understood as the absorption of Columbia College's faculty by the graduate school, generated so much hostility in Hamilton Hall.

Ever since Columbia's president Frederick A. P. Barnard and John W. Burgess, professor of political science, had embarked on building Columbia into one of the world's foremost research universities in the 1870s, the future of Columbia College had looked uncertain. In 1884, Burgess called for the abolition of the American college on the grounds that it was unable to become a research university and unwilling to become a *gymnasium*, or European-style high school.[15] Columbia College's administrators spent the next century devising ways to keep the university from making good on Burgess's plan.[16]

Columbia College's decision following World War I to set up a core curriculum was aimed not only at educating an increasingly diverse student body of young men about America's western European traditions and democratic ideals, but also at securing the college's independent identity within the university. Over the course of the next fifty years, Columbia's core courses, especially its year-long Literature Humanities sequence and its year-long Contemporary Civilization sequence, came to define Columbia College's special contribution to liberal-arts education in the United States. Colleges across the country copied the courses for their own undergraduates. Although many of the schools began to drop Columbia's approach to general education in the 1970s, as a new generation of scholars came to question the wisdom of building undergraduate education around a "canon" that excluded the experience of many of the peoples of the world, Columbia held doggedly to its tradition, both on its own merits and as its most reliable weapon in its long-term intellectual struggle with the graduate departments, in which specialized research reigned supreme.[17] There was more at stake than keeping control of the college's intellectual capital. In real-estate terms, merger would mean that faculty with offices in Hamilton Hall would be scattered across the campus to the buildings where the graduate departments were housed, buildings where undergraduates had never been made to feel particularly welcome and where college faculty were largely ignored.[18]

The administration and faculty of Columbia College had even stronger reservations about merging with Barnard College, which had rejected the core curriculum in the 1920s and by the 1970s seemed no more willing to embrace it. Notwithstanding these reservations, administrators and faculty members at Columbia often talked about ways to cooperate with Barnard to make the experience of undergraduates more coeducational. Throughout the 1970s, they worked to increase cross-registration for Barnard and Columbia undergraduates and talked about ways to open up housing and dining exchanges. But those conversations never came close to creating genuine coeducation. By the end of the 1970s, Barnard students were still taking only 20 percent of their classes at Columbia.[19] The basic problem was that Barnard and Columbia students could share few classes in their first two years, since Columbia students were required to take six courses in the core, and (because of space constraints) few Barnard students could enroll in those classes, even when they wanted to. By the time Barnard students were juniors and seniors, they tended to be heavily involved in their majors, which required them to write a senior thesis, a requirement from which Columbia students were exempt. As a consequence, Dean of Students Roger Lehecka, who had been working for coeducation since his own Columbia student days in the 1960s, despaired as he watched Columbia students "regress under conditions of an essentially all-male education."[20]

Determined to achieve coeducation, without having to sacrifice Columbia's distinctive identity, the college administration, beginning with Dean Carl Hovde in 1969, concluded that the best course would be to admit women directly to Columbia College. The chief problem the college faced in pursuing that plan was a potential firestorm of negative publicity for taking a step that would likely hurt, if not destroy, Barnard College. How could Columbia, which had forced Barnard into existence by refusing to open its own doors to women students at the end of the nineteenth century, jeopardize Barnard's future by opening its doors to women at this late date? President McGill would not hear of it, but his opposition did not put the matter to rest. In 1975, Peter Pouncey, who had succeeded Hovde as dean of Columbia College in 1972, cast caution to the winds. He called a meeting of the Columbia College faculty at which a vote was taken to admit women in 1977. A furious McGill disallowed the vote and told the trustees that the college's admitting women would spell "the end of Barnard." McGill then called on administrators and faculty at Barnard and Columbia to work out some kind of de facto coeducation.[21]

THE VIEW FROM MILBANK HALL

No one at Barnard wanted Columbia College to admit women unilaterally. But Barnard's distinctive history made most faculty, administrators, alumnae, trustees, and even students leery of taking the one step that would have avoided that result: merging the two schools. Given Columbia's fiscal crisis and hiring patterns, many feared that merger would threaten Barnard's faculty, especially its female faculty.[22] Many also believed that the premium that Barnard placed on teaching would likely be jeopardized if it united with Columbia. This feeling was so strong in the Barnard history department that the department's chair, Chilton Williamson, monitored junior colleagues for any sign that they might be "too big on research" and thus, presumably, not sufficiently committed to teaching.[23] Opposition to merger was by no means universal. Several trustees, all men, thought that coeducation was inevitable and that it was time to fold Barnard into Columbia, while some faculty, women as well as men, argued that given Columbia's repeated threats to go its own way, "almost any deal was better than no deal."[24] And some students favored merger, even if it meant sacrificing Barnard.[25] In the end, however, opponents of merger were both more numerous and more committed. They insisted that only by remaining separate could Barnard's mission be secured.

In fact, the threat of merger helped radicalize feminists on campus and gained them a voice that they had lacked. They exercised that voice in support of three projects in the early 1970s aimed at securing a place for feminist scholarship within the larger university: a women's center, a Women's Studies program, and a University Seminar called "Women and Society."

FOUNDING THE BARNARD WOMEN'S CENTER

In 1970, feminist students and faculty called for the creation of a women's center. Catharine Stimpson, assistant professor of English, suggested the idea; President Martha Peterson provided seed money; and a trustee, Eleanor Elliott (Barnard 1948), secured additional funding from a recent bequest to Barnard from her mentor, Helen Rogers Reid (Barnard 1903), the longtime trustee and staunch feminist who had championed paid maternity leave in the 1930s. A more unlikely group of co-conspirators would have been difficult to find.

Martha Peterson, a native of Jamestown, Kansas, embodied the sensible, plainspoken virtues of the American Midwest. Working her way through the University of Kansas, she earned bachelor's and master's degrees in mathematics in 1937 and 1943, and a doctorate in educational psychology and counseling in 1959. She taught math and worked in the dean's office at Kansas until 1952, when she became dean of women. Four years later, she moved on to become dean of women at the University of Wisconsin–Madison, and in 1963 she rose to the position of dean of students for the thirteen-campus University of Wisconsin system. Five years later, she accepted the presidency of Barnard College. When Columbia president Grayson Kirk met her in the spring of 1968—at a moment of peak interest in coeducation throughout the country—he indicated that he looked forward to working with her on the merger of Columbia and Barnard Colleges. Noting that they shared a background at the University of Wisconsin, he assumed that she shared his view that women's colleges were an anachronism. Barnard was, in fact, the only single-sex institution with which Peterson was ever affiliated, but her years in huge university systems had taught her the value of small liberal-arts colleges. Moreover, the fact that she had never married and her longtime companion was another woman helped her appreciate the supportive atmosphere of an institution dedicated to the interests of women. She was determined to protect Barnard from being swallowed up by its larger sibling, while acceding to what she deemed Columbia's legitimate concerns about monitoring the balance of payments and maintaining the quality of faculty.[26]

Eleanor "Elly" Thomas Elliott came from a very different social milieu. A product of New York City's Republican elite, she had initially shown no interest in college, but four days at Miss Finch's finishing school in 1944, following graduation from the Chapin School for girls, changed her mind. After a quick visit to Morningside Heights, a little tutoring in algebra, and a recommendation from a family friend, Helen Rogers Reid, she entered Barnard College. Upon graduation in 1948, she worked as a staff writer and an editor at *Vogue* until 1953, when, with the election of President Dwight D. Eisenhower, she became social secretary to a distant relative, the secretary of state, John Foster Dulles, and his wife. The late nights required for this work prompted her to return after three years to New York, where she briefly considered working at the Reid family's *New York Herald Tribune*. When that job, too, promised late nights, she declined the offer—only to be told by Reid that if she was not going to work for the *Trib*, "she had better go to work for Barnard." By 1959, she had married the advertising executive John "Jock" Elliott and had joined the Barnard College Board of Trustees. In addition to her work as a trustee, Elliott wrote for *Glamour*, worked for the New York State Committee of the Republican Party, served on the boards of a number of philanthropic organizations, and, in the later 1960s, became an active member of the National Organization for Women.[27] Years later, friends at Barnard remembered her marching down Fifth Avenue as part of the fiftieth-anniversary celebration of the Nineteenth Amendment on August 26, 1970. Others waved placards; Elliott carried a handbag.[28]

Catharine Stimpson was one of the placard wavers. Born in Bellingham, Washington, she early felt an "ambition, not to marry the boy next door."

Catharine Stimpson (b. 1936)
Graduate of Bryn Mawr College (1958),
Cambridge University (B.A. 1960, M.A.
1965), and Columbia University (Ph.D.
1967), and lecturer, instructor, and assistant
professor of English at Barnard College
(1963–1980), as photographed in 1968.
(Barnard College Archives)

That goal took her to Bryn Mawr College, where she earned a B.A. in 1958, and then to Newnham College, Cambridge, where she earned a second B.A., with honors, in 1960. Returning to the United States, she entered the Department of English and Comparative Literature at Columbia, from which she earned a Ph.D., with distinction, in 1967, with a dissertation entitled "The Early Novels of Iris Murdoch." Her career at Barnard began in 1963, when she joined the ranks of instructors in the English department while working on her doctorate. Her closest friend was Kate Millett, an instructor then as well, with whom she shared an office and with whom she encountered the world of radical feminism down on the Bowery, where they both lived. Kate "looked more conservative than I, in her long skirts, pumps, and hair drawn back in, yes, a bun. I jumped around the corridors in miniskirts, tights, and unruly, . . . naturally curly locks," Stimpson later recalled. "I might have looked the more radical," she added, "but I was, intellectually, the more conservative, prudent, and buttoned up."[29]

When the English department declined to renew Millett's appointment as an instructor following the 1968 protests, Mary Mothersill of the Barnard philosophy department hired her to teach in Barnard's Experimental College. "A child of the strike of 1968," according to Millett, the Experimental College, composed of Columbia and Barnard College volunteers, was an experiment both in coeducational living (it was housed at the Paris Hotel, at West End Avenue and Ninety-seventh Street) and in self-directed learning. Millett insisted that the students "write long papers." But, she later recalled, "mostly their idea of freedom was not to do very much," except experiment "with sex and drugs." Millett quickly went from being a "popular radical teacher to being the whipping boy of the experimental collegians." In December 1970, college officials decided not to renew her contract.[30]

The year 1970 proved difficult for Millett in other ways as well. In August, *Time* had put her on the cover of the issue scheduled to coincide with the fiftieth anniversary of the Nineteenth Amendment. An accompanying article identified her as the "Mao Tse-tung of Women's Liberation." Millett was dismayed; to be singled out as a leader violated the egalitarian spirit of feminism. To make matters worse, within months she found herself at the center of a debate over lesbianism in the women's movement. In November, at a forum on sexual liberation in Columbia's McMillan Theater, she was scheduled to discuss bisexuality. From the audience, a member of the Radicalesbians called out, "Bisexuality is a cop-out. Are you a lesbian?"[31]

In writing *Sexual Politics*, Millett had invoked the existence and response of a female reader to the sexually exploitive writings of the leading male writers of the day. But despite the personal-is-political ethos of her historical moment, she shrank from suggesting that the reader might be not only female but lesbian. To write explicitly of a desiring, female reader was dangerous enough. Millett continued to guard her own feelings in the months that followed the publication of *Sexual Politics*. An article in *Life* identified her as a member of "a radical lesbian organization." But the article also pictured Millett kissing her husband, Fumio Yoshimura, and quoted her as disclaiming a lesbian identity for herself: "I'm not into that." Angry fellow members of the Radicalesbians were determined to force Millett to claim a lesbian identity. As Millett later recalled her anguished reaction to this public outing, "Yes I said yes I am a Lesbian. It was the last strength I had."[32]

Time quickly ran a follow-up story, stating that Millett's disclosure would "reinforce the views of those skeptics who routinely dismiss all liberationists as lesbians." Among feminists, the response was mixed. Gloria Steinem defended her, but Betty Friedan denounced her. The furor over Millett's public "confession" did nothing to advance her academic career. Although she taught briefly at Bryn Mawr the following year, her academic career was effectively over. By 1971, she was buying and cultivating fields in Poughkeepsie, New York, where she founded the Women's Art Colony Farm and dedicated herself to art and writing.[33] The more politically contained Stimpson survived as an academic, winning promotion to assistant professor in 1968 after the completion of her doctorate. Stimpson was one of a small group of young academics determined to make the college—and, beyond it, the world—a place more receptive to the radical insights of modern feminism.[34]

The fact that women with such different perspectives on life could conspire to found a women's center underscores the galvanizing power of the women's movement at that moment. Peterson, Elliott, and Stimpson were soon joined by others. An executive committee of faculty, administrators, alumnae, and students planned the center. The students soon dropped out, mistrustful of a college-run project. Those who remained were faculty members (Annette Baxter, Patricia Graham, and Catharine Stimpson), alumnae trustees (Eleanor Elliott and Iola Stetson Haverstick), and administrators (Barbara Hertz and Jane S. Gould). Located in a small room on the ground floor of Barnard Hall, the center was apparently the first in the country. Stimpson became its acting director until the college could find a permanent head.[35]

On January 12, 1972, Stimpson inaugurated the Barnard Women's Center with a forum in the Barnard gym: "Male Chauvinism at Columbia: Does It Exist?" Professors Ann Sutherland Harris (who had just moved from Columbia to Hunter College) and Elaine Showalter (a future president of the Modern Language Association, then at Douglass College) moderated a panel of seven male Barnard and Columbia professors and administrators:

"Male Chauvinism at Columbia: Does It Exist?"
President William McGill with Professors Elaine Showalter and Ann Sutherland Harris,
moderators of the first event sponsored by the Barnard Women's Center, on January 12, 1972.
(*Columbia Spectator*)

George Fraenkel (dean of the graduate faculties), Eli Ginzberg (Business School), Loren Graham (history, Columbia), Clive Kessler (anthropology, Barnard), Allen Farnsworth (Law School), Menelaos Hassialis (School of Engineering), and President William McGill. All the panelists readily conceded that male chauvinism existed at the university, but the predominantly female audience was indignant to learn that most of the panelists thought that the discrimination was largely a thing of the past. Eli Ginzburg, principal author of *Womanpower* (1957) and long a champion of women, provoked a particularly negative response when he counseled, "Don't worry about what has happened in the past or even what is happening now, because new opportunities are opening up for the future." To women facing the worst job market in years and seeing no concrete strategy for opening up the higher levels of the professoriate and administration to women, Ginzburg's advice, as Showalter remembered it, "pissed us off." Of all the male panelists, only the history professor, Loren Graham—the one member of the panel with an academic spouse—made what a *Barnard Bulletin* reporter, Ellen McManus (Barnard 1973), considered a "constructive comment." Emphasizing the problems faced by married women and mothers in academe, he urged the university to grant parental leaves and to encourage the joint appointments of husbands and wives.[36]

Outraged by what they considered a failure of most men at the university to comprehend the gravity of the disadvantages under which women were laboring, leaders of the Barnard Women's Center resolved to make their center the place in New York City where scholars and feminists from across the city and, indeed, around the world could meet to debate new directions in thinking and activism on issues of particular concern to women. Although the search committee for a new director sought a leader with a Ph.D., they found no one willing to risk academic advancement on so politically engaged an undertaking. Kate Stimpson, who would have been the logical candidate, was about to come up for tenure, and continued leadership of the center, everyone agreed, would not help her case.[37]

The search committee therefore turned to Jane S. Gould, a member of the executive committee of the center and the longtime director of Barnard's Office of Career Services. A Barnard alumna (1940), a widow, and a mother, Gould had spent much of her own career helping married women reenter the workforce. Taking charge of the center seemed a logical next step, but it quickly posed some serious personal challenges for her: "I was forced to acknowledge that I wasn't at ease with all the issues I heard women raising." At first, she could not see the ways in which language reinforced sexism, and she balked at her younger colleagues' insistence that the word "girl" be applied only to females under the age of eighteen. But gradually such terms as "mankind," "brotherhood," and "man" began to seem exclusive, and she taught herself not to use them unless she meant men only. Issues relating to sexuality raised even more troubling concerns. When Gould first encountered the self-help part of the women's movement, she "thought it bordered on the ridiculous." But she agreed to allow a group of young women to use the center's space on the ground floor of Barnard Hall, in the evenings. With "the blinds pulled down, they learned how to use a speculum and see their vaginas for the first time. They took this very seriously and found it self-affirming to see that their vaginas were pink and rosy, not unsavory black holes as many had been led to believe." And then there was the subject of homosexuality: "Although I knew there were women who related only to women, I was more comfortable not talking about it, since I assumed that all 'normal' people were heterosexual." As director of the Barnard Women's Center, Gould had to confront her homophobic feelings, for many of the women with whom she worked most closely and whom she admired most fully were coming out of the closet, demanding to be accepted and insisting that their concerns have a public hearing. It was not always easy, Gould found, to fulfill the center's founding promise to become "a physical and psychological meeting place for women."[38]

News of the center spread quickly beyond Columbia University, and Gould was soon overwhelmed by requests from artists, filmmakers, writers, activists, and women's groups to hold forums on a wide range of topics. Most of the movers and shakers of the American women's movement participated in one of the center's programs during the tumultuous 1970s. And, in an updated version of Virginia Gildersleeve's outreach to university women around the world, the center attracted European feminists—including Hélène Cixous, Juliet Mitchell, and Sheila Rowbotham—and delegations of women from the Soviet Union and China. The events quickly multiplied. In any given month, the center's calendar might include, as Gould later recalled, such programs as the lecture "A View of Women as Seen Through the Eyes of Christine de Pizan," a fifteenth-century woman of letters; a screening of *Women of Wounded Knee*; a discussion of grass-roots organizing for battered women; a workshop on "lesbianism and the social function of taboo"; a women's art exhibition; an analysis of the theological question "Is There a Feminist Understanding of Sin?"; a discussion of "Perceptions of Black Women Writers"; and a talk by a Salvadoran woman about oppression by both the *junta* and the macho men with whom Salvadoran women lived. A final bequest from the Helen Rogers Reid estate provided money for the center to sponsor annual lectures to be given by women who had distinguished themselves in their fields and had shown a strong commitment to other women. One of the consciousness-raising groups that proliferated in the early 1970s used the center for its meetings for many years. A women's caucus in sociology also came regularly. A women's counseling project helped women confront issues that had long plagued them but that they had never before been able to discuss: rape, sexual harassment, domestic violence. Long after the lights in the college's classrooms dimmed, the lights in the Barnard Women's Center burned bright.[39]

Most ambitious of all Gould's initiatives was "The Scholar and the Feminist," an annual conference launched in 1974 with the hope of attracting speakers throughout the academy and even beyond its walls. The very title was provocative. To suggest that scholarship could—indeed, should—be politically engaged was to challenge a core value of the academy: its declared detachment from ideology. In the 1950s, the Columbia sociologist Daniel Bell had famously celebrated the post–World War II era as an "End of Ideology," a period free of both Marxist cant and fascist repression, an open society, in which the university could flourish as never before. Throughout the academy, scholars had long argued that intellectual inquiry should be "value-free." Many male scholars looked on the influx of self-identified feminists as a threat to that goal. Gould and her colleagues had two responses. The first was to agree that the university should be a more open place and to point to the academy's treatment of women and women's writing as a violation of its own standards. The second response was to draw on philosophical critiques of rationality and objectivity to question the viability of the value-free principle. Pointing out that all people act within an ideological framework—that is, on a set of values, beliefs, and interests—feminist scholars argued that the very claim of value-free inquiry was itself an ideology. Scholarship, they contended, was inevitably affected by one's particular situation in life—one's gender, race, religion, geographical place, and class—and that the good scholar was attuned to the beliefs that flowed from that situation, not blind to them. Their critical powers heightened by their near-universal participation in consciousness-raising groups, feminist scholars insisted that they were simply more aware than many traditional scholars of the values that informed their search. Indeed, they credited their own gender-born perspective on life with generating the idea that power, wielded disproportionately by men, structured all of life, from the state on down to the family. From the very first, "The Scholar and the Feminist" conferences included contributions in feminist scholarship from scholars who would go on to major careers in the academy: Gerda Lerner and Patricia Graham in women's history, Elaine Pagels and Carol Christ in religion, and Carolyn Heilbrun, Barbara Miller, and Nancy Miller in literary criticism.[40]

FOUNDING THE WOMEN'S STUDIES PROGRAM

Creating the Barnard Women's Center and even running "The Scholar and the Feminist" conference proved easier than establishing a Women's Studies program. As of the 1971/1972 academic year, the Barnard catalog listed ten courses on topics related to women. Given the unusual range of those offerings, one might have expected Barnard to be among the first colleges to start a Women's Studies program, but resistance to establishing a separate program, one associated so openly with feminism, was widespread. The idea of a women's college enjoyed strong support at Barnard in the 1970s, even as such support diminished elsewhere, but the idea of a feminist college was not so generally accepted. Under the pressure of negotiations with Columbia, however, those who sought to distinguish Barnard as a feminist-minded institution gradually gained strength.[41]

It helped that Barnard had such a long history of interdepartmental offerings. Unlike Columbia, where—outside the core—specialization was highly prized, Barnard had been sponsoring interdepartmental work since the 1920s, when William Ogburn in sociology and Franz Boas in anthropology championed the idea that scholarship flourished best under a system of cross-fertilization produced by interdepartmental instruction. By 1972, Barnard offered seven interdepartmental majors, among them American Studies, which from the 1950s, and especially under the leadership of Annette Baxter, had been directing attention to women's experience as part of its mission. As the executive committee of the Barnard Women's Center lobbied the Committee on Instruction for recognition of Women's Studies, the idea of a program, rather than a department, seemed more in keeping with the interdisciplinary ambitions of the advocates. A department could easily be marginalized, while a program not only fit within the history of Barnard's interdepartmental course work, but offered a way to reform the curriculum of the college generally. Women's Studies aimed at transforming knowledge throughout the college. To do so meant participating in searches in every department that might be in a position to provide faculty to the program. Such collaboration seemed the surest way to guarantee that the new scholarship on women would be represented everywhere. Throughout the early 1970s, however, that work had to be carried out informally. It took the Barnard Women's Studies Coordinating Committee six years, until 1977, to persuade the college's Committee on Instruction to allocate a page in the college catalog on which they could list the twenty-one courses they had encouraged into being in thirteen departments. The next year, the Committee on Instruction had approved a major in Women's Studies. And in 1981, the administration finally approved the hiring of a full-time, tenured faculty member to head the program.

Nancy Miller (Barnard 1961), a member of the executive committee of the Barnard Women's Center, was the first to hold the position. She earned her Ph.D. in French at Columbia in 1974, with a dissertation entitled "Gender and Genre: An Analysis of Literary Femininity in the Eighteenth-Century Novel." Apart from a few doctoral students in psychology, she was the first to use the word "gender" in the title of a dissertation. In so doing, she was among the first to suggest that the term long used exclusively as a grammatical category might serve the needs of feminist scholars far better than the word "sex," with its limiting biological associations. Here was a term that freed scholars to explore more freely the ways in which cultures create men and women, structure sexual experience, and deploy power. Following her graduate work, Miller stayed on to teach at Columbia, but like so many women (and men) hired at Columbia during the university's period of fiscal crisis, she had been warned that there was no prospect of tenure.

Fiscal constraint was part of the problem; Miller's feminist leanings, another. The offer of a position as head of the new Women's Studies program, with an appointment in the Barnard French department, came at a crucial moment for her and kept at Columbia an important new perspective.[42]

Some of the most exciting and provocative ideas in feminist scholarship were coming out of France in the 1970s and 1980s, and Miller gave voice to them in her classes and writings. As she remembered her entry into feminist scholarship in the early 1970s, the phrase "feminist criticism" was not yet an acknowledged category, at least not on the fifth floor of Philosophy Hall, where the Columbia French department had its offices and structuralism reigned supreme. "There was literary theory (what the good people did), and there was feminism (Kate Millett, English Departments)," Miller recalled. She saw the two—structuralism and feminism—working together: "I can still remember the moment when, in a study group, I understood Saussure's model of the sign: never again would I confuse the word and the thing; literature and the world; sign and referent; signified and signifier (little knowing that Lacan, not to mention Derrida, had already turned this upside down)." Just as exciting was the discovery of binary oppositions and how they organize symbolic and social universes: "Lévi-Strauss delivered the truth of this fact in person in the Barnard College gym in 1972 (poststructuralism, with a whole new set of emphases, had already unsettled structuralism in France, but colonials necessarily live according to belated cadences)."[43]

For Miller, the lesson of structuralism was that the tendency to form binary oppositions was hardwired into the brain. Here is where Simone de Beauvoir had begun, with the polarizing operations that opposed man as Same to woman as Other. And it was the intellectual beginning of a journey that Miller took, over the course of the 1970s, away from male authors and how they represented women (the strand of feminist criticism initiated by Millett), to female authors and how they constructed their own world (the strand of feminist criticism launched by Elaine Showalter in A Literature of Their Own [1977] and enlivened by French critics Hélène Cixous and Monique Wittig). It was this latter approach to feminist scholarship, which valorized "working on women," that brought Millett back to Barnard in 1981.[44]

FOUNDING THE UNIVERSITY SEMINAR
"WOMEN AND SOCIETY"

Building separate institutions dedicated to the study of women found favor in the 1970s not only at Barnard, but also among a few of the female faculty at Columbia who yearned for a space in which to pursue the new work on women. Although some departments were beginning to search for faculty whose research concentrated on women, there was no place in the university, apart from the Barnard Women's Center, where feminist scholars could gather regularly to discuss ongoing research. In 1971, discussions began between two members of the executive committee of the Barnard Women's Center—the writer Louise Bernikow (Barnard 1961) and Susan Rennie Ritner (Barnard 1961), who had just completed her doctorate in political science with a dissertation on Afrikaner racial ideology—and Marcia Wright, a Columbia historian who had helped supervise Ritner's dissertation. A 1957 graduate of Wellesley College, with a Ph.D. in African history received from the University of London in 1966, Wright had been hired by the African Institute in the School of International Affairs at a time when the Ford Foundation was still funding foreign-area studies, and she had gradually gained entry into the Columbia history department, where she won tenure in 1973, despite Fraenkel's announced tenure freeze. Meeting in Wright's apartment, the threesome talked about forming a University Seminar dedicated to the new scholarship on women.[45]

The Columbia University Seminars were one of the university's most distinctive institutions. Started in 1945 by Frank Tannenbaum, professor of Latin American history, they were conceived as a mechanism for bringing scholars together from throughout the university—indeed, from throughout the larger metropolitan area—to discuss research on topics of common concern. In a university where centripetal forces of urbanism had always made achieving a sense of intellectual community difficult, the University Seminars offered multiple sites, in Tannenbaum's words, "to merge the disciplines for the purpose of getting a unified view."[46] By 1971, there were sixty seminars in place. Bernikow, Ritner, and Wright proposed that a seminar entitled "Woman and Society" be the sixty-first.

Their timing could not have been worse. To a newly budget-conscious Columbia administration, the University Seminars presented yet another fiscal drain on the university's hard-pressed fisc. Bruce Bassett, a professor from the Business School whom McGill had brought over to Low Library to bring order to the university's finances, complained about the seminars in an August 1971 letter to James Gutmann, the director of the University Seminars. The "seminars have 1,943 members," Bassett noted, "of whom 1,319 are not associated with the university." Since a perk of membership in a seminar was the free use of the university libraries, a privilege charged at the rate of $300 a year to any other user not affiliated with the university, the University Seminars were giving away $400,000 a year. And the loss was accelerating. For years, the University Seminars had been growing at the rate of two a year. But in 1971, Gutmann, on the advice of his faculty advisory committee, had added seven new ones. Something had to be done to stanch the hemorrhaging.[47]

A chastened Gutmann and the oversight committee of the University Seminars henceforth subjected proposals for new seminars to an especially searching scrutiny. "Women and Society" was one proposal that was initially set aside. The largely male committee members viewed it as more political than scholarly in conception, and they took particular exception to the fact that all the twenty-one scholars who had signed the proposal for the new seminar were women. The signatories included Gerda Lerner, by then teaching women's history at Sarah Lawrence; Joan Kelly, a Columbia-trained historian at City College; Carolyn Heilbrun, recently recruited from General Studies to join the graduate school; Catharine Stimpson, at Barnard in English; Annette Baxter and Suzanne Wemple, at Barnard in history; Mirra Komarovsky, at Barnard in sociology; Helen Bacon, at Barnard in classics; Patricia Graham, at Barnard in history and education; Ruth Bader Ginsburg, newly arrived at the Law School; Ethel Person, at Physicians and Surgeons in psychiatry; and Renate Bridenthal, a Columbia-trained historian at Brooklyn College.[48] The University Seminars were supposed to be open to all. Where were the men?

Unorthodox and fiscally burdensome though their proposal might be, the proponents had two things going for them. First, Marcia Wright sat on the oversight committee, as the group's sole female member. Given her position, she easily made the case that women felt outnumbered in the university and needed a scholarly place of their own. Second, Susan Rennie Ritner had taken a job in the provost's office, where the primary focus of all energies in 1971 and 1972 was a feverish effort to respond to the Department of Health, Education, and Welfare's charges of sex discrimination. Ritner argued that the university would be crazy not to accept a seminar dedicated to the new scholarship on women; doing so would help the university in its ongoing negotiations with the federal agency overseeing the development of their affirmative-action plan.[49]

Both Provost Wm. Theodore de Bary and the oversight committee agreed, and in the academic year 1974/1975 the University Seminar "Women and Society" was formed.[50] In the years that followed, some of the most important new scholarship on women was first delivered at the seminar's monthly meetings. Two historians, Suzanne Wemple of Barnard and JoAnn McNamara of Hunter, led off with a joint paper on medieval women; a Columbia-trained historian, Carroll Smith-Rosenberg of the University of Pennsylvania, presented her influential essay "The Female World of Love and Ritual"; another

Columbia-trained historian, Joan Kelly-Gadol, offered a critique of male conceptions of time with her paper "Did Women Have a Renaissance?"; Sherry Ortner, an anthropologist at Sarah Lawrence, presented her provocative essay "Is Woman to Nature as Man Is to Culture?"; and the Columbia medical school psychiatrist Ethel Person spoke on changing conceptions of sexuality.[51]

One of the consequences of Columbia's fiscal problems in the 1970s was that a number of senior faculty left for other institutions. Replacements were made, if at all, at the junior level, with non-tenure-track appointees—many of them women—who stayed for only a few years and then moved on. Every department suffered as a result, but none more than English, which lost sixteen assistant professors. Maintaining the faculty's quality proved impossible under the circumstances. "We have fallen," announced the Marcus Commission, named for its chair, English professor Steven Marcus, in 1979. Columbia could no longer claim to stand in the top rank of American universities.[52] In that context, the efforts of feminists at Barnard and Columbia to build institutions like the Barnard Women's Center, the Women's Studies program, and the University Seminar "Women and Society" proved critical in enabling new ideas to develop, even as members came and went. This nascent institution building took place against the backdrop of the ongoing negotiations between the Barnard and Columbia trustees and helps explain why those negotiations became increasingly acrimonious. The debates were not just about a larger institution swallowing a smaller one, or simply about whether scholarship or teaching should dominate the undergraduate setting, but about whether feminism would find a place in the academy.

MAINTAINING BARNARD'S AUTONOMY

While negotiations continued over the establishment of Women's Studies at Barnard and the creation of the University Seminar "Women and Society" at Columbia, the Barnard and Columbia trustees reached a new intercorporate agreement, the most significant since the agreement in 1900, which had enabled Barnard to hire its own faculty. Signed in 1973, the new agreement provided for three important changes in the Barnard–Columbia relationship. First, Barnard and Columbia undergraduates would be able to register in courses throughout the university. Second, Barnard would increase its payments to Columbia to defray the rising costs of cross-registration. And third, to ensure the high quality of faculty appointments, all Barnard faculty promoted to tenure would have to go through the university's ad hoc process, under which each candidate would be judged by five senior faculty members, two from Barnard, three from Columbia—none from his or her own field.[53]

At a time when Columbia was placing a virtual freeze on promotions to tenure because of its budget deficit, many Barnard faculty and administrators feared that having to submit to Columbia's ad hoc process would inevitably limit prospects for promotion, even though Barnard faculty were paid out of Barnard's own limited, but nonetheless solvent, budget. Since two out of three faculty at Barnard were women, the long-term impact on female faculty would almost certainly be adverse.

Catharine Stimpson was among the first candidates from Barnard to be vetted by the Columbia ad hoc process. Her case pitted the emerging feminism at Barnard against traditional scholarly expectations at Columbia. Rather than publishing her dissertation or writing scholarly articles, the conventional routes to tenure, she had been building the Women's Center, seeking support for Women's Studies, writing feminist criticism, and editing congressional testimony in favor of the Equal Rights Amendment and of equal rights in education and employment in the hope of making that testimony available to a wider audience than it would generally command. Already having encountered opposition from her own department (where one colleague sought to torpedo her case with the allegation that she was having an affair with Martha Peterson), she also encountered resistance in the Columbia English department on the traditional grounds that tenure required the publication of a scholarly monograph or articles in peer-reviewed journals. Her case went better in the Barnard Committee on Appointments, Tenure, and Promotion, but at the Columbia ad hoc, she received a vote of two in favor (from the Barnard members) and three against (from the Columbia members). It cannot have helped that George Fraenkel, present at committee deliberations by virtue of his position as dean of the graduate faculties, objected that to get tenure one needed a field, and Women's Studies was not a field. Martha Peterson appealed the decision, expending a great deal of political capital in the process, and McGill reluctantly agreed to Stimpson's promotion, with the proviso, "Never again."[54] Stimpson would go on to found *Signs* (the country's leading journal of feminist scholarship), to be dean of the graduate faculties first at Rutgers and then at New York University, and to be president of the Modern Language Association. But although Stimpson's supporters anticipated a brilliant future for the charismatic feminist, her close call with the new ad hoc tenure system sent a chill through every assistant professor at Barnard, especially those just entering the field of Women's Studies.[55]

With fears mounting that Barnard was on the road to extinction, opponents of merger on the board of trustees approached Eleanor Elliott, the person they thought most likely to fight effectively for Barnard's independence. In 1973, Elliott became the board's chair, the second woman, after Helen Rogers Reid, to hold that position. Elliott and her supporters believed that Barnard had relinquished too much control to Columbia in the 1973 negotiations and blamed Martha Peterson for Barnard's loss of control over tenure decisions. Elliott admired Peterson as an administrator—for her skill in keeping lines of communication with students open during the 1968 protests and for her support in creating the Barnard Women's Center—but following the 1973 intercorporate agreement with Columbia, she concluded that the president had spent too much of her career as a dean of students in big coeducational midwestern universities ever to appreciate Barnard's mission as a college dedicated to the interests of female students and faculty or to be an effective advocate for it. In 1975, Elliott encouraged Peterson to find another job (Peterson became president of Beloit College) and set about forming a search committee to replace her.[56]

In November 1975, the search committee, co-chaired by trustees Helene Kaplan and William Golden, settled on Jacqueline Mattfeld, a musicologist and dean of the faculty at Brown University. They soon regretted their choice. If Peterson had worked too well with Columbia, in the view of some observers,

Whither Barnard?
Barnard College trustees Eleanor Elliott (Barnard 1948) and Arthur Altschul with President Jacqueline Mattfeld and President Emerita Millicent McIntosh, as photographed by Luigi Pellettieri, 1978. (Barnard College Archives)

Mattfeld came close to burning all bridges between the two institutions. As Kaplan recalled, Mattfeld proved to be a "manipulative and suspicious person," whom the board could not trust. McGill soon drew the same conclusion. Worried that Mattfeld was doing more harm than good, the Barnard board barred her from further contact and assumed full responsibility for negotiations. Mattfeld then tried to discourage the Barnard faculty from interacting with their counterparts at Columbia, a directive that made life especially difficult for those who were teaching graduate courses across Broadway. To make matters worse, Mattfeld fought constantly with the new chair of the Barnard board, Arthur Altschul, who succeeded Elliott as chair in 1976. Indeed, relations grew so strained that Altschul would not go to a meeting with Mattfeld unless Kaplan accompanied him as a witness. Mattfeld may have been making matters worse, but, as Kaplan later conceded, she did "hit us in the face with the reality of the situation" they confronted with Columbia. Barnard had more to fear than merger; the college risked losing its affiliation with the university, a fate that, given Barnard's small endowment—still the lowest of any in the Seven Sisters—had huge financial implications. Simply trying to increase the size of the library to make up for the potential loss of access to Columbia's library system would be a ruinous undertaking.[57]

In 1980, William McGill resigned the Columbia presidency in favor of Michael Sovern, who for the previous year had been serving as Columbia's provost. Seeing the opportunity for a fresh start, the Barnard board fired Mattfeld. The last straw was the board's discovery that Mattfeld had understated the extent of an increase in faculty salaries that she was proposing to the trustees. In Mattfeld's place, the board appointed one of its own, a thirty-year-old lawyer, Ellen Futter, as acting president, while they searched for a successor. The following year, the search committee concluded that no other candidate could lead Barnard as well as Futter could. The daughter of a Columbia alumnus, Victor Futter (Columbia College 1939, Law School 1942), who had long been active in Columbia affairs, Futter had grown up on Long Island and then gone to the University of Wisconsin. She had transferred after two years to Barnard, however, when she found Wisconsin "too anonymous." As a junior, she was elected to the board of trustees as a student representative, a position that had just been created. Graduating from Barnard in 1971, she went straight to Columbia Law School, where she was a student of Columbia's future president, Michael Sovern. Upon graduation in 1974, she took a job with the Wall Street firm Milbank, Tweed and won election to the Barnard board as a full member. Smart and effective, Futter was the youngest person, since the twenty-nine-year-old Emily James Smith was named dean in 1894, to be appointed to lead the college. She was also

Ellen Futter (b. 1949)
Graduate of Barnard College (1971) and
Columbia Law School (1974), lawyer,
president of Barnard College (1980–1993),
and president of American Museum of
Natural History (1993–), as photographed
in 1980. (Barnard College Archives)

pregnant, a factor that once would have been disqualifying.[58] Nothing demonstrated how much Barnard had changed since 1900, when Emily James Putnam was forced out as dean of Barnard when she announced that she was pregnant, than the board's decision to appoint Futter as president at what everyone knew was a critical moment, even though she was pregnant. Futter was favored, in particular, by Helene Kaplan (Barnard 1953), who had combined motherhood with a demanding legal career and believed that younger women, even college presidents, should have the opportunity to do likewise.[59]

Ellen Futter was not only Barnard's first pregnant president, but also its first Jewish president. That she came to office at the same time that Columbia appointed its first Jewish president, Michael Sovern, suggests that Columbia and Barnard had finally transcended the Jewish problem. The woman question, however, remained.

THE BRESLOW COMMITTEE REPORT ON COEDUCATION

In 1977, Arnold Collery, an economist from Amherst, succeeded Peter Pouncey as dean of Columbia College. Finding little support from the Columbia faculty for further cooperation with Barnard, he appointed a special committee, chaired by Ronald Breslow, professor of chemistry, to look into the possibility of Columbia College's admitting women directly. Breslow, who had a daughter nearing college age and who wanted her to have the option of attending Columbia, recognized that the chief stumbling block to

Columbia's admitting women was the fear that such a step might destroy Barnard. To address that concern, his committee examined other formerly all-male institutions near women's colleges in order to determine what had happened when they started admitting women.[60] In the grip of wishful thinking, the committee avoided the question of whether the women's colleges had begun to experience increased difficulty in recruiting students (all had) and looked to see, simply, whether any had yet folded (none had).

Reassurance that adopting coeducation did not automatically lead to the extinction of a single-sex sister school removed an important barrier to Columbia's admitting women unilaterally, but it was the committee's demographic evidence that provided a sense of urgency. The baby boom, which had fueled the expansion of higher education in the 1960s, had tapered off. By the late 1970s, educators saw a crisis looming. Demographers predicted a 40 percent decline in college-age Americans in the Northeast in the 1980s. Schools once awash in students had already begun to compete fiercely to attract them. Columbia had to do this in the middle of New York City, whose fiscal woes throughout the 1970s made it a dreary, even dangerous place to be. As of 1980, Columbia had the lowest number of applications from men of any school in the Ivy League and was forced to accept nearly half of all who applied. Only Cornell and the University of Pennsylvania were less selective. Dean of Admissions Jim McMenamin, newly arrived from Brown University's admissions department, warned that conditions were likely to worsen as the demographic crisis intensified. In the fall of 1981, he was finding that his efforts to sell Columbia as a coeducational experience by virtue of the college's affiliation with Barnard were not getting through to the eighteen-year-olds he was trying to recruit.[61]

Mindful of these facts, the Breslow Committee report recommended that Columbia not enlarge its student body, a step that had been taken by Yale in 1969, when it admitted women. Instead, Columbia should keep its class size constant, but consider females equally with male applicants. In one stroke, Columbia would become immediately twice as selective as it had been. All but one of the committee members endorsed the report's conclusion in April 1981 that Columbia should admit women immediately.[62]

The one dissenter, a professor of religion, Gillian Lindt, was also the sole woman on the committee. Born and raised in western Europe, the daughter of two freelance journalists, she spent her youth in France, Italy, Switzerland, Germany, Poland, Ireland, and England, never living for more than a few months in any one place. Lindt came to Columbia as a graduate student in sociology in 1955. One of an entering class of more than fifty students (one-third of them women), she witnessed a disproportionate attrition of the women, "several of whom were smarter than I was." Offered on average less financial support than their male peers and lacking self-confidence, they found Columbia an unwelcoming place. Lindt persevered in part because her parents had given her the confidence to believe that she could make it on her own. Her peripatetic childhood had led her to accept as a given that she was and always would be an outsider. Unlike many of her female peers in American universities, she did not expect much in the way of welcome or support. Lindt, whose primary training was under the guidance of Richard Morris in history and Robert Merton and Sigmund Diamond in sociology, developed a special interest in religious sects and wrote a thesis with them on the Moravians, for which she won the Bancroft Dissertation Prize in 1965. Interestingly, although women played major leadership roles among the Moravians, Lindt did not then regard gender as an important theme in her work; that perception came only in the 1970s, as feminism began to in-fluence research in religion.[63]

Along the way, Lindt married and bore two children, while continuing to teach and pursue her research. Her career, which included appointments at Rutgers, Columbia (General Studies, of course), Howard, and American Universities, would have come to an abrupt halt had it not been for the "un-failing support of another woman," her housekeeper, who shouldered the bulk of the responsibility for child care for more than fourteen years. When her husband accepted a research position in Washington, D.C, in 1963, she asked her mentor, Robert Merton, for advice on which of the local univer-sities to apply to. Without a moment's hesitation, he responded, "The only

Gillian Lindt (b. 1932)
Graduate of Columbia University (Ph.D. 1965), historical sociologist, professor of sociology and religion at Graduate School of Arts and Sciences and School of General Studies (1973–1998), first woman dean of Graduate School of Arts and Sciences (1983–1990), and dean of School of General Studies (1994–1997), as photographed in 1984. (Columbia University Archives–Columbiana Library)

university of quality in that area is Johns Hopkins. But they do not hire women faculty in sociology or history." As Lindt moved from one university to another, following her husband, as was customary in the 1950s and 1960s, she typically was the only woman in her department and encountered her share of sexual harassment and indignity. On being interviewed by a male dean for a tenured appointment, she was asked, "Do you plan to have any more children?" To which she replied, "Do you?" Humor, she insisted, was in those days more effective than the threat of litigation, in dealing with discrimination. Then, in 1973, the religion department at Columbia recruited her for a tenured position. Lindt taught in both the graduate school and the School of General Studies, but the chair of her department never thought to have her appointed to the Columbia College faculty. When she was named to the Breslow Committee to consider the future of Columbia College, therefore, she was not only the sole female member of the committee, but also the only professor without an appointment in Columbia College.[64]

From the beginning, Lindt felt uncomfortable about the committee's work. She was surprised to learn that the proposal to make the college coeducational had come from the college administration, not the faculty. The committee was told that coeducation was the only way to stem the rapidly deteriorating size and quality of the college's applicant pool. In the committee's discussions, support for the admission of women to Columbia College was based on purely pragmatic political considerations, not on any serious reconsideration of the ethics of excluding women from the college. More than anything else, she was dismayed by the tenor of the committee's discussions. In the context of Columbia College's ability finally to be able to house all its students on campus, one committee member called for "a bed for every College man and a girl to go with it." "They had no idea how demeaning that kind of value assumption would be to the very women they were hoping not only to attract to the college, but also to retain," Lindt later declared. She took exception as well to the suggestion of one member that Columbia impose a quota that would limit women to one-third of the student body. When told that imposing a quota would be illegal, the proponent of the idea asked, "Can we do this informally?" Lindt, who had developed friendships with several Barnard faculty—including Mirra Komarovsky, Barbara Miller, Elaine Pagels, and Catharine Stimpson—was well aware that many faculty at Barnard were deeply worried about what the admission of women to Columbia College would do to the women's college. In the end, to the distress of her fellow committee members, Lindt wrote a separate, dissenting report in which she declared that the committee had not provided sufficient evidence to show that the admission of women to Columbia College would not harm Barnard and, furthermore, that the college was not yet ready to admit women. The university, she believed, would need a year or two, rather than a few months, to prepare for a successful shift to coeducation in the college and to minimize the adverse consequences for Barnard.[65]

COLUMBIA'S DECISION TO ADMIT WOMEN

Disappointing though Gillian Lindt's dissent was to those in Hamilton Hall, it had the considerable virtue, in the minds of those in Low Library, of buying the university some time. The new president, Michael Sovern, agreed with most other Columbia administrators that single-sex schooling was an "anachronism," but he wanted to see how far Barnard and Columbia could go toward coeducation before acting unilaterally to admit women. Barnard College's new president, Ellen Futter, was a former student of his at Columbia Law School; Helene Kaplan was one of his oldest friends (she graduated from Barnard the same year he graduated from Columbia College); and one of his daughters was a Barnard alumna. He vowed to do all that he could to expand coeducation on Morningside Heights.[66]

By October 1981, the Barnard and Columbia trustees believed that they had reached an agreement in principle. Barnard and Columbia students would share housing and dining facilities, the Barnard curriculum would be modified to require that all Barnard students take Columbia's core curriculum (which would be taught, in part, by Barnard faculty), and steps would be taken to ensure cross-registration, with the aim of achieving the same level of coeducation that then existed at other coeducational Ivy League schools. In practice, that would mean that undergraduate classes would be at least 40 percent female. In October 1981, each president took the Agreement in Principle to his or her respective faculty. Neither group proved happy. To many Barnard faculty members, the agreement was tantamount to merger. At best, they could hope to spend the rest of their careers teaching a core curriculum that many did not believe in; at worst, they would see the abandonment of most of their major requirements because they would not have the staff to teach the necessary courses. On close analysis, it appeared that for Barnard to meet Columbia's terms, it would be necessary to transfer 60 percent of its enrollment and half its annual tuition to Columbia.[67] Moreover, to those faculty members and administrators who had labored throughout the 1970s to persuade female-friendly Barnard to pay attention to the new scholarship on women, the likelihood that Columbia might be ready to take seriously the interests or needs of women students seemed remote at best.

For Columbia College's part, the faculty saw the Agreement in Principle as saddling them with a faculty unprepared to teach the core and female students who were no better than the male students they already had. They still wanted to admit women and reap the possibility of doubling their applicant pool while remaining the same size. In the end, Michael Sovern's decision seems to have been based on three key considerations. First, one of his children was enrolled at Brown University, coed since 1973, with an applicant pool that was significantly larger and stronger than Columbia's. It galled him that Columbia was less selective than Brown. Second, he concluded that Barnard was not willing to sacrifice as much control over its own curriculum as would be necessary to produce the 40 percent level of female enrollment in Columbia classes that he insisted was necessary for Columbia to call itself a coeducational institution. Admitting women seemed the only possible answer to achieving the coeducation he wanted to see. And, finally, the Breslow Committee report persuaded him that, were Columbia to admit women, Barnard would survive. And yet, unless he conceded something of real value to Barnard, he feared coming to be known as "the butcher of Barnard." The Barnard negotiating team made that much clear to him. Columbia therefore agreed to remain affiliated with Barnard and to guarantee continued access to Columbia's rich resources. In addition, Columbia would no longer seek to dictate the fields in which Barnard searched for new faculty, and the university would relinquish its majority voting power on ad hoc committees. Under this revised ad hoc system, Barnard would have two votes, Columbia would have two, and a scholar from outside the university in the candidate's field would be the fifth member of each ad hoc committee. Just as important, all committees considering Barnard tenure cases would be told by the Columbia provost that, while Barnard faculty were to be held to the same high standard as Columbia faculty, their greater involvement in undergraduate teaching would be taken into account in making decisions about tenure. Finally, in an important bow toward the salutary effect that Title IX of the Educational Amendments of 1972 (which Columbia feminists had been so influential in producing) was already having on women's participation in sports, Barnard athletes would be eligible to participate in Division I sports with their Columbia counterparts.[68]

Assurances from the Breslow Committee notwithstanding, many observers on both sides of Broadway believed that Columbia's decision to admit women meant certain death for Barnard without genuine coeducation for Columbia. The reaction of the Barnard faculty to Ellen Futter's announcement of Sovern's decision was initially shocked disbelief, and the immediate effect on recruitment at Barnard was nothing short of disastrous.[69] Of women admitted to both Barnard and Columbia in 1983, 90 percent chose to go to Columbia.[70] A difficult decade followed, as Barnard competed with Columbia for female students. To make matters worse, Barnard experienced increased difficulty in retaining female faculty. The college had never been willing to match outside offers, and for decades had not had to, academic opportunity being so limited for female academics everywhere else in the country. But as the women's movement brought pressure on universities to recruit women, Barnard became a popular site for academic raiders. Elaine Pagels, professor of religion, left for Princeton in 1982; the sociologist Viviana Zelizer followed in 1988. Nancy Miller left for the City University of New York in 1987.

And yet, Barnard survived through the determined leadership of Ellen Futter in the 1980s and of her successor, Judith Shapiro, in the 1990s. Futter embarked on a major fund-raising campaign. She also accepted the recommendation in 1985 of a faculty committee on a maternity- and parental-leave policy. This policy, the first since the one that Helen Rogers Reid and Virginia Gildersleeve had formulated in 1930, but Millicent McIntosh had abandoned to save money, granted pregnant staff a semester off at half pay, with full benefits. Not as generous as the original plan of a semester off at full pay, but a start, it certainly was more generous than at Columbia, which had no maternity leave provision. In recognition of the time required to parent a young child, Futter also accepted a faculty recommendation that new parents be able to slow the tenure clock by a year following the birth of a child.[71] Futter's most daring decision as president was to embark on the construction of a new dormitory for which Barnard did not yet have the funds. Building Sulzberger Tower, as the dormitory came to be known in honor of the family that had done so much for the college and that had donated $5 million toward the project, finally made the campus fully residential, at a time when both Columbia and other colleges were moving in that direction. Barnard was helped, in turn, by the publication of a series of studies claiming that girls and women reached their potential more readily in all-female settings than in coeducational institutions.[72]

When Judith Shapiro took over in 1994, she reinforced that message. Raised in Queens, and educated in that borough's public schools, Shapiro recalled that "school was my world," and her mother—a schoolteacher turned librarian—her model. There was never any question but that she would end up in academe. Shapiro earned her bachelor's degree at Brandeis in 1963 and studied European history briefly at Berkeley, but found archival research stultifying. Returning to New York, she worked in a series of jobs in publishing and psychological research before entering graduate school at

Columbia in anthropology in 1964, "with a National Institute of Mental Health fellowship but not a single course in anthropology." She quickly sensed that the all-male faculty was more concerned with establishing men than women in careers, but she felt "well taken care of by faculty advisers" and flourished in the left-wing political culture of the department, where growing outrage over the Vietnam War united students and faculty in anti-war protests.[73]

What she did not experience, however, was any sense that gender mattered intellectually. That tradition in Columbia's anthropology department was long dead. Setting off for Brazil in 1967, she decided to focus on the social culture of the Yanomamo Indians. Influenced by the emerging feminism of the day, she noticed something for which her training had not prepared her: the chief organizing principle of the society was the differing roles of men and women. Her dissertation became "Sex Roles and Social Structure Among the Yanomamo Indians of Northern Brazil." In that golden moment before academic jobs disappeared, she took a position at the University of Chicago, where she was both the first woman ever to teach anthropology and the first person to teach a course on sex roles. She found the intellectual atmosphere at Chicago exciting, but uncomfortable, too: "I hadn't finished my dissertation. Everyone in the department was a male, senior faculty member. It was intimidating." Completing her degree in 1972, she moved in 1975 to Bryn Mawr, where she rose to the position of provost

Judith Shapiro (b. 1942)
Graduate of Brandeis University (1963) and
Columbia University (Ph.D. 1972), anthropologist, and president of Barnard College
(1994–), as photographed by Joyce Ravid,
1997. (Barnard College Archives)

before coming to Barnard as president. Having worked in both single-sex and coeducation settings and having trained as an anthropologist, she knew something about what coeducation meant in theory and in practice.[74]

As she addressed the audience at her inauguration in 1994, she summed up what she had learned. As long as women remained disadvantaged members of the larger society, she argued, women's colleges would have a place: "At a time in the life cycle when pressures of gender socialization are building, girls' schools and women's colleges function as a kind of liberated zone. . . . If too many coeducational classrooms are places where boys will be boys and girls will be girls, all-female classrooms are places where girls stand a better chance of getting to be people." But the persistence of a women's college in a coeducational university was not just about students, she continued. It was about the whole institution. Coeducation did not yet exist, she said, in an institution where men and women were not yet equally likely to study all fields. Nor was an institution coeducational if women and men were not found in similar numbers in all ranks of the faculty and administration. The remarkable thing about Barnard College, President Shapiro concluded, was that it had been a coeducational institution in the fullest sense for longer than any other part of the university and, as such, continued to have a place in a university on its way to full coeducational status.[75]

"MOVING WOMEN FROM THE MARGINS"

If Columbia University could not claim to be a fully coeducational campus—in the sense of achieving gender equity in all divisions and at all levels—it made progress in the two decades following the admission of women to Columbia College. Michael Sovern, who was president from 1980 to 1993, made a start by naming women to key administrative positions. In 1983, he appointed Gillian Lindt, the woman who had said that Columbia was not ready for coeducation, as dean of the Graduate School of Arts and Sciences. In 1985, he promoted Barbara Aronstein Black, his former Law School classmate, to dean of the Law School. And in 1988, he appointed Joan Konner as dean of the School of Journalism.[76]

When Gilliam Lindt took over as dean of the graduate school, she decided that the only way to create opportunities for female scholars was to make a structural change. Taking her cue from the role that Barnard College had long played in the university, she formed a committee, chaired by Marcia Wright, to look into the creation of a separate, women's research institute within the graduate school.[77] Wright's committee recommended the establishment of the Institute for Research on Women and Gender, and in 1987 the institute

Michael Sovern (b. 1931)
Graduate of Columbia College (1953)
and Columbia Law School (1955), lawyer
and educator, professor (1957–1970) and
dean (1970–1979) of Law School, and provost
(1979–1980) and president (1980–1993) of
Columbia University, as photogrphed in 1983.
(Columbia University Archives–Columbiana Library)

opened with Carolyn Heilbrun as its first director. Heilbrun recently had declared war on the curricular status quo in one of a series of invited university
lectures by distinguished Columbia faculty members in the Low Library ro-
tunda. Speaking on "The Politics of Mind: Women, Tradition, and the University," Heilbrun declared, "In recent years the educational establishment in
the United States, and those in charge of teaching the humanities in the universities, have insisted upon the importance of our 'legacy,' and of the connection of that 'legacy' to the 'life of the mind' and to certain unchanging
truths." In obvious reference to her teacher Lionel Trilling, who had died in
1975, she continued, "The entrance of women students into almost every formerly male college and university raises the questions of how political the protection of that 'legacy' is and what effect the changing lives of women in our
society should have upon university policy." In response, she declared, "the academic community must face the necessity of moving women from the margins of universities to their center. Not to do so will indicate the degree to
which the male tradition has dictated what questions we may ask of our universities, of our 'legacy,' and of our 'old-fashioned values.'"[78]

Heilbrun's first project was to create an undergraduate Women's Studies
program at Columbia College, which she did in collaboration with the
Women's Studies faculty at Barnard, initially adopting Barnard's courses,
since there were as yet none available at Columbia. By 2003, more than
sixty courses on women and gender were offered each year in Women's

Carolyn G. Heilbrun (1926–2003)
Graduate of Wellesley College (1947) and
Columbia University (M.A. 1951, Ph.D. 1959);
literary critic and mystery writer; instructor,
assistant professor, and associate professor
of English at School of General Studies
(1960–1972); and professor at Graduate School
of Arts and Sciences (1972–1993), as photographed in 1984. (Columbia University Archives–
Columbiana Library)

Studies and related fields at Barnard and Columbia Colleges, and well over
a hundred faculty were teaching courses in which gender was an important
theme.

The Institute for Research on Women and Gender contributed significantly to that growth, especially after Lindt agreed to provide additional leadership, through a series of interdisciplinary hires. The Columbia history department gained three new faculty members, all from Rutgers. Martha
Howell (Columbia Ph.D. 1979) was hired in 1989 and directed the institute
for the next five years. She was followed by Victoria de Grazia (Columbia
Ph.D. 1976) and Alice Kessler-Harris. Other directors included Jean Howard,
hired in conjunction with the English department, and Rosalind Morris in
anthropology. Initiatives from the Institute for Research on Women and Gender had effects throughout the university, most strikingly in history—where
Howell, de Grazia, and Kessler-Harris joined Ellen Baker, Elizabeth Blackmar, Caroline Bynum, Barbara Fields, Carol Gluck, Nancy Stepan, and
Madeleine Zelin—and in anthropology, which recovered a strong feminist
presence by recruiting five new members from the University of Michigan,
including Sherry Ortner, and Lila Abu-Lughod, from New York University.[79]

Gradually, Columbia made strides toward achieving gender balance in its
arts and sciences faculty, which was finally fully unified in 1990. In 1971,
women represented 3 percent of the tenured full professors in the arts and
sciences at Columbia; by 2000, that figure had risen to 17 percent. During
the same period, the figure for associate professors rose from 9 to 33 percent,
and that for assistant professors increased from 15 to 35 percent.[80]

Significant problems remained, however, as the Commission on the Status of Women found in its 2001 study of women at the university. First, there was a much higher rate of attrition among women students than among men in all divisions of the arts and sciences, a phenomenon that stood in the way of greater progress. Second, Columbia was attracting a lower percentage of women to its applicant pool for junior faculty positions than either the national pool or the Columbia pool of Ph.D.'s was making available. Something about New York City or Columbia appeared to be deterring women more than men from applying for jobs. This problem also manifested itself at more senior levels. While the promotion process seemed to be improving gender balance in the faculty, recruitment from outside directly into tenure did not. Most recruits from outside the university were men. Finally, as administrators reoriented the university away from the humanities and social sciences and toward the natural sciences, the overall numbers for women were affected adversely in two ways. The shift not only redirected the university toward those disciplines in which there were few female students (and therefore relatively little potential for growth in the number of female faculty), but also, by slowing growth in the humanities and social sciences, made it hard for those divisions to achieve gender balance, despite their large number of female students.[81]

Moreover, resistance to research on women, gender, race, and sexuality remained throughout the university, and battles broke out on occasion. One of the fiercest battles took place at Barnard in April 1982, at the ninth annual "The Scholar and the Feminist" conference, provocatively designated "Towards a Politics of Sexuality." The conference, planned by a committee headed by the Columbia anthropologist Carol Vance, set out to challenge the growing influence of Women Against Pornography, led by Andrea Dworkin, Robin Morgan, and Susan Brownmiller, which had inaugurated an annual "Take Back the Night" march to protest violence against women and was campaigning to outlaw pornography. To Vance and other conference planners, Women Against Pornography threatened free speech and came close to forming an alliance with the "Moral Majority" in the country. Deciding to bar representatives of Woman Against Pornography from the conference, the planners organized sessions that explored both the pleasures and the dangers of female sexuality. They also published *Diary of a Conference on Sexuality*, in which they included background on the conference, descriptions of the workshops, suggested readings, and sexually provocative images. Members of Women Against Pornography who got wind of the proceedings, and especially the pamphlet, deluged the office of the new president, Ellen Futter, with protests that she was sponsoring a "pornographic" conference. Futter, facing the novel and daunting prospect of having to compete with Columbia College for students and worried about negative publicity for Barnard, impounded the conference *Diary* and thereby produced outraged protests from the conference organizers. The conference itself went on successfully and led to the publication in 1984 of *Pleasure and Danger*, which became a classic in the study of gender and sexuality. But nervousness about the adverse publicity that could accompany any open discussion of sexuality—especially in its allegedly deviant forms—persisted.[82]

Indeed, that nervousness intensified. In the years immediately following the sexuality conference, the issue of sexual harassment claimed center stage. Long before there was a name for it, women endured pinching and squeezing, verbal sexual abuse, forced sexual intimacies, and outright sexual propositions backed by the threat of losing a job or a fellowship. Women at Cornell coined the term "sexual harassment" in 1975, and Eleanor Holmes Norton, New York City's Human Rights Commissioner, held hearings about the problem later that summer. Enid Nemy covered the hearings for the *New York Times*, and her article "Women Begin to Speak Out Against Sexual Harassment at Work" sparked a wave of magazine articles and books. In 1976, the first of a series of rulings from the Equal Employment Opportunity Commission declared sexual harassment to be unlawful sex discrimination.[83] Rosalind S. Fink (Barnard 1968), who became director of equal opportunity and affirmative action at Columbia in 1980, made the implementation of grievance procedures at the university a priority. In the decade that followed, a variety of committees and task forces worked to clarify those procedures and make it easier for victims to press claims. In 1982, Columbia's Equal Opportunity Policy Board issued a "Policy Statement" prohibiting "sexual harassment by anyone." Two years later, the University Senate defined the term as "any verbal or physical conduct of a sexual nature (homosexual or heterosexual) which is imposed by someone in a position of authority on a student, junior colleague, or employee, which adversely affects that person's learning or working environment." And in 1985, under the leadership of Karen Blank in the office of the Columbia College dean of studies, the meaning of sexual harassment was broadened to include harassment by equals, and accusers were no longer required to face those they accused. That year, every student at Columbia received a cream-colored pamphlet with "Tell Someone" written across the front.[84]

Publishing rules did not stop sexual harassment, especially where differences in cultural background came into play, as they inevitably did at a university that had come to pride itself on the internationalism of its students and faculty. Dean Gillian Lindt saw six cases against graduate faculty members reach litigation between 1983 and 1990. All the accused were white, foreign-born men; none had received instruction about changes in the rules. How to provide that instruction in an effective way became a chief challenge in the years that followed.[85]

Discussion of sexual harassment reinforced a sense of political solidarity among women at Columbia, but it was a solidarity that was sorely tested by conflicts over race. As Nancy Miller later recalled, "that interlocking sense of personal conviction and political solidarity—speaking 'as a feminist' *for all women*—had already begun to erode within the feminist community. This was the moment when white mainstream feminists finally began to pay attention to internal divisions that of course had been there from the beginning." In 1983, Miller brought Barbara Smith to Barnard to teach for a year. A black, lesbian, feminist author, educated at Mount Holyoke, Smith was a founder (together with Cherrie Moraga and Gloria Anzaldua) of the Kitchen Table, Women of Color Press. Moraga and Anzaldua had been searching unsuccessfully for a publisher for a collection of essays by women of color that they had edited. Smith persuaded them that only by founding their own press would they ever get into print. Published in 1981 as *A Bridge Called My Back*, this collection set the terms of dissent from the discourse of unity that then characterized feminist criticism. The authors refused to identify themselves as feminists because the whiteness of feminism's universal subject did not include them. In common with poststructuralism, which was then sweeping the literary establishment, they accused feminist criticism of perpetuating binary accounts of gender. Did feminists truly want to posit *femaleness* as the grounds of women's identity? At both Barnard and Columbia, African American students complained that attention to their needs was not sufficiently addressed in any of the existing departments or programs. At Barnard, they pressed for the creation of a program in Pan-African Studies in 1992 and at Columbia, for an African American Studies program in 1993. Students at both schools demanded the hiring of more faculty of color and greater attention to issues of race in the curriculum.[86]

Nowhere were the battles over gender, sexuality, and race more intense than in the Columbia Department of English and Comparative Literature. Debates over what constituted good scholarship grew ever louder, as younger scholars began to explore not just feminist criticism but also, inspired by anthropology, the related field of cultural studies. As many younger scholars failed to get tenure, Carolyn Heilbrun and Joan Ferrante objected to what they regarded as a continuing unwillingness to accept women fully into the department. In 1992, Heilbrun, holder of an endowed chair and past president of the Modern Language Association, resigned in frustration at the age of sixty-six. Explaining her decision to leave, Heilbrun told a reporter for the *New York Times*, "When I spoke up for women's issues, I was made to feel unwelcome in my own department, kept off crucial committees, ridiculed, ignored. Ironically, my name in the catalogue gave Columbia a reputation for encouraging feminist studies in modernism. Nothing could be further from the truth." Joan Ferrante, who had served for a term as department chair, volunteered that she thought Heilbrun was being too kind. "Chairing was hell, but I got my hands on some numbers," Ferrante said. "Over the last twenty years, two or three men have been tenured for every woman. A list of female talent let go from here would make a brilliant department anywhere." Many of Ferrante and Heilbrun's senior male colleagues responded that the department's attitudes toward women had improved over the past twenty years. They felt betrayed by Heilbrun's abrupt departure and could explain it only as a function of her lack of "collegiality," as well as her tendency to be "quite out of control, where women's issues are concerned," and "terribly frustrated." To which Heilbrun responded, "Of course I'm frustrated, dealing with such idiocy. If I hadn't been married for forty-seven years, with three kids, you can imagine what else they'd be whispering."[87]

The English wars could be nasty, but they reflected the growing power of women in the department. When Heilbrun resigned, Gayatri Spivak, a specialist in postcolonial feminist criticism, succeeded to her endowed chair. Some departments had too few women to generate a battle, much less a war. In the Columbia Department of Philosophy, the tradition of academic machismo persisted so strongly that no woman was tenured until the end of the 1990s. The Harvard-trained early modernist Margaret Wilson visited the department in the early 1970s but quickly left for Princeton, where she spent the rest of her career, training some of the country's leading women in philosophy. According to Christia Mercer, a student of Wilson's and the first woman to rise through the ranks at Columbia in philosophy and receive tenure, in 1999, "The ability to stand on one's feet and argue, shouting others down if necessary," defined the successful philosopher. Unfortunately, it was "harder for women to be combative without being perceived as bitchy." Besides championing combativeness, philosophy had become increasingly narrow, not just at Columbia but throughout the United States. Indeed, philosophy had been off-loading fields throughout the twentieth century. Political theory had ended up in political science; ethics, in religion; and aesthetics, in literature. With rare exceptions, women interested in theory did their theorizing in other departments. The most influential female philosopher at Columbia until the end of the twentieth century was Maxine Meyer Greene at Teachers College. A 1938 graduate of Barnard, Greene had earned her Ph.D. in the philosophy of education at New York University in 1955. The first woman to be hired in philosophy at Teachers College, in 1963, Greene carried on the pragmatic tradition of John Dewey. At a time when philosophy was becoming ever narrower, she urged a return to its interdisciplinary roots. Echoing Dewey and championing existentialism, she sought to foster a democratic, feminist engagement in philosophical discourse. Not until the end of the twentieth century, however, did feminism begin to have an impact on mainstream philosophy and to draw more women to the field.[88]

CHALLENGING THE "MALE CULTURE" IN THE PROFESSIONS

In Columbia's professional schools, as in its graduate faculties, the arrival of a female dean was usually a key factor in opening opportunities for other women. When Barbara Black assumed the position of dean of the Law School in 1985, she found a school "on which the male culture still had a grip." Black had left Columbia Law School in 1956 for Yale, where she had earned a Ph.D. in American history and had taught legal history. Upon her return to Columbia in 1984—first as a visiting professor, then as a permanent member of the faculty, and finally as dean—she encountered a student body in which women still made up less than 40 percent and general skepticism about the new scholarship being done by women. But becoming the first female dean of an Ivy League law school, Black noted, made an immediate difference.

Barbara Aronstein Black (b. 1933)
Graduate of Brooklyn College (1952), Columbia Law School (1955), and Yale University (Ph.D. [history] 1975), and professor (1984–1986) and dean (1986–1991) of Columbia Law School, the first woman to lead an Ivy League law school, as photographed in 1985. (Columbia University Archives–Columbiana Library)

Only two years after her appointment, female enrollment in the first-year class jumped to 45 percent. Two years later, an ad hoc student organization called the Coalition for Diversity called for a more diverse faculty, a more diverse student body, and a more diverse curriculum. It held a teach-in, which Black attended, and then, to emphasize its seriousness about the need for change, held a sit-in at her office. There followed a set of "nonnegotiable demands," soon abandoned—lawyers being lawyers—in favor of negotiations, which lasted through the night and finally produced a "Blueprint for Progress." By the turn of the twenty-first century, 25 percent of the faculty and between 44 and 56 percent of the students (depending on the year) were female. The faculty was engaged in a much wider array of scholarship than had once been the case—not just on contracts and constitutional law, but also on race and gender. Seminars included "Sex Equality: Family and State in Historical Perspective"; "Intersectionalities, Race and Gender"; "Selected Issues in Children and Law"; "Sexuality, Gender and Human Rights"; and "Topics in Law and Sexuality."[89]

The School of Journalism, as much a male bastion in the days of Betsy Wade as the Law School, changed dramatically under the pressure of feminism and Michael Sovern's appointment in 1988 of the school's first female dean, Joan Konner, who served until 1997. A 1961 graduate of the school, Konner had gone on to a career in journalism as a director and producer at NBC and then PBS, where she made fifty documentaries. She was the third woman to serve on the Columbia University Board of Trustees, joining the board in 1978 and resigning after her appointment as dean in 1988. Under

Joan Konner (b. 1931)
Graduate of Sarah Lawrence College (1951) and Columbia School of Journalism (M.S. 1961), broadcast journalist, member of Columbia University Board of Trustees (1978–1988), and dean of School of Journalism (1988–1997). (Columbia University Archives–Columbiana Library)

her direction, the School of Journalism, both the student body and the faculty, became more coeducational than it had ever been. The School of International Public Affairs underwent a similar change after 1996, when President George Rupp named a political scientist, Lisa Anderson, as dean. The only schools that maintained a coeducational culture despite male leadership were those like the School of Social Work (which did not have a female dean until the appointment of Jeanette C. Takamura in 2002) and Teachers College, both of which had had student bodies and faculties that were heavily female from the start.

Schools that lacked either administrative or faculty leadership tended to remain more resolutely masculine in tone. At the College of Physicians and Surgeons, for instance, although women increased from 10 percent of the student body in 1970 to 50 percent by the turn of the century, women found it difficult to challenge the dominant male culture. In 1973, Helen Ranney (Barnard 1941, P&S 1947) became the first woman to chair a department of medicine at a major teaching hospital, but it was at the University of California at San Diego, not Columbia. As of 2003, there were still only two women serving as departmental chairs: Mary D'Alton in obstetrics and gynecology and Mary Wood in anesthesiology (the department in which Virginia Apgar made her mark). While there was a growing number of female clinical professors, women only rarely succeeded in winning tenure because the demands of speedy research and publication interfered with the desire of many to have children, for whom they continued to be the primary caregivers. The relative absence of women from administrative authority affected the nature of research. In common with other medical schools, Columbia treated female patients, outside of obstetrics and gynecology, as though they were men, and scientific studies rarely included women. In the 1990s, however, a cardiologist and professor of clinical medicine at P&S, Marianne J. Legato, a 1962 graduate of New York Medical College, helped found the field of gender-specific medicine. Taking advantage of a 1990 federal mandate that all federally funded research include women in studies that look at diseases that affect females, she made a number of discoveries, including the fact that women experience heart attacks differently from men. She became the editor of the *Journal of Gender Specific Medicine*, and, in addition to her scientific articles, wrote *The Female Heart: The Truth About Women and Heart Disease* (1992) and *Eve's Rib* (2002).[90]

A male culture persisted, too, in the Business School, where only 14 percent of the faculty and 35 percent of the student body was female in 2003. But change was coming even there. Phyllis Grann (Barnard 1958), who rose through the publishing industry to become the chief executive officer and president of Penguin Putnam, came to the Business School in 2003, following her retirement from Penguin in 2001, to teach finance. Professor Heather Haverman was offering a course on women in management. And half the students pictured on the school's M.B.A. Web site were women.

COLUMBIA 250

By the time Columbia began to plan for the celebration of its 250th anniversary in 2004, the university was faring better than it ever had in its history. Its success created opportunities for women, despite continuing barriers to their full equality. In the mid-1990s, as New York City recovered from a long slump, the fortunes of the university in general, and of Barnard and Columbia Colleges in particular, improved dramatically. Columbia, which had battled Cornell and the University of Pennsylvania for last place in the Ivy League in 1980, edged out Yale to finish third behind only Harvard and Princeton in the *U.S. News & World Report* ranking of the country's most selective universities, and Barnard became the country's most selective women's college. George Rupp (a former dean of Harvard Divinity School and president of Rice University), who took over the Columbia presidency from Michael Sovern in 1993, agreed with Provost Jonathan Cole that it was past time to reverse the policy instituted a century before by Frederick A. P. Barnard and John W. Burgess, of keeping Columbia College a small and marginal unit in a university dedicated to graduate research. Instead, Rupp insisted that "the college should be at the heart of the university" and enlarged its enrollment by 15 percent to four thousand students, thereby bringing in an additional $16 million annually. At the same time, he downsized the graduate program, redirecting faculty resources to the college, and worked to rebuild departments that had slid in stature during fiscal hard times. Rupp worked, as well, to improve Columbia's relations with the surrounding community by recruiting Emily Lloyd, sanitation commissioner under Mayors David Dinkins and Rudolph Giuliani, as his executive vice president for administration. Lloyd made it a practice to consult with the local community about construction plans, and quickly won what passes in New York as high praise from Maritta Dunn, chair of Community Board 9: "the current powers that be are really trying."[91] When Lee Bollinger succeeded George Rupp in 2002, he brought with him a commitment to affirmative action developed at the University of Michigan. Indeed, it was that commitment that had especially commended him to the Columbia search committee. By the year 2003, women, who won their first position on the Columbia University Board of Trustees only in 1973, constituted 15 percent of the board, 25 percent of all department chairs in the Graduate School of Arts and Sciences, 40 percent of the entire faculty (if the faculty from Teachers College and Barnard are included), and 60 percent of the student body. While resistance to women and the issues of greatest interest to them remained, even the most recalcitrant professors found it difficult to ignore issues of gender altogether. As Diana Trilling observed in 1993, "Women's Liberation, that most successful revolution of our century, has cast a wide net. By now it reaches even the aging men of my generation. They are in their seventies and eighties and never in their lives have performed a domestic service."[92] They were beginning, nonetheless, to bow to the forces of change—change that had been shaped in significant part by the women of Columbia University.

CONCLUSION

B Y THE turn of the twenty-first century, the influence of Columbia's women had spread far beyond Morningside Heights to colleges and universities across the country. By virtue of their numbers alone, these women had a significant impact. No other university supplied as many female scholars to the country's institutions of higher learning as did Columbia in the century following Lillie Devereux Blake's effort to open the university's doors to women. But the influence of Columbia's women exceeded their numbers. In Blake's day, the academy was a male enclave in which theories of evolutionary hierarchy reigned supreme. A century later, those theories were on the defensive, as the study of gender begun at Columbia transformed the face of the academy and the subjects studied there. The questions that Columbia's women raised—about the ways in which cultures distinguish males from females and structure sexual experience—initiated that transformation and shaped it throughout the twentieth century. Along the way, the women of Columbia challenged canonical texts, attacked accepted disciplinary distinctions, pioneered new methods, analyzed the ways in which gender structured power relations, and inspired others to do likewise.

Columbia's location in New York City, with its ethnic and racial conflicts and its tradition of radical politics, ensured that debates about gender would be profoundly influenced by struggles over race and rights. The harder Columbia's leaders fought to preserve the university as a bastion of Protestant male whiteness, the more vigorous and intellectually inventive did opposition to that defensive posture become. Administrative concerns about the "Jewish problem," the "Negro invasion," and the "woman question" prompted a reaction most famously in Franz Boas's anthropology department, where work on rebutting the administration's belief in racial and gender hierarchies became a preoccupying concern by the 1920s. As part of that rebuttal, Ruth Benedict, Margaret Mead, and Zora Neale Hurston developed a feminist theory of culture (informed by literary criticism and psychological investigations) that was to influence the development of the social sciences and humanities through-out the remainder of the twentieth century. Masculinity and femininity, they argued, as well as sexuality and color, derived their meaning not from the genetic material that people inherit, but from the particular narratives into which they are born. Narratives can constrain as much as heredity, they noted, but narratives also allow for invention and change.

Introducing a feminist critique of gender, sexuality, and politics to the university beyond the anthropology department proved far more difficult. Anthropology was but a tiny enclave, led by a socialist Jewish man sympathetic to blacks and women. Larger fields, like history and literature, where assumptions of Protestant, white, male superiority were deeply entrenched, provided less hospitable terrain. History at Columbia, with rare exceptions, concentrated on past politics—with a particular focus on the efforts of southern white men to establish their dominance over African Americans. For decades, only the work of Mary Beard in history, Elizabeth Baker and Emilie J. Hutchinson in economics, and Willystine Goodsell in education built the case that women had a history of their own, one worthy of scholarly attention on its own terms. Pursued on the margins of the university (at Barnard and Teachers Colleges, in the case of Baker, Hutchinson, and Goodsell) or completely outside it (in the case, after 1904, of Beard), this work had little effect on the larger scholarly enterprise at the university. Not until the arrival of Gerda Lerner (inspired by Beard's work and the radical politics of the 1930s and 1940s) and Annette Baxter (inspired by the iconoclasm of American Studies at Barnard College) did attention to women become an important focus of historical scholarship at the university. Lerner, Baxter, and those they recruited to women's history questioned the belief that men should be the measure of all that was worthy and asked why women should have to model themselves on men to merit attention. They even began to rethink the meaning of time. As Joan Kelly-Gadol suggested in "Did Women Have a Renaissance?" events and periods important to the development of men's ideas and institutions might not be important for women. Indeed, women's experiences, values, and achievements might better be viewed on a completely different temporal grid, one modeled on female experience. The women of Columbia were not alone in calling for work on women. Pioneering work was beginning throughout the country in the 1960s, as feminism began to reemerge as a political force. But Columbia's size gave its women a critical mass; its distinctive structure gave them enclaves of concentrated support; and its location in the media and publishing capital of the country gave them visibility—all of which magnified their influence and helped ensure that attention to women would quickly spread.

Feminist critics beat a parallel path within literature, vastly expanding the number of texts available for literary analysis simply by searching for work done by women that had long been ignored. The women of Columbia engaged in more, however, than a work of reclamation. They also embarked on a radical critique of traditional methodology. Throughout much of the twentieth century, the study of literature had been overwhelmingly the study of the male hero. Following the work of Kate Millett, that view became harder to sustain. Invoking the idea of the female reader, Millett provided a new tool of critical analysis and set off an avalanche of writing on English literature, the modern languages, and the classics concerning the ways in which male authors used sex as a means of establishing male power. Millett's critique helped lay the foundation for postmodern literary criticism by revealing the interested, ideological nature of the hierarchical relationship established in the texts she examined and thereby subverting the basis of that hierarchy. In doing so, she created an audience for the work of Jacques Derrida, Jacques Lacan, Michel Foucault, and other postmodernists in the years ahead.

In addition to changing how we think about gender and sexuality, the women of Columbia challenged conventional thinking about politics. Beginning in the early twentieth century, women trained in economics, sociology, and history at Columbia joined the broader community of women in New York City to organize settlement houses, fight for school reform, campaign for suffrage, and draft legislation that would assign to the political sphere responsibility for health, housing, and social insurance. Operating from a position of weakness, they came to regard the state as an institution that could be used to protect their interests as well as the interests of any disadvantaged group that sought for its members greater personal freedom and social justice. This faith in the power of the state led a number of Columbia women to the Communist Party in the 1930s, and kept many of them there through the 1940s, when the party, under Cold War assault and losing male members, staked its future on the fight for racial and gender justice. Even into the 1950s, when right-wing attacks succeeded in silencing radical protests throughout much of the country, feminist critiques continued to find a voice at Columbia. The sociologist Mirra Komarovsky, most effectively, persisted in questioning America's failure to nurture female talent and to create social services that would free women to participate fully in civil and economic life.

The most dramatic challenge to American politics came in the late 1960s and early 1970s, as modern feminism came to full flower. Columbia's women called the university to account for its long-term indifference to women's ambitions. Products of New York City, they drew support from radical feminist groups, called on the media to publicize their grievances, and lobbied the federal government to act on their behalf. They took two ideas, affirmative action and equal protection, that had been created to benefit minority men and turned them into weapons for advancing the interests of women.

Columbia women remain an important force in American life, judged by the positions they hold and the prizes they have won. Ruth Bader Ginsburg is an associate justice of the United States Supreme Court; Harriet Rabb is vice president and general counsel to Rockefeller University; Judith Kaye is chief judge of the State of New York; and Constance Baker Motley, who began her career working on civil rights cases for the NAACP, is a senior judge emerita of the United States District Court. Barnard and Columbia alumnae also include two federal judges, Miriam Goldman Cedarbaum and Anna Diggs Taylor; Congresswoman Rosa DeLauro of Connecticut; ABC News anchor Claire Shipman; the director of HIV, STD, and TB Prevention at the Centers for Disease Control and Prevention, Dr. Helene Gayle; the president of the American Museum of Natural History, Ellen Futter; and a former secretary of state, Madeleine Albright. Gerda Lerner, Linda Kerber, and Jacquelyn Hall have each been elected to the presidency of the Organization of American Historians, and Carolyn Heilbrun and Catharine Stimpson have served as presidents of the Modern Language Association.

In recognition of their extraordinary achievements, prize committees have bestowed many honors on women who either studied or taught at Barnard, Teachers College, or Columbia. The MacArthur Foundation, where Catharine Stimpson was at one time director of the fellows program, has awarded fellowships to the chemist Jacqueline Barton, the journalist Katherine Boo, the historian Caroline Walker Bynum, the writer Lydia Davis, the historian Nancy Farriss, the historian Barbara Fields, the disarmament specialist Randall Caroline Forsberg, the anthropologist Faye Ginsburg, the novelist Rebecca Goldstein, the architect Roseanne Haggerty, the women's and children's health advocate Ruth Watson Lubic, the anthropologist Sherry Ortner, the biblical scholar Elaine Pagels, the writer Susan Sontag, the sculptor Sra Sze, the choreographer Twyla Tharpe, the law professor Patricia Williams, and the archaeologist Irene Winter. Columbia women also have figured prominently among Pulitzer Prize winners: Natalie Angier, Rose Arce, Susanne Bilello, Katherine Boo, Jhumpa Lahiri, Eileen McNamara, Judith Miller, and Anna Quindlen. Through their very success, these women illustrate how much ideas about gender have changed in America.

As the rest of America became more like New York City, in terms of ethnic and racial makeup as well as cosmopolitan interests, Columbia women could no longer remain as dramatically in the vanguard as they had for most of the twentieth century. But in persuading others of the connection among gender, sex, race, and rights, the women of Columbia achieved something of lasting value; they ensured that what was once a local story would become a national, and even an international, undertaking—one in which anyone could join.

NOTES

1. THE BATTLE OVER COEDUCATION

1. Lillie Devereux Blake described her visit to Columbia in her diary, a typed transcript of which exists in the Missouri Historical Society, in St. Louis, along with Blake's other papers. It is reprinted in Katherine Devereux Blake and Margaret Louise Wallace, *Champion of Women: The Life of Lillie Devereux Blake* (New York: Revell, 1943), 111–12. I have not been able to find Blake's original petition, but she recorded her intentions in a letter to the editor of the *Golden Age* a month later ("Shall Columbia College Be Open to the Young Ladies" [letter to the editor], November 6, 1978, *Golden Age*, November 15, 1873, reprinted in *Acta Columbiana*, November 1873, 9, Columbia University Archives–Columbiana Library [cited hereafter as Columbiana]). She also recalled her visit a decade later in Lillie Devereux Blake, *Woman's Place To-day: Four Lectures in Reply to the Lenten Lectures on "Woman" by the Rev. Morgan Dix, D.D., Rector of Trinity Church, New York* (New York: Lovell, 1883), 26–28, and in a letter to the editor of the *New York Tribune*, March 10, 1883. I am indebted to Grace Ferrell for sharing her work on Lillie Devereux Blake and persuading me of Blake's importance to the history of women at Columbia. See Grace Farrell, *Lillie Devereux Blake: Retracing a Life Erased* (Amherst: University of Massachusetts Press, 2002). For an earlier, more dismissive account, see Annie Nathan Meyer, *Barnard Beginnings* (Boston: Houghton Mifflin, 1935), 4–5.
2. Population is given for New York City as defined by the Consolidation of 1898 and thus includes the population of Manhattan, the Bronx, Brooklyn, Queens, and Staten Island.
3. Edwin G. Burrows and Mike Wallace, *Gotham: A History of New York City to 1898* (New York: Oxford University Press, 1999), 980; "Ellen Louise Demorest," "Margaret Getchell La Forge," and "Sara Payson Willis Parton," in *Notable American Women, 1607–1950: A Biographical Dictionary*, 3 vols., ed. Edward T. James, Janet Wilson James, and Paul S. Boyer (Cambridge, Mass.: Belknap Press of Harvard University Press, 1971), 1:459–60, 2:358, 3:24–25.
4. George Templeton Strong, *The Diary of George Templeton Strong, 1820–1875*, vol. 4, *Post War Years, 1865–1875*, ed. Allan Nevins and Milton Halsey Thomas (New York: Macmillan, 1952), 256; Burrows and Wallace, *Gotham*, 980–81.
5. J. C. [Jane Cunningham] Croly, *The History of the Woman's Club Movement in America* (New York: Allen, 1898), 29–30; Marguerite Dawson Winant, *A Century of Sorosis, 1868–1968* (Uniondale, N.Y.: Salisbury, 1968), 1–3, 5, 23; Karen J. Blair, *The Clubwoman as Feminist: True Womanhood Redefined, 1868–1914* (New York: Holmes & Meier, 1980), 15–31. The first members worried about what to call the group. "Bluestockings" sounded too literary; "Women's League," too political and

masculine. They wanted a name that had no negative associations, one that would suggest pride in being female, without sounding offensively "strong-minded." Croly and a friend found "Sorosis" in a botanical dictionary.

6. Ellen Carol DuBois, *Feminism and Suffrage: The Emergence of an Independent Women's Movement in America, 1848–1869* (Ithaca, N.Y.: Cornell University Press, 1978), 126–61; Burrows and Wallace, *Gotham*, 981–85.

7. Barbara Miller Solomon, *In the Company of Educated Women: A History of Women and Higher Education in America* (New Haven, Conn.: Yale University Press, 1985), 50–55; Charlotte Williams Conable, *Women at Cornell: The Myth of Equal Education* (Ithaca, N.Y.: Cornell University Press, 1977), 36–42; Rosalind Rosenberg, "The Limits of Access: The History of Coeducation in America," in *Women and Higher Education in American History*, ed. John Mack Farragher and Florence Howe (New York: Norton, 1988), 109–11; Sally Schwager, "'Harvard Women': A History of the Founding of Radcliffe College" (Ed.D. diss., Harvard University, 1982), 28, 79–99.

8. Diane Ment, "Public Schools," in *The Encyclopedia of New York City*, ed. Kenneth T. Jackson (New Haven, Conn.: Yale University Press, 1995), 955–61. Independent schools open in 1873 included Friends Seminary (founded in 1786), Packer Collegiate Institute (1845), Academy of the Sacred Heart (1846), Academy of Holy Infancy (1853), Brooklyn Female Academy (1854), and Caroline Reed's School for Girls (date unknown).

9. Selma Berrol, "City University of New York" and "Hunter College," in *Encyclopedia of New York City*, 234, 575–76; Thomas J. Frusciano and Marilyn H. Pettit, *New York University and the City: An Illustrated History* (New Brunswick, N.J.: Rutgers University Press, 1997), 46–52 (NYU admitted women in 1914); Alice Duer Miller and Susan Myers, *Barnard College: The First Fifty Years* (New York: Columbia University Press, 1939), 6; Henry M. Pierce, "Address to the First Graduating Class of Rutgers Female College" (presented at the Fourth Avenue Presbyterian Church, June 2, 1867). For challenges to the classical curriculum, see Frederick Rudolph, *The American College and University* (Athens: University of Georgia Press, 1962), 119, 123–25, 290–95.

10. Blake and Wallace, *Champion of Women*, 24; Ronald Yanosky, "Lillie Devereux Blake," in *American National Biography*, ed. John A. Garraty and Mark C. Carnes (New York: Oxford University Press: 1999); Marie A. Kasten, "Lillie Devereux Blake," in *Dictionary of American Biography* (New York: Scribner, 1964).

11. Grace Ferrell, "Lillie Devereux Blake (1833–1913)," *Legacy* 14 (1997): 146–53.

12. Blake and Wallace, *Champion of Women*, 47.

13. Ibid.; Yanosky, "Lillie Devereux Blake"; William R. Taylor, "Lillie Devereux Blake," in *Notable American Women*, 1:167–70; Kasten, "Lillie Devereux Blake."

14. Blake and Wallace, *Champion of Women*, 74

15. Ibid., 87.

16. Ibid., 105.

17. Ibid., 75–222; Yanosky, "Lillie Devereux Blake"; Helen Lefkowitz Horowitz, "Victoria Woodhull, Anthony Comstock, and the Conflict over Sex in the United States in the 1870s," *Journal of American History* 87 (2000): 403–34.

18. Barnard used the phrase "an innovation on immemorial usage," in his annual report to the trustees in 1879.

19. Frederick A. P. Barnard, *Memoirs of Frederick A. P. Barnard*, ed. John Fulton (New York: Macmillan, 1896), 340, 364–65. In 1864, the School of Law enrolled 158 students, under a faculty of 4. The newly opened School of Mines had 29 students,

with 3 professors, 5 lecturers, and 1 assistant. Undergraduate enrollment continued to fall to 116 in 1872.

20. Frederick A. P. Barnard, *Causes Affecting the Attendance of Undergraduates in the Incorporated Colleges of the City of New York* (New York: Van Nostrand, 1872), 4–5, quoted in Harold Wechsler, *The Qualified Student: A History of Selective College Admission in America* (New York: Wiley, 1977), 67.

21. William F. Russell, ed., *The Rise of a University*, vol. 1, *The Later Days of Old Columbia College, from the Annual Reports of Frederick A. P. Barnard* (New York: Columbia University Press, 1937), 341.

22. Barnard, *Memoirs of Barnard*, 4, 10, 35, 47–48, 62, 412; William J. Chute, *Damn Yankee! The First Career of Frederick A. P. Barnard: Educator, Scientist, Idealist* (Port Washington, N.Y.: Kennekat, 1978), 10. For an excellent analysis of the gender issues in Barnard's life, see Stacilee Ford Hosford, "Frederick Augustus Porter Barnard: Reconsidering a Life" (Ed.D. diss., Teachers College, Columbia University, 1991), and Robert McCaughey, "F. A. P. Barnard," in *American National Biography*.

23. Chute, *Damn Yankee*, 76–83, 136.

24. Ibid., 96–98, 104–8, 121, 286; "Margaret McMurray Barnard" [obituary], *Auglaize Democrat* (Wapakoneta, Auglaize County, Ohio), November 26, 1891, 5.

25. Chute, *Damn Yankee*, 168–73; Barnard, *Memoirs of Barnard*, 246–53.

26. Barnard, *Memoirs of Barnard*, 280–98.

27. Blake and Wallace, *Champion of Women*, 111–12.

28. George Templeton Strong, *The Diary of George Templeton Strong, 1820–1875*, vol. 3, *The Civil War, 1860–1865*, ed. Allan Nevins and Milton Halsey Thomas (New York: Macmillan, 1952), 407, 487, 510; Strong, *Diary*, 4:121.

29. Horace Coon, *Columbia: Colossus on the Hudson* (New York: Dutton, 1947). According to Strong, "He is an admirable executive officer, and leads the board admirably. Strange to say, his impenetrable deafness strengthens him in his leadership. We are a gentlemanlike board, and no one of us likes to oppose or object to any proposition of the President's, because it's rather difficult and painful to make the President hear or understand the objection. So we commonly acquiesce, unless the matter be grave" (*Diary*, 4:194).

30. Strong, *Diary*, 3:47–48; 4:194.

31. Ibid., 4:60, 214; Morgan Dix called Margaret McMurray Barnard one of a group of "fanatics" ("Diary," April 24, 1882, Columbiana); "Margaret McMurray Barnard."

32. *Acta Columbiana*, November 1873, 1, 10, 29. In her diary entry for October 4, 1873, Lillie Devereux Blake identified Ogden Rood as an old friend (Blake and Wallace, *Champion of Women*, 110).

33. Blake, *Woman's Place To-day*, 27–28.

34. Strong, *Diary*, 4:497, 471.

35. Ibid., 4:497; Richard W. Prichard, "Morgan Dix," in *American National Biography*. Dix elaborated his concern over secularization in *Lectures on the Calling of a Christian Woman: and Her Training to Fulfill It, Delivered During the Season of Lent, A.D. 1883* (New York: Appleton, 1883), 161. Although members of the Episcopal clergy had the right to marry, he had spoken out against this practice on the grounds that marriage led to divided interests. His decision in 1874 to marry a much younger woman led to something of a scandal but not to any other change in his generally conservative views (Strong, *Diary*, 4:510).

36. Strong, *Diary*, 4:497; Prichard, "Morgan Dix."

37. Strong, *Diary*, 4:497.

38. Ibid., 4:499. Strong died on July 24, 1875. Dix made no reference in his daily "Diary" to this initial effort to win admission for women to Columbia College, whereas he discussed efforts made in 1883 in some detail. He may not have taken this early application very seriously.

39. Barnard, *Memoirs of Barnard*, 423; Blake, *Woman's Place To-day*, 28.

40. *Acta Columbiana*, November 1873–February 1874, 1, 9–10, 20–23, 29–30.

41. Croly, *History of the Woman's Club Movement*, 29–30; Columbia College Trustees, Minutes, December 4, 1876, Columbiana.

42. According to Strong, in his diary entry for June 5, 1871, "Barnard produced a cord or two of closely written foolscap MS and said he would read a few brief extracts from his annual report. . . . At last Governeur Ogden got up and interrupted Barnard with the statement that, as the report would probably be printed and as some of us had urgent engagements elsewhere, it might be unnecessary to read any more of it" (*Diary*, 4:362–63).

43. Frederick A. P. Barnard, "The Higher Education of Women" [passages extracted from Barnard's annual reports presented to the trustees in June 1879, June 1880, and June 1881] (New York: Privately printed, 1882), 11, Barnard College Archives.

44. Barnard, "Higher Education of Women," June 1879, 8–11; Nicholas Murray Butler, *Across the Busy Years: Recollections and Reflections*, 2 vols. (New York: Scribner, 1939), 1:76–77, 80; Hosford, "Barnard," 95.

45. Barnard, "Higher Education of Women," June 1879, 13.

46. For an excellent account of the campaign, see Schwager, "'Harvard Women,'" 79–148.

47. Edward Clarke, *Sex in Education; or, a Fair Chance for the Girls* (Boston: Osgood, 1873), 12–13.

48. Studies critical of Clarke appeared immediately: Julia Ward Howe, ed., *Sex and Education: A Reply to Dr. Clarke's "Sex in Education"* (Cambridge, Mass.: Roberts, 1874). See especially the comments by Howe, 1–31, and by Thomas Wentworth Higginson, 35–40, and the section "Testimony from Colleges," 191–203.

49. Barnard, "Higher Education of Women," June 1879, 15.

50. Ibid., 16.

51. Ibid., 18. For a favorable response in the press, see "A University for Men and Women," *Home Journal*, August 6, 1879.

52. Butler, *Across the Busy Years*, 1:76–77.

53. Meyer, *Barnard Beginnings*, 62.

54. For Barnard's version of the 1879 board resolution, see Frederick A. P. Barnard to Caroline Choate, March 8, 1883, Frederick A. P. Barnard Papers, Rare Book and Manuscript Library, Columbia University. For more on Caroline Reed and the employment of Columbia instructors, see Sylvanus Albert Reed, *The Life of Caroline Gallup Reed* (New York: Privately printed, 1931), 11, and Butler, *Across the Busy Years*, 1:89. On concern over female applicants to the Law School, see John W. Burgess, "On Coeducation at Columbia" (handwritten, undated draft), John W. Burgess Papers, Rare Book and Manuscript Library, Columbia University.

55. Columbia College Trustees, Minutes, October 6 and November 3, 1879, Columbiana; Butler, *Across the Busy Years*, 1:76–77.

56. *Acta Columbiana*, November 7, 1879.

57. Barnard, "Higher Education of Women," June 1880, 64–77.

58. *Acta Columbiana*, March 16, 1880, Columbiana.

59. Barnard, "Higher Education of Women," June 1881, 83.

60. John William Robson, *Guide to Columbia University* (New York: Columbia University Press, 1937), 9.

61. Lindsey R. Harmon, ed., *A Century of Doctorates: Data Analysis of Growth and Change* (Washington, D.C.: National Academy of Sciences, 1978), 127.

62. William A. Dunning, *Reconstruction, Political and Economic, 1865–1877* (New York: Harper, 1907); Eric Foner, *Reconstruction: America's Unfinished Revolution, 1863–1877* (New York: Harper & Row, 1988), xix–xxvii; Peter Novick, *That Noble Dream: The Objectivity Question and the American Historical Profession* (New York: Cambridge University Press, 1988), 75–80; David W. Blight, *Race and Reunion: The Civil War in American Memory* (Cambridge, Mass.: Harvard University Press, 2001), 358.

63. John W. Burgess, *Reminiscences of an American Scholar: The Beginnings of Columbia University* (New York: Columbia University Press, 1934), 3–4; Ralph Gordon Hoxie, "John W. Burgess, American Scholar, Book I: The Founding of the Faculty of Political Science" (Ph.D. diss., Columbia University, 1950), 7–10.

64. Burgess, *Reminiscences of an American Scholar*, 294–95, 3–137, 168; Hoxie, "John W. Burgess," 7; Roger S. Bagnall, "John W. Burgess and the Birth of the University" (paper presented at the Columbia University Seminar on the History of the University, February 28, 2001); John W. Burgess, *The American University: When Shall It Be? Where Shall It Be?* (Boston: Ginn, Heath, 1884), 18; Walter Metzger, *Academic Freedom in the Age of the University* (New York: Columbia University Press, 1955), 105; Barnard, *Memoirs of Barnard*, 400.

65. Burgess, "On Coeducation at Columbia."

66. Burgess, *Reminiscences of an American Scholar*, 241–42.

67. Ibid., 242.

68. Strong, *Diary*, 4:544.

69. Reed, *Life of Caroline Gallup Reed*, 18.

70. Burgess, "On Coeducation at Columbia." Jews then constituted about 9 percent of New York City inhabitants; by 1915, they were close to 28 percent.

71. John W. Burgess, *Reconstruction and the Constitution, 1866–1876* (New York: Scribner, 1902), 263–64.

72. Frederick A. P. Barnard, President's Annual Report, 1880, 63, Columbiana.

73. Frederick A. P. Barnard to Mrs. Henry E. Pellew, November 16, 1881, Barnard Papers, quoted in Hosford, "Barnard," 129–30.

74. Barnard, "Higher Education of Women," 69 and letters that precede essays. Prominent members included the "liberal" leaders of the day, anti-Tammany and in favor of good government and free trade: E. L. Godkin (reformer, editor of the *Nation* and, after 1881, the *Evening Post*), Charles Loring Brace (head of the Children's Aid Society), Joseph H. Choate (prominent corporate lawyer, opponent of income tax), and Mrs. W. E. Dodge Jr. (wife of the heir to the Phelps Dodge copper fortune).

75. Will Irwin, Earl Chapin May, and Joseph Hotchkiss, *A History of the Union League Club of New York City* (New York: Dodd, Mead, 1952), 115–19.

76. "Proceedings of the First Public Meeting of This Association for Promoting Higher Education of Women in New York," 1882, 36, Barnard College Archives; Hosford, "Barnard," 130; Meyer, *Barnard Beginnings*, 9. According to Meyer, "Choate also said that the appeal was not for coeducation, but for equal educational privileges" (37). Given his disparaging remarks about the idea of an annex, Meyer found those words "obscure." But Choate was merely repeating Barnard's oft-made point that it was not the throwing of men and women together that he was advocating, but the extending to women of the same privileges long granted to men. If the board wanted to teach men and women in separate classrooms and was willing to foot the

expense, he would go along. If they insisted on constructing a building across the street for the separate classes, he would accept that, too, but with the sure conviction that this unnecessary duplication would not last long. He was not willing to support setting up a separate college, with its own trustees, administration, and degrees (Frederick A. P. Barnard to Caroline Choate, March 10, 1883, Barnard Papers).

77. For evidence of the close connection between New York and Cambridge, see Schwager, "'Harvard Women,'" 231. Abby Parsons, a third-year Harvard Annex student and organizer of the Appian Way Association, had lamented three weeks earlier, on March 31, 1882, that "we get the crumbs that fall from the table [and] we enjoy them all by ourselves away from our cruel brothers here on Appian Way."

78. Frederick A. P. Barnard to William F. Warren, April 5, 1882, quoted in Hosford, "Barnard," 131; Frederick A. P. Barnard to Caroline Choate, June 6 and 11, 1882, Barnard Papers.

79. Dix, "Diary," April 21–24, 1882, Columbiana.

80. "Co-education at Columbia," Columbia Spectator, May 5, 1882.

81. Ibid.; the petition can be found in the Barnard College Archives. The local papers reprinted it with the names of many of the prominent signers ("Coeducation at Columbia," New York Tribune, February 6, 1883).

82. Miller and Myers, Barnard College, 6.

83. Dix, "Diary," April 24, 1882, and January 30, 1883, Columbiana; Schwager, "'Harvard Women,'" 355.

84. Burgess, "On Coeducation at Columbia."

85. Blake and Wallace, Champion of Women, 151–57; Blake, Woman's Place To-day.

86. Dix, Lectures on the Calling of a Christian Woman, 64–66, 11, 13, 16.

87. Ibid., 68–73.

88. Ibid., 68, 81, 108.

89. Ibid., 30.

90. Ibid., 86, 97–98, 102, 108, 119–30; Burrows and Wallace, Gotham, 1071–72.

91. Dix, Lectures on the Calling of a Christian Woman, 83, 169–75.

92. Blake, Woman's Place To-day, 60–61; Blake and Wallace, Champion of Women, 126. One argument made by members of the Association for Promoting the Higher Education for Women was that a woman with a Columbia degree could obtain a better position than she otherwise could ("Columbia's Latest Step; The Exclusion of Women as Students; How the Action of the Trustees Is Regarded — Talks with Mr. Fish, President Barnard and Others," New York Tribune, March 7, 1883).

93. Blake, Woman's Place To-day, 9–23, 66.

94. Ibid., 41, 43.

95. Ibid., 41, 43, 45, 58.

96. Ibid., 71–72.

97. Blake and Wallace, Champion of Women, 152–53. Coverage of the debate in New York was extensive.

98. Dix, "Diary," March 5, 1883, Columbiana.

99. Throughout the 1870s, Dix repeatedly rejected the entreaties of coeducationists, but he never mentioned coeducation in his diary. To him the idea was so preposterous that it did not merit comment. Beginning with the formation of the Association for Promoting the Higher Education of Women, however, the topic began to figure prominently in his entries.

100. The particular views of the trustees are laid out in "Co-education at Columbia."

101. "Columbia Shuts Its Doors; Women Not Allowed to Study There; But the Trustees Vote in Favor of a System of Examinations and Diplomas," *New York Tribune*, March 6, 1883; "Women Not to Enter Columbia," *New York Tribune*, March 6, 1883; "Columbia's Latest Step." Those who wished to offer a compromise included Cornelius R. Agnew (the only other open advocate of coeducation), Hamilton Fish, John W. Townsend, Gerard Beekman, and perhaps others.

102. Columbia College Trustees, Minutes, March 5 and June 4, 1883, Columbiana.

103. Dix, "Diary," March 7 and 13, 1883, Columbiana; Blake and Wallace, *Champion of Women*, 131.

104. Columbia College Trustees, Minutes, May 7, 1883, Columbiana.

105. Dix, "Diary," April 14, 1883, Columbiana; Prichard, "Morgan Dix"; Blake and Wallace, *Champion of Women*, 158–227. In 1894, the New York Board of Education opened Public School 6 on Manhattan's Upper East Side. Katie Devereux Blake, who later achieved fame as a suffragist and pacifist, became the principal of its "girls' department." In 1911, with the departure of the boys' principal, she became principal of the entire school. In 1916, as part of a general movement in the city to name public schools after prominent New Yorkers, the board named P.S. 6 the Lillie Devereux Blake School.

106. Barnard, *Memoirs of Barnard*, 420; Frederick A. P. Barnard, correspondence with Caroline S. Choate, Barnard Papers.

107. Barnard, *Memoirs of Barnard*, 420; Meyer, *Barnard Beginnings*, 169.

108. Winifred Edgerton Merrill, interview with Roger Howson, Winifred Edgerton Merrill Biographical Folder, Biographical Files, Columbiana.

109. Barnard, *Memoirs of Barnard*, 420, 423; Merrill interview; Ray Trautman, *A History of the School of Library Service, Columbia University* (New York: Columbia University Press, 1954), 9–19.

110. Burgess, *Reminiscences of an American Scholar*, 218.

111. Columbia College Trustees, Minutes, May 2, 1887, Columbiana.

112. Trautman, *History of the School of Library Service*, 19.

113. In addition to running his new school in Albany, Dewey served as secretary to the New York State Board of Regents and helped Annie Nathan Meyer secure an expedited charter for Barnard College. With the closing of Columbia's library school, library training in New York continued to develop elsewhere. In 1902, the Library School at Albany became a graduate school requiring college graduation for admission to the two-year course. In 1912, the New York Public Library established its own library school. In 1926, both were absorbed by Columbia when a new generation of trustees agreed to reestablish a School of Library Service under the direction of Charles C. Williamson. By 1939, the school was granting the B.S. to more than two hundred students a year (75 percent of them women), and the M.S. to more than twenty a year (86 percent of them women). The large number of women in the school troubled some. When Dean Williamson retired in 1943, Carl M. White, a candidate to replace him, outlined in a letter to President Butler the conditions under which he would take the job. Those conditions included "strengthening the faculty by making appointments in the higher ranks to fill vacancies, and gradually reducing the proportion of women on the faculty." Under President Butler's assurance that he concurred in those ideas and plans, White accepted the appointment.

114. Barnard, *Memoirs of Barnard*, 88; Barnard, President's Annual Report, 1866, 29–31, Columbiana.

115. "Barnard Founders Die," *Columbia Alumni News*, November 1951, clipping, Merrill Biographical Folder, Columbiana.

116. Dix, "Diary," January 5 and 18, 1884; Winifred Edgerton to Morgan Dix [inserted in Dix's diary], January 22, 1884; Columbia College Trustees, Minutes, January 7 and February 4, 1884, all in Columbiana.
117. Solomon, *In the Company of Educated Women*, 134. By 1900, 238 women and 2,372 men had received doctorates.
118. Dix, "Diary," April 17, 1884; March 5, 1885; and February 12 and June 7, 1886; Columbia College Trustees, Minutes, June 7, 1886, both in Columbiana; Joan Sar Faier, "Columbia's First Woman Graduate," *Columbia Today*, winter 1977, 28; Merrill interview.
119. Columbia College Trustees, Minutes, June 7, 1886, Columbiana; Faier, "Columbia's First Woman Graduate," 27–29; Merrill interview.
120. Alice H. Bonnell, "Women at Columbia: The Long March to Equal Opportunity," *Columbia Reports*, May 1972, 5.
121. Barnard, *Memoirs of Barnard*, 458; Meyer, *Barnard Beginnings*, 45.

2. ESTABLISHING BEACHHEADS

1. Annie Nathan Meyer, *It's Been Fun: An Autobiography* (New York: Schuman, 1951), 9–128.
2. Annie Nathan Meyer, *Barnard Beginnings* (Boston: Houghton Mifflin, 1935), 16, 15–19; "Co-education at Columbia," *Columbia Spectator*, May 5, 1882.
3. Meyer, *Barnard Beginnings*, 19–25.
4. Ibid., 26–31, Ray Trautman, *A History of the School of Library Service, Columbia University* (New York: Columbia University Press, 1954), 7.
5. Annie Nathan Meyer, editorial, *Nation*, June 26, 1899, reprinted in Meyer, *Barnard Beginnings*, 166–74.
6. "Friends of Woman's Higher Education" to The Honorable Hamilton Fish, Chairman of the Board of Trustees of Columbia College, March 5, 1888, Barnard College Archives.
7. Frederick A. P. Barnard and Caroline S. Choate, correspondence, November 11, 1882–April 3, 1883, Frederick A. P. Barnard Papers, Rare Book and Manuscript Library, Columbia University. Joseph and Caroline Choate's daughters, Mabel and Josephine, and two of their nieces made up the first class at the school (Mabel Choate, "In the High and Far-Off Times," Brearley School Archives, New York).
8. Meyer, *Barnard Beginnings*, 47–48, appendix D.
9. At the meeting after Meyer's memorial was first discussed, the Columbia College Board of Trustees "Resolved, that this Board, in view of the great difficulties that have arisen in trying to arrange a course for the degree of Master of Arts for Women that shall not include attendance upon lectures, respectfully asks that the formation of the still more difficulty courses for the higher degrees of Doctor of Philosophy and Doctor of Letters, without attendance upon lectures, be deferred by the Trustees until the course for Master of Arts as preliminary to such higher degrees can be brought into successful operation" (Minutes, April 2, 1888, Columbia University Archives–Columbiana Library [cited hereafter as Columbiana]).
10. Trautman, *History of the School of Library Service*, 11–19; Horace Coon, *Columbia: Colossus on the Hudson* (New York: Dutton, 1947), 195.
11. Meyer, *Barnard Beginnings*, 68.
12. Ibid., 62–68; Meyer, *It's Been Fun*, 206, 201–8; "Annie Nathan Meyer" [obituary], *New York Times*, September 24, 1951.

13. Meyer, *Barnard Beginnings*, 57.
14. Ibid., 20, 120; Robert Cross, "Maud Nathan," in *Notable American Women, 1607–1950: A Biographical Dictionary*, 3 vols., ed. Edward T. James, Janet Wilson James, and Paul S. Boyer (Cambridge, Mass.: Belknap Press of Harvard University Press, 1971), 2:608–9. Annie's jealousy of her sister was so great that she never referred to her by name in her memoir, though she spoke fondly, by name and at some length, about her brothers (Myrna Goldberg, "Annie Nathan Meyer: Barnard Godmother and Gotham Gadfly" [Ph.D. diss., University of Maryland, 1987]).
15. Columbia College Trustees, Minutes, March 5 and May 8, 1888, Columbiana; Meyer, *Barnard Beginnings*, 75–79. For a record of the members of Meyer's committee, see Philip M. Hayden to Annie Nathan Meyer, March 4, 1929, Annie Nathan Meyer Papers, American Jewish Archives, Cincinnati, Ohio.
16. Winifred Edgerton Merrill, interview with Roger Howson, October 4, 1944, Winifred Edgerton Merrill Biographical Folder, Biographical Files; Winifred Edgerton to Morgan Dix [inserted in Dix's diary], May 23, 1887, both in Columbiana. According to the records of Trinity Church provided by archivists Bob Heman and Jessica Silver, Winifred Edgerton and John Merrill married at Trinity Church on September 1, 1887. In 1906, Edgerton founded the Oakmere School for girls, which she ran for twenty years. Her husband died in 1916. In 1926, she took a position as the librarian at the Barbizon Hotel for women in New York, where she resided until two years before her death at the age of eighty-eight. Edgerton's portrait, painted by H. E. Ogden Campbell on the occasion of the fiftieth reunion of the Wellesley class of 1883, was commissioned by the class, the Zeta Chapter of Phi Delta Gamma, and the Columbia Women's Graduate Club, and it was given to the university in 1933 by Barnard dean Virginia Gildersleeve. It hung in Philosophy Hall until moved to the office of Vice President Emily Lloyd. See "Columbia to Honor First Woman Student," *New York Times*, March 26, 1933.
17. Meyer, *Barnard Beginnings*, 76–79, 120–21.
18. Barbara Miller Solomon, *In the Company of Educated Women: A History of Women and Higher Education in America* (New Haven, Conn.: Yale University Press, 1985), 134.
19. Columbia College Trustees, Minutes, April 1, 1889, Columbiana; Marian Churchill White, *A History of Barnard College* (New York: Columbia University Press, 1954), 15.
20. Meyer, *Barnard Beginnings*, 120–21.
21. Nicholas Murray Butler, "On the Education of Women: A Men's Symposium," *Columbia University Quarterly*, June 1900, 226–29.
22. Meyer, *Barnard Beginnings*, 121. Margaret Barnard went on to give the college Barnard's copy of *Johnson's Encyclopedia*, which he had edited, and the portrait of Barnard that now hangs in Sulzberger Parlor.
23. Meyer, *Barnard Beginnings*, 43, 120n
24. Ibid., 80–114. The first board members were Mrs. Francis B. Arnold, the Reverend Arthur Brooks, Helen Dawes Brown, Mrs. Joseph H. Choate, Frederic R. Coudert, Noah H. Davis, George Hoadley, Hamilton W. Mabie, Mrs. Alfred Meyer, George A. Plimpton, Mrs. John D. Rockefeller, Jacob H. Schiff, Francis Lynde Stetson, Mrs. James S. T. Stranahan, Mrs. James Talcott, the Reverend Henry Van Dyke, Ella Weed, Everett P. Wheeler, Alice Williams, and Mrs. Francis Fisher Wood (White, *History of Barnard College*, appendix 2).
25. White, *History of Barnard College*, 16–17.
26. Meyer, *Barnard Beginnings*, 150.

27. White, *History of Barnard College*, 21–22; Helen Lefkowitz Horowitz, *Alma Mater: Design and Experience in Women's Colleges from Their Nineteenth Century Beginnings to the 1930s* (New York: Knopf, 1984), 135.

28. There is some dispute about the number of freshman enrolled in 1889. According to the first trustee minutes, only five students were enrolled (Barnard College, "Meeting of Trustees and Associate Members," November 11, 1891, 10, Barnard College Archives), but another source lists fourteen women, eight of whom were granted the B.A. degree in 1893 (Roll of Students Enrolled, in "Freshman Studies, 1889–1890," prepared by Barnard Registrar Elizabeth O. Abbot, and copied on April 16, 1936, by Annie Nathan Meyer, box 7, folder 1, Meyer Papers).

29. White, *History of Barnard College*, 23; Alice Duer Miller and Susan Myers, *Barnard College: The First Fifty Years* (New York: Columbia University Press, 1939), 25–26.

30. Meyer, *Barnard Beginnings*, 21–22.

31. Miller and Myers, *Barnard College*, 40.

32. Alice Duer Miller, "Social Life at Barnard," *Columbia University Quarterly*, June 1900; Sally Schwager, "'Harvard Women': A History of the Founding of Radcliffe College" (Ed.D. diss., Harvard University, 1982), 284–85.

33. Barnard College, "Meeting of Barnard Trustees and Associate Members," November 21, 1890, 23, Barnard College Archives.

34. Diane Ravitch, *The Great School Wars: A History of the New York City Public Schools* (1974; reprint, New York: Basic Books, 1988), 1–102, 107–110.

35. Esther Katz, "Grace Hoadley Dodge: Women and the Emerging Metropolis, 1865–1914" (Ph.D. diss., New York University, 1980), 1–19.

36. Thomas R. Navin, *Copper Mining and Management* (Tucson: University of Arizona Press, 1978), 13, 29, 83; Linda Gordon, *The Great Arizona Orphan Abduction* (Cambridge, Mass.: Harvard University Press, 1999), 20–21.

37. Robert Cross, "Grace Hoadley Dodge," in *Notable American Women*, 1:489–92.

38. Katz, "Grace Hoadley Dodge," 20–33; Ellen Condliffe Lagemann, *A Generation of Women: Education in the Lives of Progressive Reformers* (Cambridge, Mass.: Harvard University Press, 1979), 18.

39. Cross, "Grace Hoadley Dodge." On working girls' clubs, see Kathy Peiss, *Cheap Amusements: Working Women and Leisure in Turn-of-the-Century New York* (Philadelphia: Temple University Press, 1986), chap. 7. Peiss assails Grace Dodge's attempts at interclass contact as an insensitive failure. For less dismissive treatments, see Joanne Reitano, "Working Girls Unite," *American Quarterly* 36 (1984): 112–34, and Priscilla Murolo, *The Common Ground of Womanhood: Class, Gender, and Working Girls' Clubs, 1884–1928* (Urbana: University of Illinois Press, 1997).

40. Lagemann, *Generation of Women*, 18–24.

41. Katz, "Grace Hoadley Dodge," 35–43; Lawrence A. Cremin, *A History of Teachers College, Columbia University* (New York: Columbia University Press, 1954), 12–14.

42. Lawrence A. Cremin, *The Transformation of the School: Progressivism in American Education, 1876–1957* (1961; reprint, New York: Vintage, 1964), 134–45; Katz, "Grace Hoadley Dodge," 139–40; Richard Whittemore, *Nicholas Murray Butler and Public Education, 1862–1911* (New York: Teachers College Press, 1970), 60.

43. Katz, "Grace Hoadley Dodge," 128; David Levering Lewis, *W. E. B. Du Bois: Biography of a Race, 1868–1919* (New York: Holt, 1993), 168–69; David Tyack and Elizabeth Hansot, *Learning Together: A History of Coeducation in American Public Schools* (New Haven, Conn.: Yale University Press, 1990), 188–91.

44. Lagemann, *Generation of Women*, 25.

45. Nicholas Murray Butler, *Across the Busy Years: Recollections and Reflections*, 2 vols. (New York: Scribner, 1939), 1:59, 88–89.
46. John W. Burgess, *Reminiscences of an American Scholar: The Beginnings of Columbia University* (New York: Columbia University Press, 1934), 214–15.
47. Elizabeth Zoe Vicary, "Nicholas Murray Butler," in *American National Biography*; ed. John A. Garraty and Mark C. Carnes (New York: Oxford University Press, 1999); Albert Marrin, *Nicholas Murray Butler* (Boston: Twayne, 1976).
48. "Resolution on Coeducation," Personal Clippings, 1882–1889, Nicholas Murray Butler Papers, Rare Book and Manuscript Library, Columbia University. I am grateful to Michael Rosenthal, Butler's biographer, for calling this petition to my attention. See also Whittemore, *Butler and Public Education*, 1–15.
49. Butler, *Across the Busy Years*, 1:72–75.
50. Excerpts from Barnard's annual reports that deal with education can be found in William F. Russell, ed., *The Rise of a University*, vol. 1, *The Later Days of Old Columbia College, from the Annual Reports of Frederick A. P. Barnard* (New York: Columbia University Press, 1937), 287–94.
51. Whittemore, *Butler and Public Education*, 31.
52. Butler, *Across the Busy Years*, 1:92–93, 98–101.
53. Tyack and Hansot, *Learning Together*, 49, 83.
54. Butler, *Across the Busy Years*, 1:178.
55. Columbia College Trustees, Minutes May 2, 1887, Columbiana; Butler, *Across the Busy Years*, 1:178.
56. Coon, *Columbia*, 87–88.
57. Gerald Kurland, *Seth Low: The Reformer in an Urban and Industrial Age* (New York: Twayne, 1971), 19.
58. Ibid., 13–23; Lincoln Steffens, *Autobiography*, quoted in Thomas Bender, *New York Intellect: A History of Intellectual Life in New York City, from 1750 to the Beginnings of Our Own Time* (Baltimore: Johns Hopkins University Press, 1987), 281.
59. "Mrs. Seth Low Dies at the Age of 81" [obituary], *New York Times*, April 2, 1929; Robert C. Morris, "Benjamin Robbins Curtis," in *American National Biography*; John Dickinson, "Benjamin Robbins Curtis," in *Dictionary of American Biography* (New York: Scribner, 1964).
60. Benjamin R. C. Low, *Seth Low* (New York: Putnam, 1925), 42–44.
61. For trustee committee membership, see *Barnard Annual*, 1894; "American History Lectures by Prof. J. F. Jameson; Initiating Daughters of the American Revolution Professorship," *New York Times*, March 13, 1895.
62. Stacilee Ford Hosford, "Frederick Augustus Porter Barnard: Reconsidering a Life" (Ed.D. diss., Teachers College, Columbia University, 1991), 96–97.
63. Kurland, *Seth Low*, 5–6.
64. Ibid., 53.
65. Seth Low, "The University and the Workingman," *Social Economist*, May 1891, quoted in Bender, *New York Intellect*, 283.
66. Butler, *Across the Busy Years*, 1:158.
67. Columbia College Trustees, Minutes, March 3, 1890, Columbiana. For Columbia's expanding curriculum and decision to open graduate classes to seniors, see University Council, Minutes, June 11 and December 12, 1890, and January 17, 1891, Columbiana.
68. Robert McCaughey, "The Transformation of American Academic Life: Harvard University, 1821–1892," *Perspectives in American History* 8 (1974): 326.

69. Solomon, *In the Company of Educated Women*, 134; Schwager, "'Harvard Women,'" 291, 368. In 1890, William James agreed to work with Mary Calkins, but he was not able to secure her a degree for her work, which he judged to be exceptional.

70. For further discussion of graduate work for women, see Columbia College Trustees, Minutes, February 6 and April 2, 1888, Columbiana. The debate centered on whether women working for graduate degrees should be admitted to lectures; their right to earn graduate degrees was accepted. These were the meetings at which the possibility of Columbia's affiliating with a women's college was first discussed.

71. Rudolf Schmid and Dennis William Stevenson, "'Botanical Text Books,' an Unpublished Manuscript (1897) by Emily Lovira Gregory (1841–1897) on Plant Anatomy Textbooks," *Bulletin of the Torrey Botanical Club* 144 (1987): 307–18; White, *History of Barnard College*, 23, 29–30, 64, 193; Margaret W. Rossiter, *Women Scientists in America: Struggles and Strategies to 1940* (Baltimore: Johns Hopkins University Press, 1982), 59–63, 84–86; Columbia College Trustees, Minutes, March 3–May 5, 1890, Columbiana ; Seth Low to Emily James Smith, January 17, 1895, Central Files, Columbiana; "John Torrey," in *The Columbia Encyclopedia*, 6th ed. (New York: Columbia University Press, 2000), 2864.

72. Columbia College Trustees, Minutes, May 5, 1890, Columbiana; White, *History of Barnard College*, 23.

73. Meyer, *Barnard Beginnings*, 44.

74. Kurland, *Seth Low*, 56.

75. Columbia College Trustees, Minutes, October 5, 1891, Columbiana.

76. Columbia College Trustees, Minutes, October 5 and December 7, 1891, Columbiana. The Faculty of Pure Science was not organized until 1896.

77. John Townsend, a trustee, in *Columbia Spectator*, May 5, 1883.

78. Miller and Myers, *Barnard College*, 22–23.

79. *A History of the Faculty of Philosophy, Columbia University* (New York: Columbia University Press, 1957), 112–13.

80. Butler, "On the Education of Women," 226–29.

81. Rossiter, *Women Scientists in America*, 32–33; Solomon, *In the Company of Educated Women*, 134.

82. Barnard College, "Reports of the Dean and Treasurer," 1895, Barnard College Archives; Seth Low to John W. Burgess, January 8, 1892; John W. Burgess to Seth Low, January 12 and 14, 1892, all in Central Files, Columbiana; White, *History of Barnard College*, 24.

83. Seth Low, President's Annual Report, 1894, 19, quoted in Bender, *New York Intellect*, 283.

84. Rosalind Rosenberg, *Beyond Separate Spheres: Intellectual Roots of Modern Feminism* (New Haven, Conn.: Yale University Press, 1982), 151.

85. Virginia Crocheron Gildersleeve, *Many a Good Crusade: Memoirs of Virginia Crocheron Gildersleeve* (New York: Macmillan, 1954), 43–44.

86. Seth Low to Emily James Smith, December 20, 1895, Central Files, Columbiana.

87. President Seth Low to the University Council, October 16, 1984, University Council Minutes, Columbiana.

88. Seth Low to John W. Burgess, October 17, 1894, Central Files, Columbiana; John W. Burgess, "On Coeducation at Columbia" (handwritten, undated draft), John W. Burgess Papers, Rare Book and Manuscript Library, Columbia University. "On Coeducation at Columbia" bears a date, not in Burgess's hand, of October 16, 1896. Since the document responds point by point to Low's arguments in favor of coeducation at the October 16, 1894, University Council meeting, and since the University

Council Minutes for the December 18, 1894, meeting indicate that Burgess was present and that the motion to open classes to auditors was then tabled, the more likely date would be between October 16 and December 18, 1894.

89. Burgess, "On Coeducation at Columbia"; John W. Burgess to Charles W. Eliot, November 7, 1894; Charles W. Eliot to John W. Burgess, November 9, 1894, both in Charles W. Eliot Papers, Harvard University Archives, Cambridge, Mass. Eliot had learned the details of Columbia's opening of classes to Barnard students in correspondence with Seth Low (Seth Low to Charles W. Eliot, January 16, 1894, Eliot Papers). For the impact of this letter on the Harvard Board of Overseers, see "Report of the Special Committee," March 7, 1894, Harvard Board of Overseers Committee Reports, Harvard University Archives; Schwager, "'Harvard Women,'" 337.

90. Burgess, "On Coeducation at Columbia"; University Council, Minutes, December 18, 1894, Columbiana; R. Gordon Hoxie et al., A History of the Faculty of Political Science, Columbia University (New York: Columbia University Press, 1955), 51, 66.

91. Barnard College, "Reports of the Dean and Treasurer," 1895, Barnard College Archives; Columbia College Trustees, Minutes, February 4, 1895, Columbiana; Low identified himself as the donor but asked that the information be kept confidential in Seth Low to George Rives, chairman of the Finance Committee, Columbia College Board of Trustees, February 18, 1895; Seth Low to Emily James Smith, April 8, 1895, Emily James (Smith) Putnam Papers, Columbiana. John Bates Clark was offered an annual salary of $5,000, and both Frank Cole and James Harvey Robinson were offered $3,500. At a time when Barnard's annual budget was $21,000, the Lows gift represented the college's single biggest source of income (George A. Plimpton, "The Financial History of Barnard College," 15, Barnard College Archives). For evidence that some at Barnard would have preferred to create a separate graduate faculty in 1895, see White, History of Barnard College, 30–31.

92. Low's exact words were, "If the Columbia degree is to be given, Columbia must, as I conceive, for its own protection when it comes to positions like professorships, put behind the call to any man . . . the prestige of appointment to its own staff" (Seth Low to Emily James Smith, January 17, 1895, Central Files, Columbiana). See also Gregory's request to Low for promotion (Emily Gregory to Seth Low, May 24, 1895, Central Files, Columbiana).

93. Emanuel D. Rudolph, "Women in Nineteenth Century American Botany: A Generally Unrecognized Constituency," American Journal of Botany 69 (1982): 1346–55; Rossiter, Women Scientists in America, 59–63, 84–86.

94. An official vote did not take place until 1897, but the registrar's report lists women enrolled in the Faculty of Pure Science as of the academic year 1896/1897.

95. White, History of Barnard College, 34.

96. Hoxie et al., History of the Faculty of Political Science, 66–67; for a discussion of the importance of segregating science laboratories, see Emily James Smith to Seth Low, May 2, 1898, Central Files, Columbiana.

97. Emily James Smith to Seth Low, September 23, 1895, Central Files, Columbiana. For requirements for admission to medical school, see Regina Morantz-Sanchez, Sympathy and Science: Women Physicians in American Medicine, rev. ed. (Chapel Hill: University of North Carolina Press, 2000), 87, 232.

98. Emily James Smith to Seth Low, April 10, 1897, Central Files, Columbiana.

99. Emily James Smith to Seth Low, March 24, 1893, Central Files; Columbia College Trustees, Minutes, February 4, 1895, both in Columbiana.

100. I cannot find any instance of Smith complaining of the absence of faculty support in the administration of the college, but when Barnard acquired its own faculty in

1900, Acting Dean James Harvey Robinson noted that the "creation of a separate Faculty . . . permits a far more satisfactory system of administration than has hitherto been possible. The responsibility no longer falls upon the Dean alone but is shared by the several standing committees of the Faculty" (Dean's Annual Report, 1900, 281, Barnard College Archives).

101. I have checked the Columbia College Catalog, Smith's correspondence, and the *Barnard Annual* (which lists faculty teaching at Barnard) for the 1890s. Although the records are not complete, it seems clear that Low refused to allow Smith to hire non-Columbia faculty, except in extreme circumstances.

102. Emily James Smith, Dean's Annual Report, 1897, 7, Barnard College Archives.

103. Helen Lefkowitz Horowitz, *The Power and the Passion of M. Carey Thomas* (New York: Knopf, 1994), 195.

104. Plimpton, "Financial History of Barnard College," 4–10; Horowitz, *Alma Mater,* 137–41.

105. Miller and Myers, *Barnard College,* 51. The names of the graduates appear in *The Registrar of the Associate Alumnae of Barnard College,* 1925, Barnard College Archives.

106. Katz, "Grace Hoadley Dodge," 140–42.

107. Columbia College Catalogue. In 1900, as today, graduate schools assumed four years of undergraduate preparation as a basis for admission, but professional schools did not. As late as World War II, most of Columbia's professional schools admitted students with no more than two years of college preparation and granted a B.S. degree after an additional two years of study. Columbia offered its own undergraduates the option of the so-called professional course for those who wanted to earn both a liberal arts and an advanced professional degree. Under this program, they could begin medical or law school, for instance, while still seniors and thus shorten the overall time required to complete their education.

108. Report of the University Council and of a committee appointed by the board of trustees to consider the matter, quoted in Butler, *Across the Busy Years,* 1:182–87; Kenneth M. Ludmerer, *Learning to Heal: The Development of American Medical Education* (New York: Basic Books, 1985), 111, 113–14, 116, 141.

109. Cremin, *History of Teachers College,* 31; Butler, *Across the Busy Years,* 1:168.

110. Cremin, *History of Teachers College,* 27–28.

111. James Earl Russell, "Coeducation in the High Schools," revised reprint from *Good Housekeeping,* October 1913, in Russell, *Trend in American Education,* 165–66, quoted in Bette C. Weneck, "The 'Average Teacher' Need Not Apply: Women Educators at Teachers College, 1887–1927" (Ph.D. diss., Teachers College, Columbia University, 1996), 194.

112. Cremin, *History of Teachers College,* 27–28, 41–58.

113. Weneck, "'Average Teacher,'" 2, 51, 73–74, 119, 237, 255, 259, 285–86; Sally Jean Thomas, "'Women's Sphere' and Institutional Structure: Teachers College, Columbia University's Two School System, 1913–1933" (Ed.D. diss., Teachers College, Columbia University, 1986), 64.

114. James Earl Russell to Laura Gill, November 28, 1906; James Earl Russell to Felix Warburg, February 7, 1907; Laura Gill to George A. Plimpton, March 27, 1907, all in James Earl Russell Papers, Teachers College Archives; Bette Weneck, "'Average Teacher,'" 226, 230.

115. Seth Low to Emily James Putnam, November 28, December 13 and 20, 1899, and January 9, 1900, Central Files, Columbiana; Emily James Putnam to Abram S. Hewitt, chairman of the Barnard College Board of Trustees, January 18 and 25, 1900, Barnard College Archives; Cremin, *History of Teachers College,* 34–35; "Agreement

Between the Trustees of Columbia College in the City of New York and Teachers College, New York City, April 6, 1900," Teachers College Archives; "Agreement Between the Trustees of Columbia College in the City of New York and Barnard College, New York City, January, 1900," reprinted in Barnard College, Charters, By-Laws, Statutes and Intercorporate Agreements, with Amendments to December 4, 1930, Barnard College Archives,

116. Seth Low, President's Annual Report, 1900, Columbiana.
117. Barnard College continued to pay the salaries of Robinson, Clark, and Cole after the gift from the Lows ran out (Seth Low to Emily James Smith, February 8, 1898, Central Files, Columbiana). Low intended that "Barnard College will undertake to maintain every professorship permanently established at its instance; and when it has adequately provided for its undergraduate work it will, as its means allow, provide for the appointment of additional professors in the University whose courses shall be open to both men and women" (Seth Low to Emily James Putnam, December 20, 1899, Central Files, Columbiana).
118. "Agreement Between Columbia College and Barnard College"; Barnard College Catalogue, 1900–1901.
119. "Agreement Between Columbia College and Barnard College."
120. Harvard Board of Overseers, "Report of Special Committee," October 30, 1894, Harvard University Archives.
121. Schwager, "'Harvard Women,'" 384.
122. Caroline Bynum and Michael Walzer, "Report of the Committee on the Status of Women in the Faculty of Arts and Sciences," Faculty of Arts and Sciences, Harvard University. I am grateful to Caroline Bynum for providing me with a copy of this report. Radcliffe students would not win the right to a Harvard Ph.D. until 1963, or the right to a B.A. until 1977.
123. For a comparison between Radcliffe and Barnard, see White, History of Barnard College, 46. The much larger University of California at Berkeley and Hunter College sent larger numbers of women on to graduate work, but those numbers composed a lower percentage of their respective student bodies (Lindsey R. Harmon, ed., A Century of Doctorates: Data Analyses of Growth and Change [Washington, D.C.: National Academy of Sciences, 1978], appendix G).
124. Teachers College, "Charter for the New York College for the Training of Teachers" (1889), in Official Documents (New York: Printed for Teachers College, 1905), Teachers College Archives.
125. Cremin, History of Teachers College, 34–35.
126. Seth Low to University Council, October 16, 1894, University Council, Minutes, Columbiana.
127. Emily James Putnam to Abram S. Hewitt, January 18, 1900, box 8, folder 4, Meyer Papers.
128. These figures, taken from the 1930 Registrar's Report, do not include enrollment figures for extension classes or summer school (Barnard College Announcements, 1900–1930, Barnard College Archives).
129. Jason Hollander, "Nearing Her 100th Birthday, Alma Mater Receives a Much Needed Makeover," Columbia News, January 15, 2003.

3. CITY OF WOMEN

1. According to the 1900 census, 59 percent of African American women, 27.2 percent of foreign-born women, and 24.6 percent of native-born women in New York City

worked (Bureau of the Census, *Statistics of Women at Work*, 1900 [Washington, D.C.: Government Printing Office, 1907], 146); Edwin G. Burrows and Mike Wallace, *Gotham: A History of New York City to 1898* (New York: Oxford University Press, 1999), 1046–49; Ann Douglas, *Terrible Honesty: Mongrel Manhattan in the 1920s* (New York: Farrar, Straus and Giroux, 1995), 15. Douglas, following James Weldon Johnson, argues that New York attracted a large number of blacks because it lacked heavy industry; I think that the argument holds even better for women.

2. Report and Register of the Associate Alumnae of Barnard College, 1910–1915, Barnard College Archives.

3. Richard Whittemore, *Nicholas Murray Butler and Public Education, 1862–1911* (New York: Teachers College Press, 1970), 64; David Ment, "Public Schools," in *The Encyclopedia of New York City*, ed. Kenneth T. Jackson (New Haven, Conn.: Yale University Press, 1995), 955–61; Diane Ravitch, *The Great School Wars: A History of the New York City Public Schools* (1974; reprint, New York: Basic Books, 1988), 83–106; Sherry Gorelick, *City College and the Jewish Poor: Education in New York, 1880–1924* (New Brunswick, N.J.: Rutgers University Press, 1981), 90. Seth Low spoke often of New York City as a vast laboratory for study and investigation (Columbia College, *Proceedings at the Installation of Seth Low as President* [New York: Printed for the College, 1890], Columbia University Archives–Columbiana Library [hereafter cited as Columbiana]; Seth Low, "A City University" [address presented at Johns Hopkins University, February 22, 1895], Columbiana; James Martin Keating, "Seth Low and the Development of Columbia University, 1889–1901" [Ed.D. diss., Teachers College, Columbia University, 1973]).

4. Mary G. Dietz and James Farr, "'Politics Would Undoubtedly Unwoman Her': Gender, Suffrage, and American Political Science," 61–85; and Helene Silverberg, "'A Government of Men': Gender, the City, and the New Science of Politics," 156–84, in *Gender and American Social Science: The Formative Years*, ed. Helene Silverberg (Princeton, N.J.: Princeton University Press, 1998).

5. Whittemore, *Butler and Public Education*, 64, 114.

6. Ravitch, *Great School Wars*, 144–67. Butler helped inspire similar movements in other cities, including St. Louis, Chicago, San Francisco, Boston, Philadelphia, and Denver (David B. Tyack, *The One Best System: A History of American Urban Education* [Cambridge, Mass.: Harvard University Press, 1974], 141–76).

7. Bette C. Weneck, "The 'Average Teacher' Need Not Apply: Women Educators at Teachers College, 1887–1927" (Ph.D. diss., Teachers College, Columbia University, 1996), 285–89; Ravitch, *Great School Wars*, 144–67; Lawrence A. Cremin, *A History of Teachers College, Columbia University* (New York: Columbia University Press, 1954), 26; Nicholas Murray Butler, *Across the Busy Years: Recollections and Reflections*, 2 vols. (New York: Scribner, 1939), 1:168. A woman could double her salary by training for an administrative position.

8. Cremin, *History of Teachers College*, 66–70.

9. Columbia University Trustees, Minutes, June 6, 1904; John Angus Burrell, *A History of Adult Education at Columbia University: University Extension and the School of General Studies* (New York: Columbia University Press, 1954), 3–9; Cremin, *History of Teachers College*, 68.

10. Columbia University, Report of the Registrar, 1919–1920, 254, Columbiana.

11. Nicholas Murray Butler to Grace Dodge, October 12 and 16, 1914, Columbia University and Teachers College, Documents and Correspondence, 1915, Teachers College Archives.

12. Cremin, *History of Teachers College*, 72.
13. Grace Dodge to Nicholas Murray Butler, October 16, 1914, Columbia University and Teachers College, Documents and Correspondence, 1915.
14. James Earl Russell to H. B. Frissell, principal of Hampton Normal and Agricultural Institute, November 12, 1900, series 6, folder 505, James Earl Russell Papers, Teachers College Archives; Booker T. Washington to James Earl Russell, April 27, 1901; James Earl Russell to Booker T. Washington, May 4, 1901, both in series 6, folder 631, Russell Papers.
15. Cremin, *History of Teachers College*, 71–73; Felix Warburg to James Earl Russell, April 27, 1915, Russell Papers, reporting on lunch with Columbia trustee Francis S. Bangs and Warburg's insistence that Teachers College be granted control of faculty appointments to the Summer School. Teachers College's Jewish trustees, Warburg and James Speyer, may also have worried that whatever influence Jews had over Teachers College would end with absorption into Columbia, since the Columbia board had no Jews and seemed disinclined to name any. See Robert A. McCaughey, *Stand Columbia: A History of Columbia University in the City of New York, 1754–2004* (New York: Columbia University Press, 2003), 217–18.
16. Mary Kingsbury Simkhovitch, *Neighborhood: My Story of Greenwich House* (New York: Norton, 1938), 70–71; and *Here Is God's Plenty: Reflections on American Social Advance* (New York: Harper, 1949), 171.
17. Cremin, *History of Teachers College*, 104–5
18. Desley Deacon, *Elsie Clews Parsons: Inventing Modern Life* (Chicago: University of Chicago Press, 1997), 12.
19. Ibid., 25.
20. Ibid., 30.
21. Albert Marrin, *Nicholas Murray Butler* (Boston: Twayne, 1976), 82.
22. Franklin Giddings, *Principles of Sociology* (New York: Macmillan, 1896), 359–60, 397.
23. Deacon, *Elsie Clews Parsons*, 33–34.
24. Weneck, "'Average Teacher,'" 272. The Speyer school was organized as a "working laboratory" (James Earl Russell, President's Annual Report, 1898, 13, Teachers College Archives).
25. Cremin, *History of Teachers College*, 104–5.
26. Deacon, *Elsie Clews Parsons*, 33–34, 46; "Elsie Clews: School Inspector," *New York Tribune*, July 8, 1899; Elsie Clews Parsons, "Educational Legislation and Administration of the Colonial Governments" (Ph.D. diss., Columbia University, 1899).
27. Carol Smith Rosenberg, "Mary Kingsbury Simkhovitch," in *Notable American Women: The Modern Period*, ed. Barbara Sicherman and Carol Hurd Green (Cambridge, Mass.: Belknap Press of Harvard University Press, 1980), 648–51.
28. Burrows and Wallace, *Gotham*, 1177–78.
29. Alfred Kahn, "Themes for a History: The First Hundred Years of the Columbia University School of Social Work" (available at: www.columbia.edu/cu/ssw/welcome/history); Burrows and Wallace, *Gotham*, 1159–60, 1176–77.
30. Elsie W. Clews, "Field Work in Teaching Sociology at Barnard College, Columbia University," *Educational Review* 20 (1900): 159.
31. Paul S. Boyer, "Elsie Clews Parsons," and Allen F. Davis, "Crystal Eastman," in *Notable American Women, 1607–1950: A Biographical Dictionary*, 3 vols., ed. Edward T. James, Janet Wilson James, and Paul S. Boyer (Cambridge, Mass.: Belknap Press of Harvard University Press, 1971), 3:20–22, 1:543–45; Rosenberg, "Mary Kingsbury

Simkhovitch"; Eleanor Midman Lewis, "Mary Abby Van Kleeck"; and Charles Trout, "Frances Perkins," in *Notable American Women: Modern Period*, 648–51, 707–9, 535–39.

32. Deacon, *Elsie Clews Parsons*, xi.

33. Ibid., 50–51.

34. Ibid., 56–57.

35. Sue G. Walcutt, "Alice Duer Miller," in *Notable American Women*, 1607–1950, 2:538–40; Deacon, *Elsie Clews Parsons*, 50–51.

36. Deacon, *Elsie Crews Parsons*, 58. I have not been able to figure out why Low would have resisted such an appointment; Dodge and Agnew had already served in the 1880s, so no traditions were being threatened. See Gerald Kurland, *Seth Low: The Reformer in an Urban and Industrial Age* (New York: Twayne, 1971), 146.

37. Elsie Clews Parsons, *The Family: An Ethnographical and Historical Outline with Descriptive Notes, Planned as a Text-Book for the Use of College Lecturers and of Directors of Home-Reading Clubs* (New York: Putnam, 1906), vi, vii, 31, 95, 100.

38. Deacon, *Elsie Clews Parsons*, 62–63.

39. Parsons, *Family*, 349.

40. Deacon, *Elsie Clews Parsons*, 90.

41. "Drs. Peters and Dix Attack Book," *New York Herald Tribune*, November 18, 1906; Deacon, *Elsie Clews Parsons*, 61–69.

42. Marelene F. Rayner-Canham and Geoffrey W. Rayner-Canham, *Harriet Brooks: Pioneer Nuclear Scientist* (Montreal: McGill–Queens University Press, 1992), 44–51.

43. Deacon, *Elsie Clews Parsons*, 59.

44. Nancy Cott, ed., *A Woman Making History: Mary Ritter Beard Through Her Letters* (New Haven, Conn.: Yale University Press, 1991), 4–8, 19; Ann J. Lane, "Mary Ritter Beard: An Appraisal of Her Life and Work," in *Mary Ritter Beard: A Sourcebook*, ed. Ann J. Lane (New York: Schocken, 1977), 11–19.

45. John W. Burgess, *Reconstruction and the Constitution, 1866–1876* (New York: Scribner, 1902), 263–64.

46. James Harvey Robinson, *The New History: Essays Illustrating the Modern Historical Outlook* (New York: Macmillan, 1912), 99.

47. John Higham, *History: Professional Scholarship in America* (New York: Harper & Row, 1965), 110–16; Peter Novick, *That Noble Dream: The Objectivity Question and the American Historical Profession* (New York: Cambridge University Press, 1988), 25, 29; James Farr, "John William Burgess," in *American National Biography*, ed. John A. Garraty and Mark C. Carnes (New York: Oxford University Press, 1999).

48. Robinson, *New History*, 24; Higham, *History*, 110–16.

49. Novick, *That Noble Dream*, 107

50. Ibid., 89. Sloane included Robinson's student and junior colleague James T. Shotwell in his criticism.

51. Robert B. Westbrook, *John Dewey and American Democracy* (Ithaca, N.Y.: Cornell University Press, 1991), 117–19. For all of Robinson's enthusiasm for interdisciplinary studies, he did not take much advantage of anthropology. His examples of different social experiences never included non-European peoples (Daniel A. Siegel, "'Western Civ' and the Staging of History," *American Historical Review* 105 [2000]: 770–803).

52. Thomas Bender, *New York Intellect: A History of Intellectual Life in New York City, from 1750 to the Beginnings of Our Own Time* (Baltimore: Johns Hopkins University Press, 1987), 285.

53. Butler, *Across the Busy Years*, 1:50.

54. In 1889, Butler wrote that "the kindergarten, the movement for drawing . . . , the movement for better and more objective methods of teaching history , geography, number, etc., and the manual training movement, are . . . not distinct, but closely related, and indeed, interdependent" (quoted in Whittemore, *Butler and Public Education*, 59–60).

55. Records in Columbiana Library list Mary Beard as a student in the academic year 1902/1903, but she does not seem to have participated in any of the seminars in sociology or statistics, her announced specialty. She may have enrolled in lecture courses only, or she may have begun a seminar and found it impossible to finish the required research papers. The title of every seminar paper completed that year is listed in the dean's annual report.

56. Cott, *Woman Making History*, 10–11.

57. Payroll records for schools in Manhattan and the Bronx, 1904–1905, Teachers College Archives.

58. Robert E. Doherty, "Tempest on the Hudson: The Struggle for 'Equal Pay for Equal Work' in the New York City Public Schools, 1907–1911," *History of Education Quarterly* 19 (1979): 413–34.

59. David Tyack and Elisabeth Hansot, *Learning Together: A History of Coeducation in American Public Schools* (New Haven, Conn.: Yale University Press, 1990), 162.

60. Doherty, "Tempest on the Hudson," 413–34. In 1924, the legislature extended the principle of equal pay to teachers throughout the state and in 1947 it equalized the pay of grade-school and high-school teachers with equivalent training.

61. Whittemore, *Butler and Public Education*, 104–5, 110, 115.

62. "To Aid Married Teachers: Women Want Rule Against Them Rescinded in This City," *New York Times*, April 19, 1913; "Women Teachers Hiss Miss Strachan," *New York Times*, November 14, 1914. Only four states in the entire country permitted the hiring of married women as teachers in the early twentieth century.

63. See, for instance, "Emily Smith James; Betrothal," *New York Times*, February 20, 1899; and "Mrs. George Haven Putnam; Barnard's Dean's Resignation," *New York Times*, January 30, 1900.

64. *People ex rel. Murphy v. Maxwell*, 177 N.Y. 494.

65. New York City Board of Education, *Seventeenth Annual Report* (1915), 66.

66. June Sochen, *Movers and Shakers: American Women Thinkers and Activists, 1900–1970* (New York: Quadrangle, 1973), 41–43.

67. Henrietta Rodman, letter to *New York Tribune*, November 10, 1914; "Henrietta Rodman," *Barnard Bulletin*, November 2, 1915.

68. "Teacher Mothers Win Final Verdict," *New York Times*, January 2, 1915; New York City Board of Education, Minutes, January 27, 1915, Teachers College Archives.

69. New York City Board of Education, Minutes, December 30, 1914, and January 13 and 27, February 24, and June 23, 1915, Teachers College Archives.

70. Sochen, *Movers and Shakers*, 41–43. The press gave extensive coverage to Rodman and Piexotto's campaigns in 1914 and 1915. See Ruth Jacknow Markowitz, *My Daughter, the Teacher: Jewish Teachers in the New York City Schools* (New Brunswick, N.J.: Rutgers University Press, 1993), 133–34, 141; and Paul N. Garver, "Legal Status of Married Women Teachers," *School and Society*, October 24, 1931, 571–76.

71. Cott, *Woman Making History*, 11–12.

72. Mary Beard to Leonora O'Reilly, April 1912, quoted in Cott, *Woman Making History*, 65.

73. Cott, *Woman Making History*, 66.

74. Ibid., 14.

75. Ibid., 15.
76. Mary Ritter Beard, *Women's Work in Municipalities*, National Municipal League Series (New York: Appleton, 1915), vii.
77. Ibid., 221.
78. Ibid., 202, 45–46.
79. Ibid., 331.
80. Cott, *Woman Making History*, 20.
81. Nancy Cott, "Putting Women on the Record: Mary Ritter Beard's Accomplishment," in *Mary Ritter Beard*, 3, 33, 79.
82. Nancy Cott, *The Grounding of Modern Feminism* (New Haven, Conn.: Yale University Press, 1987), 15; Judith Schwartz, *Radical Feminists of Heterodoxy: Greenwich Village, 1912–1940* (Lebanon, N.H.: New Victorian Press, 1982), 23.
83. Deacon, *Elsie Clews Parsons*, 84–87.
84. Elsie Clews Parsons, *Social Rule: A Study of the Will to Power* (New York: Putnam, 1916), 54–55; Deacon, *Elsie Clews Parsons*, 126–29.
85. Deacon, *Elsie Clews Parsons*, 129.
86. The Brearley School was then located in a brownstone at 8 East Forty-fifth Street (Mabel Choate, "In the High and Far-Off Times," Brearley School Archives, New York).
87. Virginia Crocheron Gildersleeve, *Many a Good Crusade: Memoirs of Virginia Crocheron Gildersleeve* (New York: Macmillan, 1954), 1–65, especially 23, 58–59, 60–65; Virginia Crocheron Gildersleeve, appointment card, Columbiana; Virginia Crocheron Gildersleeve to Annie Nathan Meyer, April 8, 1935, Annie Nathan Meyer Papers, American Jewish Archives, Cincinnati, Ohio.
88. Gildersleeve, *Many a Good Crusade*, 52–53.
89. Elsie Clews Parsons to Silas Brownell, n.d., Administrative Records, Barnard College Archives.
90. Gildersleeve, *Many a Good Crusade*, 62–65.
91. Ibid., 71.
92. Barbara Miller Solomon, *In the Company of Educated Women: A History of Women and Higher Education in America* (New Haven, Conn.: Yale University Press, 1985), 112–13.
93. Gildersleeve, *Many a Good Crusade*, 99; Annie Nathan Meyer, *Barnard Beginnings* (Boston: Houghton Mifflin, 1935), 68; and *It's Been Fun: An Autobiography* (New York: Schuman, 1951), 201–8.
94. Helen Lefkowitz Horowitz, *Alma Mater: Design and Experience in the Women's Colleges from Their Nineteenth Century Beginnings to the 1930s* (New York: Knopf, 1984), 255. The membership for Barnard's chapter of the New York State Suffrage League first appears in the 1910 Barnard *Mortarboard*, which suggests that it was started at Barnard in 1909, eight years before women won the right to vote in New York State.
95. Gildersleeve, *Many a Good Crusade*, 97. By 1913, Mary Beard had joined Alice Paul in the Congressional Union, after Carrie Chapman Catt of the New York Suffrage Association refused to speak out in support of the Pankhursts.
96. The School of Architecture admitted women in 1910.
97. Horace Coon, *Columbia: Colossus on the Hudson* (New York: Dutton, 1947), 239–50. I am grateful to James Boylan of the Columbia School of Journalism, author of *Pulitzer's School: Columbia University's School of Journalism, 1903–2003* (New York: Columbia University Press, 2003), for sharing with me clippings from around the country about the controversy over whether women should be admitted.

98. Claire Howard, "Iphigene Ochs Sulzberger," *Barnard Alumnae Magazine*, March 1937, 14–15.

99. Susan E. Tifft and Alex S. Jones, *The Trust: The Private and Powerful Family Behind the New York Times* (Boston: Little Brown, 1999), 97–101

100. Ibid., 80–83, 179–80; "Choate and Twain Plead for Tuskegee," *New York Times*, January 23, 1906.

101. Alden Whitman, "Helen Miles Rogers Reid," in *Notable American Women: Modern Period*, 574–75. During the Depression, the School of Journalism became a graduate school only (it had given both bachelor's and master's degrees before that), and the faculty took steps to limit women's access. According to Dean Carl W. Ackerman, "women of superior ability . . . will be admitted to the school in numbers proportionate to the opportunities which shall develop for them in the future in professional work." Registration was cut from 180 to 65; women earned about one-quarter of the degrees (*New York Tribune*, clipping, March 10 [?], 1935, from James Boylan). Enrollment statistics from 1930 and 1940 suggest that students enrolled in the School of Journalism, but often did not earn degrees. Women were as likely to do so as men in the earlier years. The school occupied a somewhat tenuous position. Most journalists had never been to college and looked down on the journalism schools as places for pampered gentlemen and women; professors in the graduate faculty and in the more established professional schools like law, conversely, questioned the school's academic rigor. Not until the 1960s would women regain a position of influence within the school. See also Coon, *Columbia*, 244.

102. Sara Alpern, *Freda Kirchwey: A Woman of the Nation* (Cambridge, Mass.: Harvard University Press, 1987).

103. These three campaigns all succeeded during World War I.

104. Coon, *Columbia*, 266–67; Kenneth M. Ludmerer, *Learning to Heal: The Development of American Medical Education* (New York: Basic Books, 1985), 77; Helen Lefkowitz Horowitz, *The Power and Passion of M. Carey Thomas* (New York: Knopf, 1994), 236; Regina Morantz-Sanchez, *Sympathy and Science: Women Physicians in American Medicine* (New York: Oxford University Press, 1985), 87, 111.

105. Gildersleeve, *Many a Good Crusade*, 100–101; Dorothea E. Curnow, "Tribute: Gulli Lindh Muller, '21," *P&S Quarterly* 18 (1973): 29–30, Columbia Health Sciences Archives. Dental schools underwent the same upgrading in the twentieth century as did medical schools. The class admitted in 1916 had 144 members; the class admitted in 1917 had 213; the class admitted in 1918 had 100. From then on, classes at P&S fluctuated between 100 and 115 members. The unusually large number admitted in 1917 may have been in response to the war.

106. In 1920, Tennessee became the thirty-sixth state to ratify the Nineteenth Amendment, thereby making it illegal for any state to deny the right to vote "on account of sex."

107. Julius Goebel Jr., *A History of the School of Law, Columbia University* (New York: Columbia University Press, 1955), 290–91.

108. Harlan Stone to Virginia Gildersleeve, November 4, 1915, Virginia Crocheron Gildersleeve Papers, Barnard College Archives; Gildersleeve, *Many a Good Crusade*, 101–3.

109. *Shall Women Be Admitted to the Columbia Law School: Opinions of the Press and of Leading Lawyers* (New York: Women's City Club, 1917), Barnard Archives. Fordham Law School admitted women in 1918; St. John's University did so when it opened in 1925; Columbia succumbed in 1927; Harvard Law School held out until 1950.

110. Thomas J. Frusciano and Marilyn H. Pettit, *New York University and the City: An Illustrated History* (New Brunswick, N.J.: Rutgers University Press, 1997), 73. The

law school began requiring a college degree for admission in 1903, and then only for non-Columbia students. Students in Columbia College were permitted to begin law school in their senior year under the so-called professional option.

111. John W. Burgess, *Reminiscences of an American Scholar: The Beginnings of Columbia University* (New York: Columbia University Press, 1934), 12.

4. PATTERNS OF CULTURE

1. Elsie Clews Parsons, "Patterns for Peace or War," *Scientific Monthly*, September 1917), 229–38, discussed in Desley Deacon, *Elsie Clews Parsons: Inventing Modern Life* (Chicago: University of Chicago Press, 1995), 182–84.

2. *The Organization of Columbia University for National Service* [pamphlet], Columbia University Archives–Columbiana Library (hereafter cited as Columbiana). Under Butler's plan, his office would become the Staff Corps, while the schools of the university would be reorganized into the Medical Corps, the Legal Corps, the Technical Corps, and the Home Instruction and Organization Corps. The Graduate Faculty of Philosophy would become the Language Corps, while the Faculty of Political Science would be known as the Economic and Social Service Corps. The training of officers would fall to Columbia College, renamed, simply, the Training Corps. The pamphlet included no mention of either Barnard College or Dean Gildersleeve, though it did include a section on "Home Instruction," under the leadership of James Earl Russell, the dean of Teachers College. See also Thomas Bender, *New York Intellect: A History of Intellectual Life in New York City, from 1750 to the Beginnings of Our Own Time* (Baltimore: Johns Hopkins University Press, 1987), 296–300.

3. Margaret Caffrey, *Ruth Benedict: Stranger in This Land* (Austin: University of Texas Press, 1989), 99.

4. Elsie Clews Parsons, letter to *New York Times*, March 9, 1917, quoted in Deacon, *Elsie Clews Parson*, 179.

5. Deacon, *Elsie Clews Parsons*, 234; Bender, *New York Intellect*, 298; Arthur M. Schlesinger Jr., *A Life in the Twentieth Century: Innocent Beginnings, 1917–1950* (New York: Houghton Mifflin, 2000), 29–30, 34–35.

6. Deacon, *Elsie Clews Parsons*, 171.

7. Ibid., 158–59.

8. Ibid., 179–89.

9. Franz Boas, "The Background of My Early Thinking," in *The Shaping of American Anthropology, 1883–1911: A Franz Boas Reader*, ed. George W. Stocking, Jr. (New York: Basic Books, 1974), 41–42.

10. Claudia Ruth Pierpont, "The Measure of America: How a Rebel Anthropologist Waged War on Racism," *New Yorker*, March 8, 2004, 54.

11. Deacon, *Elsie Clews Parsons*, 247.

12. Daniel J. Kevles, *In the Name of Eugenics: Eugenics and the Uses of Human Heredity* (New York: Knopf, 1985), 75.

13. George W. Stocking Jr., *Race, Culture, and Evolution: Essays in the History of Anthropology* (New York: Free Press, 1968), 270–307.

14. Franz Boas to Nicholas Murray Butler, November 26, 1917; "Teaching Schedule, 1919–1920"; Nicholas Murray Butler to Franz Boas, April 13, 1918, all in Central Files, Columbiana.

15. Deacon, *Elsie Clews Parsons*, 151, 432n.13.

16. Ann Douglas, *Terrible Honesty: Mongrel Manhattan in the 1920s* (New York: Farrar, Straus and Giroux, 1995), 309–10.

17. Jeffrey S. Gurock and Calvin B. Holder, "Harlem," in *The Encyclopedia of New York City*, ed. Kenneth T. Jackson (New Haven, Conn.: Yale University Press, 1995).

18. N. W. Liggett to George Plimpton, June 20, 1906, George A. Plimpton Papers, Barnard College Archives. Any study of the "Jewish problem" at Barnard should begin with Lynn D. Gordon, "Annie Nathan Meyer and Barnard College: Mission and Identity in Women's Higher Education, 1889–1950," *History of Education Quarterly* 26 (1986): 503–22, and Helen Lefkowitz Horowitz, *Alma Mater: Design and Experience in the Women's Colleges from Their Nineteenth Century Beginnings to the 1930s* (New York: Knopf, 1984), 255–60.

19. John W. Burgess, *Reminiscences of an American Scholar: The Beginnings of Columbia University* (New York: Columbia University Press, 1934), 241–42; "Professional Tendencies Among Jewish Students in Colleges, Universities, and Professional Schools" (Memoir of the Bureau of Jewish Social Research), in *American Jewish Yearbook*, 5681, vol. 22 (September 13, 1920–October 2, 1921), 3381–93, cited in Marcia Graham Synnott, *The Half-Opened Door: Discrimination and Admissions at Harvard, Yale, and Princeton, 1900–1970* (Westport, Conn.: Greenwood Press, 1979), 16. This study put the percentage of Jews at City College at 79 percent; New York University, at 48 percent; and Hunter College, at 38 percent. Even Catholic Fordham, at 23 percent, had a greater Jewish concentration than did Columbia University. The significantly lower percentage of Jews given for Columbia, as compared with other colleges, may be the result of Columbia's including enrollment in its graduate faculties, where, as of 1918, the percentage of Jewish students may have been lower than at the College.

20. Synnott, *Half-Opened Door*, 16.

21. Adam Leroy Jones to Nicholas Murray Butler, September 30 and October 23, 1911, and March 14, 1912, Adam Leroy Jones Papers, Columbiana. The only undergraduate school that operated outside the committee was the school of practical arts at Teachers College.

22. Edward L. Thorndike, *Thorndike Intelligence Examination for High School Graduates* (New York: Bureau of Publications, Teachers College, 1922), Teachers College Archives.

23. Ibid.

24. Kevles, *In the Name of Eugenics*, 134–35. When Congress moved to cut off immigration following the war, Boas provided Brooklyn congressman Emmanuel Celler with technical advice in his losing battle against restrictive legislation.

25. H. E. Hawkes to E. B. Wilson, January 16, 1922, Central Files, Columbiana.

26. Adam Leroy Jones, "University Admissions, Report of the Director," in Columbia President's Annual Report, 1919, 236, Columbiana.

27. "Frosh Statistics Show Religious Preferences," *Columbia Spectator*, October 10, 1921, cited in Harold S. Wechsler, *The Qualified Student: A History of Selective College Admission in America* (New York: Wiley, 1977), 183n.109. Hawkes gave the 15 to 20 percent figure as the range he thought safe in H. E. Hawkes to E. B. Wilson, January 16, 1922, Central Files, Columbiana.

28. Sara Alpern, *Freda Kirchwey: A Woman of The Nation* (Cambridge, Mass.: Harvard University Press, 1987), 13–15. Kirchwey's peers voted her "Best Looking," "Done Most for Barnard," "Most Popular," "Most Famous in Future," and, significantly, "Most Militant."

29. Annie Nathan Meyer to Jacob H. Schiff, January 1, 1914, and May 25, 1915; George A. Plimpton to Jacob H. Schiff, June 2, 1915, all quoted in Harold S. Wechsler, "The Rationale for Restriction: Ethnicity and College Admission in America, 1910–1980,"

American Quarterly 36 (1984): 652; Alpern, *Freda Kirchwey*, 12; "Barnard College Puts Ban on Secret Societies," *New York Times*, June 8, 1913.

30. Freda Kirchwey, "May Jews Go to College?" *Nation*, June 14, 1922, 708–9; Alpern, *Freda Kirchwey*, 45–46. Kirchwey had just returned from "the great college tour," during which she had found administrators of women's colleges screening out working-class and career-oriented women, especially those who were Jews. See also "Too Many College Girls?" *Nation*, June 10, 1922, 647, 648.

31. Virginia Gildersleeve to Nicholas Murray Butler, November 27, 1920, Central Files, Columbiana.

32. "Minutes of Staff Conference," January 10, 1921; "Minutes of Barnard College Faculty," January 31, 1921; "Minutes of Staff Conference," November 14, 1921; "Minutes of Barnard College Faculty," November 28, 1921, all in Barnard College Archives. Henry Hollingworth, the psychologist to whom others deferred in matters of testing, regarded tests as a way of drawing bright students to Barnard (of whatever background) who might not have the means to prepare for conventional entrance exams.

33. Virginia Crocheron Gildersleeve, *Many a Good Crusade: Memoirs of Virginia Crocheron Gildersleeve* (New York: Macmillan, 1954), 89–91. For Jews at Bryn Mawr, Mount Holyoke, Radcliffe, Smith, Vassar, and Wellesley, see Barbara Miller Solomon, *In the Company of Educated Women: A History of Women and Higher Education in America* (New Haven, Conn.: Yale University Press, 1985), 144.

34. The percentage of Jews in Barnard classes in the 1930s is calculated from lists sent to Rabbi Baruch Braunstein at his request, Barnard College Archives. On New York City and Columbia, see Wechsler, *Qualified Student*, 168; and Wechsler, "Rationale for Restriction," 643–67.

35. Robert A. McCaughey, *Stand Columbia: A History of Columbia University in the City of New York, 1754–2003* (New York: Columbia University Press, 2003), 274.

36. Gilbert Osofsky, *Harlem: The Making of a Ghetto: Negro New York, 1890–1930*, 2nd ed. (New York: Harper & Row, 1971), 84.

37. John P. Clyde, "The Negro in New York City" (M.A. thesis, Columbia University, ca. 1899), 3–4, cited in Osofsky, *Harlem*, 84.

38. Douglas, *Terrible Honesty*, 311.

39. Gurock and Holder, "Harlem," 524.

40. Peter Novick, *That Noble Dream: The Objectivity Question and the American Historical Profession* (New York: Cambridge University Press, 1988), 75–80.

41. Pixley Ka Isaka Seme, "The Regeneration of Africa," *Columbia Monthly*, April 1906, 143–46. See also box on black students, Columbiana.

42. Linda M. Perkins, "The Racial Integration of the Seven Sisters Colleges," *Journal of Blacks in Higher Education*, no. 19 (1998): 104–8.

43. James E. Russell to H. B. Frissell, of the Hampton Institute, November 11, 1900, series 6, folder 505, James Earl Russell Papers, Teachers College Archives; Booker T. Washington to V. Everett Macy, October 18, 1900; James Earl Russell to Booker T. Washington, October 23, 1900; Booker T. Washington to James Earl Russell, April 27, 1901; James Earl Russell to Booker T. Washington, May 4 and December 9, 1901, and May 19, 1902, all in series 6, folder 631, Russell Papers. For scholarships awarded to Tuskegee students, see Teachers College Announcement, 1903/1904–1906/1907; after that date, the announcement no longer lists names of schools. See David Levering Lewis, *W. E. B. Du Bois: Biography of a Race, 1868–1919* (New York: Henry Holt, 1993), 262–64, 353.

44. Sarah Delany and Elizabeth Delany, with Amy Hill Hearth, *Having Our Say: The Delany Sisters' First 100 Years* (New York: Kodoshana International, 1993), 100–120.

45. Ibid.; "May Edward Chinn," in *Black Women in America: An Historical Encyclopedia*, 2 vols., ed. Darlene Clark Hine, Elsa Barkley Brown, and Rosalyn Terborg-Penn (Bloomington: Indiana University Press, 1994), 1:234–36.

46. Carney was raised in the Oklahoma Territory, and educated in the public high schools of rural Illinois. Following high school, she attended normal school for two years and became a teacher in rural schools. In 1912, she published *Country Life and the Country School*, which called attention to the inferior state of the country's rural schools. Carney's courses in "Negro life" came to occupy a central place at Teachers College, "as symbolic of the whole upward struggle of all humanity toward freedom and light, and especially of the life-grip of minority groups for recognition and place in our American social order." Courses at Teachers College were followed up by courses taught at the Hampton Institute in the summers of 1924 and 1925. In 1927, Carney founded the Negro Education Club, an organization open to both black and white students, as well as to foreign students. It produced annually eight to twelve programs for the college, at which Eleanor Roosevelt and W. E. B. Du Bois, among many others, spoke to the entire college (Richard Glotzer, "The Career of Mabel Carney: The Study of Race and Rural Development in the United States and South Africa," *International Journal of Historical Studies* 29 [1996]: 309–36; N. C. Newbold, "Lectures on Negro Education and Race Relations," February 4–April 15, 1913, Teachers College Archives; Mabel Carney, "Teachers College and the Education and Welfare of Negroes" [typescript], August 14, 1942, "Negro Education and Race Relations" folder, Vertical Files, Teachers College Archives).

47. Beginning in 1917, African American education became the subject of graduate study and research. The first doctorate went to Jane Ellen McAllister in 1929 for her dissertation "Training of Negro Teachers in Louisiana." Between 1929 and 1942, thirty-six dissertations were written, twenty-five of them by blacks, and eleven by whites (Mabel Carney, "Doctoral Dissertations and Projects Relating to the Education of Negroes," *Advanced School Digest* 7 [1942]: 41–44, "Negro Education and Race Relations" folder, Vertical Files, Teachers College Archives).

48. Katharine Du Pre Lumpkin, *The Making of a Southerner* (1947; reprint, Athens: University of Georgia Press, 1981), 201–4.

49. Ibid., 204–7. The summer seminar in which Lumpkin enrolled was probably Sociology 311, the seminar "The Socialization of Religious Institutions," taught by H. N. Shenton. This was the only seminar at either Columbia or Teachers College that dealt with the topic that Lumpkin described, and it may well have appealed to someone destined for a career with the YWCA.

50. Valerie Boyd, *Wrapped in Rainbows: The Life of Zora Neale Hurston* (New York: Scribner, 2003), 96–97; Carla Kaplan, ed., *Zora Neale Hurston: A Life in Letters* (New York: Doubleday, 2002), 55–65.

51. Virginia Crocheron Gildersleeve to Annie Nathan Meyer, June 9, 1925, box 7, folder 3, Annie Nathan Meyer Papers, American Jewish Archives, Cincinnati, Ohio.

52. Robert E. Hemenway, *Zora Neale Hurston: A Literary Biography* (Urbana: University of Illinois Press, 1977), 20–21; Zora Neale Hurston, *Dust Tracks on a Road: An Autobiography* (1942; reprint, Urbana: University of Illinois Press, 1984), 171.

53. Boyd, *Wrapped in Rainbows*, 17.

54. Zora Neale Hurston to Annie Nathan Meyer, January 1926, box 7, folder 3, Meyer Papers; Zora Neale Hurston, transcript, Registrar's Office, Barnard College Archives; Boyd, *Wrapped in Rainbows*, 106.

55. Zora Neal Hurston to Annie Nathan Meyer, December 13 and 17, 1925, box 7, folder 3, Meyer Papers; Boyd, *Wrapped in Rainbows*, 108.

56. Virginia Crocheron Gildersleeve to M. Carey Thomas, December 15, 1930, Barnard College Archives.

57. Perkins, "Racial Integration of the Seven Sisters," 104–8.

58. Pauli Murray, *Pauli Murray: The Autobiography of a Black Activist, Feminist, Lawyer, Priest, and Poet* (Knoxville: University of Tennessee Press, 1987), 66, 70–71; Dorothy I. Height, *Open Wide the Freedom Gates: A Memoir* (New York: Public Affairs, 2003), 30–31.

59. Anonymous notes from a black alumna from the class of 1947, apparently in response to Rosalind Rosenberg, "The Legacy of Dean Gildersleeve," *Barnard Alumnae Magazine*, summer 1995; Virginia Crocheron Gildersleeve, letter to the editor, *Barnard Bulletin*, March 1, 1943.

60. Deacon, *Elsie Clews Parsons*, 247.

61. Between the two world wars, half of the graduate students in anthropology were women (Deacon, *Elsie Clews Parsons*, 255).

62. Lois Banner, *Intertwined Lives: Margaret Mead, Ruth Benedict, and Their Circle* (New York: Knopf, 2003), 47.

63. Caffrey, *Ruth Benedict*, 49.

64. Bruce Kuklick, *The Rise of American Philosophy: Cambridge, Massachusetts, 1860–1930* (New Haven, Conn.: Yale University Press, 1977), 351–69.

65. Caffrey, *Ruth Benedict*, 50–53.

66. Ibid., 87.

67. Judith Schachter Modell, *Ruth Benedict: Patterns of a Life* (Philadelphia: University of Pennsylvania Press, 1983), 109–17.

68. Ruth Benedict, "The Concept of the Guardian Spirit in North America" (Ph.D. diss., Columbia University, 1923), in *Memoirs of the American Anthropological Association* 29 (1923): 84.

69. Emily Gregory served briefly as professor of botany at Barnard College, from 1895 until her death in 1897; Margaret Maltby was appointed adjunct professor of physics at Barnard in 1903. The next breakthrough came in 1910, when the university revised its teaching ladder to include the ranks of assistant professor (replacing the rank of adjunct professor) and associate professor. In that year, Virginia Gildersleeve, who had earned a Ph.D. in English in 1908, won appointment as assistant professor of English at Barnard and an invitation from Columbia to teach a graduate class in Anglo-Saxon. The first woman to reach the rank of assistant professor at Teachers College was Grace A. Cornell, assistant professor of education, in 1911. For further information, see appointment cards, Columbiana.

70. Brewster used the term "feminization" in Report on Budget from William Brewster to Virginia Gildersleeve, November 29, 1921, Barnard College Archives. But he had been issuing warnings about the state of the Barnard–Columbia relationship for at least two years (Provost William Brewster to Dean Virginia Gildersleeve, September 29, 1919; William Brewster, "Analysis of the Teaching and Administrative Personnel of Barnard, 1919," both in Barnard College Archives).

71. Brewster, Report on Budget.

72. Ibid.

73. Gildersleeve, *Many a Good Crusade*, 78–79.

74. Frederick J. E. Woodbridge, dean of the Faculties of Political Science, Philosophy and Pure Science, to William Brewster, May 31, 1922, Barnard College Archives.

75. Virginia Crocheron Gildersleeve, draft of annual report for year ending 1920, Barnard College Archives; Margaret W. Rossiter, *Women Scientists in America:*

Struggles and Strategies to 1940 (Baltimore: Johns Hopkins University Press, 1982), 163–64. Brewster resigned following this episode; the position of provost was not filled again until Millicent McIntosh succeeded Gildersleeve in the late 1940s. Harvard Medical School appointed Alice Hamilton to a position as assistant professor in 1919 (with the understanding that she would never participate in commencement exercises), but Harvard did not hire a woman to its graduate faculty until 1948, when it appointed Maud Cam, a medieval historian from Cambridge, England. The first woman to achieve tenure on the graduate faculty at Yale did so in 1959, twenty-two years after Benedict achieved tenure at Columbia.

76. Benedict was bitterly disappointed not to win the Barnard appointment, and some have suggested that Boas appointed Reichard because she was a single woman, while Benedict was married and supported economically by her husband. It may have been the case, however, that Reichard won the appointment because she finished her degree first.

77. Franz Boas to Dean Frederick J. E. Woodbridge, November 30, 1927; Frederick J. E. Woodbridge to Franz Boas, February 21, 1928, cited in Caffrey, *Ruth Benedict*, 112–14; Franz Boas to Nicholas Murray Butler, November 15, 1929, all in Franz Boas Papers, American Philosophical Library, Philadelphia.

78. William F. Jones, "Frederick James Woodbridge," in *American National Biography*, ed. John A. Garraty and Mark C. Carnes (New York: Oxford University Press, 1999).

79. Julius Goebel, Jr., *A History of the School of Law, Columbia University* (New York: Columbia University Press, 1955), 290–91; Whitney S. Bagnall, "Women at Columbia School of Law Raising Their Profile, Expanding Their Opportunities, Realizing Their Aspirations," *Columbia Law School Report*, 2003. The Law School dean, Huger Jervey, had warned Gildersleeve against giving any publicity to her victory. He did not want "the appearance created that the Law School had determined at this time generally to admit women equally with men." Gildersleeve complied, and sent only her best graduate, Helen Robinson, for admission in the fall of 1927. But word of the Law School's action got out, and two female Columbia graduate students, one with a master's degree and the other with a doctorate, sought admission. Dean Jervey found them too well qualified to be turned away. Margaret Spahr (B.A. 1914, Smith; M.A. 1919, Ph.D. 1926, Columbia) was the first to graduate.

80. Huger Jervey to Virginia Gildersleeve, December 20, 1926, Virginia Crocheron Gildersleeve Papers, Barnard College Archives; Gildersleeve, *Many a Good Crusade*, 101–3; Peter R. Teachout, "Thomas Reed Powell," in *American National Biography*. I am grateful to Columbia Law School archivist Whitney S. Bagnall for information on Margaret Spahr. New York University, which began admitting women in 1890, produced many of the early women lawyers, who might otherwise have attended Columbia: Stanleyetta Titus (who became the first woman admitted to the New York State Bar), Crystal Eastman, Harriet Stanton Blatch (daughter of Elizabeth Cady Stanton), and Dorothy Kenyon. In the years that followed, many of New York's most influential female lawyers and civic leaders trained at Columbia: Edith Spivak, Harriet Pilpel, Helen Buttenwieser, Bella Abzug, Soia Menschkoff, Constance Baker Motley, and Ruth Bader Ginsburg.

81. Boas proposed that Benedict, who "for a number of years has proved a most valuable help in the work of the department," be appointed assistant professor (Franz Boas to Howard McBain, November 15, 1929, Central Files, Columbiana), and reported to Kroeber that the "general position of anthropology" had been "brought vigorously to

the attention of the President, Trustees and Budget Committee by McBain" (Franz Boas to Alfred Kroeber, February 16, 1931, Central Files, Columbiana).

82. Marie M. Daly, "Mary Letitia Caldwell," Biographical Files, Columbiana.

83. Ruth Benedict, appointment card, Columbiana. In 1930, anthropology awarded one M.A. and one Ph.D., both to women. Chemistry awarded sixty-four M.A.'s and sixteen Ph.D.'s, one-third to women.

84. Timothy P. Cross, An Oasis of Order: The Core Curriculum 'at Columbia College (New York: Columbia University Press, 1995), 11–13; Daniel Bell, The Reforming of General Education: The Columbia College Experience in Its National Setting (New York: Columbia University Press, 1966), 12–25.

85. Barnard Faculty Minutes, May 14, 1923, Barnard College Archives.

86. Gildersleeve, Many a Good Crusade, 76–77.

87. Ibid., 82–83; Lindsey R. Harmon, ed., A Century of Doctorates: Data Analyses of Growth and Change (Washington, D.C.: National Academy of Sciences, 1978), 137.

88. Franz Boas to Nicholas Murray Butler, November 26, 1917, Franz Boas Papers, Central Files, Columbiana.

89. Gildersleeve, Many a Good Crusade, 42–43.

90. John Erskine, My Life as a Teacher (Philadelphia: Lippincott, 1948), 165; Cross, Oasis of Order, 24.

91. John Erskine, "The Moral Obligation to Be Intelligent," in The American Character and Other Essays: Selected from the Writings of John Erskine (Chautauqua, N.Y.: Chautauqua Press, 1927), 30.

92. Erskine, My Life as a Teacher, 169.

93. John Erskine, The Influence of Women, and Its Cure (New York: Bobbs-Merrill, 1936), 11, 17, 64–65, 113.

94. Franz Boas to Nicholas Murray Butler, November 26, 1917, Boas Papers, Central Files, Columbiana.

95. Gildersleeve, Many a Good Crusade, 83.

96. Susan Ware, Letter to the World: Seven Women Who Shaped the American Century (Cambridge, Mass.: Harvard University Press, 1998), 89.

97. Jane Howard, Margaret Mead: A Life (New York: Fawcett, 1984), 42.

98. Sigmund Freud, "Femininity," in The Complete Introductory Lectures on Psychoanalysis, trans. and ed. James Strachey (New York: Norton, 1966), 576–99.

99. Margaret Mead, Blackberry Winter: My Early Years (New York: Simon and Schuster, Touchstone, 1972), 111.

100. Henry Hollingworth, Leta Stetter Hollingworth (Lincoln: University of Nebraska Press, 1943), 77–81, 97–100.

101. Rosalind Rosenberg, Beyond Separate Spheres: Intellectual Roots of Modern Feminism (New Haven, Conn.: Yale University Press, 1982), 54–113; Ludy T. Benjamin, Jr., "Henry Levi Hollingworth," in American National Biography; Leta Hollingworth, Functional Periodicity: An Experimental Study of the Mental and Motor Abilities of Women During Menstruation (New York: Teachers College, 1914), 1, 11–14, 86–87, 92–95.

102. Leta Hollingworth, "Variability as Related to Sex Differences in Achievement," American Journal of Sociology 19 (1914): 510–30; Rosenberg, Beyond Separate Spheres, 99–103.

103. Chauncey N. Allen, "Studies in Sex Difference," Psychological Bulletin 24 (1927): 299, quoted in Carl Degler, In Search of Human Nature: The Decline and Revival of Darwinism in American Social Thought (New York: Oxford University Press, 1991), 132.

104. Hilary Lapsley, *Margaret Mead and Ruth Benedict: The Kinship of Women* (Amherst: University of Massachusetts Press, 1999), 69

105. Mead, *Blackberry Winter*, 111–12.

106. Kevles, *In the Name of Eugenics*, 137–38

107. Kurt Koffka, *The Growth of the Mind: An Introduction to Child Psychology*, trans. Robert Morris Ogden (New York: Harcourt, Brace, 1924).

108. Caffrey, *Ruth Benedict*, 154.

109. Ibid., 149.

110. Clifford Geertz, *Works and Lives: The Anthropologist as Author* (Stanford, Calif.: Stanford University Press, 1988), 113.

111. Caffrey, *Ruth Benedict*, 153–55.

112. Hemenway, *Zora Neale Hurston*, 63.

113. Daniel Kevles, *In the Name of Eugenics*, 137.

114. For courses Hurston took at Barnard, I have relied on her transcript, Registrar's Office, Barnard College Archives; Boyd, *Wrapped in Rainbows*, 114; Hurston, *Dust Tracks on a Road*, 123.

115. Hemenway, *Zora Neale Hurston*, 215.

116. Graciela Hernandez, "Multiple Subjectivities and Strategic Positionality: Zora Neale Hurston's Experimental Ethnographies," in *Women Writing Culture*, ed. Ruth Behar and Deborah A. Gordon (Berkeley: University of California Press, 1995), 160–62.

117. On Camp Columbia, the engineering school's summer surveying camp, see James Kip Finch, *A History of the School of Engineering, Columbia University* (New York: Columbia University Press, 1954), 51–52.

118. Deacon, *Elsie Clews Parsons*, 258–65.

119. Mead, *Blackberry Winter*, 103.

120. Lapsley, *Mead and Benedict*, 30–31, 76, 158, 308; Banner, *Intertwined Lives*, 195–98.

121. Lapsley, *Mead and Benedict*, 75–76.

122. Banner, *Intertwined Lives*, 252–53, 292–94. As Banner found in examining the scores of letters that Mead and Benedict wrote to each other from the 1920s through the 1940s, they never used the word "lesbian" in referring to each other, though Mead referred to other women they knew as lesbians. Today Mead would be regarded as bisexual and Benedict as a lesbian.

123. Franz Boas, "Anthropology," in *Encyclopedia of the Social Sciences*, 15 vols., ed. Edwin R. A. Seligman (New York: Macmillan, 1930), 2:73–110; Edward Sapir, "The Discipline of Sex," *American Mercury* 16 (1929): 417, quoted in Caffrey, *Ruth Benedict*, 198.

124. Mary Catherine Bateson, *With a Daughter's Eye: A Memoir of Margaret Mead and Gregory Bateson* (New York: Morrow, 1984), 124.

125. Lapsley, *Mead and Benedict*, 75–96; Lillian Faderman, *Odd Girls and Twilight Lovers: A History of Lesbian Life in Twentieth Century America* (New York: Viking, 1991), 62–92.

126. Gildersleeve, *Many a Good Crusade*, 105–6; Virginia Crocheron Gildersleeve, "What Are They Going to Do?" *New York Times*, June 2, 1935, Barnard College Archives.

127. Gildersleeve, *Many a Good Crusade*, 108.

128. Margaret Mead, *Coming of Age in Samoa: A Psychological Study of Primitive Youth for Western Civilization* (New York: Morrow, 1928), 171.

129. Ruth Benedict, "Anthropology and the Abnormal," in *An Anthropologist at Work: Writings of Ruth Benedict*, ed. Margaret Mead (Boston: Houghton Mifflin, 1959), 262–83.

130. Boyd, *Wrapped in Rainbows*, 127–31, 161, 224–25, 271–75.

131. Lois Banner, "Mannish Women, Passive Men, and Constitutional Types: Margaret Mead's *Sex and Temperament in Three Primitive Societies* as a Response to Ruth Benedict's *Patterns of Culture*," *Signs* 28 (2003): 833–58.

132. Zora Neale Hurston, *Their Eyes Were Watching God: A Novel* (1937; reprint, Urbana: University of Illinois Press, 1978), 17.

133. Banner, "Mannish Women," 833–56; Margaret Mead, *Sex and Temperament in Three Primitive Societies* (New York: Morrow, 1935), 296–97, 305–6; Ruth Benedict, *Patterns of Culture* (New York: Houghton Mifflin, 1934), 262–65

134. Banner, *Intertwined Lives*, 207–8.

135. Ruth Benedict to Margaret Mead, January 20, 1932, in *Anthropologist at Work*, 318.

136. Nancy C. Litkenhaus, "Margaret Mead and the 'Rustling-of-the-Wind-in-the-Trees School' of Ethnographic Writing," in *Women Writing Culture*, 193.

137. Geertz, *Works and Lives*, 102–28. See also Benedict to Mead, January 20, 1932, in *Anthropologist at Work*, 318, and Virginia Crocheron Gildersleeve to B. Lippincott, Esq., May 28, 1934, Barnard College Archives.

138. Geertz, *Works and Lives*, 106–7.

139. Ruth Benedict, "Anthropology and the Humanities," in *Anthropologist at Work*, 459, 467–70. Caroline F. E. Spurgeon argued that the study of images in literature could reveal unconscious assumptions of a writer and culture that were not otherwise accessible to the scholar (*Shakespeare's Imagery and What It Tells Us* [Cambridge: Cambridge University Press, 1935], 7).

140. Ruth Benedict, "Folklore," in *Encyclopedia of the Social Sciences*, 6:288–93; Caffrey, *Ruth Benedict*, 144–45.

141. Howard McBain to Virginia Gildersleeve, March 19, 1934, Gildersleeve Papers; Ruth Benedict and Margarete Bieber, appointment cards, Columbiana. Barnard College appointed Bieber as visiting lecturer in fine arts and archaeology in 1934, and the Columbia Faculty of Philosophy promoted Bieber to associate professor with tenure in 1938.

142. H. E. Hawkes, "Report of the Committee on Anthropology," January 18, 1937, Central Files, Columbiana; Lapsley, *Mead and Benedict*, 257. According to Lapsley, McBain wanted Columbia to be the first university to have a female head of a department; Mead thought she did not have the temperament for the job; Parsons disapproved because Benedict had never finished the Southwest concordance. For an excellent discussion of the problems that female anthropologists faced in trying to advance in the profession, see Deacon, *Elsie Clews Parsons*, 262–72.

143. Franz Boas to Dean George B. Pegram, January 28, 1937, George B. Pegram Papers, Columbiana; Adelin Linton and Charles Wagley, *Ralph Linton* (New York: Columbia University Press, 1971), 13, 34, 75; Caffrey, *Ruth Benedict*, 277.

144. Hawkes, "Report of the Anthropology Committee"; all information on appointments and promotions comes from appointment cards, Columbiana. According to Mead, who served for many years as an adjunct professor at Columbia, "The Faculty of Political Science [to which anthropology switched in 1945] . . . felt that the addition of a woman to their ranks as full professor would lower their standing in the academic community" (Carolyn Heilbrun, "Tenured Women at Columbia," *Columbia*, summer 1980, 23).

145. Caldwell won tenure in 1940 but was not promoted to associate professor until 1943.

146. S. J. Woolf, "Woman Leader of 'Key' Men," *New York Times Magazine*, March 17, 1940, clipping, Nicolson Biographical File, Columbiana.

147. Virginia Heyer Young, *Ruth Benedict's Work After "Patterns of Culture"* (Lincoln: University of Nebraska Press, forthcoming).

5. WOMANPOWER

1. Mollie Panter-Downes, "Letter from London," March 22, 1941, *New Yorker*, March 29, 1941, 53–54; National Manpower Council, *Womanpower* (New York: Columbia University Press, 1957), 143–66.

2. Virginia Crocheron Gildersleeve, "The Shortage of Trained Brains," February 1942; "Training Women for War Work, Professional Level: Statement for the Manpower Commission," December 11, 1942; "Educating Girls for the War and the Post-War World: Postscript" (speech delivered October 20, 1943); and "Professional Fields in Which New Jobs Are Developing" (speech delivered on July 17, 1944), all in Virginia Crocheron Gildersleeve Papers, Barnard College Archives.

3. Professors in the applied sciences had persuaded the trustees in 1911 to amend university statutes to permit them to exclude women from earning a degree in the School of Mines, Engineering, and Chemistry.

4. Virginia Crocheron Gildersleeve, *Many a Good Crusade: Memoirs of Virginia Crocheron Gildersleeve* (New York: Macmillan, 1954), 275, 267–87.

5. Margaret W. Rossiter, *Women Scientists in America: Struggles and Strategies to 1940* (Baltimore: Johns Hopkins University Press, 1982), 170–71.

6. For a fuller discussion, see chapter 4.

7. Marion Hunt, "An Extraordinary Doctor; An Extraordinary Woman," in Days to Remember: A Perennial Calendar, 2002, 5–13, Columbia University Health Sciences Archives; Virginia Apgar, appointment card, Columbia University Archives–Columbiana Library (hereafter cited as Columbiana).

8. For the gradual erosion of anti-nepotism rules around the country, see Rossiter, *Women Scientists in America*, 137–42.

9. Harriet Zuckerman, Jonathan R. Cole, and John T. Bruer, eds., *The Outer Circle: Women in the Scientific Community* (New York: Norton, 1991), 71–93; Registrar, Annual Report, 1958–1959, Columbiana.

10. Andrea Walton, "Women at Columbia: A Study of Power and Empowerment in the Lives of Six Scholars" (Ph.D. diss., Teachers College, Columbia University, 1995), 327–66. According to her appointment card, Hayner finally won promotion to assistant professor in 1946, to associate professor in 1952, and to full professor in 1962. For women's situation in physics in the 1920s and 1930s, see Daniel J. Kevles, *The Physicists: A History of a Scientific Community in Modern America* (Cambridge, Mass.: Harvard University Press, 1987), 200–207.

11. Walton, "Women at Columbia," 354. When both Mitchell and Hayner were instructors in the 1930s, a time when wages at Columbia remained unchanged except in case of promotion, he earned $3,700 while she earned $2,700. When he won promotion in 1940, his salary rose to $4,000; Hayner's salary was raised to $3,000 (appointment cards, Columbiana). On Rabi, see Samuel Devons, "I. I. Rabi: Physics and Science at Columbia, in America, and Worldwide," *Columbia*, summer 2001, 36–49.

12. "Maria Gertrude Goeppert Mayer," in *Notable American Women: The Modern Period*, ed. Barbara Sicherman and Carol Hurd Green (Cambridge, Mass.: Belknap Press of Harvard University Press, 1980), 466–68.

13. Chien-Shiung Wu, appointment card, Columbiana. I am grateful to have been given access to an interview with Chien-Shiung Wu, conducted by Harriet

Zuckerman and Jonathan Cole, July 8, 1981. See also Estelle Gilson, "Subtleties and Surprises," *Columbia*, summer 1980, 7–9; and William Dicke, "Chien-Shiung Wu, 84, Dies; Top Experimental Physicist," *New York Times*, February, 18, 1997. In recognition of Wu's contribution to shattering the principle of parity in 1956, Columbia University promoted her to full professor in 1958. Hayner, who had never had the research opportunities that Wu enjoyed, did not win promotion to full professor until 1963.

14. Gildersleeve, *Many a Good Crusade*, 114–15, 127–48; Carikube Niemczyk, "Dean Virginia C. Gildersleeve at the United Nations Charter Conference of 1945" (paper presented at Barnard College, November 15, 1995).

15. William Allan Neilson, remarks, March 11, 1945, Barnard College Archives.

16. Gildersleeve, *Many a Good Crusade*, 330; Virginia Crocheron Gildersleeve, "The World Is a Community" (address given under the auspices of the American Association for the United Nations, July 14, 1995), printed as a pamphlet of the AAUN, 2, Barnard College Archives. With the assistance of her aide at the charter convention, the Barnard English professor Elizabeth Reynard, Gildersleeve also drafted the first paragraph of the Preamble to the United Nations Charter: "We, the Peoples of the United Nations, determined to save succeeding generations from the scourge of war, which twice in our lifetime has brought untold sorrow to mankind." To Gildersleeve's bitter regret, less skilled wordsmiths hammered out the rest (*Many a Good Crusade*, 346–48).

17. Gildersleeve, "World Is a Community," 3.

18. Gildersleeve, *Many a Good Crusade*, 342.

19. The most famous of the popular psychoanalytic works to attack educated women in general and feminists in particular for undermining the family was Ferdinand Lundberg and Marynia Farnham, *Modern Women: The Lost Sex* (New York: Grosset & Dunlap, 1947).

20. Lynn White Jr., *Educating Our Daughters* (New York: Harper, 1950), 77–78.

21. Millicent Carey McIntosh, oral history, Oral History Collection, Columbia University Libraries.

22. Karen W. Arenson, "Millicent McIntosh, 102, Dies; Taught Barnard Women to Balance Career and Family," *New York Times*, January 5, 2001. According to one Barnard alumna, it was understood at the time that "Mrs. Mac" would not live on campus, in the Deanery, as Gildersleeve had, but would commute in her battered station wagon from her townhouse on the Upper East Side. It was also understood that she would do very little, if any, traveling for the college while her children were young.

23. Mirra Komarovsky, "Women Then and Now: A Journey of Detachment and Engagement," *Barnard Alumnae Magazine*, winter 1982, 7–11; Dolly (Komarovsky) Cheser, younger sister of Mirra Komarovsky, interview with Rosalind Rosenberg, February 6, 2001; Ana Cheser Silbert, niece, interview with Rosalind Rosenberg, July 11, 2001. Although Mirra Komarovsky spent her career studying the intimate details of others' lives, she was an intensely private person, who avoided discussing her own life and destroyed her personal papers. In the Barnard College Archives are copies of her major publications; some materials related to her research and teaching; a few letters; an essay on the 1905 Akkerman pogrom by Mendel Komarovsky; copies of passports; a few newspaper clippings; several interviews conducted with friends and family; memorial tributes by Jonathan Rieder, Herbert Ganz, and Ana Cheser Silbert; and a few pictures. Komarovsky kept a diary in Russian from June through October 1918, which has been translated into English and gives a vivid picture of her preco-

cious intellect. Ann Lowenthal, one of those who interviewed Komarovsky toward the end of her life, plans to publish an annotated version.

24. Komarovsky, "Women Then and Now," 7; copy of 1921 family passport; "High School Teachers Laud Work of Russian Refugee," newspaper clipping, both in Barnard College Archives.

25. Elizabeth Faulkner Baker, *Protective Labor Legislation* (New York: Columbia University Press, 1925); Emilie J. Hutchinson, *Women's Wages: A Study of the Wages of Industrial Women and Measures Suggested to Increase Them* (New York, 1919), and *Women and the Ph.D.: Facts from the Experience of 1,025 Women Who Have Taken the Degree of Doctor of Philosophy Since 1877* (Greensboro: North Carolina College for Women, 1929); Willystine Goodsell, *A History of the Family as a Social and Educational Institution* (New York: Macmillan, 1919), and *Education of Women: Its Social Background and Its Problems* (New York: Macmillan, 1923).

26. Komarovsky, "Women Then and Now," 7.

27. Mirra Komarovsky, "Some Persistent Issues on Sociological Polemics," *Sociological Forum* 2 (1987): 557.

28. "Class Notes," *Barnard Alumnae Monthly*, November 1933, 15; *Barnard Alumnae Directory*, 1934; Cheser interview; Silbert interview.

29. Mirra Komarovsky, *The Unemployed Man and His Family* (New York: Dryden Press, 1940), 76. For an excellent review of Komarovsky's career, see Shulamit Reinharz, "Finding a Sociological Voice: The Work of Mirra Komarovsky," *Sociological Inquiry* 59 (1989): 374–95.

30. Mirra Komarovsky, appointment card, Columbiana. The Department of Economics and Sociology at Barnard split into two separate departments in 1942.

31. Robert MacIver, *As a Tale that Is Told: The Autobiography of R. M. MacIver* (Chicago: University of Chicago Press, 1968), 98–105.

32. Ibid.; Nancy Woloch, "Helen Merrell Lynd," in *Notable American Women, a Biographical Dictionary: Completing the Twentieth Century*, ed. Susan Ware (Cambridge, Mass.: Belknap Press of Harvard University Press, forthcoming); Helen M. Lynd, *England in the Eighteen Eighties: Toward a Social Basis for Freedom* (New York: Oxford University Press, 1945).

33. MacIver, *As a Tale that Is Told*, 114–37.

34. Ibid., 141.

35. Robert K. Merton, *Science, Technology and Society in Seventeenth Century England* (1938; reprint, New York: Fertig, 1970).

36. Helen Mayer Hacker, interview with Rosalind Rosenberg, April 11, 2001, and "Slouching Toward Sociology," in *Individual Voices, Collective Visions: Fifty Years of Sociology*, ed. Ann Goetting and Sarah Fenstermaker (Philadelphia: Temple University Press, 1995), 241.

37. Hacker, "Slouching Toward Sociology, " 242.

38. Alice Rossi, "Women in the Seventies: Problems and Possibilities" (keynote address presented at Barnard College Conference on Women, April 17, 1970), in *Discrimination Against Women: Hearings Before the Special Subcommittee on Education of the Committee on Education and Labor of the U.S. House of Representative, 91st Congress, 2nd session, on Section 805 of H.R. 16098*, 2 vols. (Washington , D.C.: Government Printing Office, 1970–71), 2:1064–67.

39. Alice Rossi to Rosalind Rosenberg, February 1, 2001.

40. Alice Rossi, "Season's of a Woman's Life," in *Authors of Their Own Lives: Intellectual Autobiographies by Twenty American Sociologists*, ed. Bennett M. Berger (Berkeley: University of California Press, 1990), 307.

41. Cheser interview.
42. Ellen Schrecker, *No Ivory Tower: McCarthyism and the Universities* (New York: Oxford University Press, 1986), 43–44. On radical activities at Columbia in these years and efforts by the administration to curb them, see also "Hellery" Collection, now known as "Protest-Activism/Series 13," Columbiana.
43. Ruth E. Pathe, "Gene Weltfish," in *Women Anthropologists: A Biographical Dictionary*, ed. Ute Gacs, Aisha Khan, Jerrie McIntyre, and Ruth Weinberg (New York: Greenwood Press, 1988), 373.
44. Grayson Kirk, "Memorandum Concerning Dr. Gene Weltfish," June 20, 1952; Nomination for Appointment, April 17, 1952, both in Central Files, Columbiana; Gene Weltfish, appointment card, Columbiana; Ruth E. Boetcker, "Gene Weltfish," in *American National Biography*, ed. John A. Garraty and Mark C. Carnes (New York: Oxford University Press, 1999).
45. Tom Nolan, "Patricia Highsmith," in *American National Biography*. See also Andrew Wilson, *Beautiful Shadow: A Life of Patricia Highsmith* (New York: St. Martin's Press, 2003), and Marijane Meaker, *Highsmith: A Romance of the 1950s* (New York: Cleis Press, 2003).
46. Betty Millard, interview with Rosalind Rosenberg, August 2, 2001, and *Woman Against Myth* (New York: International Press, 1948), 3–24.
47. Millard, *Woman Against Myth*, 15.
48. Ibid., 16.
49. Ibid., 13–14.
50. Ibid., 13
51. Ibid.
52. Ibid., 22–23.
53. David Horowitz, *Betty Friedan and the Making of the Feminine Mystique* (Amherst: University of Massachusetts Press, 1998), 113.
54. Kate Weigand, *Red Feminism: American Communism and the Making of Women's Liberation* (Baltimore: Johns Hopkins University Press, 2001), 62; Gerda Lerner, *Fireweed: A Political Autobiography* (Philadelphia: Temple University Press, 2002), 254–57.
55. Weigand, *Red Feminism*, 123.
56. Ibid., 63–64.
57. Morton Keller and Phyllis Keller, *Making Harvard Modern: The Rise of America's University* (Cambridge, Mass.: Harvard University Press, 2001), 204; David A. Hollinger, *Science, Jews, and Secular Culture: Studies in Mid-Twentieth Century American Intellectual History* (Princeton, N.J.: Princeton University Press, 1996), 129–30.
58. Schrecker, *No Ivory Tower*, 169, 255–63.
59. The Committee on Conference, as it was known, included Walter Gelhorn, Thomas Drew, James Gutman, I. I. Rabi, and Mark Van Doren (Committee on Conference files, Columbiana).
60. Grayson Kirk, "Memorandum Concerning Dr. Gene Weltfish," June 20, 1952, Central Files, Columbiana; Fred Knubel, "Ex-President Kirk Is Dead at 94," *Columbia University Record*, December 5, 1997.
61. Travis Beal Jacobs, *Eisenhower at Columbia* (New Brunswick, N.J.: Transaction Books, 2001), 288–89.
62. Columbia University Trustees, Minutes, October 6, 1952, and November 3, 1952, Columbiana; Schrecker, *No Ivory Tower*, 256.

63. "Academic Freedom Question," *Barnard Bulletin*, March 26, 1953.

64. Lionel Trilling, "Committee on Conference Statement on Academic Freedom," November 11, 1953, Columbiana.

65. Mirra Komarovsky, *Women in the Modern World: Their Education and Their Dilemmas* (Boston: Little, Brown, 1953), 77, 127, 287, 299.

66. Gene N. Levine and Dale E. Ordes, "A Census of Barnard College Alumnae," Bureau of Applied Social Research, Columbia University, November 1962, Barnard College Archives.

67. Ernest Havemann and Patricia Salter West, *They Went to College: The College Graduate in America Today* (New York: Harcourt, Brace, 1952), 59.

68. Helene Kaplan, interview with Rosalind Rosenberg, March 22, 2000.

69. Havemann and West, *They Went to College*, 74; Levine and. Ordes, "Census of Barnard College Alumnae," table 1.

70. Lindsey R. Harmon, ed., *A Century of Doctorates: Data Analysis of Growth and Change* (Washington, D.C.: National Academy of Sciences, 1978), appendix G.

71. Women's College Coalition, "A Profile of Recent College Graduates," 1985; Elizabeth Tidball, "The Baccalaureate Origins of Recent Natural Science Doctorates," *Journal of Higher Education* 57 (1986): 606–20; *Baccalaureate Origins of Doctorate Recipients: A Ranking by Discipline of 4-year Private Institutions for the Period 1920–1995*, 8th ed. (Lancaster, Pa: Franklin and Marshall College, Office of Planning and Institutional Research, 1998).

72. Harmon, *Century of Doctorates*, table 42. While Columbia ranked first in the production of female Ph.D.'s, it ranked sixth in the production of male Ph.D.'s.

73. Thanks to Judith Shapiro for pointing this out to me.

74. Gildersleeve, *Many a Good Crusade*, 78–79; Mirra Komarovsky, reminiscences, recorded and transcribed by Anne W. Lowenthal, June 19, 1997, Barnard College Archives.

75. Millicent McIntosh to the Barnard Faculty, September 28, 1952, Central Files, Columbiana; McIntosh, oral history, 515, Oral History Collection.

76. "80 Years of Education for Adults: Columbia University–School of General Studies," Columbiana; Gillian Lindt, dean of General Studies (1994–1997), interview with Rosalind Rosenberg, February 27, 2004; Margaret Mead, appointment card, Columbiana.

77. Elspeth Rostow to Rosalind Rosenberg, August 28, 1995; Linda Kerber, "Angles of Vision: What American Studies Has Been; What American Studies Might Be" (keynote address presented at "60 Years of American Studies at Barnard College," Barnard College, New York, October 8, 1999, 3–4, available at: http://www.barnard .columbia.edu/amst).

78. Kerber, "Angles of Vision," citing Dorothy Kenyon, "What Women Have Done" (speech given at Barnard College, November 17, 1950), Smith College Papers, Northampton, Mass.

79. Course description, Columbia Bulletin, 1952–1953, Columbiana; Linda Kerber, "In Memoriam: John Atlee Kouwenhoven," *American Quarterly* 44 (1992): 463–66.

80. Linda Kerber, "In Memoriam: Annette Kar Baxter," *American Quarterly* 35 (1983): 455–57.

81. Kerber, "Angles of Vision," 7–8.

82. Linda Kerber, interview with Rosalind Rosenberg, October 4, 1999.

83. Nancy K. Miller, *But Enough About Me: Why We Read Other People's Lives* (New York: Columbia University Press, 2002), 5–8, 56–62.

84. Keller and Keller, *Making Harvard Modern*, 256.
85. Eli Ginzberg, interview with Rosalind Rosenberg, February 16, 2001; Robert F. Worth, "Eli Ginzberg, 91, Economist at Columbia and Adviser to Eight Presidents, Is Dead," *New York Times*, December 6, 2002.
86. Ginzberg interview.
87. As of 1960, women were only 4 percent of those working toward an M.B.A. nationwide.
88. National Manpower Council, *Womanpower*, 74.
89. Eli Ginzberg, *The Life Styles of Educated Women* (New York: Columbia University Press, 1966), 1–27.
90. Ibid., 20, 42, 94, 103, 104, 105, 143.
91. Ibid., 143, 181, 185, 186.
92. Millicent McIntosh, "New Patterns for Educated Women" (address presented at Barnard Convocation, September 1959); Rosellen Brown Hoffman, "Our Lives at Fifty" (paper presented at the thirtieth reunion of the class of 1960, Barnard College). I am grateful to Linda Kerber for bringing these documents to my attention and to Lucille Nieporent for sending them to me.
93. Columbia University Bulletin of Information, Graduate Student Guide, September 28, 1957, 59–60, Columbiana. I am grateful to Marion Elizabeth Jemmott for calling this bulletin to my attention.

6. SEXUAL POLITICS

1. According to figures from the United States Department of Education, university enrollment in 1960 stood at 900,000; by 1970, the figured had doubled to 1.8 million.
2. Registrar, Annual Report, 1960, 1970, Columbia University Archives–Columbiana Library (hereafter cited as Columbiana).
3. Commission on the Status of Women, "Part I, Officers of Instruction," report to the Columbia University Senate, March 1975, Columbiana.
4. For the full story of Columbia's financial difficulties, see Robert A. McCaughey, *Stand Columbia: A History of Columbia University in the City of New York, 1754–2004* (New York: Columbia University Press, 2003), 496–500.
5. Marion Elizabeth Jemmott, interview with Rosalind Rosenberg, July 29, 1999; Joseph Ridgley, interview with Rosalind Rosenberg, February 20, 2003; Robert Hanning, interview with Rosalind Rosenberg, March 8, 2001
6. In 1973, Nicolson wrote to Columbia's president, William McGill, complaining about his office's adoption of the honorific "Ms.": "Of all the nonsense spoken or written by what is called 'Women's Lib' (that's bad enough), this form of address is the silliest I have ever encountered" (Marjorie Hope Nicolson to William McGill, March 14, 1973, Central Files, Columbiana).
7. Marjorie Hope Nicholson, "The Rights and Privileges Pertaining Hereto," *Journal of the American Association of University Women* 31 (1938): 137–39.
8. Marjorie Hope Nicolson and Susanne Howe Nobbe, appointment cards, Columbiana.
9. Nicolson, "Rights and Privileges," George Stade, interview with Rosalind Rosenberg, February 23, 2003.
10. Ridgely interview; Nicolson hired Ridgely away from Johns Hopkins, where she had once studied, to teach the American proseminar in 1958 (Carolyn G. Heilbrun, interview with Rosalind Rosenberg, February 13, 2003).
11. Jemmott interview.

12. James Trilling, "My Father and the Weak-Eyed Devils," *American Scholar*, spring 1999, 27.

13. On the difference between graduate and undergraduate teaching at Columbia, I have found especially helpful my interview with Robert Hanning.

14. Diana Trilling, *The Beginning of the Journey: The Marriage of Diana and Lionel Trilling* (New York: Harcourt, Brace, 1993), 165, 257–80.

15. Ibid., 226.

16. Ibid., 269.

17. Ibid., 266–67.

18. Lionel Trilling, "Art and Neurosis," in *The Moral Obligation to Be Intelligent: Selected Essays*, ed. Leon Wiesletier (New York: Farrar, Straus and Giroux, 2001), 101.

19. Carolyn G. Heilburn, *When Men Were the Only Models We Had: My Teachers Barzun, Fadiman, Trilling* (Philadelphia: University of Pennsylvania Press, 2002), 51–99.

20. Heilbrun interview.

21. Heilbrun, *When Men Were the Only Models*, 113.

22. Carolyn G. Heilbrun, "The Character of Hamlet's Mother," in *Hamlet's Mother and Other Women*, ed. Carolyn G. Heilbrun (New York: Columbia University Press, 1990), 9–118; and *Toward a Recognition of Androgyny: Aspects of Male and Female in Literature* (London: Gollanz, 1973), 115.

23. Anne Matthews, "Rage in a Tenured Position," New York Times Magazine, November 8, 1992, 72–73; Hanning interview; Joan Ferrante, interview with Rosalind Rosenberg, January 29, 1999.

24. Kate Millett, interview with Rosalind Rosenberg, September 11, 2000; Catharine Stimpson, interview with Rosalind Rosenberg, April 4, 2000; Anne Prescott, interview with Rosalind Rosenberg, September 20, 2000. See also Marcia Cohen, *The Sisterhood: The True Story of the Women Who Changed the World* (New York: Simon and Schuster, 1988), 72–80, 143–254.

25. Millett, Stimpson, and Prescott interviews.

26. Kate Millett, *Sexual Politics* (New York: Doubleday, 1970), xii.

27. Millett interview.

28. Millett, *Sexual Politics*, 1, 5–6, 314, 238, 301, 56. For an excellent analysis of Millett's creation of the female reader, see Nancy Miller, *Enough About Me: Why We Read Other People's Lives* (New York: Columbia University Press, 2002), 63–64.

29. Millett, *Sexual Politcs*, 31, 23–58, 158, 362–63. For the link between racism and sexism in feminist thinking, see Nancy Woloch, *Women and the American Experience*, 3rd ed. (New York: McGraw-Hill, 2000), 533.

30. "Who's Come a Long Way Baby?" *Time*, August 31, 1970, 18.

31. Kate Millett, interviews with Rosalind Rosenberg, September 11, 2000, and March 8, 2003; Stade interview. The Columbia English department enjoyed a banner year in 1970. Nancy Milford's dissertation on Zelda Fitzgerald also become a best-seller.

32. Carolyn G. Heilbrun, "Millett's Sexual Politics: A Year Later," *Aphra* 2 (1971): 38–39.

33. Jonathan Culler, *On Deconstruction: Theory and Criticism After Structuralism* (Ithaca, N.Y.: Cornell University Press, 1982), 55.

34. Miller, *Enough About Me*, 56.

35. Stade interview.

36. Patricia Graham, "Women in Academe," *Science*, September 25, 1970, 1285. The quotation was repeated many times by members of the Columbia history department in the decades following Clough's remark.

37. Seymour Martin Lipset and Richard Hofstadter, eds., *Sociology and History: Methods* (New York: Basic Books, 1968), 358–70, 25–46.

38. Gerda Lerner, *The Majority Finds Its Past: Placing Women in History* (New York: Oxford University Press, 1979), xxi; and *The Grimké Sisters from South Carolina: Rebels Against Slavery* (Boston: Houghton Mifflin, 1967).

39. Lerner, *Majority Finds Its Past*, xvii–xxv; Carol Berkin, e-mail to Rosalind Rosenberg, May 21, 2003.

40. Carl N. Degler, "Revolution Without Ideology: The Changing Place of Women in America," 193–210; and Alice Rossi, "Equality Between the Sexes: An Immodest Proposal," 98–143, in *The Woman in America*, ed. Robert J. Lifton (Boston: Beacon Press, 1964).

41. Gerda Lerner, e-mail to Rosalind Rosenberg, February 4, 2001; Carl Degler, e-mail to Rosalind Rosenberg, March 6, 2001; Gerda Lerner, oral history, 11–14, Columbia University Rare Book and Manuscript Collection.

42. "Baxter Advocates Study of Female," *Barnard Bulletin*, October 14, 1965; "Two Departments Announce Course Revisions; Interdisciplinary 'History of Women' Established," *Barnard Bulletin*, March 7, 1966; David M. Potter, "American Women and the American Character, " in *History and American Society: Essays of David M. Potter*, ed. Don E. Fehrenbacher (New York: Oxford University Press, 1972), 277–303.

43. Estelle B. Freedman, *No Turning Back: The History of Feminism and the Future of Women* (New York: Ballantine, 2002), x; Estelle B. Freedman to Rosalind Rosenberg, March 7, 1999.

44. "Ban on Shorts Threatens Classic Barnard Couture," *New York Times*, April 28, 1960; "Administrative Regulations: Campus Etiquette," *Barnard College Blue Book*, 87–88.

45. "Women's Rights," *Columbia Spectator*, May 3, 1962.

46. *Barnard Residence Halls Guide*, 1962–1963, 14; Roger Lehecka, interview with Rosalind Rosenberg, July 1, 1999.

47. Joseph T. Lambert, "Ivy League Deans Favor Women in the Dorms," *Columbia Spectator*, May 4, 1962.

48. Alan J. Willen, "Kirk Accepts UDC Women-in-Dorms Proposal, but Says Doors in Rooms Must Remain Open," *Columbia Spectator*, March 20, 1963.

49. "Slightly Open," *Columbia Spectator*, March 20, 1963.

50. Trilling, "My Father," 22.

51. Barnard College Announcement, 1960–1961, 169.

52. Barnard College Announcement, 1967–1968, 44–46. Commuting distance to the college was defined as "one and one-half hours from the College each way" ("Barnard Housing," *Columbia Spectator*, December 11, 1961).

53. "Women's Rights."

54. Lehecka inteview.

55. Judy Klemesrud, "An Arrangement: Living Together for Convenience, Security, and Sex," *New York Times*, March 4, 1968.

56. Susan E. Tifft and Alex S. Jones, *The Trust: The Private and Powerful Family Behind the New York Times* (Boston: Little, Brown, 1999), 438, 56.

57. Editorial, *Barnard Bulletin*, March 9, 1967.

58. "Informal Barnard Poll," *Barnard Bulletin*, March 8, 1967.

59. Barbara Schmitter, then associate dean of studies, interview with Rosalind Rosenberg, March 2004.

60. Anne Hoffman, "Columbia Student Refuses Induction," *Barnard Bulletin*, March 13, 1968.

61. Beth Bailey, *Sex in the Heartland* (Cambridge, Mass.: Harvard University Press, 1999), 92, 200–201.

62. Linda LeClair, letter to the editor, Barnard Bulletin, March 13, 1968; Schmitter interview; Lindsay Van Gelder, "Coed Faces Expulsion for Living with Boyfriend," *New York Post*, April 17, 1968; William A. McWhirter, "The 'Arrangement' at College," *Life*, May 31, 1968, 56; "Students: Linda the Light Housekeeper," *Time*, April 26, 1968, 51; Bailey, *Sex in the Heartland*, 6, 91–104, 201. The college's response to the LeClair affair was widely reported in the city's newspapers (clippings, Barnard College Archives).

63. Linda LeClair, "Testimony Given by Linda LeClair at Judicial Council Hearing," April 16, 1968, Barnard College Archives.

64. "Statement of Decision of the Judicial Council Regarding the Case of Linda LeClair," no date, Barnard College Archives.

65. Letters to Barnard administrators, including the one that refers to Barnard as P.U., from "Alice" to "Dean," April 18, 1968; LeClair, "Testimony"; Martha Peterson to Linda LeClair, May 6, 1968, all in Barnard College Archives; Schmitter interview. See also Bailey, *Sex in the Heartland*, 200–205.

66. A number of black women students lived at the Harlem YWCA, which was a leader in civil-rights activities in Harlem (Cheryl Lynn Greenberg, *Or Does It Explode? Black Harlem in the Great Depression* [New York: Oxford University Press, 1991], 105–8; Elvita Dominique, "Negotiating Integration: Black Women at Barnard, 1968–1974" [senior thesis in history, Barnard College, 2003], Barnard College Archives). On the Seven Sisters, see Linda M. Perkins, "The Racial Integration of the Seven Sisters Colleges," *Journal of Blacks in Higher Education*, no. 19 (1998): 104–8. On the number of African American women students at Barnard in the 1950s, see the college yearbook, *Mortarboard*.

67. McCaughey, *Stand Columbia*, 423–61.

68. Ibid., 437.

69. Ibid., 442–50.

70. Ibid., 434–39.

71. Carolyn Eisenberg, interview with Rosalind Rosenberg, June 24, 2003.

72. Sara Evans, *Personal Politics: The Roots of Women's Liberation in the Civil Rights Movement and the New Left* (1974; reprint, New York: Vintage, 1980), 200–201.

73. Diana Trilling, *We Must March My Darlings* (New York: Harcourt Brace Jovanovich, 1977), 95.

74. Hanning interview.

75. Christine L. Edwards, "The Dilemma of the Black Student in the White University: Case in Point: My Four Years at Barnard College," May 7, 1973, Barnard College Archives; Dominique, "Negotiating Integration"; Karla Spurlock and Annette Adams, "Women's Liberation: The Black Perspective," *Barnard Bulletin*, April 28, 1970 .

76. Kate Millett, interview with Rosalind Rosenberg, July 12, 2000.

77. Harriet Zellner, interview with Rosalind Rosenberg, July 12, 2000; Alice Echols, *Daring to Be Bad: Radical Feminism in America, 1967–1975* (Minneapolis: University of Minnesota Press, 1989), 141.

78. Zellner interview; Barbara Buonchristiano, interview with Rosalind Rosenberg, January 25, 1999.

79. Cynthia Fuchs Epstein, "Personal Reflections with a Sociological Eye," in *Authors of Their Own Lives: Intellectual Autobiographies by Twenty American Sociologists*, ed. Bennett M. Berger (Berkeley: University of California Press, 1990), 357–58; interviews by author with other women who prefer to remain anonymous .

80. Rachel Blau DuPlessis includes a passage on her experience as a graduate student in English at Columbia and the founding of Columbia Women's Liberation in 1969 in "Reader, I Married Me: A Polygynous Memoir," in *Changing Subjects: The Making of Feminist Literary Criticism*, ed. Gayle Greene and Coppelia Kahn (London: Routledge, 1993), 97–111. See also Rachel Blau DuPlessis and Ann Snitow, eds., *The Feminist Memoir Project: Voices from Women's Liberation* (New York: Three Rivers Press, 1998).

81. Ann Sutherland Harris, e-mail to Rosalind Rosenberg, July 15, 1999; Rachel Blau DuPlessis, e-mail to Rosalind Rosenberg, July 8, 2000.

82. Rachel Blau DuPlessis et al., "Columbia Women's Liberation: Report from the Committee on Discrimination Against Women Faculty," *Barnard Alumnae Magazine*, spring 1970, 12–18; Columbia University Bulletin, 1968–1969, Columbiana. See also Graham, "Women in Academe."

83. DuPlessis, "Columbia Women's Liberation," 18.

84. Harris e-mail; Catharine Stimpson, interview with Rosalind Rosenberg, April 4, 2000. Greenhouse was then also covering stories on abortion reform for the *New York Times* and had friends at Barnard and Columbia who were keeping her informed as to activities on campus (Linda Greenhouse, e-mail to author, January 16, 2001).

85. Margaret W. Rossiter, *Women Scientists in America: Before Affirmative Action, 1940–1972* (Baltimore: Johns Hopkins University Press, 1995), 274; Jo Freeman, *The Politics of Women's Liberation: A Case Study of an Emerging Social Movement and Its Relation to the Policy Process* (New York: McKay, 1975), 194–95.

86. Rossiter, *Women Scientists in America*, 374.

87. Congress established the first Department of Education in 1867 as an independent agency and then transferred it to the Department of the Interior as the Bureau of Education in 1869 and to the Federal Security Agency in 1939. In 1953, Congress created the Department of Health, Education, and Welfare, and then, in 1979, created two agencies in its place: Department of Education and Department of Health and Human Services.

88. Bernice Sandler, "A Little Help from Our Government: WEAL and Contract Compliance," in *Academic Women on the Move*, ed. Alice Rossi and Ann Calderwood (New York: Russell Sage Foundation, 1973), 439–55.

89. Harris received a second call from Jo Freeman, a graduate student in political science at the University of Chicago, who was working on a similar, but more limited report on discrimination against women at Chicago (Jo Freeman, "On the Origins of the Women's Liberation Movement from a Strictly Personal Perspective," in *Feminist Memoir Project*, 172–208; for discussion of Chicago, see 188).

90. Bernice Sandler, e-mail to Rosalind Rosenberg, July 15, 1999; Bernice Sandler to George Shultz, May 11, 1970, "Women at Columbia" box, Columbiana.

91. Sandler e-mail.

92. J. Stanley Pottinger, interview with Rosalind Rosenberg, June 26, 2000; Albert A. Logan Jr., "Women Seek U.S. Action on Alleged Bias," *Chronicle of Higher Education*, April 13, 1970; Nancy Gruchow, "Discrimination: Women Charge Universities, Colleges with Bias," *Science*, May 1, 1970, 559–61.

93. Sandler e-mail.

94. The Educational Amendments Act (which included Title IX) and the Equal Rights Amendment were passed by both houses of Congress in 1972.

95. Pottinger interview.

96. McCaughey, *Stand Columbia*, 496–500.

97. Warren Goodell to John Borneman, December 4, 1969, Affirmative Action folder, Central Files, Columbiana. Goodell complained that he had been asking for the creation of an "Equal Opportunity" Office for five years, without success, and warned that the university was in serious trouble with the federal government. He wrote only of minorities and made no reference to women, except as "cleaning ladies."

98. George Fraenkel, interview with Rosalind Rosenberg, July 13, 1999. The professor was Edward Said, one of Columbia's most distinguished faculty members. But not all those granted tenure so informally would have survived a more searching review.

99. Fraenkel interview.

100. J. Stanley Pottinger to William McGill, November 3, 1971, Office of Scholarly Resources, Health and Sciences Division, Columbia University. I am grateful to Steven Novak, archivist at the Health Sciences Library, for finding this letter. Curiously, there was no copy in the university's Central Files, further evidence, perhaps, of the limitations of Columbia's record keeping in the early 1970s. See also Commission on the Status of Women, "Part I, Officers of Instruction."

101. William McGill, oral history, Oral History Research Office, Columbia University; McCaughey, *Stand Columbia*, 490–93.

102. William McGill to Columbia University Community, November 8, 1971, Central Files, Columbiana.

103. Ivar Berg, interview with Rosalind Rosenberg, March 14, 2001; Paul Carter, interview with Rosalind Rosenberg, June 19, 2000.

104. Commission on the Status of Women, Minutes, December 17, 1971, Senate Office files, Columbia University.

105. University Senate, Minutes, November 19, 1971, Senate Office files; Frances Hoffman, interview with Rosalind Rosenberg, September 20, 1999.

106. William McGill to Marion Jemmott, Janurary 24, 1988, Central Files, Columbiana.

107. William McGill to Marjorie Hope Nicolson, April 12, 1973, Central Files, Columbiana.

108. McGill oral history; McCaughy, *Stand Columbia*, 490–93; Fraenkel interview.

109. William McGill to Robert Brookhart, Jonathan Cole, Nina Garsoian, Eli Ginzberg, Patricia Graham, Charles Hamilton, Ann Hirsch, Frances Hoffman, Herbert Robbins, Ichiro I. Shirato, Gerald Thomson, and Chien-Shiung Wu, November 12, 1971, Provost's Papers, Columbiana; Patricia Albjerg Graham, interview with Rosalind Rosenberg, December 28, 1960.

110. For more on women in academe and the discrimination they faced in the 1960s, see Rossiter, *Women Scientists in America*, 361–82.

111. Geraldine Joncich Clifford, ed., *Lone Voyagers: Academic Women in Coeducational Institutions, 1870–1937* (New York: Feminist Press, 1989), 34; Graham interview.

112. Estelle Freedman to Rosalind Rosenberg, March 7, 1999.

113. Chien-Shiung Wu, appointment card, Central Files, Columbiana. The salaries rose as follows: 1970, $23,000; May 1972, $26,000; October 1972, $28,000; 1974, $30,000; 1975, $32,000; and 1976, $36,000. As of the academic year 1970/1971, the maximum nine-month salary in the sciences was $35,000; the minimum was $16,000 ("Inter-University Salary Information Exchange," fall 1970, box 08–02–02, Provost's Papers, Columbiana). Information on salary review comes from Ferrante, Graham, Jemmot, and Hoffman interviews and from Barbara Low, professor of biochemistry at P&S, interview with Rosalind Rosenberg, July 28, 1999, and Nina Garsoian, interview with Rosalind Rosenberg, January 22, 1999. Dean George Fraenkel disagreed that Professor Wu was discriminated against in salary. According to his recollection,

her salary properly reflected her contribution to the university in terms of her teaching load, departmental service, and scholarship.

114. Hoffman interview.

115. Chien-Shiung Wu, "Women in Physics," *American Physical Society*, February 3, 1971; and excerpt from autobiographical essay, both in Biographical Files, Columbiana; Rossiter, *Women Scientists in America*.

116. Eli Ginzberg to William McGill, November 29, 1971, Central Files, Columbiana.

117. Jonathan Cole, interview with Rosalind Rosenberg, February 13, 2001.

118. "Outline of Presentation to HEW," December 15, 1971," Central Files, Columbiana.

119. Heilbrun, *When Men Were the Only Models*, 64–65.

120. Burt Barnes, "Reverse Bias Alleged in College Hiring," *Washington Post*, March 5, 1973.

121. Paul Carter, interview with Rosalind Rosenberg, June 19, 2000; Low interview.

122. Carter interview.

123. Hoffman interview; "Affirmative Action Plan," April 10, 1972, Central Files, Columbiana.

124. Fraenkel interview.

125. Ferrante interview; McCaughey, *Stand Columbia*, 501, 518; "Affirmative Action Plan."

126. Memo, April 18, 1975, University Senate files.

127. Hoffman interview; Commission on the Status of Women, "Part I, Officers of Instruction."

128. Barbara Aronstein Black, "Something to Remember, Something to Celebrate: Women at Columbia Law School," *Columbia Law Review* 102 (2002): 1457; Michael Sovern, interview with Rosalind Rosenberg, July 22, 1999.

129. Whitney S. Bagnall, "The Women of Columbia Law School: A Brief History of Their 75 Years as Students and Alumnae," *Columbia Law School Report*, fall 2002, 2–17.

130. David Margolick, "Judge Ginsburg's Life: A Trial by Adversity," *New York Times* June 25, 1993.

131. Jeffrey Rosen, "The New Look of Liberalism on the Court," *New York Times Magazine*, October 5, 1997, 63; Eleanor Porter Swiger, *Women Lawyers at Work* (New York: Messner, 1978), 50–66.

132. Mitchel Ostrer, "A Profile of Ruth Bader Ginsburg," *Juris Doctor*, October 1977, 34.

133. Margolick, "Judge Ginsburg's Life."

134. Ibid.

135. Ibid.

136. Ibid.; Ruth Bader Ginsburg, interview with Rosalind Rosenberg August 1, 1985.

137. Pam Lambert, "Ginsburg and Rabb: Setting Precedents," *Columbia*, summer 1980, 12–13; Nan Robertson, *The Girls in the Balcony: Women, Men, and the New York Times* (New York: Random House, 1992), 160–63.

138. Flyers, Women at Columbia box, Columbiana; Ginsburg interview.

139. Sovern interview.

140. Ibid. Women made up 4 percent of enrollments at law schools across the country in the 1950s (Amy Singer, "Numbers Too Big to Ignore," *American Lawyer* 21 [1999]: 6).

141. The following year, Sovern worked to diversify the Columbia faculty further by appointing Kellis E. Parker, one of five students to integrate the University of North Carolina in 1960 and a 1968 graduate of Howard Law School, as Columbia's first black professor of law,

142. Ostrer, "Profile of Ginsburg," 34–38; Ruth B. Cowan, "Women's Rights Through Litigation: An Examination of the American Civil Liberties Union Women's Rights Project, 1971–1976," *Columbia Human Rights Law Review* 8 (1976): 373–412; Laura

Jones, "Columbia's Leader," *Columbia Today*, April 1975, 13–15. In 1980, Ginsburg became a judge in the United States Court of Appeals for the District of Columbia, and in 1993, she became the second woman to be named a justice of the Supreme Court

143. Lambert, "Ginzberg and Rabb," 13; Robertson, *Girls in the Balcony*, 158.
144. Robertson, *Girls in the Balcony*, 86–90.
145. Ibid., 90–92.
146. Ibid., 19–20, 114–31; Tifft and Jones, *Trust*, 173–74.
147. Susan Brownmiller, *In Our Time: Memoir of a Revolution* (New York: Dial Press, 1999), 138–46.
148. Robertson, *Girls in the Balcony*, 144–45.

7. THE BATTLE OVER COEDUCATION RENEWED

1. Chief Justice Earl Warren, majority opinion, *Brown v. Board of Education of Topeka Kansas*, 347 U.S. 483 (1954).
2. Frank Mazza, "Barnard Panel Backs Linda's Housing Plan," *Daily News*, April 18, 1968, LeClair file, Barnard College Archives.
3. Ellen Horwin, "Peterson Reviews Barnard Progress," *Barnard Bulletin*, May 8, 1968.
4. H. Sophie Newcomb maintained a quasi-independent relationship with Tulane. The two New Orleans schools had a shared faculty and, after 1979, a merged curriculum, but maintained separate admissions, deans, and staff (http://www.newcomb.tulane.edu/new_hist.html).
5. Ellen Futter, interview with Rosalind Rosenberg, July 27, 1999.
6. Alecta Arenal, "What *Women Writers?*" in *The Politics of Women's Studies: Testimony from Thirty Founding Mothers*, ed. Florence Howe (New York: Feminist Press, 2000), 183–93.
7. Eleanor Elliott, interview with Rosalind Rosenberg, July 8, 1999.
8. George Fraenkel, interview with Rosalind Rosenberg, July 13, 1999.
9. George Fraenkel, "Arts and Sciences Instructional Budget: Preliminary Five-Year Projections," June 23, 1971, Central Files, Columbia University Archives–Columbiana Library (hereafter cited as Columbiana); Fraenkel interview.
10. Fraenkel interview.
11. Robert A. McCaughey, *Stand Columbia: A History of Columbia University in the City of New York, 1754–2004* (New York: Columbia University Press, 2003), 521; Martha Peterson to Rosalind Rosenberg, September 30, 1999.
12. McCaughey, *Stand Columbia*, 519–20.
13. Fraenkel interview; Stephen Rittenberg, interview with Rosalind Rosenberg, February 2, 2001.
14. Fraenkel interview.
15. John W. Burgess, *The American University: When Shall It Be? Where Shall It Be?* (Boston: Ginn, Heath, 1884), 18; Walter Metzger, *Academic Freedom in the Age of the University* (New York: Columbia University Press, 1955), 105.
16. Lionel Trilling, "The Van Arminge and Keppel Eras," in *A History of Columbia College on Morningside Heights*, ed. Dwight Miner (New York: Columbia University Press, 1954), 14–47.
17. Daniel Bell, *The Reforming of General Education: The Columbia College Experience in Its National Setting* (New York: Columbia University Press, 1966), 12–25.
18. Michael Rosenthal, interview with Rosalind Rosenberg, April 25, 1999.
19. McCaughey, *Stand Columbia*, 536.

20. Roger Lehecka, interview with Rosalind Rosenberg, July 1, 1999; James McMenamin, former dean of admissions, interview with Rosalind Rosenberg, July 14, 1999; Rosenthal interview.

21. McCaughey, *Stand Columbia*, 527–28.

22. Kate Millett, "A Jane Crow Education," *Barnard Bulletin*, December 11, 1968; Leroy Breunig and Annette Baxter, testimony, "Transcript of Joint Columbia–Barnard Trustees Committee," May 12, 1971, Barnard College Archives.

23. Patricia Albjerg Graham, interview with Rosalind Rosenberg, December 28, 1998.

24. Elliott interview; McCaughey, *Stand Columbia*, 538.

25. "Louis Harris Surveys Barnard," *Barnard Alumnae Magazine*, winter 1978, 2, 10.

26. "Martha Peterson Papers Donated to KU," news release, Office of University Relations, University of Kansas, Lawrence; Graham interview; Martha Peterson to Rosalind Rosenberg, September 30, 1999.

27. Elliott interview.

28. Remembrances offered at twentieth anniversary celebration of the Barnard Women's Center, 1990.

29. Catharine R. Stimpson, "Feminist Criticism," in *Redrawing the Boundaries*, ed. Stephen Greenblatt and Giles Gunn (New York: Modern Language Association, 1992), 252.

30. Kate Millett, interview with Rosalind Rosenberg, September 11, 2000.

31. Marcia Cohen, *The Sisterhood: The True Story of the Women Who Changed the World* (New York: Simon and Schuster, 1988), 240–43; "Who's Come a Long Way, Baby?" *Time*, August 31, 1970, 16; "Marie-Claude Wrenn, the Furious Young Philosopher Who Got It," *Life*, September 4, 1970, 22.

32. Kate Millett, *Sexual Politics* (New York: Doubleday, 1970), 5; and *Flying* (1974; reprint, New York: Simon and Schuster, 1990), 15; Nancy K. Miller, *But Enough About Me: Why We Read Other People's Lives* (New York: Columbia University Press, 2002), 63–64.

33. Millett interview; Cohen, *Sisterhood*, 243.

34. Catharine Stimpson, interview with Rosalind Rosenberg, April 14, 2000; Catharine R. Stimpson, appointment card, Barnard College Archives.

35. Stimpson interview; Jane S. Gould, *Juggling: A Memoir of Work, Family, and Feminism* (New York: Feminist Press, 1997), 142–43.

36. Stimpson interview; Elaine Showalter, e-mail to Rosalind Rosenberg, February 12, 2003; Gould, *Juggling*, 146–55; Gail Robinson, "Forum Examines 'Male Chauvinism,'" *Columbia Spectator*, January 12 1972; Ellen McManus, "Chauvinism at Columbia," *Barnard Bulletin*, January 13, 1972.

37. Catharine Stimpson, e-mail to Rosalind Rosenberg, June 18, 2003.

38. Gould, *Juggling*, 163–65.

39. Ibid., 167–72.

40. Stimpson, "Feminist Criticism," 258–59; Gould, *Juggling*, 186–205; Susan Brownmiller, *In Our Time: Memoir of a Revolution* (New York: Dial Press, 1999), 295–330; Carol S. Vance, ed., *Pleasure and Danger: Exploring Female Sexuality* (Boston: Routledge & Kegan Paul, 1984).

41. Barnard College Announcement, 1971–1972.

42. In 1978, the French department at Columbia had lost another feminist scholar, Naomi Schor, to Brown (she moved next to Yale); in 1982, it lost still another, Alice Jardine, to Harvard.

43. Miller, *Enough About Me*, 33.

44. Ibid., 33–42; Gould, *Juggling*, 180.

45. Dorothy O. Helly, "The Founding of the Columbia Seminar on Women and Society" (paper presented at the twenty-fifth anniversary of "Women and Society," Columbia University, October 16, 2000); Marcia Wright, interview with Rosalind Rosenberg, February 9, 2001; Jill Woolman, "Susan Ritner Speaks of Columbia–Barnard Future," *Barnard Bulletin*, March 2, 1972.

46. Frank Tannenbaum, at http://www.learn.columbia.edu/cu/Usem2001/htm/usem_movement.html.

47. University Seminars, "Summary Report, 1973–74"; Bruce Bassett to James Gutman, August 5, 1971, both in University Seminars folder, Columbiana.

48. "Proposal for a University Seminar: 'Women and Society,'" no date, personal papers of Renate Bridenthal.

49. Wright interview; Helly, "Founding of the Columbia Seminar on Women and Society."

50. Ibid.

51. The author was pressed into service as the seminar's first secretary; a poor record keeper, she has had to construct the list of early presentations from memory.

52. Steven Marcus, "Presidential Commission on Academic Priorities in the Arts and Sciences," December 1979, Columbiana; McCaughey, *Stand Columbia*, 528–29.

53. Barnard–Columbia Intercorporate Agreement, 1973, Columbiana.

54. Stimpson e-mail. At the time she was considered for tenure, Stimpson had published *J. R. R. Tolkien* (New York: Columbia University Press, 1969) and "Women's Liberation and Black Civil Rights," in *Women in Sexist Society: Studies in Power and Powerlessness*, ed. Vivian Gornick and Barbara K. Moran (New York: Basic Books, 1971), 622–57. She also had edited *Women and the Equal Rights Amendment* (New York: Bowker, 1972) and *Discrimination Against Women: Congressional Hearings on Equal Rights in Education and Employment* (New York: Bowker, 1973).

55. Graham interview.

56. Elliott interview.

57. Helene Kaplan, interview with Rosalind Rosenberg, March 22, 2000; Elliott interview. As of 1978, Barnard's endowment stood at $22.5 million, and Vassar's endowment was $68 million ("Lowest Endowment of the Seven Sisters," *Barnard Bulletin*, March 27, 1978).

58. Futter interview; Toni Crowley Coffee, "President Futter Looks Ahead," *Barnard Alumnae Magazine*, fall 1980.

59. Kaplan interview.

60. Ronald Breslow et al., "Report of the Select Committee for the Study of Coeducation in Columbia College," 1981, Central Files, Columbiana; Ronald Breslow, comments made in response to Rosalind Rosenberg, "The Woman Question: From John W. Burgess to Judith Shapiro" (paper presented at Columbia University Seminar "History of the University, " February 17, 1999)."

61. McMenamin interview; Rosenthal interview.

62. Breslow et al., "Report of the Select Committee."

63. Gillian Lindt, interview with Rosalind Rosenberg, April 3, 2001.

64. Ibid.

65. Ibid.

66. Michael Sovern, interview with Rosalind Rosenberg, July 22, 1999.

67. McCaughey, *Stand Columbia*, 535–40.

68. Sovern interview; Futter interview; Kaplan interview.

69. Flora Davidson, interview with Rosalind Rosenberg, March 1, 1999.

70. Sovern interview.

71. Barnard College, *Faculty Handbook*, 1985.
72. The most influential report was *How Schools Shortchange Girls* (Washington, D.C.: American Association of University Women Educational Foundation, National Education Association, 1992), funded by the Ford Foundation and conducted by the American Association of University Women.
73. Judith Shapiro interview with Rosalind Rosenberg, January 28,1999.
74. Ibid.
75. Judith Shapiro, "Barnard College Inaugural Address," October 27, 1994, Riverside Church, New York, Barnard College Archives.
76. In 1988, Lindt became the first woman to be elected president of the Association of Graduate Schools, whose members included more than fifty of the major research universities in the United States.
77. Lindt interview; Lindt was dean of the graduate school from 1983 to 1990.
78. Fred Knubel, Office of Public Information, Press Release, April 1, 1986, Columbiana; Carolyn G. Heilbrun, "The Politics of Mind: Women, Tradition, and the University," in *Hamlet's Mother and Other Women*, ed. Carolyn G. Heilbrun (New York: Columbia University Press, 1990), 213–26.
79. Lindt interview; Columbia Catalog, 2002–2003.
80. Commission on the Status of Women," Part I: Officers of Instruction," report to the Columbia University Senate, March 1975; and "Advancement of Women Through the Academic Ranks of the Columbia University Graduate School of Arts and Sciences: Where Are the Leaks in the Pipeline?" interim report to the Columbia University Senate, April 27, 2001, both in Columbiana.
81. Commission on the Status of Women, "Advancement of Women." The figures for women were natural sciences: 33 percent of students, 23 percent of tenure-eligible faculty, 11 percent of tenured faculty; social sciences: 46 percent of students, 36 percent of tenure-eligible faculty, 23 percent of tenured faculty; and humanities: 48 percent of students, 33 percent of tenure-eligible faculty, 20 percent of tenured faculty.
82. Gould, *Juggling*, 193–205; Brownmiller, *In Our Time*, 314–16; Vance, ed., *Pleasure and Danger*.
83. Brownmiller, *In Our Time*, 279–84.
84. Anne Kornhouser, "Sexual Hrassment: Do the Statistics Reflect Reality?" *Columbia Spectator*, October 2, 1982; Margaret McCarthy, "Harassment Draws University Attention," *Acta Columbiana*, December 1, 1985, Sexual Harassment clipping files, Columbiana.
85. Lindt interview. A related problem emerged in the 1990s: what to do about consensual sexual relations between faculty and students (Columbia University, "Romantic Relationship Advisory," 2002, available at: www.columbia.edu).
86. Miller, *Enough About Me*, 42.
87. Anne Matthews, "Rage in a Tenured Position," *New York Times Magazine*, November 8, 1992, 72–74, 83.
88. Christia Mercer, interview with Rosalind Rosenberg, September 4, 2003; Maxine Greene, interview with Rosalind Rosenberg, March 22, 2001.
89. Barbara Aronstein Black, "Something to Remember, Something to Celebrate: Women at Columbia Law School," *Columbia Law Review* 102 (2002): 1451–68.
90. Marianne Legato, interview with Rosalind Rosenberg, July 10, 2003.
91. Karen W. Arenson, "Reseeding Ivy:, Columbia on the Comeback Trail from Troubles," *New York Times*, November 1, 1999.
92. Diana Trilling, *The Beginning of the Journey: The Marriage of Diana and Lionel Trilling* (New York: Harcourt, Brace, 1993), 155.

BIBLIOGRAPHY

COLUMBIA UNIVERSITY recently has devoted significant resources to the collection, organization, and preservation of its
historical records, and working in its archives has become a
pleasure. It was not always so. Until 1961, when the university established the Columbia University Archives–Columbiana Library, the records of the university were maintained by the secretary of the university, and even after the creation of the archives, sys-
tematic collecting was long delayed. Much is forever lost. The Barnard College
Archives had a similarly slow start, and the Teachers College Special Collections
Archives are now closed. Fortunately, the Rare Book and Manuscript Library of the university has preserved the personal papers of some of the key figures in Columbia's history, and the Oral History Research Office has systematically collected the reminiscences of many more. The Columbia Law School Special Collections and the Health
Sciences Archives hold the papers of their respective schools; moreover, archivists there
were sometimes able to provide documents not available in the university's Central
Files. Because of Columbia's location in New York, the city's newspapers, especially the
New York Times, proved a useful source for much of the story told in this book, as did
the university's various publications, especially *Acta Columbiana, Barnard Alumnae
Magazine, Barnard Bulletin, Columbia Magazine, Columbia Record, Columbia Spectator*, and *Columbia Today*. In addition to these sources, the secondary literature on
urban, intellectual, women's, and educational history—cited in this bibliography—
form the foundation of *Changing the Subject*.

Alpern, Sara. *Freda Kirchwey: A Woman of the Nation*. Cambridge, Mass.: Harvard
University Press, 1987.
Alperstein, Janet F. "The Influence of Boards of Trustees, Senior Administrators, and
Faculty on the Decision of Women's Colleges to Remain Single-Sex in the 1980s."
Ed.D. diss., Teachers College, Columbia University, 2001.
Antler, Joyce. *The Journey Home: Jewish Women and the American Century*. New York:
Free Press, 1997.
Arenal, Alecta. "'What Women Writers?'" In *The Politics of Women's Studies: Testimony
from Thirty Founding Mothers*, edited by Florence Howe, 183–93. New York: Feminist
Press, 2000.
Bagnall, Whitney S. "The Women of Columbia Law School: A Brief History of Their 75
Years as Students and Alumnae." *Columbia Law School Report*, fall 2002, 2–17.
Bailey, Beth. *Sex in the Heartland*. Cambridge, Mass.: Harvard University Press, 1999.
Baker, Elizabeth Faulkner. *Protective Labor Legislation*. New York: Columbia University
Press, 1925.

Banner, Lois W. *Intertwined Lives: Margaret Mead, Ruth Benedict, and Their Circle*. New York: Knopf, 2003.

——. "Mannish Women, Passive Men, and Constitutional Types: Margaret Mead's *Sex and Temperament in Three Primitive Societies* as a Response to Ruth Benedict's *Patterns of Culture.*" *Signs* 28 (2003): 833–58.

Barnard, Frederick A. P. *Causes Affecting the Attendance of Undergraduates in the Incorporated Colleges of the City of New York*. New York: Van Nostrand, 1872.

——. *Memoirs of Frederick A. P. Barnard*. Edited by John Fulton. New York: Macmillan, 1896.

Barzun, Jacques. *The American University: How It Runs—Where It Is Going*. New York: Harper & Row, 1968.

Beard, Mary Ritter. *Woman's Work in Municipalities*. National Municipal League Series. New York: Appleton, 1915.

Behar, Ruth, and Deborah A. Gordon, eds. *Women Writing Culture*. Berkeley: University of California Press, 1995.

Bell, Daniel. *The Reforming of General Education: The Columbia College Experience in Its National Setting*. New York: Columbia University Press, 1966.

Bender, Thomas. *Intellect and Public Life: Essays on the Social History of Academic Intellectuals in the United States*. Baltimore: Johns Hopkins University Press, 1993.

——. *New York Intellect: A History of Intellectual Life in New York City, from 1750 to the Beginnings of Our Own Time*. Baltimore: Johns Hopkins University Press, 1987.

Benedict, Ruth. "The Concept of the Guardian Spirit in North America." Ph.D. diss., Columbia University, 1929.

——. "The Concept of the Guardian Spirit in North America." *Memoirs of the American Anthropological Association* 29 (1929): 1–97.

——. *Patterns of Culture*. New York: Houghton Mifflin, 1934.

——. "Psychological Types in the Cultures of the Southwest." In *An Anthropologist at Work: Writings of Ruth Benedict*, edited by Margaret Mead, 248–61. New York: Avon, 1959.

Berger, Bennett M., ed. *Authors of Their Own Lives: Intellectual Autobiographies by Twenty American Sociologists*. Berkeley: University of California Press, 1990.

Black, Barbara Aronstein. "Something to Remember, Something to Celebrate: Women at Columbia Law School." *Columbia Law Review* 102 (2002): 1451–68.

Blair, Karen J. *The Clubwoman as Feminist: True Womanhood Redefined, 1868–1914*. New York: Holmes & Meier, 1980.

Blake, Katherine Devereux, and Margaret Louise Wallace. *Champion of Women: The Life of Lillie Devereux Blake*. New York: Revell, 1943.

Blake, Lillie Devereux. *Woman's Place To-day: Four Lectures in Reply to the Lenten Lectures on "Woman" by the Rev. Morgan Dix, D.D., Rector of Trinity Church, New York*. New York: Lovell, 1883.

Blight, David W. *Race and Reunion: The Civil War in American Memory*. Cambridge, Mass: Harvard University Press, 2001.

Boas, Franz. "Changes in the Bodily Form of the Descendents of Immigrants." *American Anthropologist* 14 (1912): 530–62.

——. *The Mind of Primitive Man: A Course of Lectures Delivered Before the Lowell Institute, Boston, Mass., and the National University of Mexico, 1910–1911*. New York: Macmillan, 1921.

Boyd, Valerie. *Wrapped in Rainbows: The Life of Zora Neale Hurston*. New York: Scribner, 2003.

Brennan, Joseph Gerard. *The Education of a Prejudiced Man*. New York: Scribner, 1977.

Brown, Courtney C. *The Dean Meant Business.* New York: Columbia University Press, 1983.

Brownmiller, Susan. *In Our Time: Memoir of a Revolution.* New York: Dial Press, 1999.

Buchler, Justus. "Reconstruction in the Liberal Arts." In *A History of Columbia College on Morningside Heights,* edited by Dwight Miner, 48–135. New York: Columbia University Press, 1954.

Burgess, John W. *The American University: When Shall It Be? Where Shall It Be?* Boston: Ginn, Heath, 1884.

———. *Reconstruction and the Constitution, 1866–1876.* New York: Scribner, 1902.

———. *Reminiscences of an American Scholar: The Beginnings of Columbia University.* New York: Columbia University Press, 1934.

Burrows, Edwin G., and Mike Wallace. *Gotham: A History of New York City to 1898.* New York: Oxford University Press, 1999.

Butler, Nicholas Murray. *Across the Busy Years: Recollections and Reflections.* 2 vols. New York: Scribner, 1939.

Caffrey, Margaret Mary. *Ruth Benedict: Stranger in This Land.* Austin: University of Texas Press, 1989.

Chamberlain, Mariam K., ed. *Women in Academe: Progress and Prospects.* New York: Russell Sage Foundation, 1988.

Chute, William J. *Damn Yankee! The First Career of Frederick A. P. Barnard: Educator, Scientist, Idealist.* Port Washington, N.Y.: Kennekat, 1978.

Clarke, Edward. *Sex in Education; or, a Fair Chance for the Girls.* Boston: Osgood, 1873.

Clifford, Geraldine Joncich, ed. *Lone Voyagers: Academic Women in Coeducational Institutions, 1870–1937.* New York: Feminist Press, 1989.

Cohen, Marcia. *The Sisterhood: The True Story of the Women Who Changed the World.* New York: Simon and Schuster, 1988.

Conable, Charlotte Williams. *Women at Cornell: The Myth of Equal Education.* Ithaca, N.Y.: Cornell University Press, 1977.

Coon, Horace. *Columbia: Colossus on the Hudson.* New York: Dutton, 1947.

Cott, Nancy, ed. *A Woman Making History: Mary Ritter Beard Through Her Letters.* New Haven, Conn.: Yale University Press, 1991.

Cowan, Ruth B. "Women's Rights Through Litigation: An Examination of the American Civil Liberties Union Women's Rights Project, 1971–1976." *Columbia Human Rights Law Review* 8 (1976): 373–412.

Cremin, Lawrence A. *A History of Teachers College, Columbia University.* New York: Columbia University Press, 1954.

———. *The Transformation of the School: Progressivism in American Education, 1876–1957.* 1961. Reprint. New York: Vintage, 1964.

Croly, J. C. [Jane Cunningham]. *The History of the Woman's Club Movement in America.* New York: Allen, 1898.

Culler, Jonathan. *On Deconstruction: Theory and Criticism After Structuralism.* Ithaca, N.Y.: Cornell University Press, 1982.

Deacon, Desley. *Elsie Clews Parsons: Inventing Modern Life.* Chicago: University of Chicago Press, 1997.

Degler, Carl. *In Search of Human Nature: The Decline and Revival of Darwinism in American Social Thought.* New York: Oxford University Press, 1991.

DeJean, Joan, and Nancy K. Miller, eds. *Displacements: Women, Tradition, Literatures in French.* Baltimore: Johns Hopkins University Press, 1991.

Delany, Sarah, and Elizabeth Delany, with Amy Hill Hearth. *Having Our Say: The Delany Sisters' First 100 Years.* New York: Kodoshana International, 1993.

Deutsch, Sarah. *Women and the City: Gender, Space, and Power in Boston, 1870–1940.* New York: Oxford University Press, 2000.

Douglas, Ann. *Terrible Honesty: Mongrel Manhattan in the 1920s.* New York: Farrar, Straus and Giroux, 1995.

Dryfoos, Susan. *Iphigene: Memoirs of Iphigene Ochs Sulzberger of the New York Times Family.* New York: Dodd, Mead, 1981.

DuBois, Ellen Carol. *Feminism and Suffrage: The Emergence of an Independent Women's Movement in America, 1848–1869.* Ithaca, N.Y.: Cornell University Press, 1978.

DuPlessis, Rachel Blau. "Reader, I Married Me: A Polygynous Memoir." In *Changing Subjects: The Making of Feminist Literary Criticism,* edited by Gayle Green and Coppelia Kahn, 97–111. London: Routledge, 1993.

Echols, Alice. *Daring to Be Bad: Radical Feminism in America, 1967–1975.* Minneapolis: University of Minnesota Press, 1989.

Epstein, Cynthia Fuchs. "Personal Reflections with a Sociological Eye." In *Authors of Their Own Lives: Intellectual Autobiographies by Twenty American Sociologists,* edited by Bennett M. Berger, 349–62. Berkeley: University of California Press, 1990.

Erskine, John. *The American Character and Other Essays: Selected from the Writings of John Erskine.* Chautauqua, N.Y.: Chautauqua Press, 1927.

——. *The Delight of Great Books.* Indianapolis: Bobbs-Merrill, 1928.

——. *The Influence of Women, and Its Cure.* New York: Bobbs-Merrill, 1936.

——. "The Moral Obligation to Be Intelligent." In *The American Character and Other Essays: Selected from the Writings of John Erskine,* 1–32. Chautauqua, N.Y.: Chautauqua Press, 1927.

——. *My Life as a Teacher.* Philadelphia: Lippincott, 1948.

Evans, Sara. *Personal Politics: The Roots of Women's Liberation in the Civil Rights Movement and the New Left.* 1974. Reprint. New York: Vintage, 1980.

Faderman, Lillian. *Odd Girls and Twilight Lovers: A History of Lesbian Life in Twentieth Century America.* New York: Viking, 1991.

Farragher, John Mack, and Florence Howe, eds. *Women and Higher Education in American History.* New York: Norton, 1988.

Ferrell, Grace. "Lillie Devereux Blake (1833–1913)." *Legacy* 14 (1997): 146–53.

——. *Lillie Devereux Blake: Retracing a Life Erased.* Amherst: University of Massachusetts Press, 2002.

Finch, James Kip. *A History of the School of Engineering, Columbia University.* New York: Columbia University Press, 1954.

Foner, Eric. "The Education of Richard Hofstadter." In *Who Owns History? Rethinking the Past in a Changing World,* 25–48. New York: Hill & Wang, 2002.

——. *Reconstruction: America's Unfinished Revolution, 1863–1877.* New York: Harper & Row, 1988.

Freedman, Estelle B. *No Turning Back: The History of Feminism and the Future of Women.* New York: Ballantine, 2002.

——. "Separatism as Strategy: Female Institution Building and American Feminism, 1870–1930." *Feminist Studies* 5 (fall 1979): 512–29.

Freeman, Derek. *Margaret Mead and Samoa: The Making and Unmaking of an Anthropological Myth.* Cambridge, Mass.: Harvard University Press, 1983.

Freud, Sigmund. "Femininity." In *The Complete Introductory Lectures on Psychoanalysis,* edited by James Strachey, 576–99. New York: Norton, 1966.

Frusciano, Thomas J., and Marilyn H. Pettit. *New York University and the City: An Illustrated History.* New Brunswick, N.J.: Rutgers University Press, 1997.

Gacs, Ute, Aisha Khan, Jerrie McIntyre, and Ruth Weinberg, eds. *Women Anthropologists: A Biographical Dictionary*. New York: Greenwood Press, 1988.

Garraty, John A., and Mark C. Carnes, eds. *American National Biography*. New York: Oxford University Press, 1999.

Geertz, Clifford. *Works and Lives: The Anthropologist as Author*. Stanford, Calif.: Stanford University Press, 1988.

Gildersleeve, Virginia Crocheron. *Many a Good Crusade: Memoirs of Virginia Crocheron Gildersleeve*. New York: Macmillan, 1954.

Ginzberg, Eli. *The Life Styles of Educated Women*. New York: Columbia University Press, 1966.

Goldman, Jane, ed. *Virginia Woolf: To the Lighthouse, The Waves*. Columbia Critical Guides, edited by Richard Beynon. New York: Columbia University Press, 1998.

Goodsell, Willystine. *A History of the Family as a Social and Educational Institution*. New York: Macmillan, 1919.

Gordon, Lynn D. "Annie Nathan Meyer and Barnard College: Mission and Identity in Women's Higher Education, 1889–1950." *History of Education Quarterly* 26 (1986): 503–22.

Gorelick, Sherry. *City College and the Jewish Poor: Education in New York, 1880–1924*. New Brunswick, N.J.: Rutgers University Press, 1981.

Gould, Jane S. *Juggling: A Memoir of Work, Family, and Feminism*. New York: Feminist Press, 1997.

Graham, Patricia. "Women in Academe." *Science*, September 25, 1970, 1284–90.

Greenberg, Cheryl Lynn. *Or Does It Explode? Black Harlem in the Great Depression*. New York: Oxford University Press, 1991.

Greene, Gayle, and Coppelia Kahn, eds. *Making a Difference: Feminist Literary Criticism*. London: Methune, 1985.

Gurock, Jeffrey S. *When Harlem Was Jewish, 1870–1930*. New York: Columbia University Press, 1979.

Hacker, Helen Mayer. "A Functional Approach to the Gainful Employment of Married Women." Ph.D. diss., Columbia University, 1961.

——. "Slouching Toward Sociology." In *Individual Voices, Collective Visions: Fifty Years of Sociology*, edited by Ann Goetting and Sarah Fenstermaker, 233–50. Philadelphia: Temple University Press, 1995.

Harmon, Lindsey R., ed. *A Century of Doctorates: Data Analysis of Growth and Change*. Washington, D.C.: National Academy of Sciences, 1978.

Havemann, Ernest, and Patricia Salter West. *They Went to College: The College Graduate in America Today*. New York: Harcourt, Brace, 1952.

Height, Dorothy I. *Open Wide the Freedom Gates: A Memoir*. New York: Public Affairs, 2003.

Heilbrun, Carolyn G. *Hamlet's Mother and Other Women*. New York: Columbia University Press, 1990.

——. "Millett's Sexual Politics: A Year Later." *Aphra* 2 (1971): 38–47.

——. *Toward a Recognition of Androgyny: Aspects of Male and Female in Literature*. London: Gollancz,1973.

——. *When Men Were the Only Models We Had: My Teachers Barzun, Fadiman, Trilling*. Philadelphia: University of Pennsylvania Press, 2002.

Higham, John. *History: Professional Scholarship in America*. New York: Harper & Row, 1965.

Hine, Darlene Clark, Elsa Barkley Brown, and Rosalyn Terborg-Penn, eds. *Black Women in America: An Historical Encyclopedia*. 2 vols. Bloomington: Indiana University Press, 1994.

Hollinger, David. *Science, Jews, and Secular Culture: Studies in Mid-Twentieth Century American Intellectual History*. Princeton, N.J.: Princeton University Press, 1996.

Hollingworth, Leta. *Functional Periodicity: An Experimental Study of the Mental and Motor Abilities of Women During Menstruation*. New York: Teachers College, 1914.

——. "Variability as Related to Sex Differences in Achievement." *American Journal of Sociology* 19 (1914): 510–30.

Horowitz, David. *Betty Friedan and the Making of the Feminine Mystique*. Amherst: University of Massachusetts Press, 1998.

Horowitz, Helen Lefkowitz. *Alma Mater: Design and Experience in the Women's Colleges from Their Nineteenth Century Beginnings to the 1930s*. New York: Knopf, 1984.

——. *The Power and Passion of M. Carey Thomas*. New York: Knopf, 1994.

——. "Victoria Woodhull, Anthony Comstock, and the Conflict over Sex in the United States in the 1870s." *Journal of American History* 87 (2000): 403–34.

Hosford, Stacilee Ford. "Frederick Augustus Porter Barnard: Reconsidering a Life." Ed.D. diss., Teachers College, Columbia University, 1991.

Howard, Jane. *Margaret Mead: A Life*. New York: Fawcett, 1984.

Howe, Florence, ed. *The Politics of Women's Studies: Testimony from Thirty Founding Mothers*. New York: Feminist Press, 2000.

Howe, Julia Ward, ed. *Sex and Education: A Reply to Dr. Clarke's "Sex in Education."* Cambridge, Mass: Roberts, 1874.

Hoxie, R. Gordon, et al. *A History of the Faculty of Political Science, Columbia University*. New York: Columbia University Press, 1955.

Hoxie, Ralph Gordon. "John W. Burgess, American Scholar, Book I: The Founding of the Faculty of Political Science." Ph.D. diss., Columbia University, 1950.

Hughes, Langston. *The Big Sea*. New York: Hill & Wang, 1963.

Hurston, Zora Neale. *Dust Tracks on a Road: An Autobiography*. 1942. Reprint. Urbana: University of Illinois Press, 1984.

——. *Mules and Men*. 1935. Reprint. Bloomington: Indiana University Press, 1978.

——. *Their Eyes Were Watching God: A Novel*. 1937. Reprint. Urbana: University of Illinois Press, 1978.

Hutchinson, Emilie J. *Women's Wages: A Study of the Wages of Industrial Women and Measures Suggested to Increase Them*. New York, 1919.

Irwin, Will, Earl Chapin May, and Joseph Hotchkiss. *A History of the Union League Club of New York City*. New York: Dodd, Mead, 1952.

Isserman, Maurice. "The Not-So-Dark-and-Bloody Ground: New Works on the 1960s." *American Historical Review* 94 (1989): 990–1010.

Jackson, Kenneth T., ed. *The Encyclopedia of New York City*. New Haven, Conn.: Yale University Press, 1995.

Jacobs, Travis Beal. *Eisenhower at Columbia*. New Brunswick, N.J.: Transaction Books, 2001.

James, Edward T., Janet Wilson James, and Paul S. Boyer, eds. *Notable American Women, 1607–1950: A Biographical Dictionary*. 3 vols. Cambridge, Mass.: Belknap Press of Harvard University Press, 1971.

Kaplan, Carla, ed. *Zora Neale Hurston: A Life in Letters*. New York: Doubleday, 2002.

Katz, Esther. "Grace Hoadley Dodge: Women and the Emerging Metropolis, 1865–1914." Ph.D. diss., New York University, 1980.

Keller, Morton, and Phyllis Keller. *Making Harvard Modern: The Rise of America's University*. Cambridge. Mass.: Harvard University Press, 2001.

Kerber, Linda K. "Angles of Vision: What American Studies Has Been; What American Studies Might Be." Keynote address presented at "60 Years of American Studies at Barnard College," Barnard College, New York, October 8, 1999.

——. "In Memoriam: Annette Kar Baxter," *American Quarterly* (1983): 455–57.

——. "In Memoriam: John Atlee Kouwenhoven." *American Quarterly* 44 (1992): 463–66.

——. *Toward an Intellectual History of Women: Essays.* Chapel Hill: University of North Carolina Press, 1997.

Kevles, Daniel J. *In the Name of Eugenics: Genetics and the Uses of Human Heredity.* New York: Knopf, 1985.

——. *The Physicists: A History of a Scientific Community in Modern America.* Cambridge, Mass.: Harvard University Press, 1987.

Koffka, Kurt. *The Growth of the Mind: An Introduction to Child Psychology.* Translated by Robert Morris Ogden. New York: Harcourt, Brace, 1924.

Komarovsky, Mirra. "Cultural Contradictions and Sex Roles." *American Journal of Sociology* 78 (1946): 873–84.

——. "Functional Analysis of Sex Roles." *American Sociological Review* 15 (1950): 508–16.

——. "Some Persistent Issues on Sociological Polemics." *Sociological Forum* 2 (1987): 557.

——. *The Unemployed Man and His Family.* New York: Dryden Press, 1940.

——. *Women in the Modern World: Their Education and Their Dilemmas.* Boston: Little, Brown, 1953.

Kurland, Gerald. *Seth Low: The Reformer in an Urban and Industrial Age.* New York: Twayne, 1971.

Lagemann, Ellen Condliffe. *A Generation of Women: Education in the Lives of Progressive Reformers.* Cambridge, Mass.: Harvard University Press, 1979.

Lane, Ann J., ed. *Mary Ritter Beard: A Sourcebook.* New York: Schocken Books, 1977.

Lapsley, Hilary. *Margaret Mead and Ruth Benedict: The Kinship of Women.* Amherst: University of Massachusetts Press, 1999.

Lerner, Gerda. *Fireweed: A Political Autobiography.* Philadelphia: Temple University Press, 2002.

——. *The Grimké Sisters from South Carolina: Rebels Against Slavery.* Boston: Houghton Mifflin, 1967.

——. *The Majority Finds Its Past: Placing Women in History.* New York: Oxford University Press, 1979.

Lewis, David Levering. *W. E. B. Du Bois: Biography of a Race, 1868–1919.* New York: Holt, 1993.

Lifton, Robert Jay, ed. *The Woman in America.* Boston: Beacon Press, 1964.

Linton, Adelin, and Charles Wagley. *Ralph Linton.* New York: Columbia University Press, 1971.

Lipset, Seymour Martin, and Richard Hofstadter, eds. *Sociology and History: Methods.* New York: Basic Books, 1968.

Ludmerer, Kenneth M. *Learning to Heal: The Development of American Medical Education.* New York: Basic Books, 1985.

Lundberg, Ferdinand, and Marynia Farnham. *Modern Women: The Lost Sex.* New York: Grosset & Dunlap, 1947.

MacIver, Robert M. *As a Tale that Is Told: The Autobiography of R. M. MacIver.* Chicago: University of Chicago Press, 1968.

Markowitz, Ruth Jacknow. *My Daughter, the Teacher: Jewish Teachers in the New York City Schools.* New Brunswick, N.J.: Rutgers University Press, 1993.

Marrin, Albert. *Nicholas Murray Butler.* Boston: Twayne, 1976.

McCaughey, Robert A. *Stand Columbia: A History of Columbia University in the City of New York, 1754–2004.* New York: Columbia University Press, 2003.

Mead, Margaret. *Blackberry Winter: My Early Years.* New York: Simon and Schuster, Touchstone, 1972.

——. *Coming of Age in Samoa: A Psychological Study of Primitive Youth for Western Civilization.* New York: Morrow, 1928.

——. *Sex and Temperament in Three Primitive Societies.* New York: Morrow, 1935.

——, ed. *An Anthropologist at Work: Writings of Ruth Benedict.* Boston: Houghton Mifflin, 1959.

Meaker, Marijane. *Highsmith: A Romance of the 1950s.* New York: Cleis Press, 2003.

Merton, Robert K. *Science, Technology and Society in Seventeenth Century England.* 1938. Reprint. New York: Fertig, 1970.

——. *Social Theory and Social Structure.* Rev. ed. Glencoe, Ill.: Free Press, 1957.

——. "The Unanticipated Consequences of Purposive Social Action." *American Sociological Review* 1 (1936): 894–904

Merton, Robert K., and Mathilda White Riley, eds. *Sociological Traditions from Generation to Generation.* Norwood, N.J.: Ablex, 1980.

Metzger, Walter. "Academic Tenure in America: A Historical Essay." In *Faculty Tenure: A Report and Recommendations by the Commission on Academic Tenure in Higher Education,* edited by Commission on Academic Tenure in Higher Education, 111–16. San Francisco: Jossey-Bass, 1973.

Meyer, Annie Nathan. *Barnard Beginnings.* Boston: Houghton Mifflin, 1935.

——. *It's Been Fun: An Autobiography.* New York: Schuman, 1951.

Millard, Betty. *Woman Against Myth.* New York: International Press, 1948.

Miller, Alice Duer, and Susan Myers. *Barnard College: The First Fifty Years.* New York: Columbia University Press, 1939.

Miller, Nancy K. *But Enough About Me: Why We Read Other People's Lives.* New York: Columbia University Press, 2002.

——. *Getting Personal: Feminist Occasions and Other Autobiographical Acts.* New York: Routledge, 1991.

Millett, Kate. *Sexual Politics.* New York: Doubleday, 1970.

Modell, Judith Schachter. *Ruth Benedict: Patterns of a Life.* Philadelphia: University of Pennsylvania Press, 1983.

Morantz-Sanchez, Regina. *Sympathy and Science: Women Physicians in American Medicine.* New York: Oxford University Press, 1985.

——. *Sympathy and Science: Women Physicians in American Medicine.* Rev. ed. Chapel Hill: University of North Carolina Press, 2000.

Murolo, Priscilla. *The Common Ground of Womanhood: Class, Gender, and Working Girls' Clubs, 1884–1928.* Urbana: University of Illinois Press, 1997.

Murray, Pauli. *Pauli Murray: The Autobiography of a Black Activist, Feminist, Lawyer, Priest, and Poet.* Knoxville: University of Tennessee Press, 1987.

National Manpower Council. *Womanpower.* New York: Columbia University Press, 1957.

Navin, Thomas R. *Copper Mining and Management.* Tucson: University of Arizona Press, 1978.

Nicolson, Marjorie Hope. "The Rights and Privileges Pertaining Thereto." *Journal of the American Association of University Women* 31 (1938): 135–42.

Noble, Jeanne L. *The Negro Woman's College Education.* New York: Garland, 1956.

Novick, Peter. *That Noble Dream: The Objectivity Question and the American Historical Profession.* New York: Cambridge University Press, 1988.

Parsons, Elsie Clews. *The Family: An Ethnographical and Historical Outline with Descriptive Notes, Planned as a Text-Book for the Use of College Lecturers and of Directors of Home-Reading Clubs.* New York: Putnam, 1906.

———. "Field Work in Teaching Sociology at Barnard College, Columbia University." *Educational Review* 20 (1900): 159.

Parsons, Talcott, and Robert F. Bales. *Family, Socialization and Interaction Process.* New York: Free Press, 1955.

Peiss, Kathy. *Cheap Amusements: Working Women and Leisure in Turn-of-the-Century New York.* Philadelphia: Temple University Press, 1986.

Perkins, Linda M. "The Racial Integration of the Seven Sisters Colleges." *Journal of Blacks in Higher Education,* no. 19 (1998): 104–8.

Potter, David M. "American Women and the American Character." In *History and American Society: Essays of David M. Potter,* edited by Don E. Fehrenbacher, 277–303. New York: Oxford University Press, 1972.

Ravitch, Diane. *The Great School Wars: A History of the New York City Public Schools.* 1974. Reprint. New York: Basic Books, 1988.

Rayner-Canham, Marlene F., and Geoffrey W. Rayner-Canham. *Harriet Brooks: Pioneer Nuclear Scientist.* Montreal: McGill–Queens University Press, 1992.

Reed, Sylvanus Albert. *The Life of Caroline Gallup Reed.* New York: Privately printed, 1931.

Reinharz, Shulamit. "Finding a Sociological Voice: The Work of Mirra Komarovsky." *Sociological Inquiry* 59 (1989): 374–95.

Reitano, Joanne. "Working Girls Unite." *American Quarterly* 36 (1984): 112–34.

Robertson, Nan. *The Girls in the Balcony: Women, Men, and the New York Times.* New York: Random House, 1992.

Robinson, James Harvey. *The New History: Essays Illustrating the Modern Historical Outlook.* New York: Macmillan, 1912.

Rosen, Ruth. *The World Split Open: How the Modern Women's Movement Changed America.* New York: Viking, 2000.

Rosenberg, Rosalind. *Beyond Separate Spheres: Intellectual Roots of Modern Feminism.* New Haven, Conn.: Yale University Press, 1982.

Rossi, Alice, and Ann Calderwood, eds. *Academic Women on the Move.* New York: Russell Sage Foundation, 1973.

Rossiter, Margaret W. *Women Scientists in America: Before Affirmative Action, 1940–1972.* Baltimore: Johns Hopkins University Press, 1995.

———. *Women Scientists in America: Struggles and Strategies to 1940.* Baltimore: Johns Hopkins University Press, 1982.

Rousmaniere, Kate. "City Teachers: Teaching in the New York City Schools in the 1920s." Ph.D. diss., Teachers College, Columbia University, 1992.

Rudolph, Emanuel D. "Women in Nineteenth Century American Botany: A Generally Unrecognized Constituency." *American Journal of Botany* 69 (1982): 1346–55.

Rudolph, Frederick. *The American College and University.* Athens: University of Georgia Press, 1962.

Russell, William F., ed. *The Rise of a University.* Vol. 1, *The Later Days of Old Columbia College, from the Annual Reports of Frederick A. P. Barnard.* New York: Columbia University Press, 1937.

Schrecker, Ellen W. *No Ivory Tower: McCarthyism and the Universities.* New York: Oxford University Press, 1986.

Schwager, Sally. "'Harvard Women': A History of the Founding of Radcliffe College." Ed.D. diss., Harvard University, 1982.

Schwartz, Judith. *Radical Feminists of Heterodoxy: Greenwich Village, 1912–1940.* Lebanon, N.H.: New Victorian Press, 1982.

Sicherman, Barbara, and Carol Hurd Green, eds. *Notable American Women: The Modern Period*. Cambridge, Mass.: Belknap Press of Harvard University Press, 1980.

Siegel, Daniel A. "'Western Civ' and the Staging of History." *American Historical Review* 105 (2000): 770–803.

Silverberg, Helene, ed. *Gender and American Social Science: The Formative Years*. Princeton, N.J.: Princeton University Press, 1998.

Simkhovitch, Mary Kingsbury. *Here Is God's Plenty: Reflections on American Social Advance*. New York: Harper, 1949.

——. *Neighborhood: My Story of Greenwich House*. New York: Norton, 1938.

Smith, Bonnie G. *The Gender of History: Men, Women, and Historical Practice*. Cambridge, Mass.: Harvard University Press, 1998.

Solomon, Barbara Miller. *In the Company of Educated Women: A History of Women and Higher Education in America*. New Haven, Conn.: Yale University Press, 1985.

Spurgeon, Caroline F. E. *Shakespeare's Imagery and What It Tells Us*. Cambridge: Cambridge University Press, 1935.

Stansell, Christine. *American Moderns: Bohemian New York and the Creation of the New Century*. New York: Metropolitan Books, 2000.

Stimpson, Catharine R. "Feminist Criticism." In *Redrawing the Boundaries*, edited by Stephen Greenblatt and Giles Gunn, 251–70. New York: Modern Language Association, 1992.

——. "Women's Liberation and Black Civil Rights." In *Women in Sexist Society: Studies in Power and Powerlessness*, edited by Vivian Gornick and Barbara K. Moran, 622–57. New York: Basic Books, 1971.

Stocking, George W. Jr. *Race, Culture, and Evolution: Essays in the History of Anthropology*. New York: Free Press, 1968.

Strong, George Templeton. *The Diary of George Templeton Strong, 1820–1875*. 4 vols. Edited by Allan Nevins and Milton Halsey Thomas. New York: Macmillan, 1952.

Summerscales, William. *Affirmation and Dissent: Columbia's Response to the Crisis of World War I*. New York: Teachers College Press, 1970.

Swiger, Eleanor Porter. *Women Lawyers at Work*. New York: Messner, 1978.

Synnott, Marcia Graham. *The Half-Opened Door: Discrimination and Admissions at Harvard, Yale, and Princeton, 1900–1970*. Westport, Conn.: Greenwood Press, 1979.

Thomas, Sally Jean. "'Woman's Sphere' and Institutional Structure: Teachers College, Columbia University's Two School System, 1913–1933." Ed.D. diss., Teachers College, Columbia University, 1986.

Tifft, Susan E., and Alex S. Jones. *The Trust: The Private and Powerful Family Behind the New York Times*. Boston: Little, Brown, 1999.

Torre, Susana, ed. *Women in American Architecture: A Historic and Contemporary Perspective*. New York: Whitney Library of Design, 1977.

Trautman, Ray. *A History of the School of Library Service, Columbia University*. New York: Columbia University Press, 1954.

Trilling, Diana. *The Beginning of the Journey: The Marriage of Diana and Lionel Trilling*. New York: Harcourt, Brace, 1993.

——. *We Must March My Darlings*. New York: Harcourt Brace Jovanovich, 1977.

Trilling, James. "My Father and the Weak-Eyed Devils." *American Scholar*, spring 1999, 17–44.

Trilling, Lionel. "The Van Amringe and Keppel Eras." In *A History of Columbia College on Morningside Heights*, edited by Dwight Miner, 14–47. New York: Columbia University Press, 1954.

Tyack, David B. *The One Best System: A History of Urban Education*. Cambridge, Mass.: Harvard University Press, 1974.

Tyack, David, and Elizabeth Hansot. *Learning Together: A History of Coeducation in American Public Schools*. New Haven, Conn.: Yale University Press, 1990.

Van Metre, Thurman W. *A History of the Graduate School of Business, Columbia University*. New York: Columbia University Press, 1954.

Vance, Carole S., ed. *Pleasure and Danger: Exploring Female Sexuality*. Boston: Routledge & Kegan Paul, 1984.

Walton, Andrea. "Women at Columbia: A Study of Power and Empowerment in the Lives of Six Scholars." Ph.D. diss., Teachers College, Columbia University, 1995.

Ware, Susan. *Letter to the World: Seven Women Who Shaped the American Century*. Cambridge, Mass.: Harvard University Press, 1998.

Wechsler, Harold S. *The Qualified Student: A History of Selective College Admission in America*. New York: Wiley, 1977.

——. "The Rationale for Restriction: Ethnicity and College Admission in America, 1910–1980." *American Quarterly* 36 (1984): 643–67.

Weigand, Kate. *Red Feminism: American Communism and the Making of Women's Liberation*. Baltimore: Johns Hopkins University Press, 2001.

Weneck, Betty. "The 'Average Teacher' Need Not Apply: Women Educators at Teachers College, 1887–1927." Ph.D. diss., Teachers College, Columbia University, 1996.

Westbrook, Robert B. *John Dewey and American Democracy*. Ithaca, N.Y.: Cornell University Press, 1991.

White, Lynn, Jr. *Educating Our Daughters*. New York: Harper, 1950.

White, Marian Churchill. *A History of Barnard College*. New York: Columbia University Press, 1954.

Wilson, Andrew. *Beautiful Shadow: A Life of Patricia Highsmith*. New York: St. Martin's Press, 2003.

Winant, Marguerite Dawson. *A Century of Sorosis, 1868–1968*. Uniondale, N.Y.: Salisbury, 1968.

Wittemore, Richard. *Nicholas Murray Butler and Public Education, 1862–1911*. New York: Teachers College Press, 1970.

Woloch, Nancy. *Women and the American Experience*. 3rd ed. New York: McGraw-Hill, 2000.

Zuckerman, Harriet, Jonathan R. Cole, and John T. Bruer, eds. *The Outer Circle: Women in the Scientific Community*. New York: Norton, 1991.

INDEX